THE PROBLEM OF RESTORATION

THE PROBLEM OF RESTORATION

A STUDY IN COMPARATIVE
POLITICAL HISTORY

by Robert A. Kann

UNIVERSITY OF CALIFORNIA PRESS

Berkeley and Los Angeles

1968

University of California Press
Berkeley and Los Angeles, California

Cambridge University Press
London, England

Library of Congress Catalog Card Number: 68-10380
Printed in the United States of America

To Peter

Preface

This study of a significant historical problem suggests in its first, general part some tentative principles according to which the process of restoration may operate. Perusal of this section of the book is indispensable for the understanding of the case studies analyzed in the second part. The cases were selected not to conform with any true or alleged law of history but solely to elucidate a problem of which we know very little as yet. On the strength of these or other cases, historians may come to different conclusions. Their suggestions are welcomed by one who perceives the meaning of history not in conformity to a preestablished pattern but in the reflection of the diversity of life.

Publication has been supported by faculty research fellowships from the Social Science Research Council and the Research Council of Rutgers University, two grants from the Council of Learned Societies and two from the American Philosophical Society. Due thanks are herewith expressed to these institutions.

I feel greatly indebted also to the University of California Press and its staff. Mrs. Gladys Castor's invaluable editorial help and counsel were particularly appreciated.

R.A.K.

Contents

ix

PART I
THE CONCEPTS

CHAPTER I

Change in Time

The concept of political restoration in terms of this study pertains to the reestablishment of a state of political and social affairs that was upset by previous revolutionary change. The significant problems of semantics involved here are fairly static.[1] The process of restoration itself, as it takes place in the course of time and in different social settings, is highly dynamic. Its analysis is the main objective of the following discussion.

INEVITABLE CHANGE

History operates in time, and time brings about change. Clearly the most obvious change is due to the limitation of man's life-span. Within two, or at the most three, generations, practically the whole cast on the stage of history will be entirely different. Because of the considerable increase in human longevity, at least in Western civilization, this particular kind of change takes place at a slower rate than even half a century ago. Perhaps the rapid sociotechnological transformation of our time may thus be partly offset by a psychological slowdown, since the same men will operate much longer on the social scene. The increase in the human life-span can be measured and predicted. The concept of "historical time" expressed in years, generations, and at most, centuries and millennia, can provide, therefore, a definite and stable reference to basic differences between periods of history. Even much shorter phases, measured not by generations but merely by decades or even years—according to average mortality rates in our civilization—already show a sizeable change in the age structure of social bodies as illustrated by the graphs of the population pyramid. The population base of a large number of younger people and a

[1] See Appendix: Restoration, the Terms.

3

small top structure of those of old age, as it existed up to the beginning of our century, will be gradually reversed until the population pyramid of previous generations will stand on its head. This is not the only fully predictable factor in the changing conditions of our social existence. Yet most of the changes in the realm of science, whether they pertain to changes in climate or to mutations in biological life—to cite only two obvious examples—require so much time that their effect on the brief period of human history in which we live is far less perceptible. The time element as it appears in the transition from one generation to the other remains the most immediately effective and by approximation the most precise element of historical change.

Other changes, whether they come about by the discovery or the exhaustion of raw materials, by technological invention, by innovation in the processes of production and distribution, by changes in the form of government because of war, revolution, colonization, and so forth, are the consequences of concerted or individual endeavors, and in that sense far less predictable. Any philosophy of history that has overcome a mythographic approach would hardly go beyond the admission that such changes enrich human experience and therefore make possible the interpretation of history with greater understanding—which is vastly different from predicting its course. Accordingly, if we suggest that the kind of change referred to in this paragraph should come under the concept of merely relative change, this does not mean that it may not be very effective up to a point. It does mean, however, that it can be effective only in relation to essentially unpredictable human actions. Here the question arises whether changes are reversible, or irreversible like the time element between life and death of new and old generations. The problem leads to the central theme of this study. If restoration in the social sphere means the establishment of a previous state of affairs, then the cardinal question arises whether such a reestablishment is possible at all, in view of the inevitability of change. We have found this inevitability to be absolute only in regard to the limits of the human life-span. We have assumed, on the other hand, that any changes in the social sphere are determined by the actions of men, and in that sense are unpredictable and relative, according to the standpoint from which they are judged. Certainly the further question must be asked how this relativity operates at various times, in various fields of concerted human endeavor.

INDETERMINATE CHANGE

Here an important problem appears on the social horizon. The Marxian philosophy of history and economic development, but particularly the former, has introduced the concept of inevitability into social theory in a roundabout way. In Marxian terms the basic economic needs of mankind determine the ideological superstructure of history.[2] We can recognize the vital role of these economic needs without agreeing that the whole course of history can be determined by them. As Max Eastman rightly points out in line with other critics of Marxism, "There can be no doubt that the limiting conditions and the determining cause are being interchanged without discrimination."[3] Accordingly the Marxian modes of production do not approximate the character of ironclad scientific laws. They establish probabilities in limited areas of social life, but by no means certainties in any of them.[4]

[2] Quoted by Max Eastman in the introduction to *Karl Marx, Capital, the Communist Manifesto and Other Writings* (New York, 1932), p. xii. See also Patrick Gardiner, *Theories of History* (Glencoe, Illinois, 1959), pp. 126 ff, and Sidney Hook, *Marx and the Marxists* (New York, 1955), pp. 36 ff. See further the excellent summary in Joseph A. Schumpeter, *Capitalism, Socialism and Democracy* (New York, 1950), pp. 10 ff.

[3] Eastman, p. xiii. The proposition has been frequently qualified and seemingly modified by Marx and Engels, as, for instance, in Engels' letter of September 21/22, 1890, to Joseph Bloch:

> According to the materialist conception of history, the ultimately determining element in history is the production and reproduction of human life. More than this neither Marx nor I have ever asserted. Hence if somebody twists this into saying that the economic element is the only determining one he transforms that proposition into a meaningless, abstract, senseless phrase. The economic situation is the basis, but the various elements of the superstructure—political forms of the class struggle and its results, to wit: constitutions established by the victorious class after a successful battle, etc., juridical forms, and even the reflexes of all these actual struggles in the brains of the participants, political justice, philosophical theories, religious views and their further development into systems of dogmas— also exercise their influence upon the course of the historical struggle and in any cases preponderate in determining their form. There is an interaction of all these elements. . . .

See Lewis S. Feuer, *Marx and Engels, Basic Writings on Politics and Philosophy* (Garden City, 1959), p. 397 f. This passage is successful in preventing the vulgarization of the argument, but it changes in no way its essence. See also Franz Mehring, *Karl Marx* (Leipzig, 1933), pp. 135-155, particularly on the Marx and Engels joint study, *Die deutsche Ideologie, eine Kritik der neuesten deutschen Philosophie . . .*, written in 1845, where much of the essence of the theory is already found. See also Gustav Mayer, *Friedrich Engels* (Haag), I, 220-244.

[4] Eastman, pp. xi ff. and also p. xiii, ". . . this failure to distinguish condition from cause is the most general of those unconscious devices by which Marx and

Thus Marxian doctrines give us little help, precisely because of their sweeping claims.[5] The obvious limiting conditions for the preservation of the social status quo which we have in mind would be technological advance pure and simple, which means the product of human ingenuity and discovery as separate from its practical application. In the history of human activities technological advance and discoveries in specific fields and specific cultural orbits have seldom, if ever, fallen into complete oblivion. The process of production may have deteriorated at times, demand and consumption may have been restricted; yet the basic invention itself has not been forgotten completely. This has been shown convincingly in Western civilization in the accomplishments of Greco-Roman civilization, which survived the Germanic invasions of Italy and the Saracen-Turkish conquests of the Mediterranean world. It was confirmed after the havoc of the Mongolian invasions in the thirteenth century A.D. Apart from the danger of nuclear devastation, our own world offers a superior haven for new discoveries because of exceedingly improved communications.

Technological advances, then, are bound to stay, although there may be a great variety of possibilities in their speed and spread in different areas. We are confronted here by high probabilities, not by certainties. The chance of complete loss of the achievements of technological progress, particularly in a large-scale war, must always be considered; the full validity of Marxian determinism, on the other hand, can never be conceded. Yet for all practical purposes we may admit that technological change represents a factor which in social practice has proved almost as universally valid, almost as inevitable, as the change brought about by the limiting conditions of human life itself. Any concept of the reestablishment of a social order will have to deal with one as well as the other, that is, with inevitable as well as with indeterminate change.

Determinism and the Social Revolution

Does this concept of change apply to the modes of production in a wider sense? To put it in Marxian terms: Does it refer to the control of the

---

his followers keep up the attitude of a philosopher while presenting the thoughts of an engineer." See further Hook, pp. 36 ff., and also, very much to the point, Sir Isaiah Berlin, *Historical Inevitability* (London, 1954), pp. 22 ff.

An inevitable chronological primacy of material needs in contrast to ideological needs has been questioned by an orthodox Marxian social philosopher as well. See Max Adler, *Lehrbuch der marxistischen Geschichtsauffassung*, 2 vols. (Berlin, 1930–1932), II, 176–181; see also 170–176. See further Paul Kägi, *Genesis des historischen Materialismus* (Vienna, 1965), pp. 305 ff., 335 ff., 366 ff.

[5] Hook, p. 36 f.; Kägi, pp. 309 ff.

means of production and the distribution of surplus values? At its simplest, are widespread and lasting social revolutions reversible? By this we mean social transformation where the dynamic factor—the technological improvement or invention—cannot be isolated and studied irrespective of the play or counterplay of political forces. Accordingly, we must deal with the question whether the whole interplay of concomitant political forces in a far-reaching change of the modes of production can be reversed.

Even an attempt to clarify the issue would require a definition of the word revolution. Crane Brinton, in the first sentence of his brilliant book *The Anatomy of Revolution*, calls it "one of the looser words," a notable understatement.[6]

The evaluation of the concept of revolution concerns us mainly in its juxtaposition with restoration. It should suffice to confine our discussion to two principal meanings of the term, restricted to social issues: a total or radical change, particularly in social thought and production methods, as exemplified by the Industrial Revolution of the eighteenth and early nineteenth centuries; and "a fundamental change in political organization or in a government or constitution; the overthrow or renunciation of one government or ruler, and the substitution of another by the governed."[7]

In the great Industrial Revolution, we find the classical case of a transformation brought about by technological progress and discovery per se. Technological progress is no solitary phenomenon, but depends upon important changes and developments in human thinking. In the Industrial Revolution, it has been linked to social and political consequences of great impact on our own time. Therefore it is difficult to view the social effect of technological advances without reference to the preceding intellectual development, as well as to the concomitant and ensuing social changes. Yet, as long as these changes do not involve political innovations brought about by a violent response to existing conditions, such an evaluation may be feasible. Changes in the standard of living brought about by an advanced technology could still be isolated for the purpose of social measurement. This would pertain to several aspects of the eighteenth century Industrial Revolution. But as soon as there is a violent

[6] Crane Brinton, *The Anatomy of Revolution* (New York, 1958), p. 3; also *passim* to p. 27. In addition, Karl Griewank, *Der neuzeitliche Revolutionsbegriff* (Weimar, 1955), pp. 171 ff.; Hannah Arendt, *On Revolution* (New York, 1963), pp. 13–52; Dolf Sternberger, *Grund and Abgrund der Macht* (Frankfurt am Main, 1962), pp. 23 ff.

[7] See *Webster's New Collegiate Dictionary;* also the *Concise Oxford Dictionary.* See also Arendt, pp. 28 ff.

change in the existing political system, or at least a breach in the legal order, as soon as technological advances and changes in the modes of production are directly linked to radical political upsets, it is no longer possible to study such social concepts in isolation.

In regard to this latter type of revolution, which raises the question of reversibility, Brinton's explanation is of great interest, although his observation is not limited to social transformation. "But our focus is on drastic, sudden substitution of one group in charge of the running of a territorial political entity for another group. There is one further implication: the revolutionary substitution of one group for another, if not made by actual violent uprising, is made by coup d'état, Putsch, or some other kind of skulduggery." If the change takes place without violence, we have a revolution "by consent," and the appropriateness of the term revolution, according to Brinton, may be questioned.[8]

This clarification, though valuable in terms of "group substitution," is not perfect. The reference to skulduggery does not do justice to the importance of the problem; the minimum size of the social body involved in the process of sudden transformation is not even hinted at. An act of rebellion confined to a small community will hardly be called a revolution although it may refer to "a territorial political entity." More important, reference to the time element is lacking. Thus a putsch by a military junta, which might be overthrown after a few days, would not be distinguished from the concept of revolution. We believe that a genuine revolution not only would have a long-lasting effect but would be expected to go through stages of violent transformation for more than a few days or even weeks. Estimates of the necessary time may range from the minimum time required to protect a regime from sudden overthrow and to enable it to obtain at least *de facto* recognition in international relations, up to the expectation of lasting character to which J. A. Schumpeter refers in regard to orthodox Marxism. According to him, the revolution "only comes to write the conclusion under a complete set of premises. The Marxian revolution therefore differs entirely, in nature and function, from the revolution both of the bourgeois radical and of the socialist conspirator."[9]

While Brinton ignores the time element, Schumpeter perhaps overrates it to the extent that revolutionary action and revolutionary consequence are thrown together in an indefinite process. We can draw the conclusion

[8] Brinton, p. 4, also p. 26; Griewank, pp. 119 ff.; Ardent, pp. 8 ff., 30 ff.
[9] Schumpeter, p. 58; Berlin, p. 24 f.

that there are elements of illegality or violence or both, as well as a time factor that is more than rapidly transitory.[10]

The problem of reversibility of social revolution as a transformation which includes not only lasting technological change but also an over-throw or radical alteration of the existing government and a break of legal continuity, can be approached only in a strictly pragmatic way. The history of our civilization does not show any precedent which would indicate the reversibility of widespread social and political revolutions rolled into one. Several cases in which this very problem is at issue, in particular in regard to the social changes brought about by the reforms of Solon in Athens in the sixth century B.C. and those of the Gracchi in Rome in the second century B.C., will be discussed in the case studies in Part II.[11]

Basic Limitations of the Validity of Historical Analogies

The representative character of the case studies in the second part of this book might be questioned in view of the tremendous lapse of time be-tween events of the past and those of our age. Yet this familiar objection sounds more plausible than it actually is. Examples of widespread social revolution throughout history in the specific terms discussed in the pre-ceding section, are not nearly so frequent as some may assume. Here some qualifying factors must be introduced to give the case studies full mean-ing in terms of our subsequent investigation. The first applies to the con-cept of social bodies, the second to the element of time.

[10] According to Schumpeter, there is a distinction between an inevitable, complete social transformation of society, as Marx conceived it according to his laws, and the actual political social revolution, including the Russian Bolshevik Revolution of 1917, the violence of which is not considered an essential part of Marxian social doctrine. See Schumpeter, pp. 57 f., 346 f. Yet even if one minimizes the frequent statements of Marx and Engels to the contrary as "but the particular garb in which his (Marx's) imagination liked to clothe that action" (p. 57), the point remains that in practice all the comprehensive social tranformations in which Marxian doctrines were involved, have shown also the break of legal continuity or violence or both, directly and essentially related to the purpose of the revolution. There can be no doubt, however, that a political upset brought about by violent means is in theory not less subject to a reestablishment of due process of legal continuity than is return to a state of grace in the spiritual field. The possibility of realization of such a restoration process is obviously an entirely different matter, to be answerable only by pragmatic experience.

See also Sternberger, pp. 30 ff., 81, who puts the Western and the Bolshevik concepts in juxtaposition.

[11] See chap. 8, Athens from Solon to Cleisthenes; chap. 9, Rome from the Imperial Republic to the Rise of Marius.

In classical theories of government a state consists of three basic elements: people and territory, linked by the sovereignty of the social body that establishes the political organization of the state.[12] How numerous the people, how large the territory of the state should be, is not part of any definition.[13] Experience has shown, however, that in Western civilization sweeping social changes could not be confined to small or thinly populated regions, whereas a change of executive power by violent means could well be confined within the bounds of the territory—for example, many of the coups d'état in Latin American republics before the Second World War. Enforced social changes in a small area, on the other hand, would lead, if not to the proselytizing of the neighboring regions, at least to the gradual emigration of those who do not concur in the changes.

Although cultural and social delay in isolated areas has been frequent in history, the reverse, namely, the isolation of dynamic social change, has proved to be manifestly impossible. Outstanding examples are the spread of the Albigensian and particularly the Waldensian movements from Southern France into Italy and, in the fourteenth century, even as far as Eastern Central Europe, the spread of the Peasants Revolts in sixteenth century Germany, and the advance of the social implications of the Declaration of the Rights of Man in 1789 beyond the French borders.

Social revolutions clearly affect sizeable areas and large populations. If we confine our study for the sake of clarification to those movements which have gained control in social communities of some size, endowed with the qualifications of states in the terms noted above, the number of examples diminishes rapidly. We would have to exclude the entire period of the migration of peoples, the invasions of the West, as well as the major part of the Middle Ages from the advance to the decline of political feudalism. As for the social bodies—states in the modern sense only by approximation—of the transition period from ancient history to early medieval times, they lacked at least one and perhaps even two of the basic factors of state power. Undivided political sovereignty over state territory and people did not exist in Europe after the disintegration of the Roman

---

[12] For some of the most perspicacious discussions of these factors, see Hans Kelsen, *Allgemeine Staatslehre,* (Vienna, 1925), Part II, pp. 95–228, and Georg Jellinek, *Allgemeine Staatslehre,* 2d rev. ed. (Berlin, 1905), pp. 131–176. See also Reinhard Bendix, *Max Weber* (New York, 1960), pp. 380 f., 413 f., based on a sociological concept of state which is more complex, but which does not actually contradict Kelsen's definition.

[13] As to the relative significance of these factors, see also Robert A. Kann, "National and International Systems: a Historical Comparison," (paper read to the American Political Science Association, New York, 1963).

Empire and was less than halfway reestablished in the feudal order. Advanced feudalism included a variety of state-forming elements and more often subordinated rather than coordinated federative associations, but hardly any centralized political power. With some reservations we may speak here of a clearly defined state territory. But because of conflicting loyalties, at least for the upper classes of society, we can scarcely point, even in the High Middle Ages, to a citizenry that resembled even remotely that of modern times, where undivided allegiance is expected in democratic and nondemocratic states alike.[14]

In terms of sizeable political bodies under central authority we would thus have to cut out a millennium of continental European history, from the breakdown of the Western Roman Empire to the end of the Anglo-French Hundred Years' War. Within the confines of Western civilization, including the medieval Byzantine Empire and the Middle East, our merely conceivable samples would be rapidly reduced.[15]

We might have to sacrifice the search for the realities of political life, for the sake of conformity to theoretical patterns of definition. Apart from the fact that these patterns have been strongly challenged by outstanding theorists like Hans Kelsen, who perceive the state not as an order of territory and people, but exclusively as a relationship of law, such an approach would run counter to the very idea of continuity in history.

As to the second qualifying factor, time—time in the context of social revolution—we refer again to Schumpeter's concept of the revolution "in the fullness of time." We are not concerned here, however, with comprehensive social changes taking place in politically undefined large areas throughout indefinite long periods of time. While such a concept of social revolution may be legitimate, it is not the object of this study, which confines itself to transformations in states within clearly definable periods of time. Again the question is: How much time? A few weeks, a year, a generation, a century? Is not each of these measures of time, indeed any measure of time, as arbitrary as the next? Not if we look at the problem from the standpoint of the completion of the phase of a historical process.

We assume that a genuine social revolution has taken place if and when comprehensive measures of social innovation have been put into effect, when concomitant changes in the structure of government have been es-

---

[14] See also Otto F. von Gierke, *Political Theories of the Middle Ages* (Boston, 1958), pp. 22–100; Carl Stephenson, *Medieval Feudalism* (Ithaca, 1956), pp. 75–96, and Bendix, pp. 368–379.
[15] See Steven Runciman, *Byzantine Civilization* (New York, 1956), pp. 222–240.

tablished—in our terms, by way of the breach of legal continuity and frequently by the use of violence. We would also require that the new government be in control and that the changes will be in effect as long as that government is in control. Whether it is and remains in control will, of course, depend largely on the strength of the internal opposition and also on the reaction of other governments.

We do not suggest that the aforesaid changes must be of a truly lasting character, which in historical terms is frequently measured in centuries. We assume, however, that the clear distinction between a genuine revolution and a putsch cannot be drawn immediately upon the occurrence of a change of government by an act of violence. Whether we can expect a government to topple any day or to maintain itself in power may be more likely a matter of years than of days, weeks, or even months. How many years? Certainly not so many as are necessary for the revolution to go on "in the fullness of time" to a penetration of social transformation in depth and its expansion in width. The latter process will become fully apparent only within decades, perhaps generations; the former, easily within a few years.

If we take the French Revolution of 1789, we see that it was apparent within a few months, perhaps as early as August, 1789, that the most basic social reforms were bound to stay, except for the danger of a defeat of the social revolution by intervention from abroad. This danger was certainly not removed before the military tide of the War of the First Coalition had begun to turn with the Battle of Valmy in September, 1792, and the French crossing of the borders of the Austrian Netherlands a few weeks later.

As for the Russian Bolshevik Revolution, it would be more difficult to say at what point the entrenchment of a definite domestic policy in social questions was assured. On the other hand, except for the Far Eastern situation, foreign military intervention and domestic counterrevolutionary military uprisings were substantially running out by the end of 1920. Thus we are again dealing with only a few years, in fact with about three years, in the Russian case as in the French.[16]

We drastically reduce the number of examples that raise the question of reversibility of social revolutions within definite political communities when we introduce as qualifying factors the concepts of state and time. Even if the concept of state is wider than that of the postfeudal world, we do not have many appropriate examples, and even fewer if we qualify the

[16] See also Hannah Arendt, *On Revolution,* pp. 217–285, on the revolutionary tradition.

time factor. The question is then how to make the most of tentative conclusions on the strength of a limited number of cases without unduly stretching the points that are to be made. Different propositions may or may not offer satisfactory answers, according to the historical situation.[17]

Two basic points must be recognized here. First, the existing number of restoration processes in Western history—not including those after conquest from the outside—is limited but substantially larger than the number of cases discussed here. Second, and even more important, each restoration, like every historical process, is in many ways different from any other. A review of all existing comparable cases would enable us to reach only tentative conclusions. Furthermore, we believe that the question of reversibility or irreversibility of the social revolutions that have taken place within the frame of the modern, fully sovereign state, and within a few years, cannot be answered at this point, since sufficient evidence may not yet be available. All these factors have to be taken into account in the selection of our test cases.

To sum up: We perceive that changes from one historical period to another are inevitable as far as the biological impact of the limits of the human life-span is concerned. For practical purposes we further assume that changes due to technological inventions are inevitable. Yet we deem it merely conceivable that changes due to widespread social revolutions are of equally lasting importance.

BASIC LIMITATIONS OF ANALOGIES THAT PERTAIN TO THE CONCEPT OF RESTORATION

Discussion of the question of reversibility may lead to interesting results, in regard not only to what we do not know and cannot know as yet, but to what we do know, as well. True, the number of cases pertinent to the study of reversibility of social revolution within a definite political body is too limited to clarify the issue. Here the question arises: To what extent can this insight be used for the direct study of the restoration process?

The answer is, to a wide degree indeed. As a social and political phenomenon, the restoration process, as much as the revolutionary process, can be studied only within the frame of a sizeable, clearly definable

[17] On the use of sample cases in historical analysis, see Karl W. Deutsch, Sidney A. Burrell, Robert A. Kann and others in *Political Community and the North Atantic Area* (Princeton, 1957), pp. 15-21. On the possibilities and limitations of the historical case study in relation to scientific method, see also Crane Brinton, *Anatomy of Revolution*, pp. 8-27. See also Robert A. Kann, "Public Opinion Research: a Contribution to Historical Method," in *Political Science Quarterly*, LXXIII/3 (September 1958), p. 374 ff.

political body that comprises the basic elements of a clear-cut concept of state, although not necessarily that of the postfeudal world. There is no difference here between the limitations pertaining to the analysis of the revolutionary process and to that of restoration. In both cases, the largest part of the medieval feudal era in regard to the relationship between subject and government, and a substantial part of ancient history concerning the territorial factor in the city-state would have to be eliminated as bases for comparison. Thus application of this qualifying factor will certainly reduce the number of cses which could profitably be used for our study.

With regard to the revolutionary process, we have noted another qualifying factor pertaining to the question of time, in particular in the French Revolution of 1789 and the Russian Bolshevik Revolution of 1917. Does this teach us anything about the restoration process as well? Obviously, any kind of social and political reestablishment which is overturned again after a very short time, perhaps after only a few days, would not fall under the concept of a genuine restoration. Such a putsch can be regarded as an insignificant phenomenon in the restoration process. The analogy with the putsch within the revolutionary process is far-reaching. It may be argued that in revolution as well as in restoration, the new regime must have reasonable expectations of a certain stability in domestic and foreign affairs before one can speak of genuine revolution or restoration. Again, this would not necessarily mean stability of a lasting character or, to use Schumpeter's phrase once more, one "in the fullness of time." With regard to the subject matter of restoration processes, it does mean a further, drastic limitation of the cases which may be subject to our analysis.

Beyond this we would not like to go at this point. First, this writer is not equipped to deal with cases beyond the borders of Western civilization. The cases have been widely drawn already and include one of Jewish history at its cradle, and one of Byzantine history at its border. We will discuss later whether, within Western civilization in this broad meaning, more accurate estimates are possible in regard to the element of time in a restoration period.

We should be aware of one basic difference between the discussions of revolution and restoration in this study. We have thus far looked at revolution only within the narrow context of the problem of reversibility. Restoration must be discussed in the wider frame of a greater variety of problems. Accordingly, more opportunities will be given for new insights from pragmatic experience. Whether it might be possible to establish a system of pragmatic probabilities or at least possibilities approximating a social law, is open to question. Be that as it may, the establishment of certain analogies common to a number of well-selected cases would be something better than complete failure. If this could be done, it would seem to be of secondary importance whether such findings be classified as probabilities, possibilities, or reasonable expectations. No claim will be made that a social law in this sphere has been charted.

CHAPTER II

Change and Content

THE THREE SYSTEMS

We have thus far considered the question of inevitable change in relation to three factors: biological change, technological change, and social revolution. We assumed that the impact of the first two is unconditional, irrespective of a determined human effort to effect social change. With regard to social revolution, the existence of subjective efforts appears obvious, unless we accede to the doubtful proposition of broad and rigid socio-economic laws. Yet since technological and social changes cannot be separated, the question of inevitability and irreversibility will remain open.

The problem we will now discuss is related to the previous one, and yet it is markedly different. Again we are concerned with sociopolitical change, but this time exclusively with change initiated by planned human action and effected only by determined and concerted human endeavors, without reference to any true or alleged socioeconomic laws. We may put the matter differently: the problem of the inevitability of change pertains to the form of change, irrespective of human efforts; the question of conscious human effort as pertaining to change is one of content. We may ask: is there any innate relationship between the concept of restoration and human progress, and conservatism? If we refuse to accept without further scrutiny the highly problematical idea that in political terms revolution is necessarily progressive and the response to it inevitably reactionary, we must raise the fundamental question of the relationship of restoration to revolution and to reaction. In doing this we stress the conflict between the demand for dynamic change and the desire to retain the status quo. This question would concern itself not only with the forms of change but with the content of change as well.

This then is the question: Is the concept of restoration, seen as a sociopolitical phenomenon, linked to the idea of conservatism, as is frequently assumed? May it apply equally well to progress or—this seems unlikely—may it at times even be associated predominantly with progress? One way to tackle these problems is to analyze individual cases, with the purpose of drawing some conclusions from experience.

At this point, a purely theoretical question, separated as far as possible from case histories, should be examined. Does the fact that a sociopolitical system or order is replaced by another, through radical transformation, and is restored again after a number of years, indicate anything about the kind of change between the original system and the restored one?

Crane Brinton refers to these original systems as "the old regimes." [1] This suggestive terminology is deliberately not used in this study. First, the question of how old the old regime to be replaced actually is, would be ambiguous, since, according to classical logic, the relationship between old and new is contrary, that is, a pair of concepts in opposite position to each other, each placed at the opposite end of a row of an indefinite number of intermediate concepts.

Even more important than this logical objection is a semantic one. *Regime* and *system* or *order* in a sociopolitical sense are clearly overlapping terms; nevertheless, each distinctly emphasizes different main aspects. Both may refer to the sociopolitical structure as a whole. Yet the word *regime,* far more than *system,* pertains to the actual compostion of government and its administration. A *new regime* may signify merely that a new administration, backed by a new majority party, elected through a truly democratic process, has taken over; but it may also mean that in a nondemocratic country a military junta has replaced a previous one. It is true that the term *ancien régime,* referring to the state of affairs in 1789 at the beginning of the French Revolution, has a much broader meaning. Yet this refers to a specific French situation and not even in French to the general meaning of the term.[2] System, on the other hand, comprises not only parties, executives, cabinets, military leaders, and so forth. In our context it does not pertain merely to a shift from one group

---

[1] Crane Brinton, *The Anatomy of Revolution* (New York, 1958), pp. 29–69.

[2] Thus the Bourbon regime on the eve of the July Revolution of 1830, and the Orléans regime on the eve of the February Revolution of 1848—to cite only two examples—are generally not referred to as ancient regimes. See also Karl Griewank, *Der Wiener Kongress und die europäeische Restauration 1814–15* (Leipzig, 1954), pp. 362 ff.

of officeholders to a new one. It stands for a whole set of laws, governmental procedures, principles, and ideas, in short for a comprehensive political philosophy, such as the American democratic, the Russian Communists, the Fascist, the National Socialist systems of government and so forth. The factor of comprehensive ideology is accordingly much more strongly identified with the concept of system than with that of regime.

This ties in precisely with our overall purpose to study a process of change of government and policies by law and ideas rather than by men alone. In this sense the terms *system* or *order,* rather than *regime,* are used. If reference is made to the original system and not just to the old system, we do not presume to indicate precisely how old it may be. Nor would we maintain that the term *original,* in our context, has any absolute meaning in the sense of primeval or first.

There is, however, a very clear, unambiguous meaning in a relative sense. A system is original in relation to the restored new system, which strives to resemble it in most important aspects. How far it can do so in reality we will discuss at a later point. Here it must suffice to state, that we refer to an original system or order only in relation to the restored, or in a formal sense, a new system. Between the two we find a system, which by radical change has overturned the original system, and was superseded later by the restored one. The question whether this second process of supersedure or supersession would take place by radical, perhaps revolutionary means, will have to be deferred. Here we are concerned merely with the terminology applied to this in-between system.

Within the frame of this study, the intervening system would have a limited stability, be endowed with a comprehensive social and political philosophy of its own, and be superseded eventually by the restored system. It is more than a regime, since in action and purpose it goes far beyond the mere change of officeholders from one phase of governmental activities to another. Quite naturally this in-between system is a truly new one in relation to the original system, just as the restored system is new, in a formal sense, in relation to the in-between system. Precisely for the reason that every system is new in reference to the one it succeeds, the qualification *new* carries here no clear connotation as to the content of the succeeding system. The adjective *new* can also refer to a novel set of principles and ideas. The word itself, however, does not indicate whether we refer only to form, that is, the replacement of a previous system, or to content as well, that is, a novel set of principles. A qualifying phrase would have to be used every time the word is used. Yet if we refer to either the in-between system or the restored system as new, this might be understood as reference to content and therefore as prejudgment of the results of this study.

The same kind of criticism could be levied if we called the in-between system revolutionary, and the succeeding, restored one counterrevolutionary. It is well to remember here that we have not yet determined the precise character and ways and means of seizure and control of power by the in-between or intermediate, and by the restored systems. For this reason, and until the main problem—the nature of the process of restoration —has been clarified further, we shall use the term "the original system" according to the terms discussed above. It will be replaced by an intermediate system, no matter what its specific political and social coloring may be. This in turn will be followed by the restoration, the restored system.

For the sake of simplification, these three formal concepts will hereafter be referred to by code letters wherever the meaning of the terms and the frame of reference in which they are used are perfectly clear. Hence the original system will be called (A), the intermediate system will be called (B), and the restored system, (C).

It is our task now to give these formal concepts, original system (A), intermediate system (B), and restored system (C), fuller and distinctive meaning in reference to content, to show an innate relationship to a certain kind of social order, rather than the means of achieving such an order. The means would tell us only how the changes from (A) to (B) and finally to (C) were brought about: by revolutionary overthrow of government, by a Caesarean *Staatsstreich,* by a dictatorship of the proletariat or some other part of a class or caste, as the case may be. The same type of means may lead to diverse, sometimes directly opposite political results. A merely formal analysis tells us something only about the phenomenon of greater or lesser change in itself, but nothing about its evaluation.

A survey of the process leading from system (A) through (B) to the restored system (C) cannot be confined only to this question of the effectiveness of change. Here the observer may take a neutral position. But as soon as the issue of the objectives of change is raised, a value system becomes indispensable. The discussion will then have to be polarized around concepts such as conservative or progressive, according to the observer's choosing, but definitely in social terms.

The word polarize is used here advisedly. The interpretation of our terms may be almost as subjective and as strongly colored by these value judgments as the notions of freedom and liberty. Yet this ambiguity or even distortion of terms does not pertain so much to definition as to interpretation. And the ambiguity and possible misapplication of such interpretation is far more obvious in terms generally applied to concepts to the left of center than in those to the right of it.[3] The reasons are obvious.

The real or alleged broadening of mass participation in government demands that any governmental measures should be directed—actually, supposedly, or even fictitiously—to an ever-increasing share by the masses in the stocks and earnings of the "common wealth" in its literal meaning. Hence the bow to general progress of some sort. Vague as this goal may seem, it is more specific than Bentham's objective of the greatest happiness for the greatest number. Measures which promote true or alleged "progress," greater "equality," economic freedom in the sense of a greater share in the common good, are not necessarily concerned with ultimate objectives. In many instances these measures have become almost meaningless by their vagueness. Accordingly, they may allow for general support by almost the whole political spectrum, and the significance of the final goal is thereby voided. "Progress" however, in general, still expresses the idea of a means or at least a movement toward an end. In that sense it is fully endorsed by Western democracy and paid lip service to by the phony plebiscitarian character of Caesarean Bonapartism. Wherever this idea does not directly conflict with the racist concept of an élite, progress is emphasized also in the service of passive mass support by fascism and is manipulated by communism. True enough, under communism the loss of liberty means not only more guns but—if available—a more equal distribution of butter as well. This is secondary, however, to the needs of power politics.

In any case, progress, either as the genuine or as the merely professed advance toward an objective, a forward movement toward an improvement in social conditions, requires considerable change. It is fair to assume that such a movement toward change of some kind—even in the abuse of the term—is not satisfied with the inevitable change based merely

[3] A particularly conspicuous, though by no means isolated case in point, are the party labels under the Third French Republic, where, for instance, the Radical Socialists, the Republican Socialists, the Independent Left, and the Radical Left represented the nonsocialist center of the political stage, whereas the so-called Republican Left, for instance, belonged very definitely to the political Right. See also Frederick L. Schuman, *War and Diplomacy in the French Republic* (New York, 1931), pp. 14 ff.

on the biological limits of the life-span of man, or with the relatively inevitable change of technological progress per se.[4]

This is probably the main reason why progress, if understood as something more specific than the course of time from past to future, is usually not associated with the notion of a restored regime or a restoration. Apart from its political connotation, this concept of progress is confined primarily to the idea of a continuum of change, implied in biological and technological terms. Admittedly, value judgments come into play here. Progress cannot be determined by any quantitative scale: how much change as to content matter and, in the widest sense, how much movement within the continuum of time there may be in the transition from system (A) to system (C).

No doubt, the idea of the transition to (C), to restoration, is frequently associated with a concept of conservatism. This conclusion, however, needs some clarification. Conservatism is generally understood in the social sphere as a tendency to maintain existing conditions and to oppose change in institutions and methods. In practice this is contrary to progress. Yet the frequent assumption that progress and conservatism stand in positions opposite each other must not be accepted without proof. True, the generally held view of progress is alien to the concept of restoration, but this does not mean that the latter is linked to conservatism by necessity. Here an entirely new factor enters the picture. Conservatism perceives itself as opposed to change for change's sake, and within the realm of the possible—and, according to its adherents, the reasonable—wants to preserve the status quo with no more modification than is inevitable.[5] It does not rule out social change in principle, although it believes in the necessity to curb a sweeping application. The same would be true by and large for restoration, insofar as system (C) in general would reestablish system (A) with no more changes than necessary. Yet this conclusion applies to the ends, to the objectives of restoration, not to

---

[4] Particularly pertinent to this discussion are the classic studies by John B. Bury, *The Idea of Progress,* quoted here from the Dover ed. (New York, 1955), particularly pp. 2–7, 236 f., 334 ff., and by Ernst Cassirer, *The Philosophy of Enlightenment* (Princeton, 1951), pp. 234 ff. See further Hannah Arendt, *The Origins of Totalitarianism* (New York, 1951), pp. 143 f., where progress is discussed in the sense of the continued accumulation of power; also Robert L. Heilbroner, *The Future as History* (New York, 1960), in particular on the notion of the inevitability of progress, pp. 33 ff. In its broad social sense it is perceived here as a product of the optimistic views of the Enlightenment. See further *ibid.,* pp. 190 ff., 197 ff.

[5] For a discussion of the concept, see also Robert A. Kann, *A Study in Austrian Intellectual History* (New York, 1960), pp. 259–302.

the means of establishing it. Conservatism refers to a concept which wants to maintain itself, restoration pertains to one that strives for the reinstatement of a previous condition. This notion not only includes change—change is, in fact, its very essence. Only by change, by a dynamic movement, can restoration be established—if it can be established at all.

It might be held here that a conservative movement might try to advance the restoration of a previous system, and such an argument does not lack pragmatic validity. It trespasses, however, beyond the strict confines of semantics. Conservatism in the main is still properly identified with the preservation of the status quo; restoration, with its recuperation. To serve its purpose, conservatism has to fight change beyond certain limits; restoration, whether it agrees or not with conservative objectives, has to make the fullest use of the means for change to achieve its aim, the shift through an intermediate system back to the original system.

Change and Image

The problem is simply, how much social and political change does the restorative power allow? The restored system, on the one hand, has to be similar to the original system. Were it different, there would be neither a motive for the restorative process, nor any *raison d'être* for the accomplished state of restoration. Yet change to some degree is inevitable, whether the social forces working for restoration will it or not.

We have noted that this inevitability pertains primarily to biological and technological change. It may be added that a measure of change would be forced intentionally on the advocates of restoration by the champions and defenders of the intermediate system (B). If they had to yield they would obviously try to preserve as much as possible of their social and political achievements, and would attempt to incorporate them into the restored system. Whether they would do so with the intention of working for a reasonable compromise, or of preparing the means to fight another day for their objectives, is immaterial at this point. The forces fighting for restoration may have to yield to some degree to leaders and adherents of system (B), yet they also may voluntarily accept and even further the preservation and entrenchment of some of the political and social gains and achievements of (B). The question now is, what are the motivations and consequences of such actions?

As far as the adherents of (B) are concerned, their purpose would be quite clear, namely, to make the restored system safe and livable from their point of view. Furthermore, they might want to lay the groundwork for a later fight against the system, if and when the occasion arose. As for the supporters of restoration, their purpose would be rather different. Concessions to system (B) would be granted either by volition or compulsion to make restoration possible, and above all, to make it durable. The reasons are obvious. Restoration is chiefly concerned with the resumption of legal continuity. Consequently any system of government based on evolutionary, well-reasoned law would rest, at least to some extent, on the consent of the governed. Submission to long-established legal standards and procedures clearly implies this. Such deduction would hold true no matter how conservative the restored regime might be otherwise. Yet it could not be entirely conservative. The trend of progress, in the terms discussed previously, demands general advance toward betterment, in breadth as well as in depth, and since such concept of progress signifies a continuum, the movement must be perceived as one of lasting character. It may be distorted and perverted by Caesarean and totalitarian regimes of all kinds. This does not change the innate impulse toward social betterment among the articulate masses of modern times. It could well be held, however, that dictatorship by open or underhand means may be opposed to such progress. But we are not concerned primarily with dictatorship when we discuss the restorative process and objectives. The desire to work for the resumption of legal continuity in the case of restoration, and the revolutionary rejection of such continuity by all brands of dictatorship allow here for a clear-cut distinction.

In view of what has been noted in regard to government by law and the urge for social progress, it should become clear that (C) needs a measure of support from the people, a measure of consent on the part of the governed, brought about by the introduction of the principles and institutions of (B) into (C). Again the decisive question is one of degree. Just how far-reaching should be the impact of (B) and the popular support of (C) in a successful restoration, which does not at the same time obscure the latter's true character?

We do not propose to answer this question categorically. Indeed, an attempt to set up a social formula to such effect would be utterly naïve. It may be useful, however, to survey individual cases of restoration from this angle at a later point. This would mean that the success or failure of the incorporation of social and political institutions of (B) into (C) would be tested at a later point by (C)'s durability in individual cases.

A more general approach to this question will not tell us what specific laws and institutions the restored system should adopt from the intermediate system, but it may indicate what conditions restoration has to meet to be successful in the accession and the durability of power. The restored system (C) must preserve the image of the original system (A) without identifying it in the minds of the governed with reaction. Reaction in our context means a movement toward a former political or social policy, a policy that does not recognize the desirability or even necessity of social change. If the restoration movement and the restored system are to avoid these pitfalls, they will have to do more than revive and resume the tradition of the original system (A). They will have to take into consideration the fact that, unless there had been major external aggression, (A) would hardly have fallen from power without major ailments in its social body, reflected also in the memories it transmitted. These memories too would have to be not only revived but reshaped as well. To what degree? Again the answer would be: to preserve the image of (A) and to prevent the possibility that the people will associate or even identify restoration with reaction.

The notion of a Hegelian synthesis may suggest itself here. In this sense system (C) on a higher plane would represent the synthesis of the thesis and antithesis of (A) and (B). Such line of reasoning is certainly arguable, but we will not commit ourselves to it. The test of a successful restoration is its durability, not its rationality in terms of closer approximation to the world spirit. Reason and rationality in Hegel's terms are highly abstract concepts.[6] To achieve durability by preserving the image of system (A) and at the same time absorbing basic institutions of (B) requires, on the other hand, very concrete political skill.

Its difficulty in political practice may largely account for the fact that successful cases of restoration within the previously established terms of reference seem to be so rare in the history of our civilization. Certain features must be emphasized in order to keep the idea of system (A) clearly before the people. Others may be blurred or even conveniently forgotten, to be replaced by traits more in line with the necessary demands of change and social progress. Since the degree of required or desired change will be dictated largely by social pressure, which cannot be easily manipulated, we would still arrive at roughly the following situation. Restoration of a state constitution in broad principles would be of cardinal importance to preserve the form, the conception of (A) in the minds of those striving for restoration. In particular this means the return from a republican regime to a monarchial one, including the concomitant social changes which convert a regime to a system.

---

[6] Karl P. Hasse, ed., *Hegels Philosophie* (Berlin, 1917), pp. 17 ff., 112 ff.; Paul Kägi, *Genesis des historischen Materialismus* (Vienna, 1965), pp. 51 ff., 123 ff.

There may in fact be greater social and even political differences in various types of republics than between a republic and a restored monarchy. The republican structures of an aristocratic and of a democratic commonwealth have entirely different political structures and social philosophies. But the disparities between the peasant democracy of the late medieval Swiss forest cantons and the patrician republic of Bern have much less impact on the general public than has the image of a monarchy with its far more widely recognized conventional accessories and symbols.

This symbol-laden character of the monarchy, plus the fact that up to the end of the First World War most states in our civilization were monarchies, helps explain why the restorative process in history generally moves from monarchy to monarchy, and not, as would be entirely possible by definition, from republic to republic.

To help retain the image of the original system (A), certain symbols and paraphernalia of a type-forming character, such as crowns, coats-of-arms, anthems, and so forth, would be of great importance, as can be easily demonstrated in any restorative process, whether successful or not.

Undoubtedly there are more subtle, more profound, and in the end more effective factors as well. Of these the most important would presumably be those related to the concepts of legal continuity, long-established mores, and in several cases of restoration, moral, in particular religious, values—a deviation from the religion of the fathers and a gradual return to it.

All these factors are undoubtedly of a more spiritual character—in the true sense of a more reasoned nature—than is the mere restoration of external symbols. In fact, a restoration movement which puts the primary emphasis on outworn symbols and outdated semisymbolic privileges of system (A) is not likely to succeed. As experience shows, the spiritual values and type-forming features of (A) which meet a positive response among large strata of the population will have a more lasting effect on restoration. This does not mean however that the impact of the symbols, particularly in emotionally tense situations, should be denied.

Here a new difficulty arises. The more profound spiritual factors of restoration from (A) to (C) are at the same time far less obvious than superficial emblems or an obvious imitation or likeness of the past. How does a successful restoration movement communicate them to those who are expected to support restoration?

Certainly there is no easy, fully satisfactory answer to this question. Allowance should be made for the fact that certain type-forming features and values may vary from case to case. Furthermore, we must remember that the restorative process is based on a combination of diverse elements. Some of them seem to be effective without direct human intervention. Others reveal the straight intent of men. Still others indicate emotional, not fully rational motivations to which the supporters of restoration may be highly susceptible.[7] All these factors, separately or in combination, emphasize external symbols. They may be conveniently summarized under the concept of the forces of tradition. It is appropriate to confront them at this point with the idea of restoration and legal continuity.

[7] Less than fully rational motivation does not, of course, preclude full consciousness of action. In other words, emotional behavior and behavior which is perhaps in part not fully rational, (though not necessarily irrational) should in no way be equated with the Freudian concept of subconsciousness.

CHAPTER III

Ways and Means of Restoration

TRADITION

The emotional and rational power of restoration rests on three main pillars; from the general to the specific they are tradition, legal continuity, and legitimacy. These three terms stand in a descending relationship to each other, for not only is the first broader than the second and the second broader than the third, but the first also comprises the other two, and the second includes the third.

Tradition—the transmission from generation to generation of information, beliefs, customs, legal principles, and unwritten laws, as well as moral doctrines in a religious sense—is indeed comprehensive in regard to all three concepts. Legal continuity—the nonrevolutionary flow and development of the legal system, on which not only the governmental structure but the whole social order is based—includes legitimacy as more specific. Legitimacy, like legal continuity, means principles and attitudes in accordance with law, but also, in a narrower sense, the lawful principles of governmental authority, and in an even more restricted sense, the monarchic hereditary principle.

Such are in general the semantics and semantic relations of the three concepts. To what extent and in what specific manner do they pertain to the problem of social and political restoration? The distinguished philosopher of history R. G. Collingwood makes a telling point relevant to this discussion, in a discourse of Greco-Roman historiography and in particular of the Hellenistic historian Polybius in the second century B.C. The people of Rome

> had a kind of historical consciousness quite different from that of the
> Greeks. History for them meant continuity; the inheritance from the

27

past of institutions scrupulously preserved in the form in which they were received; the moulding of life according to the pattern of ancestral custom. The Romans acutely conscious of their own continuity with their past, were careful to preserve memorials of that past . . . they preserved ancient traditions of their own corporate history to an extent unknown to the Greeks. These traditions were undoubtedly affected by the inevitable tendency to project the characteristics of late republican Rome into the history of her earliest days. . . .

After referring to the danger in distortions of this kind, Collingwood continues: "It is to the Romans . . . that we owe the conception of a history both oecumenical and national, a history in which the hero of the story is the continuing and cooperate spirit of a people. . . ."[1]

True, the national tradition of Roman historiography does not represent the only kind of historical tradition conceivable. In fact, Collingwood rightly points out that almost two thousand years after Polybius, Gianbattista Vico observed that we may conceive of a far more complex tradition which does not imply the straight handing down of customs, beliefs, and laws from generation to generation. We have to take tradition "not as literally true but as a confused memory of facts distorted through a medium whose refractive index we can to a certain extent define. All traditions are true, but none of them mean what they say; in order to discover what they mean, we must know what kind of people invented them and what such a kind of people would mean by saying that kind of thing."[2] Undoubtedly a very different but simpler and at the same time grander tradition, one of dominant spiritual ideas, exists also in the *Civitas Dei* of St. Augustine or in the early Romantic ideas of Herder, to mention only two outstanding examples. Yet we are primarily concerned here with the Roman type of tradition, for two principal reasons. We have to deal only with the effect of a tradition within the state, not with one of lasting metaphysical or philosophical systems transgressing far beyond it. Furthermore, we are concerned here with the direct effect of tradition from one generation to the next, not with one throughout ages measured by centuries and millennia.

Perhaps no political thinker has investigated the political implications of that concept of tradition as widely and as keenly as Max Weber. In his classical studies of political sociology and in particular of the origins and authority of power, he holds that "traditional domination is based on the belief in the legitimacy of an authority that 'has always existed.' The per-

[1] R. G. Collingwood, *The Idea of History* (New York, 1957), pp. 34, 37 f.
[2] Collingwood, p. 70; see also pp. 63–71; and Henry P. Adams, *The Life and Writings of Gianbattista Vico* (London, 1935), pp. 94 ff., 147 ff.

sons exercising the power of command generally are masters who enjoy personal authority by virtue of their inherited status."[3] This certainly represents tradition in a very wide political sense, though not nearly as wide as notions based on the religious heritage of St. Augustine or the *Volksgeist* of Herder. They clearly and consistently transcend the socio-political sphere. Weber, on the other hand, narrows down his concept as he moves along. "The content of commands is bound up with and limited by tradition. A master who violated tradition without let or hindrance would thereby endanger the legitimacy of his own authority which is based entirely on the sanctity of that tradition. As a matter of principle it is out of the question to create new laws which deviate from the traditional norms. . . ."[4] Accordingly, this "legitimation of traditional domination occurs, wherever the 'authorities' claim obedience on the basis of established usage. . . ." Thereupon the "combination" of patrimonial and feudal elements characteristic in the West results in the modern state.[5]

We cannot here probe into the history of traditional social bodies. It must suffice to note that the impact of tradition pertains as much to general rational and more specific legal values as to a feudal institutional heritage. All of these values have to be blended into a comprehensive image of forces that mold society. Within this image certain features are of particular significance, in a positive as well as in a negative sense.

Wide as the impact of tradition is, even in the political sense alone, certain governmental and social systems are not compatible with the social relationship of restoration as understood in this study. This applies first of all to the question of personal, often despotic rule wherever the claim to rightful succession is challenged, the ruler of the old dynasty is overthrown, and the old dynasty or even the dispossessed ruler himself is eventually reestablished, as in the English Wars of the Roses in the fifteenth century, for instance, or in the Russian succession conflicts during the so-called "time of troubles" centering around the false Dimitri in the early seventeenth century. Numerous examples could be found in Ottoman Turkish history well into the nineteenth century. In none of the examples of this kind can we speak of restoration by appeal to a broad, ancient tradition beyond that of legitimate succession. Important as

---

[3] Reinhard Bendix, *Max Weber* (New York, 1960), pp. 298 ff., as discussed in Max Weber, *Wirtschaft und Gesellschaft,* Vol. I, Part II.

[4] Bendix, p. 332, quoted from Max Weber, *Staatssoziologie,* p. 101.

[5] Bendix, *ibid.,* and pp. 379 ff. The last conclusion, although based strictly on Weber's deductions, must be attributed to his interpreter, Reinhard Bendix.

legitimate succession was to contemporaries ideologically, in political practice it was an issue merely in terms of personal ambition and the defense against it on grounds of personal privilege. Modern historians are, of course, fully aware of basic social and psychological causes and implications of these struggles.

As to genuine restoration, or to restoration processes which come close to restoration, it makes little difference whether the return is to a system under the same or under different individuals. What happened in England in 1660 and in France in 1814 would have been genuine cases of restoration, even if Charles I and Louis XVI had not been executed but had been banished and later returned to power, like their successors Charles II and Louis XVIII. Irrespective of these purely personal facts, the return of the Stuarts and Bourbons represented, or approached, the restoration of systems and the revival of issues, regardless of the individuals involved. As long as these basic issues remained substantially unchanged, even the transition from an extinct dynasty to a new one would make little difference. On the other hand, the transition in England from the reign of Richard II to that of Henry IV Bolingbroke, and from that of Henry VI Lancaster to that of Edward IV of York, and the related issue of legitimacy mainly concern just persons. This is even more obvious in the case of the accession of the Romanov dynasty in Russia in 1613. Now, there is no question that the Lancaster–York warfare in England, and in particular its beginnings, the deposition of Richard II Plantagenet, was as deeply connected with the Wat Tyler peasant revolt and Wyclif's influence on relations of state and church as the rise of the Romanov dynasty in Russia was associated with growing insight into the political weakness of Russian feudalism. However, the political consequences—the replacement of previous rulers or dynasties by new ones—appeared for some time to be only incidental to the causes of unrest. Political and social disturbances unleashed the forces which were eventually to cause change. Yet it was by no means possible to visualize a concerted effort to match new programs against old concepts of power. Conflicts were crystallized not primarily in issues but in personnel problems, in symptoms, not in causes. Seemingly the deep-seated social struggle and the dynastic contests ran just parallel.[6]

Despotism and absolutism, as far as they merely imply the rule of one

[6] A lucid discussion of these matters can be found in George Trevelyan, *History of England*, Vol. I, Book II, various editions; John R. Green, *A Short History of the English People*, Vol. I, chap. 5, various editions; and in Bernard Pares, *A History of Russia* (New York, 1947), pp. 127–162.

individual rather than of another, can never, either for better or for worse, establish a tradition, because such changes completely lack comprehensiveness in regard to social, cultural, and spiritual ideas. This does not mean that any kind of tradition is good; it does mean that any tradition is comprehensive, and without such a comprehensive tradition we can speak of the replacement or reinstitution of men or even of governments but never of the restoration of systems as we use the term here.

The obvious notion that a tradition does not necessarily have to be positive—good in a moral sense, or progressive in a social one—raises another question. What about dictatorships? Dictatorships surely may be evil, yet there is no denying that they may be far more comprehensive and deeply rooted in regard to institutions, ideas, and values than such dynastic problems in modern history as whether the main line of the house of Bourbon or its Carlist branch should have been restored to power in nineteenth century Spain.

We refer here primarily to dictatorship as an institution which intends to perpetuate itself, and not to a mere administrative device for dealing with an emergency situation, as in republican Rome. Consequently some distinctions are in order. The existence of three main types of dictatorship in modern Western history is suggested. The first one would be the type frequently, but not exclusively, observed in the overthrow of presidential governments in Latin American countries, particularly before the First World War. While this political phenomenon has by no means disappeared, its intimate connection with the major social and ideological conflicts of our times has become far more obvious. It was neither obvious fifty years ago nor, in some cases, in existence at all. We would have to admit that this type of dictatorship has existed and still exists frequently in countries administered by regimes classified as democratic in purely constitutional terms, but which are politically not well prepared for democracy. Change in the top echelons of government has hardly more social significance than the revolutions which made or unmade the successions to many an Ottoman sultan in the Seraglio of Istanbul. Thus the most common kind of dictatorship lacks an issue, as does the removal or reinstitution of any brand of monarchial despotism. It is therefore not a legitimate subject of a discussion of restoration. No tradition exists, and a false appeal to one comes to nothing.

A second type of dictatorship is far more interesting from our point of view. It is related to but not identical with what Hannah Arendt refers to as "non-totalitarian dictatorships," as they came into being after the First World War in Rumania, Poland, the Baltic states, Hungary, Portugal, and Spain and, it may be added, in Austria in 1933 as well. According to Arendt, "These countries simply did not control enough human material to allow for total domination and its inherent great losses of population. Without much hope for the conquest of more heavily populated territories, the tyrants in these small countries were forced into a certain old-fashioned moderation lest they lose whatever people they had to rule." [7]

Although the word tyranny may be too strong, this evaluation of dictatorship may be true as far as it goes, which is not far enough. The "non-totalitarian dictatorships" to which Arendt refers may have a much smaller popular base than genuine totalitarian dictatorships, not necessarily because of weakness, but perhaps because of difference of purpose. The Caesarean type of dictatorship (in modern times represented by Bonapartism, and far more by the regime of Napoleon III than that of Napoleon I), differs from genuine totalitarianism not merely in degree but also because of limitations of purpose. The fact that in several of the dictatorships that followed the First World War these limitations were based on authoritarian restraint resulting from weakness, cannot obscure the basic fact. The Caesarean type of dictatorship, much of it still traceable in these postwar dictatorships, differs from the merely personal type of dictatorship in that it is based to a degree on mass support. Furthermore, its objectives go beyond the simple aim of perpetuating power. This kind of rule is distinguished from true totalitarianism by the fact that the popular support which it hopes to secure is limited to certain social groups. Unlike genuine totalitarianism, the political and social objectives of such a regime are not really comprehensive but are limited or, perhaps more correctly, selective.

In the case of true totalitarianism, the third type referred to, coercion, propaganda, and illusionary promises are aimed at the support of the people as a whole. The fact that such systems need an internal enemy—capitalists, traitors to the interests of the working class, true or alleged Communists, Jews, as the case may be—as much as an external one does not contradict the aim of comprehensive mass support. To put these groups beyond the pale does not simply mean discrimination against one group or another as occurs continuously throughout history. In a thirst for aggression, essential to fully totalitarian dictatorships, this political strategy strives for the complete destruction of one part of the population in order to establish a new kind of nation or *Volksgemeinschaft*. It still remains comprehensive after its own hideous fashion.

[7] Hannah Arendt, *The Origins of Totalitarianism* (New York, 1951), p. 303 f. See also Ernst Nolte, *Three Faces of Fascism* (New York, 1966), pp. 13 ff. (translated from the German).

We return to the pretotalitarian, or rather minor totalitarian, brand of dictatorship with its merely selective aims, to which Arendt refers, and to the older one of Caesarism. They are alike in the limitation of objectives and popular support, but in Caesarism these limitations are ordinarily due not to the weakness of the regime but to a different philosophy in kind. Bonapartism would be a case in point. It stands for the establishment of absolute state power linked to a modernized economic system which sustains the abolition of economic feudalism and shifts the center of social gravity of a system (A) from the rural nobility to the urban industrial and commercial upper middle class and middle class. Increasingly affiliated with this political philosophy is a plebiscitarian endorsement by pseudodemocratic institutions, which under Napoleon III, includes limited social welfare legislation to gain the support of industrial labor.

What does tradition have to do with the possibility of restoration of regimes of this kind? Undeniably they have stronger popular support and a more vigorous ideological foundation than the Latin American military junta dictatorships. Can they also cement their establishment with a stronger appeal to tradition, as they have frequently attempted? In Bonapartism under Napoleon I, there are frequent, obvious allusions to the grandeur of the Roman Empire in the constitutional experiments of the Consulate and in fact in the whole legislative work of the Napoleonic order. This notion was merged with the Holy Roman Empire idea of Charlemagne, to serve as emotional basis of the French empire of 1804.

Italian Fascism, roughly until the assassination of Matteotti in 1924, might be called a semitotalitarian rather than a fully totalitarian regime, and here the appeal to the tradition and expectations of rejuvenation of the Roman Empire was particularly strong. The appeal to somewhat similar reminiscences of a glorious past can be observed in Austria, particularly from 1933 to the German occupation of 1938, in relation to the bygone Habsburg power; or in semiauthoritarian Poland in the 1930's, in regard to the reestablishment of her late medieval and early modern position as a Great Power. These and other examples emphasize the effect of tradition in line with a clear-cut appeal to the idea of restoration.

In the sense in which we perceive the problem of restoration, such an interpretation warrants great caution. For one thing, the concept of restoration is based on the doctrine of legal continuity and its resumption after a revolution. This means that the break of such legal continuity, which occurs in every type of dictatorship, precludes a genuine and not merely propagandistic identification with a previous system. Yet the very concept of restoration is based on the idea of legal continuity between an original and a reestablished system. The dictatorship in our terms may follow system (A) by way of revolution and will then take the place of system (B). It may, as in France under the Napoleonic Consulate, follow (B) by way of counterrevolution and establish some new kind of government, but it will never establish true restoration. Not only is genuine restoration based on the consecutive order of three systems of government; it also requires system (C), following (B), to resemble (A) in its social and political doctrines to a marked degree.[8]

There is, however, a more specific reason why tradition does not play a part in the establishment of semitotalitarian dictatorships. Here we cannot speak of a true process of restoration because no true association with tradition exists. The semitotalitarian regimes are instilled not with a full but only with a good measure of totalitarian spirit and doctrine. Thus they deny by implication what they frequently proclaim loudly—a genuine respect for tradition. When Napoleon I equated the new French empire with that of Charlemagne and with many tenets of the ancient Roman Empire; when Mussolini boasted that he had brought the imperium back to the City of the Seven Hills; and when Dollfuss claimed that the Austrian republic of six million people had a European mission comparable to that of the Habsburg empire in the main battles of the Occident against the onslaught of the Ottoman Turks, a more or less effective emotional appeal was made to the glories of the past. Yet beyond the aim of reaching the hearts—rather than the minds—of the people, such appeals to the past had little practical meaning. Napoleon I was too farsighted to burden his governmental system with ancient or early medieval social and political principles. They would have impeded an imperialism whose success was largely based on administrative, technological, and economic modernization. Mussolini in his heyday was a politician far too shrewd and crafty to pursue a policy of unlimited imperialism in terms of global strategy. As soon as he lost touch with reality, the opportunity to achieve even limited objectives slipped from his hands. Dollfuss and his successor, Schuschnigg, could not seriously believe that they could restore the tradition of a great empire to any practical purpose. They were chiefly concerned with the modest and far too difficult task of preventing small Austria from being overrun by the German National Socialists. Endeavors to make the struggle against the evolution of the social welfare

[8] In several cases one could refer to the intermediate *era* rather than to the intermediate *system*. A good example would be France from the Thermidorian reaction in 1794 throughout the whole Napoleonic regime, where we can speak of numerous intermediate regimes and perhaps even systems until 1814, the time when the true restorative process in relation to system (A) fully succeeded for some time to come.

state more palatable by an appeal to semimedieval corporate ideas were doomed to failure in Austria as they were in Italy. In substance they never went beyond an imperfect blueprint stage in either case.

This is not the tradition we have in mind when we speak of genuine political and social restoration. In that case success is based on the proclamation of the vigor of the original system's institutions. Such an appeal, though not always well founded in history, is made in good faith. Semitotalitarian dictatorships, on the other hand, represent only a dubious imitation of such restoration. Their regimes succeeded to some extent when and where they paid only lip service to tradition, provided they could also play a skillful game of power politics. They became ridiculous, however, wherever they took this game too seriously. This is as true for the coronation of the great Napoleon I under the actor Talma's guidance as for the proclamation of Vittorio Emanuele III as emperor of Ethiopia.

The genuine, integral dictatorships of our times, National Socialism and Bolshevism in its Stalinist stage, are linked as clearly to sweeping revolution as to restoration. This revolutionary aspect of the problem will not be discussed at this point. Even so we are faced with a number of complex methodological problems. These two basic types of modern dictatorship, however, widely divergent as they are, hold a great deal in common in regard to tradition and restoration. Naturally, Communism cannot be equated with National Socialism due to the latter's racist tenets of denying the equality of men and to its tactics of genocide. Yet both are based on the aim of total, vociferous, but in effect only passive, mass support. We have referred to their comprehensive drive to annihilate the internal enemy. In other respects they subordinate all social activities to the complete control of the governing regime. The fact that National Socialism in social respects has proved to be far inferior to Russian communism, particularly in the latter's post-Stalinist stage of development, makes little difference for our specific purpose. Apart from very small islands of human freedom in a totalitarian sea, the objectives of either regime are all comprehensive and radical in regard to tradition, though different movements may not proceed at the same speed. From the very beginning of the Bolshevik revolution there was a complete break with the past in regard to social objectives. Later, somewhat positive allusions to political history perceive men like Peter the Great or Kutusov in 1812 not so much as forerunners of a glorious future but as capable tools serving unwittingly and inevitable development.

In the beginning of the National Socialist era we find, it is true, an abundance of associations and affiliations with the spirit and above all the expansion of the idea of the Holy Roman Empire and the old Prussian military virtues. Yet, even before the outbreak of the Second World War these propagandistic links with the past were withering away. There can be little doubt that wartime National Socialism wanted to destroy them as mere semifeudal recollections of a historical caste system. The move in the direction of a national "bolshevik" chaos without the benefits of social planning and methodology was undeniable. The issue should be clear. Notwithstanding loud propagandistic concessions on the part of the National Socialist regime in its beginning and more subtle ones on the part of Russian communism in its later history, both deny the impact and significance of tradition.

This essence of genuine tradition stands by no means for mechanical or, in a literal sense, reactionary imitation of the institutions of the past. It does stand for respect for these institutions and the intelligent reappraisal and readjustment of their values. Totalitarian philosophy, however, even though it may pay lip service to tradition, actually wants to destroy the heritage of the past and has succeeded, in varying degrees, in doing so. In any case, tradition plays no major rational part in either system and no important emotional one. Systems of this kind, as well as the semitotalitarian regimes, may easily demand the recuperation of former and bygone political power, but obviously their imperialism is not limited by historical boundaries. Beyond these false appeals to faded glories, the far more important associations with the past through mores, laws, and social and spiritual values, in which genuine restoration is based, mean little to them.

In regard to the incompatibility of the totalitarian systems with genuine restoration, two other points should be noted in which the two basic types again show an amazing similarity. They will make use of pseudotraditional invocations wherever it serves their purpose. Yet this purpose is usually served only by an appeal to a far distant past, with utter rejection of the measures and accomplishments of an immediately preceding era, be it the Weimar republic or the administration of Prince Lvov and Kerensky. Indeed, several of the feeble semitotalitarian governments of the period between the two world wars also rejected with utter contempt the notion of building their flimsy structures on the embers of intermediate regimes.[9]

[9] To avoid confusion, the term "system" is here avoided since it is used in this study only in reference to truly restorative processes. Obviously this does not mean that changes brought about by the Communist revolution in Russia or the National Socialist one in Germany are less sweeping than changes from any system to any other referred to so far.

Here again true restoration is genuinely different. It may be, in major aspects, entirely averse to the policies of (B), yet a genuine restorative movement will always try to repress such an aversion in order to bridge a wide political and social gap between (A) and (C). Restoration does not want to lose the image of identification with system (A), but neither does it intend to sever the links with (B) and thus with a limited accommodation to the needs of the future. True restoration, and that means successful restoration, aims for accommodation if not reconciliation with the intermediate past, not for its outright repeal. Totalitarianism and semitotalitarianism, on the other hand, will pay lip service to the distant past and, at the same time, may be ready to crush the intermediate regime in a bloodbath since it represents the last roadblock barring its accession to power.

An analogy between Right and Left totalitarian systems seems justified in reference to the cult of personality, which actually comes closer to the concept of oriental despotism than to the hero glorifications of other kinds of dictatorship. The military junta dictatorship of the Latin American brand is clearly too transitory even to make an attempt in this direction.[10] The semidictators of the period between the World Wars and some of those after the Second World War as well, generally cut such sorry figures and had such feeble power that an often attempted cult of personality was doomed to failure and ridicule. The cult of personality in the Great Power dictatorships on the other hand, while morally no less reprehensible, can be organized and backed up by such a huge power apparatus in foreign and domestic relations that it arouses fear and disgust but hardly ridicule. In this respect too there is a strong internal relationship between the different brands of integral totalitarianism. This attitude, it is true, has been superseded in Russian communism since Stalin, but not yet in Chinese communism. Frequent appearances to the contrary, genuine restoration, on the other hand, is in essence based on the preservation of the idea and not of the person, as expressed in the principle "Le roi est mort, vive le roi!"

Totalitarian movements, therefore, can never represent genuine restoration. Whether they themselves can or could be reestablished seems to be, in the case of the firmly entrenched power of Bolshevism, an academic

[10] The obvious should be noted here to avoid misunderstanding. Péronism in Argentine under Juan Péron, where a cult of personality showed itself rampant, and the present Castro regime in Cuba, where it still is, both have stronger and broader foundations than military junta regimes. Whether Péronism holds the middle ground between a semitotalitarian and a genuine totalitarian regime, or whether it represents integral totalitarianism is debatable; there can be little doubt that Castro's regime stands at present for full totalitarianism.

question. As far as National Socialism is concerned, the question seems more or less remote. Any past regime may, of course, be succeeded at some point by another one with similar objectives. This is, however, not identical with restoration. In theory the question is simply: Can a movement which denies genuine tradition and which owes its rise to power—not necessarily in form but in substance—to a break with the past, itself establish a tradition? It is fortunate for mankind that our historical experience with the "philosophy" of an order of "scientific" genocide is too limited to answer this question. On the basis of pragmatic experience the question can be answered in the negative.

Restoration, sometimes for better and sometimes for worse, stands for the revival and adjustment of tradition. Tradition is in this respect a means to an end, but also in a much revised form an end in itself. Totalitarianism, on the other hand, is always a means and never an end because as such it would devour itself as the proverbial revolution devours its children. Yet, while as a means it may look back to many precedents in the far distant past of history, it must at the same time deny, minimize and excuse their existence. Unlike tradition, totalitarianism, whose adherents in the deepest layers of their minds are bound to be ashamed of themselves, can be instrumental neither in building nor in rebuilding a free society.

LEGAL CONTINUITY

"Legal domination exists where a system of rules that is applied judicially and administratively in accordance with ascertainable principles is laid for all members of the corporate group." [11] This view of Max Weber does not say how the ascertainable principles are ascertained. Legal domination may indeed refer to statute law, but also to law founded upon customs; it may pertain to historic law as well as to the immanent principles of natural law; and any one of them may be codified or focused on case law.

These distinctions have considerable bearing on our problem. If we assume that the driving force which leads to restoration is the desire to heal the break in the legal continuity between system (A) and the revolutionary intermediate system (B), then the idea of legal continuity is a specific, clearly marked aspect of tradition. This is obvious in reference to law founded upon custom, and to the equation of such law with tradition. The denial of these principles means a clear break with that tradition. The stages of the French Revolution of 1789, which are char-

[11] Bendix, *Max Weber,* p. 297; see also pp. 391-411.

acterized by recognition of an immanent natural law as the enlightened philosophers perceived it, would be cases in point.

It might be argued that a revolutionary system, at least in theory, could introduce a new set of legal principles based on a different interpretation of historic law. On a large scale such an attempt does not seem likely. In a technical sense the codification of French law under Napoleon I as consul and emperor, which actually had already progressed very far under the revolutionary regime of the Convention, means the replacement of a set of heterogeneous historic laws by another, older set of such laws, namely, by the principles of Roman law. Yet Roman law, as it was molded by the so-called "Reception"—that is, its readmission combined with readjustment in Germany after the eleventh century and particularly in the fifteenth and sixteenth centuries,[12] and in very different ways and far more clearly again in late eighteenth century France—was not perceived any longer as the product of a distant history. It was seen and studied as the incarnation of reason, discovered, comprehended, and protected, from the Twelve Tables of the early Roman republic to the Age of the Philosophers and beyond. In short, it was subjectively understood as an eternal system of law, but it actually represented historic law like any other. This difference between historic law and natural law would be accepted as one of subjective interpretation except—and this is a major exception—where natural law is understood as the direct outgrowth of divine law. Whoever affirms and believes in such divine law will naturally see it in a legal system different from historic law in kind, not merely in interpretation. This is a question of faith which need not be argued here.

Prior to the rise of the Marxian philosophy of history, however, no revolutionary regime would emphasize its legal foundations with explicit reference either to a very distant historic past nor usually to the legal principles of a recent past controlled by a hostile system. The spirit of revolution—in our context, system (B)—likes to refer to permanent, though generally not metaphysical, principles of law, which are allegedly more lasting and more obvious than any set of historic laws.[13] This

[12] Although the Reception took place in other West European countries even earlier, it was far less comprehensive there than in Germany. See Heinrich Brunner, *Deutsche Rechtsgeschichte* (Munich,1927), pp. 258 ff.; Georg Dahm, *Deutsches Recht* (Hamburg, 1944), pp. 36 ff.; Heinrich Mitteis, *Deutsche Rechtsgeschichte* (Munich, 1960), pp. 174 ff.

[13] Literature on this subject is overpowering in quantity. For brief general information the reader is referred to the following excellent works: Ernst Cassirer, *The Philosophy of the Enlightenment* (Princeton, 1951), pp. 234–274; Karl Petras-

general, largely emotional attitude of the true revolutionary is beautifully expressed by Schiller in *Wilhelm Tell,* when a representative of the original forest cantons in their revolt against Habsburg power states:

> Nein, eine Grenze hat Tyrannenmacht,
> Wenn der Gedrückte nirgends Recht kann finden,
> Wenn unerträglich wird die Last—greift er
> Hinauf getrosten Mutes in den Himmel
> Und holt herunter seine ew'gen Rechte,
> Die droben hangen unveräusserlich,
> Und unzerbrechlich, wie die Sterne selbst— [14]

Yet Marx proclaimed that the revolutionary takes the laws not from heaven, as Schiller says, but from economic inevitability embedded firmly in the setting of history. Does this contradict the previous observation that the revolutionary appeals to natural law rather than to historic law? We do not think so. We have noted that—except for the religious metaphysical sphere—the difference between historic law and natural law is one of subjective interpretation and, we may add, one of historical distance on the part of the observer and interpreter. What Marx actually did was to claim the discovery of a historic law of general social, though not specific legal, nature. He firmly believed that this doctrine was one of scientific precision. In fact, he held, contrary to the more modest views of many a modern scientist in his own field of research, that this meant more than high probabilities that could be tested by pragmatic experience.

This belief is nothing but a version of an alleged historic law elevated to natural law by subjective interpretation. The fact that Marx would certainly have contested such a statement indicates only that he, like many of his contemporaries and predecessors in the enlightened age, equated natural law exclusively with metaphysics, a concept that he firmly rejected. Yet if natural law is comprehended in a wider sense of modern legal philosophy as the existence of permanent, self-evident principles of moral law, then there is no reason to exempt Marxism from the widespread identification of revolutionary principles with a system of natural law.

Perhaps one might also suggest in this context that the revolutionary trends are toward codified rather than case law, for the simple reason that

chek, *System der Rechtsphilosophie* (Freiburg i/B, 1932), pp. 75–152; Gustav Radbruch, *Grundzüge der Rechtsphilosophie* (Leipzig, 1924), pp. 3–9. See further Otto Gierke, *Natural Law and the Theory of Society, 1500–1800,* 2 vols., trans. Ernest Barker (Cambridge, 1934), I, 166 f.

[14] Schiller, *Wilhelm Tell,* Act II, Scene 2. It should be noted that the "heaven" of Schiller, student of Kant, is free of any specific religious connotation.

a greater opportunity is thereby given to change the legal system in a comprehensive way. Certainly the French Revolution of 1789 would offer evidence to that effect. However, the evolution of law in the modern history of Western civilization outside of the Anglo-Saxon world is associated in general with statute law. Neither the two English Revolutions in the seventeenth century nor the American Revolution imply a complete break with tradition and in particular legal tradition; they all took place in the more flexible realm of case law. Accordingly this line of investigation appears not to be sufficiently specific—except in one sense. The fact that neither the English Restoration movement of 1660 nor the French one of 1814—and here we return to statute law—substantially changed the basic principles of the legal system in regard to civil law, criminal law, and procedure in a technical sense, helps to explain why these great historical transactions had at least a measure of success. Extreme change, outside of the constitutional sphere, did not take place in England and in France either between systems (A) and (B) or between (B) and the restoration movements (C).[15]

The main point to be stressed here is that legal continuity indicates social continuity as well. In no way does it prevent or generally even impede far-reaching social reform. On the other hand, it is inconceivable that a totalitarian revolution could operate for any length of time unless it practically eliminated the previous legal system. This holds fully true for the change in the Russian legal system after the October Revolution of 1917, and in the Italian Fascist and German National Socialist revolutions, with regard to criminal law, inevitably the first concern of any totalitarian system with its strategy of terror. In both Italy and Germany we also find far-reaching changes in civil law. Because of the outbreak of the war, however, these were incomplete at the time these regimes collapsed. Irrespective of the relatively lesser—though in themselves not minor—differences between the civil law systems of these powers and those of the Western "bourgeois" democracies, it can safely be surmised that further changes in civil law would have been drastic indeed if the fascist regimes had not fallen. The salient point in any system of civil law, as in other law, is not the question of property rights in itself but the related question of the freedom of the individual versus the power of the state. In that respect much similarity existed between the totalitarian regimes to the

[15] An objection in regard to radical French changes under the regime of the Convention may be answered with reference to the fact that these changes pertained to only two of the twenty-two years of the intermediate regime—from 1792, the fall of the monarchy, to 1814.

Right and Left, despite other, wide differences in their social philosophies.

If we thus equate legal continuity in a wider sense with social continuity and believe that the resumption of such continuity is a *conditio sine qua non* of a successful restoration, we must allow for a relatively broad sphere of possible social change embedded in the content of laws. This does not conflict with the objective of restoration, as long as procedural rights and the freedom of decision of the individual are safeguarded.

The most obvious questions to be raised here are the following: In view of the foregoing, would it be correct to say that legal continuity pertains to a much wider sphere of social and legal action than transactions deriving from constitutional changes? Does the concept of legal continuity require or should it require the legal structure of system (A) itself to have been lawfully established? How much change can we allow in system (C) and still maintain that the legal system of (A) has been reestablished by restoration? And finally, a most important issue, to be discussed in chapter 6: Can the legal and social principles of the revolutionary system (B) be sanctioned simply by the course of time, and if so, how much time?

As to the first problem, the topical range of the concept of legal continuity must not be reduced to the change of ruling groups who just happen to be in or out of power. Although the change from monarchy to republic and back to monarchy may be full of meaning, on the other hand it may not represent more than a storm-in-the-water-glass revolt in the Merry Widow type of country often associated with nineteenth century Balkan politics. There would be little difference between this interpretation of constitutional change and that of the Latin American dictatorships noted before. In neither case is a major part played by powerful social ideologies, or indeed by the whole massive problem of the extent and inevitability of social change. Any revolution and any restoration which limit themselves to the constitutional upset and its later revision would not stand for more than a putsch associated with a personal regime of absolute despotism or petty dictatorship.

The revolutionary and restorative processes we are concerned with here would certainly not shy away from profound changes in all spheres of social activity. This implies all spheres of public and private law as well. It does not mean that the basic principles of the legal system, whether those of the Magna Charta in England or the Declaration of the Rights of Man in France, would have to be abandoned by the restored system. Here again we refer to our previous conclusion that a restorative process which plainly voids instead of revises all the legal—and to a large extent social —changes brought about by system (B), will have very little chance to succeed. The issues involved in the break in and the resumption of legal continuity in the process of change between the three systems warrant a broad, extensive interpretation, not one that is narrow, legalistic, constitutional.

The same approach would be necessary in regard to the second problem, whether the question of legal continuity could be raised only if the original system had been lawfully established. The more ancient a political body—generally a monarchic political entity—the more difficult, indeed often impossible, would be the proof of lawful establishment. This might lead to a paradox. Few governments preceding those established after the two world wars could be considered legally constituted, on the strength of available evidence. Monarchical states and ancient republics going far back into the Middle Ages, on the other hand, would be deprived of the moral justification of government established by law.

This argument might be carried even farther. While in a number of cases the historic creation of a medieval state may be obscure from a legal point of view, there are others where no doubt exists that there was aggression in their early history. This applies equally to the Norman conquest of England, the break of the Union of Kalmar between the Scandinavian countries by Sweden in the sixteenth century, the establishment of independence of the Netherlands from Spain, down to the unification of Italy and Germany in the second half of the nineteenth century, which involved, quite apart from the question of external aggression, a whole string of unconstitutional acts. Obviously it is much easier to find examples of a break in legal continuity than cases of uncontested legal establishment in the development of modern states. Whether they have been set up by formal agreement between sovereign powers or, more recently, under United Nations auspices, is certainly not decisive. Were it different, our present system of an international community of states, badly shaken as it is already, would collapse.[16] According to state practice it is obvious that if the population of a country submits to the authority of the state and if the state itself receives *de jure* recognition from other

[16] As examples of an abundant literature on the problem see Arthur Nussbaum, *A Concise History of the Law of Nations* (New York, 1947), pp. 52 ff., 86 ff., 126 ff., 178 ff., 238 ff.; Hugo Krabbe, *The Modern Idea of the State* (New York, 1922), pp. 12–34; Alfred Verdross, *Die Verfassung der Völkerrechtsgemeinschaft* (Wien-Berlin, 1926), pp. 115–56; Joseph G. Starke, *An Introduction to International Law,* 4th ed. (London, 1958), pp. 237 ff.

states, its sovereignty is not questioned, even though it may have controversial antecedents.

Not quite so obvious are some corollary questions. What it the connection between the concept of legal continuity and the authority of system (A) in regard to length of time required to make it lawful? In what way, if any, would the consent of the governed have to be expressed for the same purpose? In the first place, according to Western political theory and the practice of modern states, the length of tenure of a government order does not in itself maintain legal continuity unless it has been endorsed by the consent of the governed. This certainly need not be an explicit recognition of the lawful origins of any national state on the part of its population, or by any other sovereign political body. In fact, even *de jure* recognition from the outside as a sovereign body implies only the permanent validity of such legal action in international relations. It does in no way determine the lawfulness of the origin of the state now recognized as sovereign.[17] According to Western doctrine, the establishment of constitutional government of lasting character, which implies the consent of the governed, would be essential. Later, the righting of previously unlawful government by way of plebiscites, referenda, or general elections would be recommended. Expression of the popular will in regard to the lawful origin of the state would not be required. Constitutional government may thus be fairly recent or of long standing. Provided its legal system operates within an orderly constitutional procedure, that is, one not imposed by unlawful violence, a government's authority cannot be challenged, irrespective of the true or alleged shortness of its rule.

Such is the reasonable position of the Western democracies, a position with strong support among modern states. It cannot hope for the genuine support of today's totalitarian powers, whose unchanged revolutionary aims are pursued with ever-varying opportunities to acknowledge or deny the lawful character of a state. As for despotic absolutism of ancient origin, it has no claims to justification by legal continuity, no matter how long its rule, colonial or otherwise. Yet the absolute monarchy, whether of medieval feudal character or more in line with the despotic absolutism of early modern times, may gradually change without violence into a regime of constitutional government. Most likely this would mean a constitutional or parliamentary monarchy, but today peaceful transition to a democratic republican regime without intermediary stages would be entirely feasible as well. In neither case could the new order be challenged on

[17] See Verdoss, pp. 137–144; Starke, pp. 104 ff.

the grounds of legal authority and legal continuity. Restoration of such an order, if overthrown, would not present any theoretical problem.

Entirely different is the case of the powerful totalitarian dictatorships of modern times, which are fully recognized in international relations but whose claim to rule by the consent of the governed is either contradicted by facts or cannot be tested. In the previous section, where we have dealt with the effect of tradition in general, we have noted that the rejection of genuine tradition by such regimes voids the possibility of their restoration in case of their downfall. They might well be succeeded immediately or subsequently by other dictatorships, but the link of basically the same image, so essential for the restorative process from system (A) to (C), would simply not exist.

Consequently we may at this point turn to the third problem. How much change of (A)'s legal order by way of the restorative process could be allowed without invalidating thereby the very essence of the restoration? This is actually only a somewhat more specific question in relation to the general problem of the retention of the image in the restorative process. Again we must refer to the previous discussion concerning the inevitability of social change, the significance of the form of government, in particular monarchic or republican, or the value of symbols. All these factors have a bearing on the question raised here, which refers in essence to the problem of image in legal continuity. Any change in the concept of legal continuity which does not conflict with main features of tradition embedded in the body politic is compatible with the restorative process. Such a change might go far indeed if the issue could be confined to the legal problem alone, and if accompanying social changes could be disregarded.

This, however, is not the case. Legal continuity in a technical sense is concerned chiefly with the formal, procedural character of law, not with its substance, its content. Accordingly any change which reflects due process of law in line with statutes providing for possible lawful change would be fully in line with tradition, fully in accordance with the principle of legal continuity. Substantive changes, however great, as long as they will be lawfully brought about, are likewise compatible with restoration. Just how compatible they may be without losing the image of system (A) in system (C) is a problem which must be approached case by case.

Finally the question arises: what if the restoration movement cannot succeed without resorting to violence against the revolutionary system? This raises a grave problem in regard to legal continuity, and it is clearly related to one briefly posed before. It has been said that the time element, the duration of a regime, is of little consequence so long as it is based on the consent of the governed and its establishment is not due to violence. The question now arises, what about legal validity where violence has not been righted by an action decisively expressing the consent of the governed? Is it in that case a matter of no consequence whether a process of violent overthrow of government has taken place two months, or two, twenty, or two hundred years ago? Can violence, the violence of either a revolutionary or a counterrevolutionary regime, be sanctioned by time? As specifically applied to the restorative process, can a system the essence of which is the fight against change by revolutionary means, resort to the same devices? We must keep these basic questions well in mind, when we turn to further specifications of the ways and means of restoration.

LEGITIMACY

Legitimate and *legitimacy* are concepts that may be understood in a wide sense to mean accordance with law, conforming to standards or type; yet they may also be perceived as synonymous with *legitimist* and *legitimism,* that is, the adherence to principles of hereditary monarchism. The supporters of restoration movements of such kinds are indeed frequently, and with a clear political overtone, referred to as legitimists.

We will not confine the issue of legitimacy, in this section, to so narrow an interpretation, even though there may be some historical justification in associating political tradition predominantly with hereditary monarchical tradition and hence with legitimacy in a very restricted sense. Yet such usage does not take account of the main streams of history of the last half century.

If we accept the wider interpretation of legitimacy, we can again refer to the authority of Max Weber. He perceives it as "power derived from established authority that allocates the right to command and the duty to obey." The obedience of the ruled is obtained to some extent through the idea that the rulers and their commands constitute a legitimate order of authority.[18] Weber's interpretation differs in one respect from the one traced here. By inference he comprehends legitimacy not as a specific

[18] Reinhard Bendix, *Max Weber,* pp. 294, 296; the qualification "to some extent" refers here to other aspects of rule such as power in general, "domination," etc., which do not concern us here. Weber's reflections are taken from his *Wirtschaft und Gesellschaft,* I, 122 and 328. For an unorthodox legal position according to which state power can never receive legitimacy by way of law, since this would mean the confounding of legal and social factors, see Hans Kelsen, *Reine Rechtslehre* (Vienna, 1934), p. 127 f.

concept of tradition but as something basically different from it. He refers to legal domination as "a system of rules that is applied judicially and administratively in accordance with ascertainable principles . . . valid for all members of the corporate group," whereas traditional domination is based on the belief in the legitimacy of an authority that "has always existed." [19] One might say that this distinction is not so much typical of Weber as it is typical of a sociological view in general, which perceives the difference between natural law and law based on customs as far more basic than it is ordinarily seen by a legally trained mind. Weber acknowledges, however, that "like the other types of authority, legal domination rests upon the belief in its legitimacy," which means that "laws are legitimate if they have been enacted; and the enactment is legitimate if it has occurred in conformity with the laws prescribing the procedures to be followed." [20] Here the legal point of view, which sees the essence of legitimacy as conformity with the law, is in agreement with the sociological approach, which is focused on purpose and value of the community.

Up to this point, however, we have been concerned only with a concept of legitimacy that pertains to any kind of political and social order, not specifically to that of restoration. If we focus our attention on restoration, we must avoid a concept of legitimacy either so narrow that it is limited to the monarchic principle alone or so wide that it does not apply to our subject at all.

Here the theory of the eminent student of the concept of legitimacy, Guglielmo Ferrero, comes in, as he developed it in many of his writings, above all in his *Principles of Power* published in 1941. Several of Ferrero's ideas are as challenging as they are controversial, yet his occasionally antiquated conservatism pertains primarily to his moralistic judgments in regard to historical facts and characters. There is no need to follow him along such lines. Here we are concerned not with the history of legitimacy as Ferrero sees it, but with its concepts and doctrines as he has keenly perceived them. His theory is not as sweeping as those of sociology which sees no difference between the concepts of government by law in general and legitimacy, nor is his view so narrow to be confined to the legitimist principle of hereditary monarchism. Ferrero presents a workable though debatable doctrine. As he sees it, the principles of legitimacy operate under the guidance of two main ideas, to which that great master of Roman history refers as "the genii of the city." In a narrow sense this means the protective local gods of the city of Rome but in a wider one those of any

[19] Bendix, pp. 297, 298.
[20] Bendix, pp. 413, 414.

orderly political community in general. These gods represent the aristo-
cratic-monarchic and the democratic principles.[21]

These guiding stars of orderly government operate at varying times in
the history of our civilization according to four principles of legitimacy:
the elective, the hereditary, the aristo-monarchic, and the democratic. The
elective, the hereditary, and the democratic principles are self-explanatory.
The aristocratic is generally associated with the hereditary monarchy,
namely, the co-rule or in a sense joint rule of a number of aristocratic
families, but it existed also in aristocratic republics of which the best
working example would be that of Venice in its heyday. A less obvious
one in early modern times would be Poland, nominally an elective kingdom, actually a republic of nobles.

> These four principles of legitimacy—the elective and the hereditary,
> the aristo-monarchic and the democratic—have for centuries been inter-
> mixed, either in conflict or in collaboration. The aristo-monarchic prin-
> ciple has always been inseparable from the hereditary principle. The
> democratic principle is irreconcilable with the latter and has only reluc-
> tantly tolerated a few remnants of it; the elective principle, fundamental
> for democracies, has also been utilized by monarchies, by aristocracies
> and by certain authoritarian institutions like the Catholic Church. A
> great many monarchies have accepted the election of diets, estates, par-
> liaments, or municipal councils. . . . In short, principles of legitimacy
> are justifications of power. . . .[22]

Ferrero perceived the reestablishment of the Bourbons in 1814, brought
about by the brilliance of Talleyrand and his alleged intellectual equal,
Louis XVIII, as a conspicuous example of a highly successful restoration.

---

[21] Guglielmo Ferrero, *The Principles of Power* (New York, 1942), pp. 12–19, 160.
The following quotations are from this main source of Ferrero's view on legitimacy.
Much, though not always fully crystallized, material on the problem is to be found
in other of Ferrero's writings as well: *The Reconstruction of Europe* (New York,
1941), pp. 47–61; *The Gamble: Bonaparte in Italy, 1796–97* (London, 1939), pp.
37 ff., 296 ff.; *Les Deux Révolutions Françaises, 1789–1796* (Paris, 1951), pp. 13–36;
see also *Between the Old World and the New* (New York, 1914).

It is interesting to note that two well-established authorities on the history of the
Congress of Vienna, where this problem stood in the foreground of discussions, per-
ceive legitimacy merely as an expedient employed in the service of Talleyrand's
French comeback policy. See Sir Charles Webster, *The Congress of Vienna* (New
York, 1963), p. 166, and Harold Nicolson, *The Congress of Vienna* (New York,
1946), pp. 142 f., 157, 176.

[22] Ferrero, *Principles of Power*, p. 22; see also pp. 20–27 *passim*. For an entirely
different but interesting approach to political legitimacy based on the process of political learning by the population, see Richard M. Merelman, "Learning and Legitimacy," in *American Political Science Review*, LX/3 (Sept., 1966), 548–561. This is
clearly a theory of social psychology in terms of semantics, not of history.

This has frequently led to a complete misunderstanding and distortion of his views as an uncritical glorification of the ancient regime in France and its restoration in all specifics. Nothing could be farther from the truth. Ferrero's writings abound in criticisms of institutions in France and in other countries under similar regimes in the two centuries preceding the revolution of 1789. He points to a number of weak spots in the alleged rally and reform after 1814 and to a new and more rapid decline after 1848.[23] Beyond the particular weakness of the hereditary principle apparent in modern times, Ferrero admits also the mixture of inevitable imperfections of any system on which the legitimate order is based, all this despite his admiration for the personality of Louis XVIII. The values of a system of legitimacy are not measured primarily in terms of efficacy. "A power is legitimate when the methods used first to establish it and then to exercise it, are conformable to these principles and to the rules drawn from them. It is that conformity and not the degree of efficacy, that establishes the right to govern. . . ." In fact, to define legitimacy in terms of efficacy would be outright dangerous. "According to the doctrine of efficacy, every government is legitimate when it has the strength to exact obedience and loses its legitimacy when it no longer has the strength. Might then would be right and every government in power would be as good as the next. The question of legitimacy would be solved by ignoring it. . . ."[24] On the other hand, legitimacy is never wholly irrational, since it was responsible for the system of orderly exercise and transition of power. "Every principle of legitimacy therefore, at least in part, is a rational implement that men may use to create an efficacious government if they want to. That is why chance is inadmissible as a means of bestowing power." Accordingly, "even the most unusual principle of legitimacy implies a minimum of rationality."[25]

Here the enlightened, conservative Ferrero comes actually somewhat closer to the ideas of a student of the restoration problem on the Left, Karl Griewank, than to those of the two Western liberal historians Sir Charles Webster and Harold Nicolson, who comprehend the legitimacy question as just one diplomatic expedient among many others.[26]

---

[23] Ferrero, *Principles of Power*, pp. 110 ff., 124 ff., 140 ff., 153 f., 281 f.; in regard to the restoration of 1814, see in particular Ferrero, *Reconstruction of Europe*, pp. 47 ff., 138–351 *passim*. See also *The Correspondence of Prince Talleyrand and King Louis XVIII During the Congress of Vienna*, M. G. Pallain, ed., 2 vols. (London, 1881), I, ix ff.

[24] Ferrero, *Principles of Power*, pp. 134, 135.

[25] *Ibid.*, p. 25.

[26] See n. 20.

Griewank agrees with them insofar as he too believes that Talleyrand used legitimacy as a lever to force the entry of France into the inner councils of the Congress of Vienna. Yet he attaches far more importance to this device than either Webster or Nicolson. At the same time he does not deny the significance of its ideological foundations.

According to Griewank's analysis, "All the practical experts of the policy of European diplomacy of equilibrium were fully conscious of the fact that the European order had to be built upon the restoration of legitimate monarchies. Yet eighteenth century diplomacy had frequently put the joint 'expediency' ('Konvenienz') of the Great Powers before individual rights of princes." When countries were divided and princes were transferred from one to another, contemporary statesmen were inclined to make concessions in the interest of a rational order among states and at the expense of the principle of legitimacy. "Emperor Alexander, who liked to dream about the creation of royal thrones, wanted least to hear about legitimacy. The dialectics of Talleyrand on the other hand . . . attempted to elevate 'legitimacy' to the central concept of political order and with Gallic realism to link the joint ideas of the diplomats to French interests. He perceived legitimacy with a characteristic French modification as rights of sovereignty based on treaties; in public law he equated it to the right to property in civil law." It was necessary to replace expediency by equity, force by law. In this way Talleyrand formulated the principles of the new French foreign policy. Therewith he made use of moral weapons which permitted a weaker power to question the right of conquest proclaimed by the victors. On this basis Talleyrand could demand the return to the relationship of the powers as of old. Yet, as Griewank sees it, this does not mean that " 'legitimacy' was more deeply entrenched in Talleyrand's political thinking than in Metternich's." This at least is the picture as Talleyrand himself presented it later.[27] There is no question that legitimacy in Griewank's interpretation is a central theme in the restoration process. It comes close to the previously discussed concept of legal continuity, but partly overlaps it. It is undoubtedly much narrower than Ferrero's in our opinion correct interpretation.

And yet, even according to Ferrero's much broader views, the principles of legitimacy remain "limited and incomplete and are of use only in certain situations in history, determined by the orientation of thought which is subject to change." This means, of course, in the latter part of

[27] Karl Griewank, *Der Wiener Kongress und die europäische Restauration 1814/15,* 2d rev. ed. (Leipzig, 1954), p. 139 f.; see also *ibid.,* n. 19 (author's translation).

the nineteenth and the early twentieth century the increasing transition from the hereditary monarchic to the democratic and elective principles. This, however, does not represent permanent truth. "If man succeeded in finding the principle of legitimacy that was absolutely rational and just, the problem of government would be solved for once and all. . . . There would no longer be the need for any reforms. . . . The social order is a structure perpetually to be reconstructed." Man accepts the imperfections of these principles only "after he has become accustomed to them, and then only for the time being; since he accepts them through habit, he gets tired of them and forsakes them. Being incomplete and limited, they wear out, which explains why they are born and die, have a childhood and an old age." Nevertheless these principles of legitimacy represent "the condition of the greatest good that mankind as a collective being can possess—government without fear." [28]

To Ferrero, legitimate government, like all earthly achievements, is a limited good, while government by fear—and that to him is revolutionary government—is an unlimited evil. This revolutionary type of government is devoid of a legitimate foundation for its rule. It is motivated by the fear of those whose legitimate rights it has overpowered. It accordingly attempts to suppress its own fears through the fear it arouses in others under the illusion that it could thus protect itself from opposition and assuage its guilt feelings and apprehensions. Yet this revolutionary evil is by no means necessarily caused by the content of its institutions. In some cases, as in the legislation of the English Glorious Revolution of 1688 and that of the French Constituent Assembly of 1789, their achievements are in substance strongly approved by Ferrero.[29] Basically he is concerned with the method, that is with the principle of the exercise of power and the evil and corrupting influence of illegitimacy in government, which eventually will spread from the methods of rule to its contents.

Government, of course, cannot exist without authority which, in absolute monarchies and democratic republics alike, comes from above. "But in monarchies as in democracies"—and this is a decisive point— "legitimacy comes from below. The government only becomes legitimate and is freed from fear by the active or passive, but sincere consent of the governed. . . . If that unity does not exist, the right of opposition becomes a battle ground for a struggle to the death." [30] Violence will ensue and the result again will be revolutionary government. Yet a gov-

[28] Ferrero, *Principles of Power*, pp. 314, 315; see also 286.
[29] *Ibid.*, pp. 49–81; see also Ferrero, *Les Deux Révolutions Françaises*, pp. 37–69.
[30] Ferrero, *Principles of Power*, p. 295.

ernment not only is based on authority from above and, if legitimate, on the consent of the governed from below. It also is anchored in the recognition of hereditary rights in the case of the monarchy, in majority rule and minority protection in the case of democracies. According to the principles of legitimacy, a regime also needs time for its proper recognition and functioning. In regard to this time element Ferrero is not at his clearest. As noted before, time is crucial in the whole restoration process, and in particular to the unchallenged legal standing of a government. Here Ferrero resorts to two auxiliary concepts, prelegitimacy and quasi legitimacy. Legitimacy "is preceded by a preparatory condition which may be called prelegitimacy. Prelegitimacy is legitimacy still in its cradle. Every government began by being a government that had not yet won, but was attempting to win, universal acceptance and had a good chance of succeeding; it became legitimate the day it succeeded in conciliating the opposition aroused by its advent." Accordingly "prelegitimate government . . . is a government in which the power is bestowed and exercised according to rules and principles not yet accepted by the people but observed by the government. . . ."[31]

The three examples which Ferrero offers to elucidate his concept are not very fortunate. One is the Weimar republic in the 1920's, which, according to Ferrero, never reached the stage of legitimacy; one is the French Third Republic between 1870 and 1890, which did reach it after a new generation grown up under the modern order had accepted it; the third case is that of the Spanish republic of 1931, where "the good chance" to succeed was exposed as plain illusion in hardly more than five years. Thus, according to Ferrero, it took the Weimar republic more than three times as long as the republic in Spain to arrive at the same stage of failure, while in the French case we can speak of success only if we attribute the downfall of the Third Republic exclusively to external aggression.

Yet the main point of criticism is not Ferrero's evaluation of these regimes but the impossibility of including three so widely different cases in the same definition. They are different largely because the question of failure or success is relative, determined primarily by the time element involved, that is, the duration of a system of government. Only if we could find a common denominator that would enable us to test success or failure of such a structure, would a definition like the one attempted by Ferrero be useful.

[31] *Ibid.*, pp. 139, 188.

Thus we will have to return later to this all-important question of the test of time. Ferrero certainly has not answered it in a fully satisfactory way. Yet he has focused it more clearly with the insertion of the concept of quasi legitimacy between legitimate and illegitimate governments. Quasi-legitimate governments are those "which, without being legitimate, are able to count on a large enough acceptance so as not to be obliged, like illegitimate governments, to make use of corruption, deception, and violence alone. They are assured of this consent partly by the elements of legitimacy they contain, partly because they are necessary to prevent anarchy." [32]

Ferrero offers in this category an incongruous number of governmental systems, including the Roman Empire at the time of Caesar, the Orléans monarchy in France under Louis Philippe, and the Italian monarchy under the house of Savoy up to the beginnings of Mussolini's usurpation of power in 1922. These cases—clearly disparate as to duration of the regimes, but even more so as to the degree of popular sovereignty and principles of government by law in operation—show the difficulty of historical classification. And yet the resort to controversial auxiliary concepts like prelegitimacy or quasi legitimacy illustrates not only the weakness but also the strength of Ferrero's line of reasoning, insofar as, unlike a Toynbee or a Spengler, he is willing to correct his dogmatism, although unfortunately only with controversial dogmas of another kind. Despite these shortcomings, his theory is of great help in an approach to the concept of legitimacy in the restoration process.

Restoration is as much dependent on legitimacy as on the resumption of legal continuity. While legal continuity refers to the status after restoration has been established, legitimacy pertains to its causation, to the motivation for the restoration process. Legitimacy is associated primarily with the resumption of the restoration process by which legal continuity is resumed. Legal continuity then stands for the extension of that process in time. These two concepts, legitimacy and legal continuity, mean something more specific than tradition in general, though undoubtedly both concepts are part of tradition. They also mean something more specific than Weber's concept of government by law. Legal continuity and legitimacy apply to the principles of the legal system of the past, and this means, perhaps more than anything else, laws of procedure. They do not bar change; indeed, up to a point they require it, yet this point is reached as soon as the principles are compromised by authoritarian methods and

[32] *Ibid.,* p. 217; see also pp. 213–376 *passim.*

aims. As to these original principles, they are genuine principles of legitimacy. Therewith we return to Ferrero's categories, to be taken up more thoroughly in the following chapter.

In the context of this discussion it is not necessary to approve or to challenge separately or collectively the four principles of legitimacy: "the elective and the hereditary, the aristo-monarchic and the democratic."[33] What matters here is not so much what the principles are but that they are observed—in other words, that the rules of the game are obeyed. We owe a great deal to Ferrero, who has defined the parental concept of legitimacy lucidly and firmly as the premise of the establishment of an orderly society, no matter how controversial may be the specific principles on which it is built. We fully support the contention that this premise pertains also the restoration of an orderly political and social system.

[33] *Ibid.,* p. 22.

CHAPTER IV

The Cycles

Gianbattista Vico is frequently credited with the first fully developed cyclic theory of history in modern times. Emphasis is on the recurrence of certain phases of history according to predetermined social laws. Such stages, developed in the broadest ideographic terms—the divine, the heroic, and the human—are, of course, conjectural. This is not meant to be derogatory. The test of these ideas, strangely implemented two centuries later in Pareto's sociology, is to be found in intellectual history, not in political history. They do not claim to deal with actual social situations. The cycle is one of thought, not of politial reality.

A much wider concept of a cyclic theory, which is frequently referred to, asserts that history proceeds according to foreordained regular stages, as stated in the Book of Daniel in the second century before Christ, in *De Civitate Dei* by St. Augustine, in Dante's *Divine Comedy,* down to Marx, Spengler, and Toynbee. With the latter three the concept of a regular pattern of historical development is sustained; that of preordination is replaced, however, by premeditation of alleged historical laws on the part of the historian. This secular concept of a cyclical theory in Western civilization goes back, of course, to Aristotle.

The argument is quite feasible that the theories of Marx, Spengler, and particularly of Toynbee could be perceived as genuine cyclic theories in a more specific sense as well. With Marx the cycle of revolutionary development reaches a definite terminal stage with the establishment of the classless society. According to Spengler and Toynbee, civilizations believed to be doomed will be replaced by others. Yet although these new civilizations must go through the same process of bloom, decline, and disintegration as their predecessors, they may otherwise be entirely different in kind. Thus it is questionable whether they represent genuine examples of recurrence as they are predicted in secular theories of premeditation or religious ones of preordainment.

The question arises whether the cyclic theories in this wider sense are more closely related to reality than those of the "cyclists" in strictest terms. We do not intend here to join the dispute whether such theories, in particular that of Toynbee, are—as claimed—based largely on pragmatic knowledge or only on philosophical speculation cemented by sweeping historical analogies. Certainly a theory that history has followed a regular pattern thus far is based on less conjecture than a theory that such a pattern will inevitably be repeated.

Yet, whether or not we recognize laws of history, the identification of an allegedly predictable stage of development with an actual historical situation must be arbitrary. It may be compared to a situation in which one is shown a picture of Shakespeare or Napoleon and is then asked who in his circle of acquaintances resembles it. Even if we grant the correctness of the basic concepts—which we do here only for the sake of argument—the measure of possible identification of such concepts with reality remains controversial.

This brief introduction is necessary to show the basic difference between the cycle we are concerned with in this study and the various, often brilliant types of cyclic theories of history noted above. In dealing with the restoration process we are confronted, not with conjectural and speculative cycles, but with real cycles, provable by historical evidence.

We need not question the reality of obvious stages of sociopolitical development as reflected in the three systems from (A) to (C). Here we are concerned with the kinds of system (A) which have existed, by what types and means of system (B) they were overthrown, and how and in what way they were restored to system (C). We do not attempt any prediction about the operation of the three systems in the future.

A significant question might be posed at this point: Is not the relation of system (C) to system (A), in spite of the inevitable biological and social changes, based on arbitrary judgments of association and identification? We challenge the validity of such criticism. To be sure, deductions in a historical study are based largely on value judgments, as is any selection of facts which the historian deems essential. Were it otherwise, history would be a dull discipline indeed! Yet it is claimed here as provable that the main phases shown in the restoration process are based on solid facts; therefore, certain tentative deductions seem justified. They pertain in particular to the analysis of basic factors in system (A), their suppression in

(B), and their revival in different form in (C). If we base our subsequent investigation of such historical developments on reasoned value judgments, we follow the regular process of historical research. We are then no more involved in speculative argument than is any kind of historical analysis which goes beyond the mere ascertainment and description of facts. In this sense any serious theory of history can be justified as working hypothesis, though certainly not as oracle.

MONARCHY AND REPUBLIC

The idea of restoration, if confined to actions within independent political bodies, is in history primarily connected with the reestablishment of monarchical systems of government. Causes for this pragmatic rather than purely rational association are easy to find. In the first place, most sovereign states in Western civilization until the end of the First World War were monarchies. In the second, restoration is concerned with the reestablishment of conditions which under the original system had lasted for some time—at least for several decades. In our civilization the bygone monarchies are the primary political bodies which were almost universally in existence at least that long and usually longer. They are still in many ways close to political reality. They may therefore justly be called the foremost objects of the restoration process.

There are exceptions to this, in time as well as place. The dominant rule of hereditary monarchical government, which had reversed a previous republican trend with the rise of the Julian house to the imperial dignity of the Roman Empire in the first century B.C., began to decline steadily by the end of the eighteenth century with the Declaration of Independence of the United States of America in 1776. It was followed by the establishment of a French republican system in 1792 and within a year by the establishment of a number of French satellite republics of brief duration, such as the Batavian Republic of 1795, the Cisalpine and the Ligurian republics of 1797, or the Parthenopean of 1799. Yet here, quite apart from the arbitrary territorial limitations of these establishments, one could not speak of the possibility of restoration. These artificial political contraptions, unlike their Renaissance models, did not last long enough to establish the image of original systems that could be restored. On the other hand, the two great republics created at the end of the eighteenth century, the United States and France, have survived. They can look back on such a long stretch of history—more than five generations—that one could well speak of a republican restoration if there had been a genuine interposition of monarchical government. This obviously never happened in the history of the United States. The contention that it happened in French history only in regard to the Bourbon Restoration and its corollary, the Orléans monarchy, is debatable. We hold here that the regimes of the two Napoleons were Caesarean dictatorships rather than genuine monarchical systems. Unlike the Bourbon–Orléans era, Bonapartism could not rely on a long-established tradition. The reign of neither Napoleon I nor Napoleon III lasted long enough or penetrated deeply enough into the social order to provide a genuine new pattern of monarchical regimes that could have established social and political original systems subject to genuine restoration.[1]

In Bonapartism the question is not nearly as clear-cut as in other dictatorships. Even Guglielmo Ferrero, an outright opponent of the concept of Napoleonic legitimacy, admits that if the empire of the first Napoleon "had lasted, time and the prescription of which Talleyrand speaks"—time measured in centuries—"might have legitimized it. It is possible to imagine the second or third generation acknowledging Napoleon IV or V as the legitimate sovereign of France."[2] There are so many if's in the supposition that prelegitimacy in Ferrero's terms might eventually have become true legitimacy that such an assumption does not weaken the previous evaluation of Bonapartism and the chances for an entirely hypothetical monarchical restoration in the United States of America. According to this opinion, European civilization and its extension to North America offered in theory the possibility for a number of years of the reemergence of hereditary monarchy. Sufficient time, from the latter part of the eighteenth century onward, was not lacking; yet actual conditions, institutions, and ideas, blending successfully into new traditions, worked clearly against such a development. Thus the predominance of the cycle from monarchy to monarchy remains on the whole unshaken. We may disregard the rapid fluctuations of government in the Balkan

---

[1] Probably the best historiographic study dealing largely with the evaluation of the regime of Napoleon I as either an incipient hereditary monarchy or a dictatorship is Pieter Geyl, *Napoleon For and Against* (New Haven, 1949). The evidence largely supports the dictatorial thesis. See particularly pp. 426 ff., 448 f.

This is definitely the view of Guglielmo Ferrero. See *The Reconstruction of Europe* (New York, 1941), particularly pp. 47–75, and the *Principles of Power* (New York, 1942), pp. 102–123 and 207–212; on Napoleon III, see *ibid.,* pp. 123 ff. See also George P. Gooch, *History and Historians in the Nineteenth Century* (London, 1952), on Napoleon I, pp. 241–263, and on Napoleon III, p. 263. See also Karl Griewank, *Der Wiener Kongress und die europäische Restaurations, 1814/15,* 2d rev. ed. (Leipzig, 1954), pp. 24–42; Ernst Nolte, *Three Faces of Fascism* (New York, 1966), p. 308.

[2] Ferrero, *Principles of Power,* p. 188; see also p. 138.

states from the second half of the nineteenth century onward, for there was no time for the full development of stable sociopolitical systems. Even pseudo-stability under duress was established only after the Second World War.

Here we face again some outright dictatorships whose structure conflicts with the premises of this investigation. We may also forego a discussion of the concepts of the elective monarchy and the aristocratic republics, for though in principle they may be germane to the subject, in practice they are anachronistic. Neither the unstable situation in the Renaissance states in central Italy, nor the more stable one in the republic of Venice, nor finally conditions in the elective monarchies of the Holy Roman Empire or Poland have much to offer for the understanding of the cycle under discussion.

More pertinent would be a glance at the development in Latin America, where within a period of some twenty years in the early nineteenth century the present system of republics was *in nuce* established. Here we have a century and a half of republican government, in a continent-wide area, penetrated well below the surface by a monarchic tradition. Yet, quite apart from the impact of the Monroe Doctrine as impediment to such changes, real chances for the reestablishment of the monarchical Spanish or Portuguese governments and subsequent republican restorations remained almost as remote as in the United States though not for the same reason. In the United States it has been the combination of a strong rational and emotional appeal of the democratic republican idea which from the outset has barred any reestablishment of the monarchy and subsequent republican restoration. In Latin America the weakness of the former colonial powers was a deterrent. Yet here one might contemplate the existence of numerous restoration processes from democratic republican government to military junta dictatorship, back and forth, and frequently welded into a mixture of both. We must remember, however, that the junta type of Latin American dictatorship represents in general only a change in the governmental order, not a genuine transition from one social and political system to another. We do not have to deal with such ephemeral movements. We must remember, however, that a wide area, fairly homogeneous in ethnic and geographic terms, has been in existence for almost a century and a half. There the time factor alone would have allowed a cycle of restorations from a democratic republican system through an intermediate monarchical one to the reestablishment of a republican structure. Sufficient time would have been at hand for the change from mere governmental regimes to regular sociopolitical systems.

Since other factors did not favor such a restoration process, the significance of this one potential factor remained academic.

On the other hand, the time factor in our civilization, through thousands of years up to the First World War, heavily favored hereditary monarchical government. This fact appeared even more striking from the aspect of greater power potential on the part of these monarchies than from the viewpoint of their numerical prevalence over republics. Only about half a century ago there were only two republican Great Powers, France and the United States, as against six monarchies, Austria, England, Germany, Italy, Japan, and Russia.

Of primary interest here is tradition—not economic or military strength—and not only in the sense that the history of the ages is reflected in that of the monarchies. Tradition is perceived here as a most effective means in history to rally around the executive, particularly in an age of lawlessness in international relations and the resulting fears and other emotions in times of crisis.

The possibility of identification of one system with another, while both differ markedly from a third, appears most impressive and simple if it is associated with a change of government as exemplified not merely by statutes but by personalities. In fact, this impact of personal association and its symbols might be so powerful that men would be willing to accept very far-reaching social and political changes if this psychological factor were restored. The English Stuart and the French Bourbon restorations show that such process may come fairly close to success if the restored system allows for far-reaching social and political change, and most conveniently if it offers the emotional compensation of the clearly visible, revived personal symbol.

A monarchical symbol must be restored, however, not arbitrarily created or imported, as it was in some Balkan kingdoms with German dynasties. The monarchical shell of a new dynasty of princes can never be substituted for long-lasting tradition. The few exceptions merely confirm the rule. The most prominent one is the Bernadotte dynasty in Sweden, where extraordinary political skill and the blessings of neutrality in a war-torn world gave this royal house, in Ferrero's terms, the unique opportunity to reach the safe port of legitimacy through the treacherous waters of prelegitimacy.

Related to this is another point. The unique symbolic value of the monarchy, particularly in a time of crisis, may easily lead to a confusion with the notion of a cult of personality as it exists in the totalitarian and semitotalitarian dictatorships. The personality of a ruler, particularly in an anachronistic setting of epigones of the divine-right theory, may be inordinately and in a vulgar sense glorified. The pathetic figure of the Kaiser, Wilhelm II, is a striking case in point. While in the four centuries of modern history alone the number of mediocre and poor rulers is fairly large, examples like the Kaiser, of glaring weaknesses covered up and at the same time blown up by sycophantic propaganda, are not numerous. On no account should they be confused with the position of a Roi Soleil in the seventeenth century. The extolling of Louis XIV, however exaggerated, expresses the attitude of his contemporaries toward the exalted royal institution, as well as his own. This after all is the true meaning of *l'état, c'est moi,* namely that the king represents something greater or, as he would see it, "even greater" than his earthly reflection. In a less spectacular manner the same applies to rulers under the system of centralized despotic absolutism in general. The glorification of Louis XIV, inordinate even by the standards of his time, represents in a sense a kind of last-ditch defense against the impending age of the philosophers and the coming regimes of enlightened absolutism with their combination of police and welfare doctrines. Still there can be little doubt that seventeenth century absolutism, even in its extremes, stands for an institution still fully in command, whereas the regime of the Kaiser's braggadocio merely alleges such a position. In that sense, imperial Germany in the last decades before the First World War represented an outdated system in a kind of schizoid position. The major strata of society paid lip service to an anachronism they no longer truly believed in. The figure of the last bearer of the crown thus stands merely for the hopeless attempt to justify the weakness of a decaying institution by the pompous antics of its chief representative.

The Kaiser and his fawning courtiers misunderstood not only the future but, what is more surprising, the past in which the personality of the monarch always had to yield to the far greater importance of the system of hereditary monarchic rule.[3] It is superfluous to enter here into a discussion about obvious shortcomings of the hereditary monarchical system. Yet except for the distortions of the system in its declining stage in the West, an extreme cult of personality is not among its more conspicuous faults. By and large this has been true ever since the Roman concept of the divine ruler was reduced to the Christian idea of the mere divine claim to rule.

[3] This idea has been lucidly developed in its full legal and historical context in Ernst H. Kantorowicz, *The King's Two Bodies: A Study in Medieval Theology* (Princeton, 1957); see particularly pp. 3–83, 323–450.

The issue of a cult of personality is one of the outstanding differences between a hereditary monarchic system and a totalitarian dictatorship. In one the ceremonial and the symbol value lies primarily in the institution and its permanence, while the ruler is its almost incidental representative; in the other the dictator in person and as person stands in the limelight. The laws of the dictatorial regime, and in particular its rules pertaining to the transfer of power from a dictator to his successor, are of secondary importance and are either subject to frequent change or by intent not clarified at all. The history of the three primary totalitarian dictatorships of our time, the Italian Fascist, the German National Socialist, and the Russian Communist up to the death of Stalin, offer in different ways abundant supporting evidence in this respect.

The same cannot be said with assurance about the elective monarchy or more recent attempts to reestablish hereditary monarchies. The elections of sovereigns could obviously be manipulated, whether by a college of princes, as in the Holy Roman Empire, by a corporate body of nobles, as in the Polish kingdom, by national assemblies, or by dubious Bonapartist plebiscites in the nineteenth century. Here, however, a distinction must be made. The election of rulers, particularly in the Holy Roman Empire, but also in the Polish-Lithuanian kingdom, was effectuated by such narrow social strata—in Poland not necessarily a narrow group of persons— that a propagandistic glorification of the ruler rather than of the sacredness of the royal institution would have made little sense.

The artificial creation or attempts at creation of new dynasties in the nineteenth century in Balkan countries, and intermittently in Spain and Mexico, are a different matter.[4] Here the situation was frequently similar to the type of Latin American military junta dictatorships before the First World War. The monarchical institutions of nineteenth century Greece and Bulgaria, or twentieth century Albania, were of such fluctuating and flimsy character that they defied major propagandistic efforts to bolster them through a widespread cult of personality.[5] In any case, the briefness of the time factor eliminates these artificial creations of monarchy from

---

[4] This means in particular the "election" of the duke of Aosta (Amadeo I) as king of Spain in 1871. See, for instance, Salvador de Madariaga, *Spain, a Modern History* (New York, 1960), p. 68; also the proclamation of Archduke Maximilian as emperor of Mexico in 1864 on the basis of a fraudulent plebiscite should be perceived in this context.

[5] The situation in Serbia and Montenegro, on the other hand, differed not by way of greater political stability, but by a measure of historical tradition cementing the rule of the Karageorgevich, Obrenovich, and Petrovich-Njegosh dynasties. In Rumania the distinguished personality of the first king, Carol I, was likewise a differentiating factor.

the range of genuine monarchical systems and true restorations. The contention still stands that a cult of personality is in essence incompatible with a true, that is, long-lasting, hereditary monarchical system.

This does not mean at all that true monarchy, even in contemporary history, should be identified primarily with mere ceremonials and symbol values. Hereditary monarchy is by no means incompatible with democratic representative government. The transformation of the Western European monarchies in the last decades of the nineteenth century and early in the twentieth fully supports the assumption that the constitutional monarchy, particularly in a setting with a tradition of representative institutions, may adjust quite well to modern conditions.

What about the parliamentary monarchy where, as in the United Kingdom, the legislative branch of government through the cabinet, which is in effect its executive committee, holds supreme executive power as well? [6] Is a monarchical system in a parliamentary monarchy, in which the sovereign reigns but does not govern, subject to the process of restoration? Can we speak of the restoration of merely symbolic power? The answer should be a clear No. The monarch's jurisdiction as chief executive may in a long-drawn-out evolutionary process be constantly reduced. His powers may be gradually transferred almost completely to the legislature and a cabinet responsible to it; yet the symbol of the monarchical institution, by the very strength of tradition, may survive for a long time. This would be particularly true in England, where royal power has been painlessly reduced by the force of precedent. Yet this symbolic status of the crown could probably never be re-created. Its restoration would be meaningless. The *raison d'être* of the monarchy is the executive power of the ruler even more than the legislative power, but either one must be supported by predictable and orderly succession and symbols with emotional value. Such power can be shared or the symbol can be preserved as a kind of museum piece for a long time. Yet the establishment or reestablishment of a monarchy without any executive power at all would deprive an ancient institution of its very core and remove the possibility and even the motivation for survival.

This factor of inherent personal power in the hereditary monarchical system raises it from an archaic, emotional level of action to a far more rational sphere of human relations. For better or for worse, this truth is the premise of a genuine monarchical restoration.

We have attempted to show why the idea of restoration is associated

[6] See, for instance, Sir William Ivo Jennings, *Cabinet Government,* 3d ed. (Cambridge, 1959), pp. 328–393.

predominantly with monarchical government. We have noted that the cycle from republic to republic has hardly become practical,[7] in spite of the fact that, as far as tradition goes, quite a few republican regimes would have been long enough in power and strongly enough entrenched to make their restoration possible *if* these republican regimes had been overthrown. Since this has not been the case, we might conclude that republics in modern history have shown greater stability against attack, more resilience in the face of a threat against their constitutions than the systems working under the cycle from monarchy to monarchy.

In a sense such a conclusion is correct, as far as it is based on the relationship between monarchies and republics. The interchange between monarchies and republics in ancient history may have fluctuated heavily and the same may have been true for small city-states and principalities of the Italian Renaissance type, where an association of the ruler as patriarch in the minds of the subjects kept alive the idea of a monarch even in a highly pluralistic society. Yet as far as medium-sized and large states in modern times are concerned, there can be little doubt that the turning of the tide favors the transition from monarchies to republics. Changes in this direction have generally proved to be durable—durable, that is, as far as the relationship of the republic to the hereditary monarchy is concerned: extremely unsteady, on the other hand, if we observe the connection between republic and dictatorship—whether under a monarchical disguise or not. It may well be argued that a republican government based on some kind of popular representation has, within the last generation, succumbed to dictatorship almost as often as, in the preceding generations, it triumphed over monarchies.

It can be pointed out, of course, that often, particularly in the Latin American presidential dictatorships, a republican superstructure is preserved, but so was a monarchical one in Mussolini's Italy, Primo de Rivera's Spain, or the Greece of Metaxas, to name only a few examples. Leaving the outdated model of the aristocratic republic aside and concentrating our attention on a republic with a genuine measure of popular representation, at least in the legislative branch of government, we find that the typical republican cycle would be not from republic through monarchy and back to republic, but from republic through dictatorship and back to a republican regime.

---

[7] Provided one does not stretch the point unduly, this would be the case, for instance, if one were to consider the revolutionary intervals between long monarchical reigns in the nineteenth century Balkan countries as cases of genuine republican restorations.

As for the rarity of the cycle from republic through monarchy back to republic, we might consider the case of the French Second Republic from 1848 to Napoleon III's dictatorship of 1851, to its reestablishment as the Third Republic in 1870. Perhaps even the earlier relationship between the republic of 1792 and that of 1848 might be a case in point. The difficulty with both these examples is obvious. Supposed, but not granted, that we are dealing here with regular systems, and not with regimes, the situation presents itself as follows. The original system in the first case lasted for only three years, or for four, if we add the time until Louis Napoleon accepted the imperial title. In the second example, not only is the restored system of the very short duration of three and four years respectively, the original one was brief as well, that is, from 1792 to the establishment of the Directory in 1795 or, if we stretch the point somewhat, to 1799, the setting up of the Consulate. Unlike genuine monarchical restoration, the intermediate system was in both cases in existence for a disproportionately long period: almost twenty years in the case of Napoleon III, thus at least five times as long as the intermediate system from 1848 to 1851. In the second example the half century from 1799 to 1848 is nearly five times as long as both the original and the allegedly restored systems combined.[8] The qualification "allegedly" is used deliberately. A governmental order which has lasted only a few years, particularly in comparison with that of a much longer intermediate period, can hardly be called a social and political system. If time confers legitimacy on any governmental structure, it would in these cases naturally rest with the intervening rather than with either the original or the restored system.

To return to the cycle republic to monarchy to republic—its rarity in modern history may possibly be explained as follows. Under stable social conditions at home and abroad a generally efficient republican regime based on popular sovereignty corresponds to the spirit of the times so well that, if it has been successfully established, its overthrow will appear to be a remote danger. Quite clearly, neither in 1792 nor in 1848 did such stable social conditions exist. In 1792, the French social reforms effectuated and those planned for the future represented far less of a direct danger to the government than the impossibility of adjusting the new regime to the prevailing order of international relations. In 1848 the opposite may have been true: the domestic problems appeared to be more controversial than those pertaining to foreign policy.

Republican regimes of this kind, more or less as exceptions to the rule,

[8] Namely, 1792–1799=7 years, plus 1848–1851=3 years; altogether 10 years as against the intervening period of 49 years.

were not firmly established in the first place. Yet, whenever they could overcome the crises of their early history, wherever they could draw on the consent of the governed without creating a deep-seated division in their own society or in international relations, they were successful. Such regimes have succeeded as long as they have avoided the dangers of extreme social divisiveness and the corresponding evil, the restriction of civil liberties in the attempt to curb radicalism. As long as these conditions hold true, republican regimes can adjust to modern conditions more easily than the hereditary monarchies.

More complex is the cycle republic to dictatorship and back to republic. We must remember that the use of the republican nomenclature of the presidency by a dictator as cloak for his totalitarian actions and designs makes little difference for our purpose. The issue is rather the overthrow by a totalitarian regime of a system based on truly representative government and the feasibility of its restoration, irrespective of the legal terminology employed. It is obvious that the elimination of genuine republican government in Central Eastern Europe, East Asia, and other parts of the globe is not due to any basic weakness in republican government itself. It would be difficult to think of a single totalitarian government whose access to power could have been prevented if it had faced a monarchical regime rather than a well-established republican one. Whether a firmly anchored monarchy in Germany could have stopped the National Socialist onslaught more effectively than the Weimar republic, may seem debatable. The point is, however, that a regime as discredited as the monarchy under the last Kaiser could hardly have been firmly anchored after 1918.

Any system with an unstable foundation may be doomed. Reasons for its overthrow may include inability to raise low standards of living, with no hope of change for the better, combined with totalitarian pressure from the outside, subversion from the inside, and lastly, sheer external aggression. We do not include the previous existence of totalitarian regimes of a different kind, as in Cuba, for instance, since in that case one could not truly speak of transition from a republican regime to dictatorship, but merely of the replacement of one dictatorship by another more sweeping in its designs and powers. As to the true cycle, republic to dictatorship to republic, there is one obvious explanation why it has become so much more frequent than that from monarchy to dictatorship and back again: monarchies are rare today; republics are not.

Still, the cycle republic to dictatorship to republic remains a problem. And again there is the factor of time. Let us take the example of the

Weimar republic of 1919, replaced by the Hitler dictatorship of 1933, and—if we leave aside the question of the artificial division of present-day Germany—allegedly restored after the Second World War by the German Federal Republic, with the seat of government in Bonn. Yet, did the Weimar republic represent a well-established social and political system? Ferrero refers to it as a typical example of prelegitimacy and writes thus in 1941:

> During the period between 1920 and 1930, in discussing legitimacy and its forms, I was often asked this question: Is the Republic of Weimar a legitimate government? My reply would be along the following lines: "No, the Republic of Weimar is not yet a legitimate government." Rightly or wrongly, there still is too large a part of Germany that refuses to accept republican institutions and the democratic form of legitimacy that justifies them; universal suffrage and popular sovereignty. A vigorous, passionate, vehement opposition by different groups and influences, blowing over the country like a tempest, prevents the crystallization of the general consent, whether active or passive, that creates legitimacy.[9]

Again we may challenge Ferrero's concept of "prelegitimacy." Yet his basic view that the republic lacked the general consent necessary to become an effective system is shared by a distinguished historian near the opposite end of the political spectrum, the Socialist Arthur Rosenberg.[10]

Somewhat similar examples might be the partially representative democratic republican regimes in Latin America that were overthrown by dictatorships and later restored. But there too the original republican systems stood on shaky foundations, several of them in fact even flimsier than the Weimar republic. The "restoration" of these regimes, wherever it took place, was more often than not destroyed by dictatorships, and new genuine republican regimes did not, and unfortunately do not, look stronger than the original ones.[11] There are, of course, a few cases where

---

[9] Ferrero, *Principles of Power*, p. 139; see also Dolf Sternberger, *Grund und Abgrund der Macht* (Frankfurt am Main, 1962), pp. 174 ff.

[10] Arthur Rosenberg, *Entstehung und Geschichte der Weimarer Republik* (Frankfurt am Main, 1955), p. 479. See also Arnold Brecht, *Aus nächster Nähe, Lebenserinnerungen,* Vol. I, 1884–1927 (Stuttgart, 1966), pp. 309 ff.

[11] The regime of Gabriel Terra in Uruguay in the nineteenth century might be considered here as the possible exception which confirms the rule. A better interpretation would probably be that the Terra administration in the traditionally most democratic Latin American state never established a genuine dictatorship, since minority rights were curtailed but never fully destroyed. Hence we cannot speak here of a real cycle. See for instance Helen M. Bailey and Abraham P. Nasatir, *Latin America* (Englewood Cliffs, 1960), p. 624 f. See also Wilhelm von Schoen, *Geschichte Mittel- und Südamerikas* (München, 1953), p. 608 f.

genuine though imperfect democratic republican regimes were overthrown by authoritarian or pseudodemocratic regimes and these in turn
succeeded by foreign dictatorships. Czechoslovakia from the Munich
agreement in 1938 to 1945 would be a case in point. But although
there was a kind of republican restoration in Czechoslovakia immediately
after the end of the Second World War, the new dictatorship established
in 1948 changed the picture again. Furthermore, restoration after conquest
from outside raises entirely different problems, which will be discussed
briefly in the following chapters. Then there are those democratic republican systems, Switzerland and the United States of America foremost
among them, where the republican democratic structure has been so
firmly established and has been cemented by so strong a tradition that
genuine restoration could come about if the almost inconceivable need for
it should ever arise.

Here we face a curious paradox. Monarchical restoration may be conceivable because of the strength—or more correctly, perhaps, length—of a
century-old tradition alone. Whether the original system was efficient and
to some degree socially enlightened is not a negligible factor in this
category, but not necessarily of decisive importance either. As to republican regimes grounded on popular representation, the possibility of a
genuine restoration appears to exist only if and so long as these systems
are based on the consent of the governed and a socially responsible government. But short of defeat in war against a totalitarian aggressor, the
case of republican restoration will presumably never arise. In general,
republican systems will stay in power, and if they are based on the consent of the governed, this is all to the good.

CYCLES OF IDEAS

Restoration will be discussed in this study only within the frame of the
sociopolitical body known as the state, as we have said. If we want to
comprehend major trends of social and cultural development within such
states we must deal either with political entities of some size or with communities whose significance is so great in many other respects that size is
unimportant. This would apply to the first two cases in Part II, the Jewish
state and the Athenian city-state, both in the sixth century B.C. Apart
from these obvious exceptions, with their great contribution to the
history of the West, the range of the size of states that we are concerned
with is difficult to determine. Its sweep reaches from the world powers of
today to political bodies which, in the prenuclear age, were in some way
capable of defending themselves but which are unable even today to solve

their own economic problems. States of the size of the majority of the three hundred of the Holy Roman Empire, the so-called "Duodez-staaten" would in general be excluded from this investigation.[12]

Yet, if we disregard these very small states—with the exceptions noted above—and consider only the larger political units, another question arises. Should not broad ideological movements which cut across political boundaries be discussed as an intrinsic part of a study of cycles? The argument would run as follows. True, we are dealing with movements within the frame of the state, and this should limit consideration to the sociopolitical sphere, since purely spiritual, cultural, and artistic trends transgress state borders and frequently even continents. Barriers imposed by government to stop the traffic of ideas existed in the Middle Ages as much as today or even more so. From a long-range point of view, however, such cultural exchange is not very much impeded by political frontiers. Should we not therefore discuss broad ideological movements that generally cut across state boundaries, provided they have political repercussions in individual countries and are subject to the restoration process?

This last point is actually the crux of the matter. We may recognize the existence of spiritual cycles in history. In a previous study on Austrian intellectual history I attempted to trace such a cycle, in which a conservative era is generally replaced by a briefer, more liberal one. Conservatism and liberalism in the broadest possible terms are to be understood there in a relationship of action and reaction, whereas the direct influence derives always from the period which precedes that of the immediate past. Some of the conclusions about the nature of such cycles, as exemplified by Austrian intellectual history, are germane to our current discussion.

> Barring extreme revolutionary change, the institutions and customs of any age are of course primarily influenced by the preceding one. This observation must be qualified to some degree in relation to the era since the industrial and agricultural revolutions, but it appears rather obvious in previous periods of far less rapid change in technology. . . . As to intellectual-spiritual influences in a new era, the situation is quite different. Here the future development is not simply the outgrowth of a straight and simple evolution from the recent past—that means, of course, to some degree in opposition to prevalent thought. . . . Hence, more often than not new ideas thrive on the ground of the era just preceding the recent past. . . . In this way, neo-Liberalism reveals an

---

[12] It may be remembered that the term *Duodezstaat,* literally translated twelve-state, derives actually from the notion of a small-sized book, which has not eight but twelve pages to the sheet (hence duodecim = twelve, in Latin).

obvious ideological connection with the Enlightenment, Franciscan conservatism with the Baroque, the Enlightenment with the Renaissance,
and the Renaissance in a wide sweep across the Middle Ages with classic
Hellenic and Roman history. . . . Spiritual achievements are not
molded and determined by any specific set of thoughts, but . . . they
grow and rise as the product of a compromise between different sets of
ideas, developed in different times and under different conditions.

Such a compromise is no mathematically balanced resultant of forces
of equal strength. It is the product of the beautifully varied inequality of
organic human life. By reason of this inequality, the intellectual influence
of the period preceding the one just passed will be stronger than that of
the intervening period. Yet the danger of its assuming an inordinate
supremacy will be checked by the ideas of the recent past as well as by
those of the one antedating this preceding era. Thus the effect of the
Enlightenment wil be furthered by that of the Renaissance and even
classical antiquity, yet it will be checked by those forces that hem it in
the future as well as in the past, i.e., Baroque and in the case of the
Renaissance, the high-medieval spirit. The strength of Franciscan conservatism is controlled by neo-Liberalism in the future and by that of
Enlightenment in the past. Its supporting force, the Baroque era, in the
past is again checked by Enlightenment and Renaissance, strengthened
by the medieval spirit but impeded in effect by classical antiquity, and so
it goes back in past and future in an unending chain. . . .[13]

This certainly is meant to be a system of cycles, although one that is not
confined within political borders. Furthermore, it clearly shows strong
elements of a restorative process of recurring historical trends. Does this
also mean that it is adaptable to our purpose, the study of the process of
restoration in terms of sociopolitical entities? Fairly strong analogies with
the restorative process as it has been discussed so far undoubtedly do exist.
Still the answer to this question would have to be in substance negative,
though with important qualifications. The main reason for this position is
not so much predominant concern with political and social issues in the
frame of the state. The lines to be drawn between a political and a social
or sociocultural issue are not clear-cut. They may be widely overlapping,
as in the political impact of Romanticism on the Restoration period after
the Congress of Vienna, or perhaps in the influence of so-called social
Darwinism on the late nineteenth century imperialism and colonialism of
the Great Powers. Furthermore, it is clear that ideologies of a political nature, like Marxism, fascism, racialism in general, or spiritual ones with political implications, like the Protestant and Catholic Reformations, may

[13] Robert A. Kann, *A Study in Austrian Intellectual History: From Late Baroque
to Romanticism* (New York, 1960), pp. 299, 300, 301, 302; see also pp. 294–302
passim.

have a definite and measurable impact on the political history of individual countries. Our chief concern here is with particulars.

If we were to extend this study to a survey of recurring or analogous trends, we might have to write a history of Western civilization with emphasis on social and intellectual factors in which the restoration problem would be overwhelmed—for a very simple reason. Cyclic recurring trends in general may lead to fairly analogous historical situations in a very broad sense. They may pertain to such questions as human values, intellectual freedom, state church versus religious diversity, a free or a more or less controlled economy, degrees or denial of popular representation in government, to name only a few outstanding issues. The recurrence or fading away of these trends would become apparent. Yet in no sense would their existence in the history of ideas appear to depend on the condition that onetime abolished institutions be reestablished and the near image of a previous social and political system, verifiable by facts, be restored. But this proof positive of restoration is indeed what we are after, and it is the main reason we are resolved to pursue our objectives within the frame of the state. We may add further that the student of cycles in intellectual history is concerned with general concepts, and the student of the restoration problem is interested in very specific facts, which, to be sure, may reflect general trends as well.

What about the definite, measurable political repercussions of general ideological movements in individual countries? Suppose they have led to a destruction of system (A) and after the revolutionary period to its restoration. Would such a process not be fully germane to the objectives of this study? The answer is a clear Yes, with the proviso, however, that in a majority of cases such a process should be part of our analysis anyway, without particular emphasis on social cycles. Suppose traditional government in any country were overthrown by a Fascist or Communist revolution, and the previous type of government were eventually restored. The discussion of such a case would be entirely within our province but it would make little difference whether we started from the state and called attention to the broad ideological movement across its borders, or whether we worked the other way, from the general to the specific. In a sense, every genuine transition from one system—not merely regime—to another and back is linked to broad ideological trends, and every broad ideological trend is related to events in individual political entities. The cases in twentieth century history, the age of "isms," may not always be as clear as the impact of totalitarian movements, but the problem is easily discernible.

There is, however, one type of combined broad social, ideological movement which poses a somewhat more complex question. It concerns the relationship between ideological and political trends in more or less strictly limited areas. We think here for instance of the connection between Reformation and Counter Reformation or Catholic Reformation as it was reflected in individual countries.[14] Here the predominantly spiritual movement may reveal a clearly traceable regional political impact. Its external manifestations might later be eliminated by political power, and the original status could be restored to a wide degree. Such development would be within the scope of our investigation, provided it can be focused on definite political bodies. In this sense a very real restorative process took place, for instance, in the Alpine hereditary Austrian lands in the late sixteenth and early seventeenth centuries, when the overwhelming majority of a Catholic population became largely Protestant and then returned to the fold of the Church. The political and social aspects of this restorative process are here almost as clear-cut as the spiritual ones. Accordingly it would be superficial to assume that the problem is outside our province because the consequences cannot be evaluated simply in terms of a change of the governmental system.

Borderline cases, where ideological changes in limited areas can be unearthed even though they may not lead to revolutionary political upheavals, may not be numerous. They should receive our attention as particularly interesting phenomena of the obvious interchange of factors of political and intellectual history. In principle we will, however, adhere to the method we have outlined. We will begin with the state and will study phenomena of the restorative process as they are primarily reflected in its structure.

[14] In line with more and more widely accepted usage by historians the term Counter Reformation stands here for the reaction to the Protestant Reformation in a spiritual as well as political sense. "Catholic Reformation," on the other hand, is perceived as an original spiritual movement of religious renascence, particularly manifest at the time of the Counter Reformation and the latter part of the Protestant Reformation, yet actually deeply rooted in the Middle Ages. See also Kann, *A Study in Austrian Intellectual History*, p. xix. See *ibid.*, also chap. 1, n. 11.

CHAPTER V

The Sanction of Time

Violence, legitimacy, and political generation

Four principles of legitimacy are perceived by Guglielmo Ferrero, as we have seen: "the elective and the hereditary, the aristo-monarchic and the democratic" in various combinations.[1] Revolutionary dictatorship conflicts with every one of these principles, separately as well as combined.[2] A dictatorial regime may, of course, be fully recognized *de jure* in international relations, it may last for an unpredictably long time, yet it can never be restored, in terms of this study, since it is hostile to tradition in general. If destroyed, it could be replaced by some other system or by a new dictatorship, but the dictatorship of old could never be revived. Of the systems subject to the process of restoration, the important ones in our time are the democratic republic (though too often not fully democratic) and the constitutional hereditary monarchy. The aristocratic republic, the absolute hereditary monarchy, the rare semiabsolute elective monarchy, or the constitutional elective monarchy are merely of historical significance. The parliamentary monarchy, on the other hand, is still very much in existence but, as outlined previously, is hardly subject to restoration, since the sovereign there represents but a symbol of executive power.

Modern man in Western civilization, accustomed to the values of a pluralistic, largely democratic society, prefers to live under a democratic republic or a hereditary constitutional monarchy. Yet it is clear that even the democratic forms of government, most attractive to Western man anxious to preserve a free society, may have their origin in war, in revolution, that is, in violence, and frequently violence in a not very distant past.

---

[1] Guglielmo Ferrero, *The Principles of Power* (New York, 1942), p. 22.
[2] *Ibid.,* pp. 3 ff., 119 ff., 284 ff.

It is generally assumed that when an orderly transfer of power has been established by one of these systems of government, no further questions are asked about its lawful origin. Yet not only a constitutional monarchy but even an absolute hereditary monarchy, irrespective of a revolutionary origin, would be considered fully legitimate after the succession from sovereign to heir had taken place unchallenged a number of times—we can assume that this means at least twice. A precedent—such as the unchallenged succession—or a custom can logically be established only if an event recurs. By analogy the same principle of recurrence could be applied in different ways to republican regimes of revolutionary origin with particular regard to regular elections. Since emphasis here would be put on the true or alleged consent of the governed, this factor of recurrence would probably be considered important if the legitimacy of the regime would be seriously challenged by an internal or external enemy invested with the potential power to destroy it.

No questions about the legitimacy of a system would be asked for any practical purpose, however, until its power was seriously challenged. Such challenge would not apply indiscriminately to any warlike or revolutionary situation but only to those where the very existence of a system is threatened. Thus a relatively large number of hereditary monarchies have survived for many centuries with no serious challenge to their legitimacy. On the contrary, their questionable legal foundations were mended and strengthened by time, which created tradition and therewith a new legitimacy. A number of these monarchies have been peacefully transformed into constitutional monarchies. They have added to the legitimacy brought about by the passing of time a new element, legitimacy by way of consent of the governed.

A larger number of monarchies, constitutional ones included, yielded to revolution and were succeeded by revolutionary regimes. Apart from conflicts over a specific dynastic succession, the issue in these major-scale nineteenth century revolutions was hardly ever the doubtful legal foundation of a monarchy of yore. In modern times it would have been a specious argument on the part of republican revolutionaries. The issue of revolution, though not necessarily the objective of revolution, has rather consistently been the assertion or the allegation that the monarchical system to be overthrown lacked the full consent of the governed at the time of the revolution. Historical legitimacy was of little consequence.

The situation changes when the current structure of a social and political system, the doubtful legal origin of which has been considered legitimated in the course of centuries, is seriously challenged. We must assume, however, that the revolutionary regime is strong enough to maintain itself in power for some time, otherwise the proposition would not be practical at all. Yet, if it stays in power, then the first question arises: can the course of time, either as predominant factor or by itself, legitimate revolutionary rule? And if so, how much time would be needed to legitimate, to sanction revolution?

This problem takes us back to the issue raised but not answered in the section on legal continuity, in chapter 4. We will reword the twofold question, because on the answers to it depend a number of other vital questions. Can revolution be legitimated by the course of time alone, which means without any manifest political and constitutional changes? If the answer is affirmative, can we establish any standards for the length of time needed to sanction revolution?

The important corollaries to this key question are the following. Assuming that revolution in one way or another can be sanctioned by time, would not the concept of restoration in such instances lack meaning? Restoration strives for the resumption of legal continuity, yet legal continuity becomes an absurdity if it replaces a system that has become lawful. Obviously there cannot be two comprehensive lawful systems in force and enforced in the same place and at the same time. Suppose that a now lawful system (B) should be replaced by (C), would that not mean a new break in legal continuity instead of its repair?

To rephrase the question: If an intermediate system can be legitimated by time alone, would not its subsequent elimination or an attempt to that effect mean counterrevolution rather than restoration, the destruction rather than the sustaining of the legal order? What after all is the precise relationship between counterrevolution and restoration?

We can approach the problem from a different angle, that of the restoration movement, and ask: Can the restoration movement be justified by the established legality of (A), despite the supposedly new legality of (B)? Would this mean emphasis on objectives rather than on means employed?

From a broad question dealing with the sanctions of revolutionary proceedings by time, and some directly related, more specific problems, we turn to two major issues which deal with the problem of force and violence. First we ask whether force used in the restorative process is necessarily linked to resistance and opposition within a country, or whether restoration may be initiated by organized attack from foreign bases, even by a foreign power and its troops. This may frequently be the case if the original system (A) has been overthrown not by domestic revolution but by conquest from outside. We conclude with a basic question, again a twofold one: As the restoration process moves through the three systems —the original, the intermediate, the restored—at what point does the permissible application of force become the unlawful use of violence? [3] Under what conditions does the opposite take place, namely, the change of unlawful violence to lawful exercise of force?

For a better understanding of these six related questions we will reformulate them briefly at this point. (1) Can the course of time sanction a claim to rule? If the answer, with or without qualification, is Yes, then we must ask (2) How much time is needed to sanction illegitimate rule?

The following two questions are likewise dependent on an affirmative answer to question (1). (3) Is the attempt to remove an intermediate, revolutionary system sanctioned by time an act of counterrevolution rather than revolution? Is it a new break in legal continuity rather than its repair? (4) On the other hand, could a restoration movement that challenges a system (B) supposedly sanctioned by time be justified by its objectives rather than by the means employed?

The last two questions, related to the other four but not dependent on an affirmative answer to question (1), are (5) Is the use of force in a restoration movement solely or primarily linked to the home base? May it start from foreign soil—may it even be initiated by a foreign power? (6) In surveying the whole restoration process through the three systems, how do we determine the precise difference between the lawful exercise of force and the illegal use of violence?

The first question dealing with the sanction of time for revolutionary action is quite clearly a key problem in our investigation, and must be approached from a pragmatic basis. If a political and social system has been accepted for a long time, which may well run into centuries, the whole issue may become altogether academic. Mainly historical curiosity prompts questions today about the legitimacy of the Norman conquest of England or of the conquest of Granada by Castille. We believe that the time factor is indeed of decisive significance here, but only if the corollary questions are closely examined: How did government act during the time in question? How is nonresistance to it to be interpreted in a specific situa-

---

[3] While the general meaning of violence is ". . . exertion of any physical force considered with reference to its effect on another . . . ," the specific connotation pertains predominantly to its unlawful character, "profanation, infringement, outrage assault" (*Webster's New Collegiate Dictionary*), "unjust use of force or power, as in deprivation of rights" (*Webster's New World Dictionary*), "unlawful exercise of physical force, intimidation by exhibition of this" (*Concise Oxford Dictionary*).

tion?[4] According to Ferrero's line of reasoning, nonresistance implies a measure of consent which, together with the more active support by a minority, fully satisfies him as long as the essential time element per se is guaranteed. Ferrero therein follows the view of Talleyrand, who stated rather broadly: "I speak of the legitimacy of governments in general, whatever their form, and not only that of kings, because it must be applied to everything. A legitimate government, be it monarchical or republican, hereditary or elective, aristocratic or democratic, is always the one whose existence, form, and mode of action have been strengthened and sanctioned over a long period of years. I might even say over a period of centuries."[5]

The point which Talleyrand makes here rather succinctly—and for democratic regimes as well as for monarchic absolutism—seems to refer not so much to the sanction of time deduced from the absence of resistance. It pertains apparently to the absence of resistance to the questionable legal foundations of government either as a whole or in regard to some of the territories under its administration. In this sense the rationalization of aggression by mere appeal to the past has been destroyed by one of its chief perpetrators, Frederic II of Prussia, who confessed in his memoirs that he would have started the first Silesian war irrespective of carefully presented historical claims.[6]

Today even the most radical totalitarian opposition, leftist or rightist, would not bother to attack a regime on account of political actions taken centuries ago. Arguments of this kind might pertain to the loss of certain territories—the German claim to Alsace-Lorraine in 1870 and 1871 would be a case in point—but hardly to a country as a whole. In this respect charges by the opposition would be based on what happened in the days, months, or years—but not the centuries—preceding the crisis. Century-old

[4] For Ferrero's views on this question see *The Reconstruction of Europe* (New York, 191), pp. 138 ff., where he discusses Talleyrand's instructions as French representative to the Congress of Vienna, drawn up by himself jointly with King Louis XVIII; and *Principles of Power*, pp. 131 ff., in particular p. 140 f. where time is considered the main element of legitimacy, though not the only one. See *ibid.* also pp. 187 ff., 294.

[5] Talleyrand, as quoted in *Principles of Power*, p. 138. For similar views by Talleyrand's intellectually equal counterpart at the Congress of Vienna see those of Friedrich von Gentz, in Golo Mann, *Secretary of Europe* (New Haven, 1946), pp. 280 f., 301 f. See also Karl Griewank, *Der neuzeitliche Revolutionsbegriff,* (Weimar, 1955), pp. 248 ff., 255 ff.; and in Karl Griewank, *Der Wiener Kongress und die europäische Restauration 1814-15,* 2d rev. ed. (Leipzig, 1954), Talleyrand's report to Louis XVIII, pp. 387 ff.

[6] See for instance Reinhold Koser, *Friedrich der Grosse,* (Stuttgart, 1911), pp. 77 ff.

legal foundations of a state power would seem immaterial to all concerned, and in this sense we could indeed speak of a sanction by time in terms of centuries.

Yet if we cannot attach more meaning to this sanction by time, the question is of little consequence. Events of centuries ago would not be the cause nor with few exceptions even the pretext for political attacks now. Hence the legitimacy or illegitimacy of political actions centuries ago, whether they have in the course of time received a full pardon or not, would be quite immaterial. To give the problem some meaning we will have to look for interests closer to the present and more directly linked to the restoration problem.

It is frequently stated that restoration has a chance to succeed only as long as the adherents of the original system are still active in the social life of their times. The easily provable contention is here that no restoration can succeed which is in the main supported only by overage veterans, former dignitaries of a bygone regime and their sympathizers. They may be inordinately concerned either with the symbols of the original system or, practically perhaps more important, with the paraphernalia and privileges of their former social status. It is a reasonable assumption, therefore, that restoration could become a real issue only within the relatively short phase dating from the replacement of the supporters of the original system as active political force to the time when they become vigorous supporters of the newly restored system. They would have to be at an age when they were still in full possession of their mental and physical powers. We may disregard here the large number of opportunists, recent political converts, and adventurers who will be found in the wake of the establishment of any seemingly successful new or renewed system. These could never form the core of a genuine, at least partly successful restoration movement of any kind. Accordingly the following conclusion is suggested.

The adherents of system (A) could not have played an active part in the political life of their time had they not been at least in their early twenties when system (B) took over. Those, on the other hand, who would still be in a position to sponsor and inaugurate system (C) actively, could hardly be much older than sixty to sixty-five years of age. After this generation had passed from the active political scene, there would be only aged veterans and flunkeys as the pitiful protagonists of restoration. Thus restoration would have a chance to succeed only within the approximate age limits of the system's adherents, from twenty-five to sixty-five years of age at the outside. Classical literature has always figured that the length of a generation is about a third of a century. With the much longer period of education and occupational training in our time which works against early marriage, it would be quite reasonable to set up forty years as time limit for the life-span of a political generation. This is, of course, something very different from the concept of a biological generation, that is from the time a child is born until such time as it procreates offspring. There is, naturally, no assurance that restoration will be successful, even if the reestablished regime is not seriously challenged within the course of one political generation. At the end of this period, the full effect of tradition is not yet felt. We may assume, however, that after thirty-five to forty years it should become apparent whether the restored system can reasonably be expected to endure.[7]

To sum up: We do not suggest here that the chance for restoration is necessarily limited by the life-span of a political generation of thirty-five to forty years, but we can make two deductions at this point. The political generation argument may not be conclusive and, without further evidence, not fully convincing, yet it is certainly not arbitrary. On the contrary, it is based on a reasonable presumption as to the practical potentialities of political activism. *If* we accept this conclusion, we arrive at a far more comprehensive, tentative one pertaining to revolutionary changes in general: If the intermediate revolutionary regime has not been seriously challenged within thirty-five or forty years after its accession to power, it will become fully stabilized and therefore sanctioned by time.

Such a far-reaching conclusion certainly requires close scrutiny. There is in the first place Ferrero's passionate argument that revolutionary dictatorship can never become legitimate because it is based on rule by a minority without the protection of the dissenting majority. This is even worse than rule by a majority without protection of the minority. In addition, according to Ferrero, the claim of the dictatorial revolution that it is based on consent of the governed is always false, and legitimacy can never be based on a premise of such kind. Compared with the clamor for fraudulently construed popular support through organized mass demonstrations,

[7] It should be clear that the average length of human life itself must not be confounded with the concept of either the biological or the political generation. For the discussion of the generation problem in relation to the question of restoration, see Robert A. Kann, "Was heisst Restauration? Begriff und Wirklichkeit eines geschichtlichen Vorganges," in *Wort und Wahrheit,* annual, XVI/5 (May, 1961), p. 353 f. Several of the points raised in the present study are sketched in that essay, pp. 345–360 *passim.*

the demand of absolutism for mere passive obedience, bad as it is, appears in a relatively favorable, because more honest, light.[8] We endorse here his condemnation of revolutionary dictatorship which may become fully recognized in international relations without ever becoming legitimate in a moral sense. Ferrero of course, perceives this concept of revolution only in a political sense, and a dictatorial one at that. Movements such as the English Glorious Revolution of 1688/89 or the French Revolution in 1789—and some aspects of it even until 1792—were not recognized by him as revolutions, since they were based substantially on the consent of the governed. This narrow interpretation of the concept of political revolution as confined exclusively to its dictatorial forms or stages is the privilege of a stimulating thinker like Ferrero, but it has found little support by the great majority of political theorists in very different camps.[9]

Another argument which deviates in some way from that of restoration within a political generation carries much more weight. We assume that the factor which lends the strongest moral support to the idea of restoration is the resumption of legal continuity as part of tradition. The lawful state, the *Rechtsstaat,* with predictable consequences in regard to administration and dispensation of justice, represents the noblest issue in an effective restoration process. Here we have indeed a clear break with the revolutionary past, or to put it differently, the healing of a previous revolutionary break with the past. In other matters such clear-cut differentiation between past and present is frequently neither required nor even desired.[10] Indeed, in general a restoration movement will be successful only if it can establish some kind of common denominator between the social patterns of systems (A) and (B) and (C). By that means alone it

---

[8] Ferrero, *Principles of Power,* pp. 187–213 *passim;* Ferrero, *Reconstruction of Europe,* pp. 47–75; Ferrero, *Les Deux Révolutions Françaises, 1789–1796* (Paris, 1951), pp. 17–36; for a contrary view see Karl Griewank, *Der neuzeitliche Revolutionsbegriff,* pp. 231–239, Dolf Sternberger, *Grund und Abgrund der Macht* (Frankfurt am Main, 1962), pp. 81 ff.

[9] See for instance Robert R. Palmer, *The Age of the Democratic Revolution: A Political History of Europe and America, 1760–1800* (Princeton, 1959), I, 3–24; Crane Brinton, *The Anatomy of Revolution* (New York, 1958), pp. 97 ff.

[10] One of the seemingly rare exceptions to this statement would be Bismarck's indemnity bill, introduced in the Prussian diet after the successful war against Austria in 1866. Bismarck's unconstitutional administration from 1862 to 1866 was then in a sense retroactively righted by express parliamentary action. Yet while Bismarck's previous actions certainly had represented a break with legal continuity, one would stretch the point unduly by referring to this political technique as revolutionary break in the generally accepted sense of the word. See for instance Erich Eyck, *Bismarck* (Zurich, 1943), II, 277 ff; Otto Pflanze, *Bismarck and the Development of Germany* (Princeton, 1963), I, 323 ff.

may be possible to take due cognizance of the inevitability of social change in the course of time. Were it otherwise—and frequently it has been otherwise in history—a restoration movement backed by the small entourage of a dethroned ruler and their specific interests could be doomed to failure from the start. Thus, as noted previously, a successful restoration movement is based on the reestablishment not simply of tradition but of a much revised tradition, and stabilization of such a kind of tradition surely needs time. How much time is difficult to say, though one thing is clear: revised tradition can begin to assume shape and to take root only after a restored system has come to power again, and considerable time will be required to make such a tradition secure.

It is our belief that tradition which establishes a fair measure of social continuity in the three systems will come into being only where and when, through time, the immediate connection has ceased to exist between those who have lived and worked under the old system (A) and those who have been indoctrinated by them directly under the new system (C). The success of adjustment by tradition will be real only after the people who had worked under the old institutions, and who directly indoctrinated the new generation, have passed from the scene. Otherwise, where customs and practices were passed on through direct contact between adherents of succeeding regimes, we could speak only of preservation of institutions, not of establishment of a tradition. Tradition will be created neither by order nor by intentional adoption of previous rules and mores, but by their unheralded, unplanned, frequently even unconscious change into ways and modes of conduct and customs by which everybody commits everybody else without direct intent.[11]

It is an important point indeed. If tradition is only established by habit, irrespective of the deliberate action of the parties concerned, do we not have to deal then with time in quite different measures? We would have to assume that such tradition can be established at the earliest after direct contact has ceased, either by death or retirement from occupational life, between those who have restored the continuity of law and their disciples

---

[11] This idea has been presented by the author in a paper read to the American Historical Association in Chicago, December, 1962, titled "Change and Continuity in the Danubian World after the First World War." On the concept of customs see Robert M. MacIver, *Society* (New York, 1937), pp. 15 ff., 358 ff.; see also Robert L. Sutherland and Julian L. Woodward, *Introduction to Sociology* (Philadelphia, 1937), pp. 24 ff., 31 f.; and particularly Gustav Radbruch, *Grundzüge der Rechtsphilosophie* (Leipzig, 1924), pp. 72 ff.; see also G. Radbruch, *Einführung in die Rechtswissenschaft* (Leipzig, 1929), p. 13: "In der Sitte gebieten alle jedem einzelnen, im Rechte ein einheitlicher Wille allen—in der Sittlichkeit jeder nur sich selbst."

and subordinates. Another generation will have to pass into oblivion, after political restoration has been initiated and legal continuity has been reestablished, before we can speak with full assurance of truly successful restoration. Until such time we have only seen the political reestablishment of a previous regime; only a generation afterward could the true restoration of a revised and reformed social system truly come into being.

We may assume that it takes one generation, the one still actively involved in the public life of systems (A) and (C), to establish reasonable expectations for the success of restoration. Another generation is necessary to assure its full success through the influence of tradition. It would seem unreasonable, on the other hand, to go further and to test success or failure of a system in a fast-moving world by even longer and for that reason highly speculative time limits.

In a sense this line of thought qualifies the previous tentative hypothesis that the intermediate, revolutionary regime, provided it is not of dictatorial nature, may become stabilized for good. This may indeed be so if no serious attempt is undertaken to drive system (B) from power. In that case the sanction of time, as far as it pertains to reasonable expectations—not assurance—of success, may take place within the thirty to forty years of a political generation. This, we repeat, would be the case if three conditions are met: System (B) is no longer of a dictatorial nature; [12] it has been in power for at least thirty-odd years; and its efficacy to rule has not been seriously challenged by sizeable strata of the population and a potentially powerful political apparatus. Only then could the revolutionary regime be said to be sanctioned by strength of the consent of the governed. If rule by the majority and protection of the minority could appear to be secured, the breach in legal continuity would be healed. Where and when this actually may have taken place in specific cases will be discussed in the second part of this study. The necessity of a time span of an additional generation, to insure that tradition becomes habitual by folkways and mores, would apply here as much as under a restored system.

The answer to the first two questions would thus be in essence in the affirmative: Sanction by time, though not by time alone, is possible if due

---

[12] Ferrero, in *Principles of Power,* p. 205, denies the possibility of such transition, but this is only because of his peculiar semantics. If the revolutionary regime changes its character, either from one based on the consent of the governed, as the French regime of the National Assembly of 1789 to that of the Convention in 1793, or vice versa, from Robespierre's dictatorship to the beginnings of the Directory in 1795, he speaks of different systems and different revolutions. See *ibid.* pp. 102 ff., and particularly Ferrero, *Les Deux Révolutions Françaises,* pp. 13 ff., 151 ff.

regard is given to content matter. The required length of time can be estimated within certain limits.

Revolution and Counterrevolution

For the sake of clarity the problem will be restated.

Let us suppose system (B) has been sanctioned by time; would not an attempt to supersede it by restoration be a counterrevolutionary rather than a restorative movement? In other words, would it not be a new break in legal continuity rather than the healing of the old break? Should we not—thus runs the counterargument—judge a restoration movement by the evolutionary content of its objectives rather than by the revolutionary, or perhaps more correctly, counterrevolutionary means employed?

Obviously the answer hinges primarily on the interpretation of the meaning of counterrevolution. Here we must go beyond the rather clear semantic meaning of "a revolution opposed to a former one," "a political movement or revolution against a government or social system set up by a previous revolution; a movement to combat revolutionary tendencies." [13] The first two meanings quoted here do not imply any basic difference between revolution and counterrevolution; the third meaning leaves the key question open. This is the issue then: whether counterrevolution is a legitimate act; and whether it restores or destroys legal continuity.

The problem would be simpler if we could assume that the issue hinges on the lawful or unlawful character of the means employed to overthrow a regime. Naturally, pragmatic experience, which means fallible, human judgment, is involved here. Just for that reason the introduction of the objective factor of time is of great importance. It has been duly noted that an initially illegitimate revolutionary regime may eventually be sanctioned in the course of time and become a genuine sociopolitical system, endowed with the strength of tradition. It has become lawful, and the restoration movement which intends to overthrow it has in turn become unlawful, since there cannot be two lawful sociopolitical systems opposed to each other which hold power at the same time and in the same place. Any other interpretation would have to deny the possibility of the sanctioning of a regime by time. Yet, with certain qualifications, we have affirmed just this possibility.

We have looked thus far at the relationship of revolution and restora-

[13] *Webster's New Collegiate Dictionary, Webster's New World Dictionary.* For a recent study which offers an interesting terminological analysis, see James H. Meisel, *Counter-Revolution* (New York, 1966), pp. 209–220.

tion from the standpoint of the means employed to replace one system with another. If we assume, however, that the decisive factor is one not of means but of sociopolitical content, the situation may be entirely different. According to such an interpretation, one system might remain permanently illegitimate and revolutionary; the one opposed to it would then be legitimate and counterrevolutionary. The decisive factor would be the radical or conservative character of the regime. This then would mean the affirmation of a stabilized system, legitimate or illegitimate, largely impervious to time. It is primarily this consideration which forces us to investigate the true meaning of the term counterrevolution.

Does the term counterrevolution refer primarily to antirevolutionary form or to content? Assuming—but not admitting—the latter, is such content absolute in character or does it change with the times? It is fair to say that from the Right to the Left most prominent students of the problem believe in a dynamic concept of revolution and, since counterrevolution is understood as its direct counterpart, in a dynamic concept of counterrevolution with reversed objectives as well. This means, of course, that absolute standards in regard to content and methods of revolution are not recognized. It does not mean, however, that we should deny the existence of typical trends in either the expansion of popular sovereignty or more equal distribution of wealth and better opportunities to gain it, linked to an apparatus initiated by the avant-garde, extremists, or, in Marxian terms, revolutionary elites.

To put it differently, counterrevolution is identified, far more often than not, with "reaction" of varying content. Only in the first, most general sense do we find reaction defined simply as "reciprocal"; or return action or [counter] influence; the return to a previous condition after [the interval of] the opposite. In the second sense, in the realm of politics, reaction would be understood as "a counter tendency, especially in politics, a movement toward a former political or social policy," as "a retrograde tendency especially in politics," "a movement back to a former or less advanced condition, stage, etc., counter tendency, especially such a movement or tendency in economics or politics"; extreme conservatism. "A 'reactionary' would be accordingly 'characterized' by favoring reaction or return to an old order, one who favors reaction in politics or policies." [14]

---

[14] *Webster's New Collegiate Dictionary, Oxford Concise Dictionary, Webster's New World Dictionary.* This is also the rather narrow definition accepted by Hannah Arendt in *On Revolution* (New York, 1963); see pp. 8, 38 f., 42 f., 184, and particularly 287 with the reference to Antoine Condorcet, *Sur le Sens du mot Révolutionaire.*

In the literature on the subject, Crane Brinton, in his *Anatomy of Revolution,* searches clearly for the common features in various revolutions such as the Cromwellian English, the American, the French one of 1789, and the Russian Bolshevik revolutions. The great diversity of these revolutions to the contrary notwithstanding, he strongly emphasizes analogies in the course of their developments. Yet, as he rightly emphasizes, far-reaching analogies must not be equated with ironclad social laws.[15]

Karl Griewank, one of the foremost and most knowledgeable students of revolution and restoration, is unfortunately caught in the Marxian traps of the inevitability of revolution and the counterrevolutionary reaction. He believes in its course according to a principle of necessity amounting to a kind of social predestination, on which the issue is focused.[16] The whole historical process may be dynamic in its content; in its method it remains strictly formalized by the alleged rigidity of social laws.

Recently, Hannah Arendt has dealt with the subject extensively. She takes up an idea of Griewank's according to which revolution was originally conceived in the general sense of the eternally recurring motion of the planets. This concept includes at the same time the idea of inevitability. While the Marxian doctrine banks heavily on the latter concept, the idea of revolution, up to the times of the American and French revolutions at the end of the eighteenth century, is attached primarily to the idea of liberation from servitude of one kind or another. This means, in other words, either the reestablishment of a previous condition, or one presumed according to the doctrines of a natural law, whether that of Rousseau's enlightened pre-Romantic views or St. Augustine's Christian patristic philosophy. Revolution is thus equated with restoration, and this interpretation still holds true for the English revolution of 1688/89—but not for the American and the French revolutions. Here a novel element, the break with legal continuity, enters the stage of history. Revolution will be perceived, from here on, as a break in the continuum of history. Yet up to the later stages of the great French Revolution, that is, prior to the regime of the Convention, revolution is still seen as a movement steered primarily

---

[15] Brinton, *Anatomy of Revolution,* pp. 3–5, 216–222. See also Max Nomad, *Aspects of Revolutions* (New York, 1959), pp. 232 f. See at this point also Friedrich von Gentz's classic study, *The French and American Revolutions Compared,* transl. by John C. Adams (Chicago, 1955), pp. 3–84 *passim.*

[16] Griewank, *Der neuzeitliche Revolutionsbegriff,* in particular pp. 238–279; see also Griewank, *Der Wiener Kongress . . . ,* pp. 374–377. For a study of revolutionary concepts from a leftist though not an orthodox Marxian point of view see further Nomad, pp. 9–126.

by enlightened human action. The notion of the true inevitability of the revolutionary pattern develops actually under Robespierre's dictatorship and reaches its culmination only in Marxian-Leninist doctrine. Such is Hannah Arendt's interesting theory, which to a point merges revolutionary content and methods with the restoration idea in a historical frame.[17]

It is interesting to compare these views with those of Ferrero, which are already familiar to us in principle. As an enlightened conservative he naturally looks, in regard to content, far more favorably on the Thermidorian reaction of 1794–1795 than on the preceding stage of the revolution under Robespierre's leadership. Nevertheless, he admits that this reaction was essentially as illegitimate as the Regime of Terror. In fact, according to Ferrero none of the regimes from 1792 to 1814 could claim that it would guarantee either rule by the majority or protection of the minority. Again, appearances to the contrary, Ferrero's concept of counterrevolution is primarily a formal one, in spite of his personal predilections. As in Hannah Arendt's theory, the break in continuity plays a major part, though in different ways.[18] The link to the problem of a rigid doctrine of social revolution, foremost with Arendt, is lacking, however. A much stronger emphasis on the restoration concept takes its place, not so much as modified return to previous conditions but as goal in itself.

A somewhat different emphasis, namely, on the concept of counterrevolution, is to be found in Jacques Godechot's views. He perceives it as a type of movement of very specific content and not as mere complementary reaction to previous action. The peasant movement in the Vendée in March, 1793, as protest against the revolutionary war, would be a conspicuous example. Godechot further contends that counterrevolutionary tendencies do not conflict with the necessity for reforms, either in principle or in practice.[19] In this respect we find much common ground with the previous discussion of the inevitable partial adjustment of the social sys-

---

[17] Arendt, *On Revolution*, pp. 14–54 *passim*, 217 ff. For an excellent critical summary of Arendt's views, see also the review article in the Sunday edition of *Neue Zurcher Zeitung*, August 4, 1963, which is superior to most professional reviews. Griewank, *Der neuzeitliche Revolutionsbegriff*, pp. 171 ff; Nomad, pp. 150 ff.; Palmer, *Age of the Democratic Revolution*, I, 5–13; Sir Isaiah Berlin, *Historical Inevitability* (London, 1954), pp. 37 f., 66.; Sternberger, *Grund und Abgrund der Macht*, pp. 118 ff.; Meisel, *Counter-Revolution*, pp. 189 f., 215.

[18] Ferrero, *Principles of Power*, pp. 187–212 *passim*, and particularly 191 f; see also Ferrero, *Les Deux Révolutions . . .* , pp. 194 ff.

[19] Jacques Godechot, *La Contre-Révolution, doctrine et action, 1789–1804* (Paris, 1961), pp. 7–55, 218 ff., 407. See also Louis Madelin, *La Contre Révolution sous la révolution, 1789–1815* (Paris, 1935), pp. 360 ff. See, on the other hand, Arendt, pp. 8, 307. See also Nomad, pp. 189 ff.

tem of a successful restoration to a previous revolutionary system. Yet Godechot's interesting views are related to the specific conditions of the French Revolution up to the time of the firm entrenchment of the Consulate; they are not concerned with general findings. Frequently they deal only with social counterprograms on the part of those forces that reject the revolution in principle from the outset. Originally affirmative social ideas and propositions outside the cycle of revolution and counterrevolution are not germane to Godechot's theory. Thus the case for counterrevolutionary programs of a possibly type-forming nature as to content is not presented as persuasively by this author as might have been attempted.

In general, however, the bulk of the evidence, by no means confined to the few authorities listed here, perceives revolution according to methods. This always implies a breach of legal continuity. If such a breach should have been healed by the sanction in time [20] and by the consent of the governed, if thus a new legitimacy had been established, then counterrevolutionary action would be as illegitimate as the previous revolutionary action. In other words, the objectives of the counterrevolution could not legitimate a movement against an intermediate system which in the course of the years and by strength of the consent of the governed has meanwhile established its legitimacy. Thus we answer our third and fourth questions.

Implied at the same time is a rebuttal of the argument that the importance of counterrevolutionary objectives should take precedence over the use of revolutionary methods, that the former should justify the latter. Here the answer is clear and obvious. Objectives, however laudable in themselves, are and always will be compromised and distorted by illegitimate means. Time and the explicit—or at least clearly implied— consent of the governed could eventually sanction a system, though these facts might be unpredictable for some time. The use of revolutionary or counterrevolutionary means without at least a reasonable chance for the essential support of time and consent in the future, will never justify objectives, however sound these may be.

INTERNAL AND EXTERNAL FORCE

In question (5), on the origin of force in the process of restoration, in the first section of this chapter, we find an obvious difference in the pro-

---

[20] The use of "in time" rather than "by time" should indicate that this sanction does not simply refer to the course of time but to the evaluation of human action during a given period.

cesses of revolution and restoration. There is little doubt that revolution, if viewed as a movement within the political entity of the state, has to be initiated and has to gain mass support on the home grounds. To be sure, this does not exclude the possibility and frequently the reality of open or subversive outside support. The techniques of modern totalitarianism are only the most obvious cases in point. Nevertheless, while the revolutionary forces do by no means neccessarily represent a majority, there is little doubt in political theory and practice that they stand for hard-core groups of interest within the country where the revolution takes place.[21] Supporting forces from the outside might be superior in power, but they would be considered inferior in revolutionary zeal and interest. Where the situation is different in that respect, we may well speak of foreign aggression and occupation supported by subversion and rebellion within a country, but hardly of revolution, within the generally understood meaning of the term.

When we discuss question (5) concerning the relationship of forces working for restoration from the inside and the outside and ask ourselves whether the predominance of the latter is at all compatible with the concept of restoration, the problem is more complex. Certainly it is far more dependent on pragmatic experience. First of all, restoration is usually focused on forces that were once driven from power, whereas revolution is centered upon groups that were not previously in power. This in turn means that the forces working for restoration will frequently have to operate from political exile, whereas revolution usually starts from underground activist forces within the country. Numerous exceptions on either side do exist. Yet, if our assumption is true in general, we could not possibly link the restoration process by definition to a center of operation within the home country without denying the reality of the restoration idea altogether.

Here brief reference will be made to the two classical cases associated with the restoration concept, the Stuart Restoration in England in 1660, and the less fortunate Bourbon Restoration effort in France in 1814. Each will, of course, be analyzed in the second part of this study in some detail. It is important to note that both restorations were initiated on foreign soil. The English Restoration started not from England but from Scotland, where the headquarters of General Monck's army were situated. Further-

---

[21] The obvious inference can be drawn from authors as widely differing in their views as Crane Brinton and Robert Palmer on the one side, and Karl Griewank on the other. See Brinton, *Anatomy of Revolution*, pp. 3 ff., Palmer, *Age of the Democratic Revolution*, I, 20 ff., Griewank, *Der neuzeitliche Revolutionsbegriff*, pp. 230 ff. These references could easily be multiplied.

more, it was supported—though, by clear intent, not conspicuously—by a foreign Great Power, France.[22]

Foreign intervention in the French Restoration movement of 1814, and particularly after Waterloo in 1815, is far more obvious. Not only did Louis XVIII return from foreign soil, but it was frequently and derisively held that in 1815 he returned to France in the baggage train of the victorious foreign armies of the four Great Powers. The alien share in this restoration was thus far more conspicuous than in the English one, although the domestic activities toward restoration prior to the occupation of Paris by the Allied troops in March, 1814, were far less obvious than in the British case.

Yet in one as well as in the other we cannot doubt the provable historical fact that restoration was backed by substantial forces within the country. More than that, while the great symbolic value of the king in exile should not be minimized, it is obvious that the idea of restoration and the incentive to the restoration movement originated with the social strata driven from power in England in the 1640's and in France after 1789. In both cases the crown represented the nucleus and rallying ground of the forces fighting for restoration; but if they had not had their chief source of emotional and ideological strength within the country, neither restoration could have succeeded.

This certainly does not mean that a ruler could not be reinstalled in a different way, namely, by sheer force of foreign bayonets alone. But in our terms this would not be genuine restoration, which must be based on the solid support, indeed the initiative, of fairly broad groups representing specific traditions, sentiments, and social interests in the home country. Were it otherwise—and it has frequently been otherwise in history—we might speak of puppet and quisling regimes, installed or reinstalled by foreign forces of occupation with or without the help of political cliques or gangs within the country. To draw the line between this type of pseudorestorative putsch system and genuine restoration may not be easy in theory, but it should be quite feasible in political practice.

[22] It might be argued that Scotland was not actually a foreign country, since after the accession of James VI, king of Scotland, as king of England in 1603, the bearer of the English crown by right of hereditary succession was also king of Scotland. Against this it could be held that the formal Act of Union between the two countries took place only in 1707. We want to rest our case far less, however, on this formal argument than on the entirely different course of English and Scottish history under the Cromwellian revolution. See for instance George M. Trevelyan, *History of England* (New York, 1953), II, 206 ff., 236 ff.; Cecily V. Wedgwood, *Oliver Cromwell* (New York, 1956), pp. 85 ff., 102 ff., and numerous references in chap. 15 of this study.

Here we must touch upon the problem of so-called restoration after a regime has been overthrown by outright conquest by foreign power. It is, of course, by no means identical with the question of restoration originating in the home country and supported by foreign interests. Both contingencies may overlap, and each case, particularly each borderline case, must be judged on its merits. Yet in principle the difference is very clear. Restoration supported by outside forces—be it the English Restoration of 1660, the French one of 1814–1815, or in an even more complex manner, the transition from the Weimar republic in Germany to the Federal republic of today—originate in movements within the country of substantial group interests which run parallel to the design of foreign powers. Conquest originating from outside, though frequently supported by groups within the country, is simply a war between various powers. All our suggestions concerning the interplay in the three systems, above all the import of the passage of time, would still fully pertain to a restoration process supported by outside forces but not requiring actual foreign conquest. In this latter contingency neither the structure of revolution, the force of tradition, nor the influence of time are decisive. Above and before everything else is the impact of military power, which voids some other conditions or preconditions. To be sure, the course of military history and its effect on a conquered country is worth investigating, but it is not the problem that this study is concerned with, although the domestic restorative process and the one after military conquest by outside power are, of course, interrelated in more than one way.

Altogether the answer to the fifth question raised in this chapter may be summed up as follows. In restoration as compared with revolution we must take a broad view in regard to the center of activities and the forces which put a restoration movement back into power. They may have to operate far more frequently from exile than the groups working for revolution. They may be very largely supported by foreign interests and even be decisively supported by foreign military power. While the same may be true of revolution, it will be more conspicuous in a restoration. Yet, we can speak of true restoration only if these forces are rallied around a movement anchored in tradition, sentiments, and interests of the home country, where the last stage of the restoration process will have to take place after all. Without this indispensable precondition we are confronted by nothing more than a counterrevolutionary putsch.

FORCE AND VIOLENCE

The difference between putsch and restoration has some bearing on the sixth and last question raised in this chapter. We refer here to the proper distinction between the lawful exercise of force and the unlawful use of violence. In theory and under ordinary, that is, nonrevolutionary political conditions it is easy to establish what is the lawful or unlawful use of force in matters politic. The difficulty arises only when a regime is overthrown by revolutionary or counterrevolutionary means. At what point do the forces that are successful in their attack on the regime become legitimate, if they become legitimate at all? It is again our opinion that the difficulty in answering this question lies in the determination of facts, not principles.

In the initial stage of almost any kind of revolution, ignited by an active minority and expanded by a kind of snowballing effect, it may be impossible to foretell the eventual success of the movement. But it would be almost as difficult to predict whether the movement will have the openly expressed consent of the governed. Until the *de facto* answer to these questions is established, we can reasonably presume that the original system (A) uses lawful force to defend its power. The movement which attacks this system by physical strength makes use of unlawful means. When system (A) is overthrown, we still do not have the final answer to our question. If the victorious revolutionary regime shuns the test of asking for majority approval and fails to protect the minority, it will never become legitimate, even if it receives *de jure* recognition in international relations. Only if it strives for and obtains majority approval and offers protection to the minority, will it have the chance to become fully legitimate and to be sanctioned eventually by time. In this respect we have introduced the concept of a political generation. After one generation of this kind has passed from the political scene, reasonable chances exist for full legitimacy and preservation of the civic order. The influence of tradition in the life of a following generation will assure its full legitimacy and durability. A reservation concerning the predictability of historical development is, of course, in order.

The measure of time required to sanction the legitimacy of a system has nothing to do with the question when the process of legitimating the revolutionary regime, or similarly the counterrevolutionary restoration movement, ought to be initiated in political practice. Here, from the standpoint of Western political doctrine, the answer should be unequivocal: at the first conceivable opportunity. The successful revolutionary regime that has superseded system (A), as well as the successful restoration movement that replaces (B) ought to secure the consent of the governed as soon as law and order is established to a degree that assures the free expression of the will of the people and the protection of dissenters.

How long should such a process take, as viewed from the testing ground of legitimacy? No delay in seeking expression of the popular will should be allowed, nor should mere words be substituted for deeds. Whether it may take days, weeks, or at the outside, months to establish the consent of the governed beyond reasonable doubt, will depend on the conditions of the individual case. Yet we know from more than one experience of our times that less than a year may be amply sufficient for establishing a powerful dictatorship of indeterminate duration and at the same time flagrant illegitimacy. On the other hand, only after the consent of the governed has been secured to the widest possible extent can the final test get under way, namely, the sanctioning of a revolutionary or reestablished order in time. While mere statutory declarations can never replace action on the rights of the majority and the protection of the minority, such action without express protection by constitutional law is less than a fully satisfactory solution. A solution is only the manifestation of the consent of the governed by due constitutional process *and* the sanction by the course of time—not any arbitrary course but one in which the doctrine of the consent of the governed is not only preached but practiced.

This point, repeated here intentionally, cannot be stressed too strongly. Yet it is equally important to remember that the enactment of these imperative requirements will establish only the preconditions for the long-drawn-out process of at least two generations which may make a revolutionary or counterrevolutionary regime fully legitimate and, as far as human predictions go, durable. Only after a political generation that was successful in the sense of democratic philosophy, has passed into history, will the new order—whether intermediate, revolutionary, restorative, or plainly counterrevolutionary—become a genuine system with reasonable chances of success. Its stability, in human terms, will be established for certain only within a second generation. Revolutionary or counterrevolutionary, intermediate or restorative, the use of violence in its lasting effects can be undone by the expressed or at least unequivocally inferred approval of the new regime by consent of the governed. Its permanence can be established only by the sanction of time and in time. Obviously the same strict requirement does not exist in regard to the original system, the foundations of which may be in history long past. Otherwise a new regime that wants to become a true system must be actively endorsed through the consent of the governed—preferably by deeds and words but never by words alone.

The overall question raised has accordingly to be answered as follows. The course of time linked to the consent of the governed and its practical affirmation in time may eventually sanction a regime and convert it into a genuine political system. As to the question of legitimacy and the healing of the break in legal continuity, a counterrevolutionary or restorative movement and regime is bound by the same threefold requirements as a revolutionary one: (1) the enactment of the preconditions of rule by the majority and protection of the minority at the earliest possible moment; (2) the establishment of reasonable expectations within one political generation to make the new or reestablished order legitimate; (3) the achievement of durability of the new or restored system within another generation through the influence of tradition.

There are no reservations concerning preferential requirements for the counterrevolutionary restorative process. It cannot ask for special privileges in the reestablishment of legal continuity. Not the social content of a system but the means employed for its establishment will determine the question of lawfulness and legitimacy. Revolutionary or counterrevolutionary violence likewise requires remedial action by appeal to the people at the earliest possible moment to decide on the legitimacy of the regime. Therewith violence is neither approved nor condoned, but the rule of law accepted by the community is established for the future. In regard to content, we may add to this our previous assertion that restoration will be the more successful, indeed only successful, if it takes account of inevitable social reforms. The better the restoration succeeds in finding a common denominator for the social content of original system, intermediate regime, and restoration, the brighter will be its prospects for a lasting reestablishment.

CHAPTER VI

Summary

Here we will review and abstract the analysis and propositions put forth in the previous chapters. The object of this summary is to clarify the criteria for the comparison of historical theory with practice which will be met as the concepts developed in the first part of this study are applied to the cases described in the second.

We decided to deal with a movement and with conditions directed at the reestablishment of a state of social and political affairs after a protracted intermediate period. Some key questions were raised at this point. Is political restoration a mere countermovement to reestablish the precise duplicate of previous conditions destroyed by an intermediate revolutionary order? Should this not be so—and historic experience seems to support this negation—to what extent could we allow for social and political change between the original and the restored order without destroying the very image of restoration? Furthermore, if violence should be employed in the process of restoration, would it not likewise endanger an image which is linked to the concept of due process of law and the reestablishment of legal continuity? These problems led to a discussion of the inevitability of political and social change in time, in the first chapter.

There, three aspects of change in time have been dealt with: inevitable change, indeterminate change, and the relationship between determinism and social revolution. In regard to the first, attention is called to the increase in the life-span of man and the gradual change in the population pyramid, trending toward complete reversal of the statistical relationship between older and younger generations. This should be considered one of the rare precisely measurable criteria that determine the nature and scope of social change. This raises the question to what extent change must be considered inevitable in a restoration process. In this respect it is held that a further factor of social inevitability lies in steady technological progress with all its social repercussions. Any other social changes appear to be in varying degrees not clearly determinable and largely dependent on unpredictable human actions. For this reason we have rejected the social determinism inherent in Marxism. This factor must not be confused, however, with the question of social reversibility of revolutions. It has been argued that political revolutions leading to the overthrow of government by violent means are in theory always subject to restoration of the legal order. The where and when of such restoration can be answered by political practice alone. The broad social process itself, on the other hand, understood in such terms as "industrial revolution" or "agricultural revolution," is considered clearly irreversible, not excluding some of its political applications.

This led to a brief discussion of the basic limitations in studying problems of this kind by reference to pragmatic test cases. We have assumed that, apart from exceptional cases of rare spiritual and social significance, the very small state, whose course of action may be influenced primarily by neighboring powers, does not lend itself well to selection as such a test case. We believe further that it would not be advisable to go beyond communities within the area of Western civilization or at least within the sphere of its direct influence. We have found that, contrary to first impressions, the problem of sampling will be not the superabundance but the relative paucity of appropriate test cases. Still, a selection has to be made.

Concerning the even more important issue of analysis, the concept of the revolutionary process pertinent to our study had to be limited. The mere putsch, the transitory overthrow of a government run by a narrow political group of insiders, by an equally petty group of outsiders, is perceived as a subject of minor ideological and social implications, and consequently extraneous to the purpose of this study. We are dealing here only with political and social processes which imply a reasonable expectation of stability in foreign as well as domestic affairs. This important qualification limits again the number of test cases applicable to the subject matter.

From here we proceed, in Chapter II, to the evaluation of sociopolitical change as far as it pertains to content beyond the purely formal aspects of the restoration process. Since the political and social transitions discussed in this study are based on substantial change of content, they are henceforth frequently referred to as systems rather than as regimes. In this sense we perceive an original system (A) which is overthrown by the intermediate system (B) and reestablished in the restored system (C). Terms like old and new are avoided as ambiguous; the word original is used in a relative sense, namely, in regard to the connection between system (A) and systems (B) and (C). A discussion of the concepts of conservatism and progress follows. Neither term is employed in an absolute, rigid sense. While conservatism is generally reflected in systems (A) and (C), and progress truly or allegedly in (B), positions could possibly be reversed. Furthermore, both concepts could exercise an influence on any one of the three systems at the same time, though hardly to the same degree.

The next question raised in regard to the content of change is how much social change is feasible without destruction of the image of the original system (A) in the restored system (C). If the restored system wants to maintain itself, it must accept some social change as inevitable, and at the same time pay attention to the values, and in particular to the emotional values, of the past. How the restored system will have to balance these divergent factors can be answered only by pragmatic experience. Yet, inasmuch as restoration should represent foremost the idea of the resumption of legal continuity severed by a revolutionary interlude, it ought to be firmly linked to the concept of government by law. In that sense it can never become outright reactionary if it wants to succeed.

From here we proceeded, in Chapter III, to the discussion of ways and means of restoration, and this required the analysis of three main concepts: tradition, legal continuity, and legitimacy. Each of these concepts is wider than the next one. Tradition, the concept which comprises the other two, is understood as the idea of historical continuity operative, in our terms, within the state. Loud partisan claims to the contrary, it is not involved in transitory overthrow of government brought about by the machinations of ambitious cliques. It cannot be taken too seriously in the feeble semidictatorships, in particular those of the period between the two world wars. It has little relevance to Caesarism, Bonapartism to wit, since there the appeal to tradition is merely selective. The impact of genuine tradition is also completely incompatible with the cult of personality in the modern, fully totalitarian dictatorship of the Right and the Left, even though these dictatorships are in many other respects by no means equated. Despite frequent aberrations, true tradition as it is represented in monarchical restoration, on the other hand, must be focused not on the person of the monarch but on the institution. True tradition appeals in good faith to the memory of achievements of the past. Totalitarianism, on the other hand, in the deeper layers of conscience ashamed of the means employed by the regime, wants to obscure if not to destroy the links with the past.

Legal continuity, which embraces legitimacy, is perceived as the essence of transition from the original to the restored system. Without the reestablishment of legal continuity, restoration can never be successful, largely because of the close relationship between legal and social continuity.

In this context four basic questions were raised and discussed. First, does the problem of legal continuity pertain to a wider sphere of social action than that of constitutional change alone? The answer would be decidedly in the affirmative. Mere changes in the form of government without concomitant social transition may reduce the significance of the problems under study almost to zero.

Does the concept of legal continuity require that system (A)—the original one only in relation to (B) and (C)—was lawfully established? Here the answer is in the negative. Were it otherwise, the many new states established within the last generation—totalitarian, semitotalitarian, some still semifeudal, few completely democratic—would have to be considered fully lawful in origin, whereas the antecedents and, by inference, also the present structures of political communities anchored in a medieval past would appear highly questionable. But primary factors in the determination of the lawfulness of a political system should be—irrespective of recognition in international relations—the efficacy of rule linked to the indispensable consent of the governed. The latter should be expressly declared and clearly tested by governmental actions taken in the course of time. Yet time alone is not a factor that establishes lawfulness in terms of this study. Neither does lawfulness rest in mere declarations on behalf of rule by the majority and protection of the minority, but in declaration *and* action. A choice between them, through necessity, would be permissible only for a brief transition period, and in that case deeds would be far more important than words alone.

How much change can we allow in the restored system and still maintain that the original system has been reestablished? This question, similar to, but by no means identical with the one raised previously in connection with the retention of an image, is to be answered in line with the foregoing. Substantive, even extensive changes of the content of law are entirely compatible with restoration if they are lawfully brought about and if they are in line with the tradition that is the spirit of law.

Finally, perhaps the most basic question to be raised here is this: Can the legal and social principles of the intermediate system—frequently the revolutionary one as to content—be sanctioned simply by the course of time, and if so, by how much time? This question, which must be kept constantly in mind, is answered subsequently but only tentatively in Chapter V.

An analysis follows of the concept of legitimacy as formulated by Max Weber, who perceives it as pertinent not merely to the monarchical principle but to any power derived from established authority. Thereupon Guglielmo Ferrero's concept of legitimacy is discussed. The doctrine of this authority is understood to be based primarily on the time element, the efficacy of government, and the means employed to establish government, rather than on its content. Issue is taken with Ferrero's further, somewhat controversial concepts of prelegitimacy and quasi legitimacy. The former is understood by him as a type of rule which may become legitimate in the course of time; the latter is actually considered to be an illegitimate government which has, however, a sufficiently broad base of support to forego the use of violence. Our own conclusion is that restoration depends primarily on the joint influence of legitimacy and legal continuity. Both are considered more specific than tradition in general.

From here we proceed, in Chapter IV, to a discussion of the cycles leading to restoration. First the interchange between monarchical and republican government is evaluated. It is followed by an examination of cycles of ideas. After a brief glance at cyclical theories in the philosophy of history in general, the question is raised whether cycles from republic through monarchical government and back to republic have as much reality as the far more frequent occurrence of cycles from monarchy through republican government back to monarchy. The reasons for the rarity of this historical process in political practice are scrutinized. Quite apart from the general monarchical background of the community of states in Western political history, it has become evident that in the few cases of transition from republican government to monarchy and back to republican government, the intermediate period was usually much longer than the tenure of the republican systems. Accordingly, no republican tradition could be fully developed, hence it could not be restored. In a successful monarchical restoration the opposite is generally true. The monarchical tradition is long, the republican brief. Yet, particularly in modern times, there is undoubtedly a very positive reason why the cycle from republic to republic is so rare. While the constitutional monarchy has in some cases stood the test of time, and while its compatibility with democratic institutions cannot be questioned, republican government has on the whole proved more efficient, less susceptible to overthrow in terms of long-range consequences. Above all, it has been supported more frequently and more unmistakably by the consent of the governed. On the other hand, because of the predominant relevance of republican government in our times we have found that the cycle republic to dictatorship to republic has become quite frequent. Often the hoped-for termination of such cycles is not in sight. As far as we can judge, this has nothing to do with any inherent inadequacy of republican government. It seems to be due rather to a specific curse of this age of the masses: totalitarian dictatorship based on manipulated mass support. This phenomenon occurs in an age where republican government prevails, but hardly because it prevails.

As to cycles of ideas in the broadest sense, the question arises whether ideological movements, which generally transgress political borders, should find room in a study of developments within individual states. Here follows the discussion of a theory of spiritual cycles according to which the ideology of an age is generally opposed by the one immediately preceding and the one immediately succeeding it, while it is supported by the ideologies which antecede and follow these immediate phases. This direct influence of a preceding—though not immediately preceding—and a succeeding—though not immediately succeeding—ideology must not be confounded with Hegel's dialectic method. We refer to continuity of past and present after an interruption rather than to a synthesis of them in a future period. Furthermore, bygone phases of history are not considered equal in their effect: the influence of the period preceding the immediate past is considered to be strongest. This ideological process, which crosses the political borders of our civilization, is too complex to be fully understood within the relatively narrow frame of political institutions. If this were attempted, the specific meaning and concept of restoration within a political entity would be lost. On the other hand, the analysis of an ideological movement may be germane to our study in the rare cases where it can be reviewed within the confines of a definite political entity.

Finally, the complex question of the time element is discussed in Chapter V. Here several basic concepts are examined: violence, legitimacy, and the political generation; revolution and counterrevolution; internal and external force; and finally, the juxtaposition of force and violence. The question of practical significance of the restoration problem is reduced to the concepts of hereditary monarchy and democratic republic. Within this restricted frame six questions are raised; the second, third, and fourth depend on an affirmative answer to the first question. The last two questions, which are focused on the problem of force, stand by themselves.

The first question, which asks whether the course of time could sanction a claim to rule, can be answered only in a pragmatic way. The problem may appear entirely academic when a system has been accepted for centuries. Yet nonresistance to a system alone does not necessarily imply consent of the governed. Action which confirms this spirit is necessary, as traced in the answer to question two in Chapter IV.

We suggest that restoration has reasonable expectations of success only if it can be accomplished in the course of a political generation of some thirty-five to forty years. The generation active in the public life of the original system must still be able to take an effective part in that of the restored system. Though this is only one important element in successful restoration, pragmatic experience should show that in the absence of this influence the prospects of restoration are rather dim.

In order to have reasonable prospects of succeeding, restoration should be established within one political generation; but its success can be tested only after another generation, that is, after tradition has come fully into play. And tradition becomes fully effective only if customs, mores, and social practices are passed on through habit and no longer by direct instructions from the political community of system (A) to that of system (C). This can be tested, however, only after another generation— the one which still could pass on social practices by direct reference to personal memories—has passed from the political scene.

But the intermediate system, too, even if it is revolutionary, may become legitimate. This suggests a response to the question raised but not answered in Chapter III. Reasonable expectations to that effect would exist under the threefold conditions that system (B) is not, or not any longer, dictatorial in nature, that it will stay in power for at least one political generation, and, in Ferrero's term, that it must possess the efficacy to rule.

In questions three and four we ask: Is the attempt to overthrown an intermediate revolutionary system that has been sanctioned by time an act of counterrevolution rather than of restoration? Would this attempt imply a new break in legal continuity rather than its repair? On the other hand, could a restoration movement which challenges an intermediate system sanctioned by time be justified on the strength of its evolutionary objectives in regard to content, irrespective of the revolutionary means?

This complex of questions leads us into the discussion of counterrevolution, which is first approached from the angle of semantics. The opinion is held that the employment of revolutionary means with the purpose of overthrowing a government is always unlawful, though sanction in time of such violent action may be possible if the conditions outlined in Chapter II in regard to the consent of the governed are met. In the content of counterrevolutionary change, the time element has not the same importance. Here the issue is conservatism embedded in legal continuity versus radicalism that implies its break.

The issue adds up to just this: Does the counterrevolutionary concept, if correctly interpreted, refer primarily to form—that is, method—or to content?

Here follows a review of the opinions of authorities in the field which indicates that absolute, rigid standards are rarely accepted. In the survey of the views of Crane Brinton, Hannah Arendt, Guglielmo Ferrero, Jacques Godechot, and Karl Griewank it is found that some of them may believe in analogous developments of very different types of revolution, but that Karl Griewank is the only one who claims that such analogies can be raised to the level of rigid social laws.

It is deduced then that counterrevolutionary action cannot legitimate a movement directed against the former revolutionary system if the latter has meanwhile become legitimate under the conditions outlined previously in this chapter. Restorative objectives cannot in themselves justify the use of revolutionary, or for that matter, counterrevolutionary, means. This should answer in substance questions three and four.

Question five raises the important point whether a restoration movement must operate primarily within the home country, or whether it may start from abroad and be directed by outside forces. The first assumption can be affirmed easily for the revolutionary process in which groups inside the country try to obtain the control of government which they did not previously possess. Here outside support, though frequently forthcoming, is not the key issue. On the other hand, where the forces fighting for restoration are driven from power and a good part of them have to go into exile, the situation may be quite different. The conspicuous, but not the only, examples are the seventeenth century Stuart Restoration and the nineteenth century Bourbon Restoration movements. On the basis of ample pragmatic experiences it must be granted that forces fighting for restoration may start their operations from abroad. They may even be decisively—though preferably not conspicuously—supported by foreign power. If, however, the movement is not centered in the home country on significant groups with distinct traditions, emotions, and social interests linked to the restoration idea, we have a mere counterrevolutionary putsch. The very core of restoration and of its supporters must be in the home country. A restorative process which is directed primarily by the military force of an outside power is not prima facie subject to the influence of revolutionary and traditional forces, and above all not to the influence of time. Admittedly there are borderline cases between domestic restoration and so-called restoration after conquest from the outside. They demand our attention in individual cases, but this interesting subject is in principle outside of our province.

Question six poses a problem more easily stated than answered. How do we determine the precise difference between the lawful use of force and the illegal use of violence in the course of the restorative process throughout the three systems?

This issue will have to be judged by the facts of individual cases and not by abstract principles, even though we can justify the preliminary presumption that the defensive movement in a revolutionary situation is lawful, the offensive one unlawful. Suppose the so-called original system (A) is overthrown, then the further test for lawful intention—but not yet accomplished lawfulness—of the revolutionary system (B) would be its willingness and readiness to ask for the consent of the governed and to introduce protection of the minority. This process must start immediately if reasonable expectation to achieve legitimacy should ever be established. As experience has frequently shown, delay in this respect can lead to the establishment of dictatorships which may be dislodged only after years of suffering, if at all.

During this entire transitional period, action and declaration with regard to rule by the majority and protection of the minority are strongly desired, but if declaration should be postponed, action is immediately required under any condition. Only after the preconditions outlined in this chapter have been met, can the process of sanctioning by time in the course of two generations begin. Revolutionary government thus may eventually become legitimate.

If the revolutionary system fails to establish the preconditions of democratic government, either during the immediate stage of dynamic change or in the following decades, then restoration has its chance. It too will have to pass through the three phases outlined above. (1) Action must be taken to secure immediate rule by the majority and protection of the minority. (2) The generation active under the original system and again active under the restored one must establish reasonable expectations for success of the restored system. (3) Restoration will be fully accepted and permanently secured only when habit eventually replaces declared intent in the course of a following generation. Like all predictions concerning the future, this one too must be considered only as a presumption supported by evidence, and by no means as a certainty.

All this pertains to counterrevolutionary as well as to revolutionary action. The question of legitimacy in both is very largely one of methods and not of content. As to the latter, restoration has to take social change duly into account. It must look for a common denominator in the three systems as one of the very first premises for its success.

This summary concludes the general part of this study.

PART II
THE CASES

CHAPTER VII

Jewish Homeland and Babylonian Exile

Original system (A) 638–609 (continued until 597) B.C.

Intermediate system (597) 586–538 B.C.
(B)

Restored system (C) after 538 B.C.

Readers who are familiar with the main events discussed and interpreted in this chapter may not be fully conscious of their historical chronology. Therefore, the following summary is offered.[1]

It is generally assumed that David, king of Judah residing in Hebron, became ruler of the whole of Israel in about 1033 B.C. According to this premise the partition of the kingdom into two states took place after the death of the second great king, Solomon, in 932 B.C. The northern kingdom, by far the larger one, known as the kingdom of Israel, was conquered by the Assyrians under Sargon in about 722, and this act of conquest and destruction is linked to the exile of some thirty thousand Israelites. The state now ceased to exist as an independent political entity. The far smaller southern realm, the kingdom of Judah, with a population that never exceeded 500,000, lasted until 586 B.C. It became first a vassal kingdom of the Assyrian power and, after a brief flare-up of independence, a tributary to Nebuchadrezzar, the mighty ruler of the Neo-Babylonian Chaldean empire. Judah was already restricted to the rule of Jerusalem and its immediate vicinity in about 597 B.C., but according to general historical opinion, only the destruction of Jerusalem in 586 B.C. marks the end of the southern kingdom.

From here on, chronological factors are of major importance in our analysis. The Babylonian exile of the Jews is generally assigned to the period from 586 to 538 or 537 B.C., that is, from the destruction of Jeru-

---

[1] The classic history of the Jews by Heinrich Graetz, though outdated in some ways as to interpretation and command of some newly discovered original sources, still offers valuable information on chronology. Reference here and in the following is made to the original German edition, which contains the full scholarly apparatus not included in the English edition. As to chronology, see Heinrich Graetz, *Geschichte der Juden von den ältesten Zeiten bis auf die Gegenwart* (Leipzig, 1902), I, 427–452, II, Part I, 392–400. See also the excellent recent study by Jack Finegan, *Handbook of Biblical Chronology* (Princeton, 1964), pp. 58 ff., 277 ff. See further the great 10-vol. history of the Jewish people by Simon Dubnow, *Weltgeschichte des jüdischen Volkes* (Berlin, 1928–1930), the shortcomings of which are not germane to our problem. See I, 457–470. See finally the comprehensive standard work by Salo W. Baron, *A Social and Religious History of the Jews* (New York, 1952), I, 116 ff.

According to these authorities, differences between the Jewish calendar and chronology and our present one would not be substantial enough to affect the following conclusion.

salem to the return of a substantial number of exiles to the Holy Land. This requires some qualification. The loss of the independence of the kingdom of Judah was more or less sealed by the outcome of the battle of Megiddo in 609 B.C., when the king of Judah, Josiah, fell in the struggle against the advancing Egyptians under Necho.[2] Since the victorious Chaldeans under Nebuchadrezzar became heirs to the Egyptian claims against the Jewish state, the political disintegration of Judah started almost a generation before the downfall of Jerusalem.

Following a revolt and subsequent surrender to the Chaldean empire in 597, a semblance of independence was preserved for another decade, though the deportations to Babylonia started immediately. On the other hand, the conquest of Jerusalem in 586 was not quite the end. A substantial number of citizens of Judah continued to live for some time, in complete legality and with limited autonomy, in the vicinity of Jerusalem. This state of affairs is known as the regime of the Jewish governor Gedaliah, with the seat of government in Mizpah. If the Chaldean appointee Gedaliah had not been murdered by the leaders of dissenting Jewish factions after only four years of his rule, Judah and not the Jewish colony in exile might have remained the center of Jewish life. Thus the year 586 is only a convenient middle date, selected undoubtedly on account of the high symbolic significance of the conquest of the Holy City.[3] Yet a certain vagueness pertains not only to the beginning of the Babylonian captivity but to its end as well. The Neo-Babylonian empire of Nebuchadrezzar fell in 538 to the milder rule of the Persian Cyrus the Great, but the Jewish return did not start before 537 and then continued intermittently beyond the middle of the fifth century. The status of the Jewish communities in the former Babylonian domains was substantially different under the Persian kings, from Cyrus the Great through Darius I to Xerxes II, from that under the Chaldean successors of Nebuchadrezzar, Nabonidus and Belshazzar. This does not pertain so much to specific intentions to oppress the Jews under the Chaldean rulers as it reveals the influence of the moral climate of the Persian empire, which was far

---

[2] Concerning this somewhat controversial date, see John Bright, *A History of Israel* (Philadelphia, [1959]), p. 305, and the sources quoted there in n. 40.

[3] See also Baron, I, 104 f.; Graetz, II, Part I, 369 f.; Dubnow, I, 317–321; Cecil Roth, in his penetrating *Short History of the Jewish People* (London, 1948), p. 38; and, equally valuable, Abram L. Sachar, *History of the Jews* (New York, 1946), p. 60. See also Josef Kastein, *History and Destiny of the Jews* (New York, 1931), pp. 63, 69 f., and Bright, pp. 302 ff. Concerning the chronology at this point see also William F. Albright, *From the Stone Age to Christianity* (Baltimore, 1940), pp. 247 ff.

higher than that of the Neo-Babylonian.[4] This affected above all the Jewish community life, whose character changed after 538 from the status of tolerated deportees to that of a well-protected minority.

In this context it is important to clarify the concept of restoration, though only from a chronological viewpoint. The phase of historical development of the Jewish people frequently referred to as restoration is the period from the time when a substantial number returned from the Babylonian exile until the days when the new settlements in the old homeland were fairly well established. That would mean from the return under Cyrus beginning with the year 537 B.C. until the completion of the restored Temple, presumably in 516 or 515. There can be no doubt that during this period of about two decades a new Jewish social, and in a limited sense also political, body was reestablished in Palestine. Few of those who had to leave the country at the beginning of the century could have been among those who, according to the Scriptures, returned from Babylonia, Egypt, and other countries. Many of them, particularly their descendants, must have been the offspring of marriages with daughters of other tribes. Nevertheless, this social and political resettlement, half a century after the old kingdom was destroyed, was so strongly linked to the tradition of the recent past that it conforms in many ways to the concept of restoration discussed in Part I.

The situation is rather different in regard to the period sometimes referred to as the second restoration, namely, the era under the spiritual leadership of Ezra and afterward of Nehemiah, from about 458 to 420. Here, and this is in particular Simon Dubnow's interpretation, the concept of restoration is no longer associated with the return to and re-identification with the land of the fathers, which after 538 was already established. Restoration is now understood largely in a sense of national separation and segregation from other tribes and their ethnic-racial influence.[5] Obviously these two concepts of restoration overlap in several important ways. As to the time element of the restoration process discussed in chapter 5, it should be clear that the return and the reestablishment in the homeland of Jewish autonomy, if not sovereignty, took place within the time span of two generations. The same could not be said for the so-called second restoration, unless we were to perceive the regime

---

[4] See Graetz, I, 2, 43–70; Dubnow, I, 344–360; Bright, pp. 305 ff., 323 ff.

[5] See particularly Dubnow, I, 357–384 and 466, who perceives two eras of restoration, one from 536 to the consecration of the new Temple in 516, the other under Ezra and Nehemiah, from 458 to 420. See also Bright, pp. 356 ff. and Max Weber, *Gesammelte Aufsätze zur Religionssoziologie*, Vol. III: *Das antike Judentum*, (Tübingen, 1923), pp. 372 ff.

established by the first restoration as overthrown and reestablished by Ezra as royal governor of the Persian King Artaxerxes I. Notwithstanding the major changes in the conditions prevailing in Judah between 537 and 458, this would be a far too sweeping, indeed an artificial assumption.

To return to the starting point of this analysis: for a picture of Judah in the last decades prior to its final destruction attention must not be focused only on the last, incapable kings, particularly on the tragic Zedekiah These rulers were briefly tributaries of the Egyptian and later the Chaldean empires, and their sovereignty extended over only a small part of the small kingdom of Judah. The great Josiah, 638–609 (probably), was indeed the last king who governed the country in its fullest extent, including parts of Samaria, the territory of the former northern kingdom. He was also the last sovereign who pursued an independent policy.

These two factors, the independence of Josiah's rule and the range of his domain, both diminished rapidly after his death, allow us to consider the religious, social, and political structure of the Judah of his time as the original system (A). Josiah's goal of a grand national policy striving for the unification of the kingdom of David was the main reason not only for his invasion of Samaria, but also indirectly for his doom. To block the attempted invasion of Syria from the East he tried to check the Egyptian advance, which threatened the territory of the former northern kingdom, to which he himself laid claims. His death in the war against the Egyptians actually helped to pave the way for the future victors over the Egyptians and Jews alike, the Chaldeans. Unfortunate as this foreign policy was, it is closely related to the king's overriding aim of national and spiritual unification. Neither one is clearly separable from the other, but John Bright refers to the overall effort as "by far the most thorough-going" reforms "in Judah's history." [6]

If Josiah's aim in foreign policy was the unification of the scattered ten tribes in the kingdom of old, in domestic policies it was the unification and centralization of religious worship. In the Jewish state, even in its pre-theocratic stage, this also meant social and legal centralization.[7] Shrines were destroyed where idols, in particular the golden bull, were still worshipped, and religious services were centralized and in a sense standardized in the Temple of Jerusalem.

But obviously the greatest event in this field, as indeed in any of Josiah's

[6] Bright, *History of Israel,* pp. 295 f. About the reign of Josiah and in particular the social and religious reforms see Baron, I, 83 ff., 330 ff.; Dubnow, I, 283–298; Graetz, II, Part I, 271–295; Kastein, pp. 57–63.

[7] On the evolution of the theocratic concept see Baron, I, 152 f., 221 ff.; Albright, pp. 184 ff. and Weber, *Das antike Judentum,* pp. 81 ff.

reign, was what is usually referred to as the discovery of the Book of Deuteronomy, the last of the Pentateuch, and its proclamation as the Law of Moses and therewith the law of the land. It is not important in this context to discuss whether Deuteronomy represented the Mosaic Law in its original or its revised form, or a combination of the latter with the laws of Josiah's own reign, or perhaps only the king's own code of law. What is decisive for our purpose is the fact that Deuteronomy was proclaimed as the Law of Moses and thus sanctified by the full force of ancient tradition.

According to an able summary by Heinrich Graetz, the four main thoughts in the new—or perhaps only newly proclaimed—law were the emphasis on the sublimeness of God, the greatness of the mission of Israel, the low moral character of the people of Judah in Josiah's time, and the realization of the consequences of this contrast between exalted mission and contemporary misconduct.[8] In this respect idolatry and mixed marriages with neighboring people and non-Jews settled in Palestine were denounced with varying severity—stronger in the case of immigrant people like the Ammonites and Moabites than in that of the neighboring Egyptians. They apparently presented a lesser threat to the country's mores and traditions.

Centralization of the formal religious services in the Temple in Jerusalem showed only the external aspect of far-reaching social changes, which led to the restriction of sacrifices altogether, to the rendering of the tithe in favor of the poor, and to the wiping out of debts every seventh year. This in turn led to the proclamation of even more radical changes, particularly in regard to the status of the king, who was as much pledged to obey government by law as were any of his subjects. Symbolic of this was the restriction of personal wealth.

As to warfare, no mercy was to be shown to heathen people settled within the land, whereas the life of a defeated foreign enemy should be spared and the obligation to pay tribute would suffice. Here again, as in the annulment of marriages with women from other tribes, the overriding principle was the preservation of the national and religious identity and purity. Whenever this principle was not involved, the law revealed remarkable social concern, whether in regard to charity toward the poor, as strict social obligation, or to the freeing of slaves after seven years, and even endowing them with property. These laws, solemnly read to the people and expressly acknowledged by them as binding, were to be strictly enforced by an expanded and improved judicial system, which

[8] Graetz, II, Part I, 272.

included also a kind of supreme court in Jerusalem. The particular strictness of the law courts was directed against any offense threatening the purity of the people's ethnic composition, such as adultery or by implication disobedience to the parents.[9]

These laws were by no means fully adhered to. The teachings, warnings, and prophecies of the great contemporary prophet Jeremiah (from between 645 and 640 to between 580 and 570) attest to this. On the other hand, the doctrines of the great prophet of the doom and ultimate spiritual purification of Israel must not be taken too literally. In the first place, Jeremiah was concerned primarily with the moral decay from the death of Josiah to the destruction of the city under Zedekiah. And Jeremiah's standard, like that of all the great prophets of any age and place, was perfection, yet nowhere and at no time could the people achieve it. Thus only a very sensitive conscience could link the destruction of the kingdom primarily to moral disintegration. Others might attribute it primarily to external factors entirely beyond the control of the people of Judah. On the other hand, the fact that under Josiah the law of Deuteronomy was proclaimed not merely as a guide of moral principles, but as the enforceable law of the land, may suggest a more positive attitude. In any case, we feel entitled to take this code and the conduct of the people who lived under its command as the social basis of the original system (A) and begin here the discussion of the restoration process. We must make allowance for the fact that the sublime character of this law—in spite of its features of down-to-earth, concise reasoning—made it very difficult for the people to fill the gap between the commandments of ethics and government in practice. To fail partly or not to succeed fully in that respect was evidence not of human depravity but only of frailty.

In dealing with the period of the exile from 586 B.C. at the latest to 537 B.C. at the earliest we assume, but do not yet accept, its identification with the intermediate system (B) in the restoration process. The discussion of pertinent data is in order here. The forced deportations to Babylon started on a large scale with the surrender of the feeble young King Jehoiachin in 597 to Nebuchadrezzar. The tragedy of the conquest of Jerusalem under his uncle Zedekiah in 586 lay not so much in the numbers of emigrants but in the severance of the traditional ties with the homeland. Even this, however, because of the continuance of the viceregal regime of Gedaliah, was by no means complete for the next few years in a political sense and never complete in an ethnic sense.

[9] The principal provisions touched here are to be found in Deuteronomy, chaps. 4, 7, 12, 13, 15–17, 19–26.

As to the return from exile, that is, the end of the intermediate system and the beginning of the restoration, the year 537 is merely the starting point of a legalized exodus from Babylonia to Palestine. It continued in various waves well beyond the second half of the fifth century, the times of Ezra and Nehemiah. In Dubnow's terms this is the period of the second restoration under King Artaxerxes I.

Were the numbers involved in deportations and return large enough, in proportion to the whole population, to justify the use of the terms *exile* of the Jewish people and, in regard to their return, *restoration* in the home-land? Or was the Babylonian exile, on the other hand, in terms of numbers a mere sideshow in Jewish history? To be sure, numbers, even if they could be ascertained accurately, are only one weighty factor among several. Yet their analysis may lead to the evaluation of further significant problems.

Heinrich Graetz assumes that the majority of those "military leaders and their followers" who managed to escape from Jerusalem in 586 pre-ferred to stay in the country at all costs. Only after the murder of Gedaliah and against the counsel of Jeremiah did another large-scale emigration take place, this time to Egypt and under far less favorable auspices than the previous ones to Babylonia. Less than a thousand of those left in Judah were now banished by Nebuchadrezzar to Babylon. The remaining Jews in the former kingdom of Judah as a body seem to have lost social significance by this time.[10]

On the strength of computations based largely on the Book of Jere-miah, Graetz assumes the existence of three main waves of deportations. One in 597 comprised some 10,000 people from Jerusalem and around 3,000 from the countryside; a second, in 586, may have amounted to about 15,000 from the city and less than 1,000 from the country; and finally the third, after the assassination of Gedaliah, involved less than 1,000 Jews.[11] Unfortunately these deductions leave the main question open: How large a percentage of the population that survived the downfall of the city was altogether subject to the deportations? Probably Salo Baron's cautious estimates are the best answer we may expect on this issue. "The local population was seriously depleted by successive deportations in the years 597–586 (602–582), and by the numerous wars and semi-voluntary migrations. It appears indeed, that fully one-third of the total pre-war population of Judah was forcibly removed by the conqueror, while many thousands died of hunger and destitution. Thousands of others . . . fled

---

[10] Graetz, II, Part II, 366–383; Dubnow, I, 325 ff.
[11] Graetz, II, Part II, 345–350.

the country before the approaching Chaldaean armies and only a part of them returned after peace was restored . . . ." The assumption in Jeremiah that all the Jews had returned after the installment of Gedaliah as governor cannot be accepted on the strength of the available archeological evidence either in full or in major part.[12]

Although numbers do not tell the whole story, in view of the crisis of national purification after the return from exile we may assume that major sectors of the undeported population, through religious and ethnic mixture with neighboring or host peoples, were lost to Judaism altogether. No contrary evidence exists in this respect. More convincing is of course the supposition, backed by all available accounts, that those who were sent to exile included, in a spiritual, economic, and social sense, the most substantial segment of the Jewish survivors. It is fair to assume that this selective process was closely related to interests of the Babylonian conqueror. On the strength of these combined factors it may be concluded that the exile represented the industrious, skilled, and propertied Jewish people. In this sense the Jews in exile may be considered to be the substance of the intermediate social system in the restoration process.[13]

Historians are generally agreed that the Babylonian captivity, if it can be called captivity at all, was amazingly mild. It gave the Jews considerable opportunity to acquire new skills, economic affluence, and what is more important, the freedom to preserve their traditions and develop them in line with the new conditions. All this is of interest to this study primarily as it pertains to change. This is less conspicuous in the social field, where adjustments were frequently of a temporary nature, than in the religious one. Apparently the social stratification of the exile generation ranged rather widely from a privileged kind of nobility to half-free subjects to slaves. The Jews entered commercial and industrial life on a much larger scale than in the home country. Merchants and bankers prospered. Farmers found it more difficult to adjust to changed conditions, but they were not impeded in their work by any legal restrictions. As Baron puts it, "On the whole, there hardly was any important vocation, including public office, in which Jews and other non-Chaldaeans were not represented." [14] But there were changes not only in affluence and skill but in social and legal status as well. The rights of women—in

---

[12] Baron, *Social and Religious History of the Jews,* I, 105 f. See also p. 344, where Baron considers his estimate of the number of deported people to be conservative.

[13] See also Baron, I, 105 ff.

[14] Baron, I, 110, 115; see also pp. 108–129 *passim;* Dubnow, I, 332–356; Graetz, II, Part II, 1–70; Kastein, pp. 64–72; Bright, pp. 323 ff.; Weber, *Das antike Judentum,* pp. 360 ff.

particular in the independent administration of property—were considerably strengthened. At the same time, mixed marriages became more and more widespread—quite natural under exile conditions in a foreign country. This problem, heightened by the numerical preponderance of men over women, revealed its full significance only after the restoration. Altogether friendly feelings toward foreigners were developed and strengthened, particularly where and when the need of the Jewish people for national identification was not endangered. Community autonomy, which replaced the lost sovereignty, served this purpose for the time being quite effectively.[15]

At the same time many of the social privileges and practices of the old landed families continued. Idolatrous religious practices increased and were castigated in the visions of the great prophet of exile, Ezekiel. Similar ideas were expressed during the last period of exile by Deutero-Isaiah.[16]

Undoubtedly the great prophets are largely responsible for the remarkable fact that people in the multinational and multireligious polytheistic Chaldean empire preserved, by and large, their national and religious identities. And this is all the more extraordinary as national self-identification was more difficult to achieve where there was no pressure from government or environment to merge with the main stream of Neo-Babylonian civilization. In other words, national consciousness did not need the incentive of a protest against national suppression. The great achievement is here the development of a net of communities on an ethnic and cultural rather than on a territorial basis. A number of devices, such as stricter observance of the Sabbath, closer study of the Pentateuch, the Five Books of Moses, could be mentioned here, but the important fact was the development and at the same time decentralization of communal life, "which in place of the ancient temple forced" the exiled Jews "to establish a new, revolutionary institution: a house of worship dedicated to prayer without sacrificial offerings." [17] All these factors combined to develop an image of a Jewish community linked as much to the preservation of the national religious tradition as to the evolution of national concepts that transgressed all political frontiers. The initial formation of this image, which has been of such far-reaching importance in the history of the Jewish people until our day, is the outstanding phenomenon of

[15] Baron, I, 136 f.; Dubnow, I, 334; Weber, *Das antike Judentum,* pp. 363 ff.

[16] The great unknown prophet to whom the second part of the book Isaiah is generally attributed. The first Isaiah lived presumably in the eighth century B.C. See also Weber, pp. 363, 379 ff.

[17] Baron, I, 132 f. See also Graetz, II, Part II, 115 f.; Dubnow, I, 334 f.

change in the analysis of the intermediate system in the process of Jewish restoration.

In dealing with the restored system (C) attention is focused here on what historians like Simon Dubnow and Salo Baron call either the first restoration or the territorial restoration. This was the return to the homeland and the resettlement there—under a statute of autonomy but still subject to the sovereignty of the Persian world empire, which had now replaced Chaldean rule. This first restoration period may be considered to have terminated with the consecration of the rebuilt Temple. There is little disagreement in the literature that the spiritual and social development during this period was far less penetrating and sweeping than that under the so-called second restoration under the great leaders Ezra and Nehemiah, roughly between 458 or 460 and 420 B.C. Nevertheless, as seen from the angle of this study, the great reform period in the fifth century is a genuine restoration only if the meaning of the term is considerably stretched. This period was removed from the original system that ended with the destruction of Jerusalem in 586 B.C. by well over a hundred years, far beyond the two-generation limit discussed in Part I. Even more important is the fact that the physical act of reestablishment in the homeland was completed long before the two great reformers returned to Judah. Their followers, in no way directly associated with either the original or the intermediate system from 597 to 538, could in no sense be considered to be exiles. They did not restore an old system under new leadership, they transformed it, with their eyes more on the first restoration than on the fateful events under the old kings from Josiah to Zedekiah. Thus although we do not challenge the tremendous importance of this period in the history of the Jewish people, it is on the fringe of the historical process this study is concerned with.

The restoration in our terms refers to the exiles or their descendants deported between the two defeats of 597 and 586 and the few years after, until the death of Gedaliah. The return approved by Cyrus under Sheshbazzar or Zerubbabel or both,[18] with the former probably as regular appointed viceroy, began in 537, and the first and main wave of emigrants reached the homeland within the next few years. This was, according to Graetz's estimates, about 40,000 persons, according to Baron some 50,000, including about 7,000 slaves, as compared to a return of a mere 5,000 under Ezra. Again, according to Graetz, the number of people who returned under Cyrus the Great was about three times that of the original exiles. Computations to deduce, from the number of those who returned,

[18] For their relationship, see n. 23.

the Jewish population figures during the two generations of exile have been attempted, but they are necessarily vague. The change in the birth-rate under new conditions and an assessment of the number of slaves in the statistics are particularly vexing problems. Some facts stand out, however, and may be accepted more easily. The returning people represented a very sizeable sector of the former exiles and their descendants. At the time of Ezra and Nehemiah some three generations later, only a small minority of the Jewish colonists abroad returned. These colonists, the descendants of the former exiles, at that later period must have numbered several hundred thousand. Furthermore, the returning Jews in the sixth century certainly did not lack property, measured in terms of slaves, cattle, and even precious metals. Yet their numbers probably included few of those who had become especially wealthy in exile. This did not mean that the most prosperous emigrants, who had done very well in the new country, disassociated themselves completely from the destiny of their kinsmen. One may assume that even the latest emigrations under Ezra in about 458 B.C. were supported by donations of rich descendants of the former exiles.[19] Re-emigration was not restricted to the empire of Cyrus. Descendants of exiles returned also from the Greek islands, Asia Minor, Egypt, and Phoenicia, indeed as the prophet Zechariah put it at the end of the century, "from the east country, and from the west country."[20]

All this leads to the conclusion that the first re-emigration, in contrast to the second main phase of the re-emigration process under Ezra, in-cluded a very substantial group of the Jewish people. They were also socially and ethnically representative. This conclusion is strengthened by the fact that a return movement also took place very soon from other areas of the Middle East and North Africa. It is not particularly weakened by the presumption that only a small number of very wealthy people participated in the emigration process.

The social stratification of old was restored sooner and to a wider degree than might have been expected. The re-emigration controlled only a small country devastated by war. The influx of settlers from neighbor-ing peoples such as Moabites, Ammonites, Edomites, Philistines, and particularly Samaritans seems to have been substantial. It was natural that the standards of living, compared with the conditions of exile, dropped

---

[19] The catalog of numbers and wealth of the participants in the re-emigration of 537 is to be found in the second chapter of Ezra. See also chap. 7 in Nehemiah. The return of Nehemiah and his retinue involved a numerically even lesser fraction of the re-emigration. See in this context also Graetz, II, Part II, 71 ff., 112 ff., 348 ff., Baron, I, 110 f., 161 f.; Bright, pp. 341 ff.; Weber, pp. 372 ff.

[20] Zech. 8: 2–8.

markedly during the first years after the return. Only a primitive kind of agriculture could be maintained in the beginning. Yet, "with few exceptions, those who returned could trace their ancestry for several generations, and in many cases knew in what part of the country their family property had been situated. . . . As the caravans successively entered the country, one may imagine that they dispersed, each family going to reassert its claim on the plot of land which it previously owned." [21]

Nevertheless, in this ring of some thirty small rural communities around the destroyed capital we do meet changes of far greater consequence for the future than is apparent in the immediate present. The ancient territorial organization, following roughly the settlements of the ten historical tribes, disappeared. In the Babylonian exile the Jewish emigration, enduring the havocs of war, could not possibly settle according to the ecology of the historic tribes. Compared with standards of later, supposedly more enlightened millennia, the exiles could consider themselves fortunate to be kept together as families.[22] This replacement of the tribal organization by a policy of settlement according to families, abroad as well as at home, could indeed be considered to be a lasting result of the threefold process of deportation, exile, and return.

A change, similar in significance and consequences, can be seen in the struggle for leadership. Here a group under the leadership of Sheshbazzar, installed by Cyrus as royal governor largely because of his presumed descent from the House of David, faced another faction under the High Priest Jeshua, who could claim a relationship to the tradition of Aaron, the first High Priest.[23] Apparently a conflict revolved around whether Judah should eventually become an independent kingdom following the great tradition of David or whether it should remain a Persian province in which the Jewish autonomy would be represented by the equally deep-rooted tradition of the office of High Priest.[24]

This surely was not an issue of mean significance, as far as it touches upon the question of full sovereignty versus mere autonomy under Persian overlordship. Far more important, however, was the underlying

---

[21] Roth, *Short History* (see n. 3 above), pp. 53 f., 57. See also Baron, I, 125; Bright, pp. 323 ff.

[22] Graetz, II, Part II, 100 f.; Roth, pp. 56 ff.

[23] Whether this conflict took place between Sheshbazzar and the followers of the High Priest or more likely the former's nephew Zerubbabel, or whether the two names refer to the same person, is far less important than the struggle itself and the outcome. See Baron I, 110 f.; Roth, pp. 53–56;; Graetz, II, Part II, 101 ff. See also Dubnow, I, 355, n. 2; Weber, pp. 365 ff.

[24] See particularly Dubnow, I, 363 ff.; Graetz, II, Part II, 101 ff.; Weber, pp. 365 ff.

ideological problem, namely, the question of secular state versus theocracy. Taking a long-range view, we see the latter, unlike the former, political concept, as related not to the notion of the territorial state but to the rising universalist tradition of Judaism.[25] This new theocratic concept which began to replace the political one, just as the family organization superseded the tribal structure, pointed toward the future problems of Judaism: the Diaspora as social foundation but at the same time as the very essence of a supranational philosophy with spiritual bonds.

Compared with these administrative and political developments, with their far-reaching spiritual consequences, the purely ritual religious measures followed rather traditional lines. The outstanding external factor of obvious great symbolical meaning was the rebuilding of the Temple. Factional differences delayed its consecration until about 516 B.C.—just within the two-generation limit discussed previously. The rededication of the Temple meant also the negation or rejection of semi-idolatrous or fully idolatrous practices. These were fed from all directions, where re-emigrants had entered the country. Similar influences pertained to the tribes who had settled in Judah during the exile period and had intermarried there with tribes from Samaria, the domains of the former northern kingdom. Their offer to participate in the rebuilding of the Temple was rejected because the sincerity of their monotheistic beliefs was in question. This indicated the beginning of the national and even nationalistic renaissance movement under Ezra and Nehemiah two generations later. As it was, the rebuilding of the Temple and the resumption of sacrificial services followed rather strictly the old tradition, though now by necessity on a more modest scale. However, here too we find an emphasis on the legal rather than merely the ritual aspects of religion and in this sense a restoration of the enforcement of religious, moral, and social law under the great king Josiah prior to the fall of the kingdom.[26]

No doubt about it, these laws were in a magnificent way further enhanced, expanded, and raised to a higher plane under the great leaders of the coming century, Ezra and Nehemiah. Yet both were "zealous nationalists," and "they stressed the national element above all others."[27] If by saving their own people they also rendered an important service to mankind, as Salo Baron believes, then they did so in a roundabout way. Their notable achievements in the strengthening of military security law

[25] See also Baron, I, 157 f. and Weber, pp. 323 ff. on Jewish universalism.
[26] See also Graetz, II, Part II, 100 f.
[27] Baron, I, 157 f.; Bright, pp. 356 ff.

enforcement, in religious purification, and above all in ethnic-racial self-identification and, indeed, isolation can be as little questioned as the harshness of their means. Yet their chief objective was to preserve the nation on a territorial basis. No doubt the generation that had returned from exile under Cyrus almost a century earlier had worked and toiled on a lower intellectual and technological level, yet, as dimly visible from a long-range point of view, on a higher spiritual plane. With their looser social organization they had helped to preserve the nation for the task of linking the homeland to the colonies of descendants of exiles abroad. Far more important, however, was the evolution of the spiritual foundations of the Diaspora in the transition from mere tribal or relative monotheism to the absolute monotheism of one God for the whole world.[28] The importance of this factor as link with the colonies abroad, which increasingly surpassed the Jewish people in the home country in population and wealth, cannot be overestimated.

True enough, the elevation of monotheism is also closely linked to the reforms of Ezra and Nehemiah, that is, as far as they associated religion with the observance of Mosaic Law. Yet inasmuch as the reformers related the law to strict ethnic segregation and expulsion of the wives of foreign extraction and their children from their Jewish husbands and fathers, they fought actively against the very concept of Jewish universalism.[29] This is no insight after the events, based on the attempt to inject modern social and ethical standards into the judgment of an entirely different historical situation. The philosophy of the leaders of the fifth century reforms were even at that time related exclusively to the idea of the preservation and enhancement of the national state. Under existing conditions this implied at the same time the loss of the Jewish colonies abroad for Judaism. More important, in view of the precarious position of the homeland within the Persian empire, it meant that the loss of semi-independence in the homeland under a less benevolent Persian king than Cyrus the Great or Artaxerxes I would see the destruction of Judaism altogether. The lifework of the first generation of those who returned after 538 B.C. tended in the opposite direction. By eliminating the tribal organization and developing the theocratic tradition of Josiah further, they traced the channels along which a nation—held together for two thousand years by only cultural and spiritual bonds—could survive and

[28] See also Dubnow, I, 329 ff.; Albright, *From the Stone Age* (see n. 3 above), pp. 240 ff. and Weber, 323 ff.

[29] See particularly Ezra 9: 2–6, 12–14; 10: 3–11; Neh. 9: 2; 12: 1–4, 23–28. See also Baron, I, 96 ff., 157 f.

develop. It will not be denied that the reformers of the fifth century, despite their basically contrary policy, made a great contribution to the observation of the law itself. It is doubtful whether the followers of either trend were fully conscious of the long-range consequences, but full consciousness of historical action over long stretches of time is not given to man.

How does this whole process tie in with the restoration system traced in the first part of this study? We assume that the original system is represented by Judah under the king, Josiah, at the end of the seventh century. Under him the concept of government by Mosaic law was firmly implanted. The brief rule of puppet kings acting under foreign stress until the destruction of the city in 586 is of relatively little significance in the context of the then existing Jewish social structure.[30] The intermediate period of exile meant the end of statewide government, but at the same time an expansion of the social stratification from the predominance of agriculture to trade and commerce. It meant the end of the tribal territorial organization and a new code of worship based on small-group prayer meeting rather than on the centralized ritual of sacrifices in the Temple in Jerusalem.

It is perfectly true that these transitions were due not only to an internal Jewish revolution but to changes brought about by tremendous external pressure, above all by the power of the Chaldean king. Yet inasmuch as the Chaldean regime and, even more, the succeeding Persian regime, left to the Jews the freedom of autonomous domestic development, it may be held that the primary force toward change came from the Jewish people themselves and only on the surface from the pressure of a foreign power.

Change within the two generations of exile from 597 to 537 B.C. was sweeping and, as to be expected, a substantial part of it went into discard with the coming restoration after the return. The territorial basis of the state—though neither its boundaries nor its full sovereignty—was established, as was the predominant agricultural structure in the social field and, more important, the tradition of the Temple in the religious one. Most important, however, the transition from the tribal religious and political organization based on territorial autonomy to that of a social and religious life based on the personal autonomy of individual affiliation with the family and the law, combined features of original and intermediate system. Government by reinforced Mosaic Law can be traced to the original system of Josiah. On the other hand, government by individual

[30] Bright, pp. 302 ff.

links to spiritual rather than to tribal bonds is associated with the intermediate exile regime. The new Jewish vassal state in Palestine had preserved setting and image of the territorial state of old and had developed it further after the restoration and under the influence of inevitable change brought about by the experiences of the two exile generations. Their contribution, which helped so much to accomplish national survival by spiritual means, is indeed the key issue in this restoration process. These people established a firm bond between the original system of Josiah and the poor, reestablished vassal state in which those who had returned sweated and toiled with admirable devotion.

Precisely such a close tie of the intermediate system to past and future is lacking when we look almost four centuries ahead to what seems at first glance a far more conspicuous, more demonstrable restoration. We refer here, of course, to the gallant Maccabean revolt. The great experience of the Hasmonean state does not unite Jewish life under the then largely disparate forces of Hellenism and Roman rule in the same sense as is true for the relationships between the Babylonian exile generations, the old kingdom of Judah, and the new beginnings after 538 B.C. The return at that earlier time heralded the departure of the Jewish people into the world; the lights kindled at Hanukkah illuminated the path back to the homeland. These trails, though perhaps equally steep and hazardous, are different in direction. Yet the very existence of both gives each more meaning and promise.

CHAPTER VIII

Athens from Solon to Cleisthenes

CHRONOLOGY

ca. 682 B.C.	Introduction of annual archonships
594/93 B.C.	Solon archon; presumable initiation of his reforms
580's possibly 570's B.C.	Probable period of continuation of reforms under special appointment
ca. 560 to 510 B.C.	Rule of the Peisistratidae (Peisistratus and his sons)
Until ca. 540 B.C.	Struggle for power
540–527 B.C.	Administration firmly entrenched
527–510 B.C.	Rule of Peisistratus' sons (Hippias until 514, then Hipparchus. Violent overthrow of the administration and expulsion of Hipparchus in 510)
ca. 508 B.C.	Cleisthenes' administration firmly established
Original system (A)	From ca. 682 or 594/93 to 590 or 570 B.C.
Intermediate system (B)	560's to ca. 510 B.C.
Restored system (C)	ca. 508 B.C.

A restoration process that might conceivably pertain to the emergence, overthrow, and entrenchment of democracy in Attica must be discussed in relation to basic chronological data.[1] It is generally assumed that

[1] In this discussion Attica is the geographic term for the peninsula ruled by the city of Athens. In the period which this analysis is concerned with, this means a *pars pro toto* reference already. Athens stands for the whole of the Athenian state, later the Athenian empire. Attica has become a mere geographic concept. See on this

Athens was in control of the best part of Attica by 700 B.C. at the latest, though it is difficult to determine the exact time when this process of *synoccism*—the merger of numerous independent small communities and aristocratic family domains with a larger political body—took place. In principle it was effected in about 682 B.C. when the office of annual archon (highest magistrate) probably was created. This happened before Solon assumed a commanding position in the Athenian state in about 594 B.C. Solon's decisive influence on legislation in Athens continued for several years after his one-year tenure of office as archon, presumably exercised in part by special appointment or, for a time, by successors favorably disposed toward his reforms.[2] The later accounts of Solon's activities are not quite clear. Presumably he traveled a great deal for a number of years, then lived under the regime of the tyrant Peisistratus for some time and died in 560 or 559 B.C.[3]

point John B. Bury, *A History of Greece to the Death of Alexander the Great* (New York), quoted from Modern Library edition, pp. 157 ff.; Michael I. Rostovtzeff, *Greece* (New York, 1963), pp. 81–97; Helmut Berve, *Griechische Geschichte* (Freiburg i.B., 1951), I, 170 f.; Nicholas G. L. Hammond, *A History of Greece to 322 B.C.* (Oxford, 1959), pp. 153 ff.; Charles Hignett, *A History of the Athenian Constitution to the End of the Fifth Century B.C.* (Oxford, 1952), pp. 34 ff., 41 ff.

[2] Hignett, p. 321, assumes, in a penetrating and rather unorthodox analysis of the Athenian chronology of Solon's legislation that "Solon carried his laws actually not in his archonship but as late as the third decade of the sixth century and that he received from the people for this purpose special powers under an extraordinary appointment." See also pp. 316–321 *passim*. Ivan M. Linforth, *Solon the Athenian* (Berkeley, 1919), pp. 265–268 and Alfred E. Zimmern, *The Greek Commonwealth*, rev. ed. (Oxford, 1931) perceive the enactment between 594 and 591. Hammond, p. 160 f., assumes likewise that Solon held full legislative powers at least until 592. Karl Hönn, *Solon* (Vienna, 1948), p. 119, agrees that the legislation remained in force for several years after the termination of Solon's tenure of office. The consensus seems to be that Solon did not enact the major part of his legislation during his one-year term as archon but that he held special powers for several years afterwards.

[3] Apart from Solon's own writings, less than 300 verses, the main ancient sources dealing with his life are Aristotle's accounts in his *Constitution of Athens* and the so-called *Historical Library* of Diodorus Siculus, written at the end of the first century B.C. with a rather sketchy reference to Solon's lifework. Most extensive but chronologically even farther removed from the events is Plutarch's biographical essay, written in the second century A.D. Notable is also the picture given by Diogenes Laertius in the third century A.D.

See for a discussion of these and other sources Charles Gilliard, *Quelques Réformes de Solon* (Lausanne, 1907), pp. 17–61; Linforth, pp. 3–26; William J. Woodhouse, *Solon the Liberator* (Oxford-London, 1938), pp. 9–30; Antony Andrewes, *The Greek Tyrannis* (New York, 1956), pp. 78 ff.; Hignett, pp. 1–33. Werner Jaeger's classical study *Paideia* is focused on the cultural aspects of Solon's ideas; as to sources in this respect see Vol. I (New York, 1965 [1939]), pp. 449–453.

Peisistratus' (or Pisistratus') regime is likewise, though in a much more transitory

The tyrannis of Peisistratus was established by a number of random operations about 560 B.C. It was apparently quite firmly entrenched by 540 or 539 and not challenged until his death in 528 or 527. According to most sources that would be roughly within sixty years after Solon had relin· quished the reins of government. The rule of Peisistratus' older son Hippias continued until about 510, and Cleisthenes was firmly in control by 508. The end of the latter's regime seems more uncertain. The story that he was banished—a victim of the institution of ostracism which he himself may have introduced—is doubtful. But the tenure of Cleisthenes' administration—the end of which certainly did not lead to radical change—is far less important for our purpose than the time factor in regard to Solon, Peisistratus, and his sons. Solon, though his administration was not actually overthrown, left Athens presumably under the pressure of an opposition which saw its vested interests greatly impaired by his reforms. The tyrannis of Peisistratus' sons was destroyed by violence. Yet the regime of Cleisthenes led to the more or less democratic regimes of Themistocles, Aristides, and Cimon, and culminated in the golden age of Pericles.

If we assume that Solon exercised some political influence until his death in 560 or 559—at least in foreign affairs—then a restoration under Cleisthenes would have taken place within about half a century. Unlike so many subsequent great Athenian statesmen, Solon did not die in political disgrace. There is in fact sufficient ground to assume his continuing influence. Yet even if we support the extreme supposition that his influence had ended definitely about 590, the restoration under Cleisthenes would still have been initiated with the fall of Peisistratus' older son, Hippias, in 510 and would have been completed by 508, when Cleisthenes

fashion, discussed by Aristotle and Plutarch. See the analysis of sources in Hönn, pp. 216–221; Hignett, pp. 2 ff., 326 ff. See Plutarch, *The Life of the Noble Grecians and Romans* (New York, Modern Library, n.d.), pp. 115 ff.

Aristotle and Herodotus both refer to Cleisthenes, the latter also to Solon. For a discussion of the original sources pertaining to Cleisthenes, see Henri Francotte, "l'Organisation de la cité Athénienne" in *Memoires couronnés*. Vol. XLVII of the Royal Academy of Belgium (Brussels, 1892–1895), pp. 101–121; Hammond, pp. 183 ff.; Hignett, pp. 124 ff., 331 ff.; Hönn, p. 221. On Peisistratus and Cleisthenes see also *The Politics of Aristotle*, ed. Ernest Barker (Oxford, 1948), Bk. V, chaps. 5 and 11 (Peisistratus), Bk. I, chap. 2, and Bk. VI, chap. 4 (Cleisthenes). See also Bk. II, chap. 12 (Review of Ideal States); Bk. III, chap. 11 (The Theory of Citizenship and Constitutions.)

For Plutarch's essay on Solon and his comparison with Publicola, see Plutarch, *op cit.*

was firmly in control. This would mean restoration within about eighty years or roughly within the two-generation limit.[4]

"The early history of the Athenian constitution resembles that of most other Greek states in the general fact, that a royalty subjected to various restrictions passes into an aristocracy."[5] There is no doubt that this stage had been fully reached by the seventh century. The position of the king was severely infringed upon by that of the polemarch, the commander in chief, elected by the nobles. The office of archon, the highest executive, probably originally a lifetime position, had changed first to a ten-year term and finally to one of only a year. This indicated a clear turn away from the patriarchal state as far as the administration was concerned. The same did not hold true for the social order in general, in which the tribal structure was still very much alive. The union of the Attic communities comprised several tribes, possibly four, each of which presumably was divided into three brotherhoods or clans. Each was originally ruled by a tribal chieftain and later by a regular officer, an archon. Members of these brotherhoods or clans were exclusively noble families, which could trace their origin to a common ancestor. The lower classes—peasants, traders, and craftsmen—were organized in a different way. Since they could not prove to be descendants from landed nobles, they associated increasingly on a partly ritual, partly occupational basis. Yet admission to these brotherhoods of a lower order, like those of the landed nobility on a higher, was based on citizenship. By the early seventh century the Athenian commonwealth may be considered to have been a kind of nobles' republic, inasmuch as the king had become a mere figurehead. It seems that most of the executive, judicial, and military functions were divided between archon and polemarch, whereas the king, apart from religious ritual duties and privileges, was little more than a presiding officer in the council of elders. This council, later known as the Areopagus, was as much a deliberative body as it was a court in capital cases. It was completely controlled by the landed aristocracy, even though the chief officers presumably were elected or at least nominated by the popular assembly of all citizens, the ecclesia.

Members of this council were originally the landed aristocracy, but inasmuch as craftsmanship, trade, and commerce rose in importance, this

---

[4] See Bury, pp. 184 f.; Hignett, pp. 113 ff.; Hönn, pp. 119 ff.; Linforth, pp. 303 ff.; Andrewes, pp. 89 ff. See also n. 2.

[5] Bury, pp. 160 f. See also the still very readable Ernst Curtius, *History of Greece,* trans. from German (New York, 1871), I, 326 ff.

aristocracy of land was gradually converted into one of wealth, the notorious timocracy. It is reasonable to assume that the lower strata of the population were dissatisfied with the clannish rule of the landed nobles although this class ruled by clearly established standards of ancestry and domain, hallowed by tradition. No rigid line could be drawn, on the other hand, between a nobility of wealth and a rising middle class of traders and craftsmen. Here we find one important source of dissatisfaction linked as much to social status as was the increasing burden of debts on the part of the small farmers to economic discontent.[6]

The social order was clearly changing. In place of the old division of big landowners, who cultivated their land with the help of others, the small farmers, and traders, merchants, and agricultural laborers, free but not endowed with citizenship rights, we are faced by a very different situation in the second half of the seventh century.[7]

Status was measured now primarily though not exclusively by wealth, or perhaps more correctly, by income. In the first class were those whose income amounted to at least five hundred measures in corn, wine, and oil; in the second, between three and five hundred; in the third, at least more than two hundred, which still included fairly prosperous peasants.[8] All these standards pertained to landed income, and the highest offices in the state were still duly reserved for those who drew their revenues from their landed estates. But soon enough, and in fact prior to Solon's administration, the issue no longer was the returns from land but any income amounting in value to the equivalent of agricultural production in terms of five hundred, three hundred, or two hundred units.[9] Claim to office was now based on wealth. In practice it was still largely landed wealth, but a certain mobility to acquire such wealth and become thus eligible to hold high office existed for all three classes. Not so for the fourth, the small free peasants with an income below two hundred measures, the so-called *thetes*. They could not possibly earn an adequate livelihood from their share of the yield of the land. Neither did they have a chance to move gradually into the ranks of the governing classes as long as they

[6] Hignett, pp. 47 ff.; Hammond, pp. 153 ff.; Woodhouse, pp. 74–87, 117–144; Bury, pp. 165 ff.; Andrewes, pp. 84 ff.

[7] Bury, pp. 166 f. The agricultural laborers received a generally insufficient share of one-sixth of the yield of the lands, hence they were called *hektemoroi*, that is, sixth partners. Gilliard, pp. 91–111; Andrewes, pp. 85 ff.; Hignett, pp. 74 ff., Hammond, pp. 157 f.

[8] The measures referred to here are the medimnos for corn, perhaps the equivalent of roughly one and a half bushels, and the metretes as measures of liquid amounting probably to slightly more than ten gallons.

[9] Berve, *Griechische Geschichte*, I, 173 f.

stayed in their line of work. The rise of naval trade, the slow shift from agriculture to commerce, and the increased need for skilled workers did not offer many openings.

All this helped to create an agricultural crisis of long duration and wide sweep. It naturally hit the small peasants hardest and led to much unrest. An unsatisfactory response to this state of affairs was the extremely harsh code of law, and in particular of criminal law, known by the name of the high judge Draco. The extremely stiff sentences, including capital punishment for acts of petty larceny, undoubtedly belong in this context. The same is true for the statutes which made the insolvent debtor the debt slave of the creditor. In the long view, the very fact of the codification itself implied some protection for all the people. The immediate effect was unquestionably the exacerbation of the lives of the poor and the heightening of inequality between them and the rich. Such was the unwholesome state of affairs when Solon took office.[10]

What is known throughout the history of the Western world as the reforms of Solon was not at all a complete revamping of existing conditions. It was the injection of new principles into the government by a man with a rather positive attitude toward pragmatic experience. What were these principles of the well-traveled young aristocrat and man of letters, interested equally in politics and commercial and cultural problems when he became archon between 594 and 593?[11]

There may be some truth in John Bury's conclusion that "For him the first of the virtues was moderation and his motto was 'Avoid excess.' "[12] And yet this prescription sounds a little colorless. More precise seems to be Solon's adherence to two basic concepts of Greek political theory, *eunomia* and *isonomia.* The former means the good law, and at the same time the spirit of compliance with the law, as opposed to *dysnomia,* that is, lawlessness. The second concept, *isonomia,* means equality of civil rights.[13] Solon's interpretation of these terms can be deduced from the fragments of his own writings as well as from the interpretation of Aristotle and Plutarch. *Eunomia* includes obviously the idea of a kind of

---

[10] See Robert J. Bonner and Gertrude Smith, *The Administration of Justice from Homer to Aristotle* (Chicago, 1930), I, 83 ff.; Hignett, pp. 306 ff.; Hammond, pp. 156 ff.; Hönn, pp. 43–48; Curtius, I, 333 f.; Bury, p. 172.

[11] On the principal facts of Solon's life see Hignett, pp. 86 ff.; Hönn, pp. 50–57, 116–119, 127–132; Gilliard, pp. 150–166; Linforth, pp. 27–45, 46–102; Bury, pp. 173 ff. Concerning the evaluation of his personality see particularly Jaeger, *Paideia,* I, 136 ff.

[12] Bury, *History of Greece,* p. 180.

[13] Hönn, pp. 67–73, 106 ff.; John E. Rexine, *Solon and His Political Theory* (New York, 1958), pp. 19 f.; Andrewes, pp. 87 ff.; Jaeger, I, 94 f., 108.

general welfare clause to conduct public affairs in the interest of the community. Furthermore, Solon understood this in a way that is as obvious in our times as it was startling in his. He believed that aristocracy—and the aristocracy of landed wealth at that—was not necessarily good and that the poor were not necessarily bad.

A commonsense evaluation of the highly sophisticated Greek mind suggests that even before Solon the concepts of good or bad pertained in public life to outstanding or poor qualifications rather than to moral or immoral character. A new application of the sweeping idea of *isonomia,* does not mean, however, the introduction of equality—in the egalitarian terms of the French Revolution—into Greek public life. Solon recognized the old tribal and clan organization as the font of wealth and prestige of aristocracy. He was opposed to the idea of a general income tax in peacetime. He fully recognized the distinctions between classes, let alone those between free men and slaves, though he granted all of them protection from physical injury. Yet the idea of the equality of the different estates in society irrespective of genealogy and tradition was as alien to him as the idea of an equal distribution of landed property or even of political equality irrespective of property. *Isonomia* meant to him that each should be judged equally according to the law that pertained to his class, but that far beyond and above this, certain inalienable rights applied to everyone. This is Solon's concept of equality and it meant as much in his time as it would mean little in ours. It is the idea of the state, though by no means the egalitarian state, as the mediator between the social classes. As Ernest Barker puts it: "This is perhaps the chief conception which the legislation and the elegies of Solon bequeathed to the Greeks. The neutral State, which the Greeks were to seek so long, and in so many different ways, in order to escape the strife that raged between the different sections of their society, found in him its first exponent." [14]

Recognition of these principles should help us to understand why, in the following, we perceive Solon's regime—and not those of preceding decades or archons—as original system (A). Greek public and economic life, in the centuries before Solon, underwent continuous and dynamic, indeed violent, change without pointing to a clear pattern of evolutionary development. Solon, on the other hand, had come to power in a peaceful and lawful manner. All the sweeping but evolutionary changes of his reform had the strength of tradition behind them. It is precisely this evolutionary pattern which the administration of Solon was to shape. The decisive issue is not that Solon's reforms stood for unequivocal progress

[14] Ernest Barker, *Greek Political Theory* (London, 1961), p. 51.

but that they were continued and developed further, after a revolutionary interlude, well into the era of Pericles in the second part of the fifth century. The restoration process moves from stability through instability back to stability. Hence we start this discussion with an evaluation of the system of Solon, which later history restored and rehabilitated fully as a stable regime, despite its brief duration prior to a revolutionary interlude.

The growing debt burdens and mortgages of the small peasants, linked to an irregular but distinct rise in interest rates, led to Solon's sweeping agricultural reforms. The most famous and comprehensive of them, the *Seisachtheia,* freed debt slaves from bondage, and in a separate statute debt slavery was outlawed for the future as well. This applied to mortgages on land and also to personal debts. Debt slaves sold abroad were retroactively redeemed at state expense. In another law Solon prohibited the export of agricultural goods in order to keep prices of food for the poor within reasonable limits. Only oil, which apparently existed in abundance, was exempted from this rule.

We have evidence that Solon introduced another, perhaps less conspicuous but far more radical, piece of legislation, which struck at the aristocracy, to which he himself belonged: The curtailment of the free sale of land in an Attica of some 200,000 people, where fertile soil was becoming scarce.[15]

Yet the social reforms of Solon meant not only extension of human freedom but also, in more than one way, the preservation of the status quo. The requirement of the retention of one-sixth of the land's yield as income for agricultural laborers is only one striking example. In fact, Solon's administration imposed new restrictions such as sumptuary laws and stringent provisions against idleness, which barred those members of the lower classes who had neglected to have their sons trained in some kind of trade from claims to alimony.[16] On the other hand, the establishment of an Athenian currency separate from that of Aegina, the furthering of Athenian naval aspirations, and the extension of citizenship rights to skilled foreign craftsmen, pointed in the direction of greater economic freedom.[17] Altogether a kind of balance was struck between such trends

---

[15] Plutarch, . . . *Noble Grecians and Romans* (see n. 3 above), 132; Hönn, pp. 78 f.; on the whole agricultural legislation see Hönn pp. 73–78 *passim;* Woodhouse, *Solon,* pp. 67–97; Gilliard, pp. 175–178, 188–213; Hignett, pp. 6 ff., 87 ff., 106 f., Hammond, pp. 159 f. As to the extent of land holdings in Solon's time see M. I. Finley, *Studies in Land and Credit in Ancient Athens* (New Brunswick, 1951), pp. 58 f.

[16] Berve, *Griechische Geschichte,* I, 174 ff.; Hönn, p. 82.

[17] Berve, I, 177 f.; Hönn, pp. 91 ff.; Gilliard, pp. 242–259; Bonner and Smith, *Administration of Justice,* I, 158 ff.; Hignett, pp. 98 f.

and the demands of a state whose paternalistic spirit was in other ways on the rise. This holds true for the whole governmental system far beyond the strictly constitutional issues. Here, too, we find a compromise, not so much, as in the economic field, between a free economy and a welfare state as between tradition and reform. Solon did not touch upon the principle of stratification of the people in four classes according to income.[18] He gave to the fourth class, however—the *thetes,* by tradition not eligible to hold high office and to serve in the cavalry in war—the right to participate in the popular assembly and to vote there in the election of magistrates. Whether he meant this to be a terminal state of affairs or merely a point of departure to further reforms is uncertain. Yet he surely opened the gate for a steady extension of citizenship rights. Equally important, he admitted the *thetes* also to participation in the principal court, the *Heliaea,* as part of a comprehensive citizen jury panel. Thus all the people had their say now in the selection of holders of public office and in the handling of capital cases in court.[19]

When Solon relieved the Areopagus, the council of elders, of its function as a kind of deliberative council of state he at the same time raised its status to that of constitutional court and supreme guardian of the ritual judicial functions of government. The fact that the archons, after the expiration of their term of office, became members of this court increased its importance further. Its counseling functions and the legislative initiative were taken over by an entirely novel institution, the council of four hundred. One quarter of this body was to be taken from each of the tribes, which Solon retained as well as the whole brotherhood clan organization. In the same spirit he still barred the *thetes* from participation in the new council. The assembly operated in fact on the basis of direct democracy. It did so in juxtaposition to the council as an instrument of representative democracy. This combination is indeed the crowning piece of Solon's political legislation.[20]

Inasmuch as the fourth estate, marked as such on account of its meager resources, did not enjoy equal political status with the others, one could hardly call this system, taken as a whole, more than halfway democratic. Yet, if judged according to the standard of the times, it could hardly be called a timocracy.[21]

[18] Hignett, pp. 100 f.; Hammond, p. 164.

[19] *Politics of Aristotle,* ed. Ernest Barker, pp. 145 f.; Plutarch, pp. 107 f.; Gilliard, pp. 215–241; Bury, *History of Greece,* pp. 169–177; Andrewes, pp. 87 ff.; Hignett, pp. 97 ff.; Hammond, pp. 162 ff.; Bonner and Smith, II, 152 ff., 232 ff.

[20] Berve, I, 174 ff. *Politics of Aristotle,* pp. 145 f., 103 ff.; Bury, pp. 200 f.; Hönn, pp. 100 ff.; Andrewes, pp. 87 ff.; Hignett, pp. 92 ff.

[21] Bury, p. 180.

The success and lasting fame of Solon has, of course, many causes. His deep social understanding, which led to the repeal of the bulk of Draco's harsh code of criminal law, is foremost. A less obvious reason for fame is his enlightened conservatism in regard to the status of his own class. This is also apparent in his reforms of the ritual. He merged the religious associations of the nobles with those of the common people—again, as is typical of his whole legislation, not without reservations. Reform in the sphere of religious ritual probably had an emotional value as great as the social value of political reform. Both were intrinsic parts of the gradual emancipation of the lower classes.[22]

Considering the fact that Athens in Solon's time was already involved in the struggle for leadership among the Greek states, this would not have sufficed to establish his position safely in the ancient world—the association of his name with success in foreign policy was essential. Here we think above all of the acquisition of the island of Salamis from Megara in about 565, when Solon had been out of office for many years. Plutarch in particular ranks this accomplishment inordinately high in the overall evaluation of the great reformer. Curiously enough, this successful move to wrest the Helgoland of Athens from Megara is linked to Solon's accomplishments as man of letters rather than as statesman, since it is embodied in the survival of a few lines of his elegy "Salamis." When the naval victory of Salamis against Persia, almost a century later, became the signal and lasting monument of Athenian glory, the hallowed name became at the same time a memorial to the man who had heralded this triumph three generations before.[23]

Yet it is strange that Salamis is connected not only with the rise of the myth of Solon but also with the shadow cast over it. The campaign against Megara not only enhanced Solon's fame further, but it also established that of a young general, a descendant from a noble house, Peisistratus, whose early career may have been furthered by his elder relative Solon.[24] Peisistratus, the conqueror of the port of Nisaia, was only indirectly involved in the acquisition of Salamis. The prestige gained in the Megara campaign enabled him to seize dictatorial powers only a few years later and therewith to destroy the very essence of the Solonian original system. This evaluation is used here advisedly. As will be discussed below, the content of the Solonian reform was to a very large

[22] *Politics of Aristotle,* pp. 103 ff.; Plutarch, pp. 107 f.; Hönn, pp. 83–88; Bury, pp. 162 f.; Hignett, pp. 104 f., 113 f.

[23] Hönn, pp. 122 ff.; Gilliard, pp. 157–166; Bury, pp. 182 ff.; Hignett, pp. 103 ff.; Hammond, pp. 164 f.; Curtius, *History of Greece,* I, 342 ff.

[24] On the relationship between Solon and Peisistratus see Plutarch, pp. 115 ff.; Hönn, pp. 121 f.; and particularly Linforth, *Solon the Athenian,* pp. 303 ff.

extent preserved and even expanded under the coming tyrannis of Peisistratus. Yet the factor which in importance overshadows all others was Solon's resolve to achieve success through elective office without resort to self-perpetuation by way of the tyrannis. John Bury's conclusion seems entirely correct: "Solon had done his work boldly, but he had done it constitutionally. He had not made himself a tyrant, as he might easily have done, and as many expected him to. . . . He had not even become . . . a legislator who for a number of years suspended the constitution in order to reform it, and rule for that time with the absolute power of a tyrant. He had simply held the office of archon, invested, indeed, with extraordinary powers." [25] After the expiration of his term of office he was apparently commissioned as extraordinary lawgiver (*nomothetes*) to reform the governmental structure. In view of the fact, amply proved by pragmatic experience, that an autocratic form of government soon enough changes its content, the far-reaching democratic setting of the Solonian system remains the premise of its substance and in terms of this study the very essence of the original system (A).

The rule of Peisistratus and his sons, initiated in about 561 and ending only in 510, will be perceived in its entirety as the intermediate system (B). This is perhaps less obvious than it may seem. Peisistratus was twice driven from power, once in about 556 and restored in about 550, and within a year driven out of Athens again to return only in about 540. From that time he ruled unchallenged until his death—presumably in 527—and transmitted the tyrannis to his sons, of whom the elder, surviving one, Hippias, was overthrown only in 510. One might thus speak of a restoration process within the restoration process.[26]

In line with the discussion of the restoration process in Part I we take the position, however, that a mere putsch undertaken only by the immediate partisans of a true or would-be dictator, and successful only for a few months or years, does not meet the standards of a genuine system with far-reaching changes of lasting significance.

Otherwise the brief and transitory periods of Peisistratus' first two attempts to establish himself in power are of considerable interest. His first try may well revive the memory of recent dictatorial techniques. The young general of fresh military glory rallied a group of discontented men

[25] Bury, *History of Greece* (See n. 1 above), p. 179. See also Andrewes, pp. 100 ff., Hignett, pp. 321 ff.; as to sources see Plutarch, pp. 131 ff.

[26] Plutarch, pp. 115 ff.; Hönn, pp. 120 f.; Bury, pp. 180 f.; Andrewes, pp. 100 f.; Hignett, pp. 114 f. The Hipparchus elected archon for 496/95 was presumably a relative, but certainly not the son of Peisistratus.

around him. They were not only poor farmers from the hills in Attica, justly dissatisfied *hektemoroi*, but also impoverished nobles, who had lost or alleged they had lost their fortunes through Solon's reform of the debt system. Charging that his opponents had attempted to assassinate him, Peisistratus persuaded the assembly to vote him a bodyguard. With the help of these henchmen and the *discomisados* around him, he seized power. The large majority of big landowners, middle-aged farmers, merchants, artisans and fishermen turned immediately against the dictator and forced him into exile, after not more than five years of unstable rule.

While the opposition to Peisistratus probably represented the large majority of the Athenian people, this majority was socially not much more homogeneous than the supporters of Peisistratus. With the help of the leaders of the wealthier coastal people, associated equally with agriculture and commercial interests, he managed a comeback in about 555. Soon Peisistratus fell out with the leader of that group and was forced back into exile within a year. This second exile lasted about a full decade and was not unprofitably spent in raising resources and troops in the north. Peisistratus now established a firm rule over a dissatisfied state. His reforms had not gone far enough to meet the demands of the landless or nearly landless small peasants and agricultural laborers, but they had gone much too far to please the landed aristocracy.[27]

Before we discuss Peisistratus' regime an examination of the concept of tyrannis in the sixth century is in order. We have Julius Beloch's penetrating evaluation of the situation.

> This new type of royalty was something entirely different from the old monarchy of the times of the heroes. The new rulers were well aware of this and did not dare to call themselves kings. Contemporaries refer to them as monarchs or as "tyrants", which term at that time had not yet the derogatory meaning of modern times. The tyrants acted as representatives of the people. . . . The forms of the republican constitutions remained as far as possible in force. However, the rulers took care that the most influential offices were always to be held by their relatives or followers. Naturally the position of the "tyrant" in the state had to be determined according to some kind of constitutional procedure, generally by the transfer of supreme military power . . . [either for lifetime or for a number of years to be conveniently renewed.]
>
> There is no question that the tyrannis furthered the economic and the intellectual development of Greece tremendously. It liberated the masses from pressures which had lasted for centuries; it smashed the old estate prejudices; it effected for the first time the equality of noble

[27] *Politics of Aristotle,* pp. 253 f.; Julius Beloch, *Griechische Geschichte* (Strassburg, 1893), I, 327 ff.; Curtius, I, 377 ff.; Bury, pp. 184 ff.; Andrewes, pp. 107 ff.

and pauper before the law. The state acknowledged for the first time the obligation not merely to protect the people but to be concerned with their material welfare as well. . . .

Notwithstanding this splendor . . . tyrannis could not last in Greece. Subjection to the will of a single person, even if camouflaged, finally became equally intolerable to all strata of the population. The deeply rooted hatred against the monarchy, which distinguishes the Greeks of the classic period, is largely a consequence of the tyrannis.[28]

Much of what has been said here could be qualified but in general it fits well the characterization of that remarkable man Peisistratus, whom Michael Rostovtzeff sees as an even more important personality than Solon. According to him, "His tyranny did not destroy a single one of the democratic foundations which Solon had laid. His power was a mere superstructure on top of Solon's constitution." Yet within the frame of that superstructure he weakened the power of the aristocracy and strengthened that of the poor—partly, it is true, by banishing his opponents and distributing their land among his followers.[29] Here we find an unfortunate confusion as to unwholesome means and laudatory objectives, but particularly a certain insensitivity to the pernicious potentialities of any dictatorship, even the most benevolent. This is not uncommon in classical interpretation of French and Roman history. John Bury, like Rostovtzeff, lacked experience with the full spectrum of modern dictatorships and thus he follows the same line. "The rule of Peisistratus may be described as a constitutional tyranny"—a contradiction if there ever was one. "He did not stop the wheels of the democracy, but he guided the machine entirely at his own will. The constitution of Solon seems to have been preserved in its most essential features," [30] which implies that the democratic features were nonessential. Charles Hignett puts particular emphasis on the comprehensiveness and speed of Peisistratus' reforms, which "hastened and facilitated the transition from the aristocratic state to democracy. . . . But the greater achievement of Peisistratus was the effective unification of Attica." [31] Quite clearly the objective of the reforms in regard to effectiveness not in regard to democratic intentions is emphasized. Karl Hönn, however, sets the record straight by observing

[28] Beloch, *Griechische Greschichte,* I, 313 ff. (author's translation from the German). See also Hignett, pp. 110 ff.

[29] Rostovtzeff, *Greece,* pp. 91 f. See also Andrewes, pp. 113 ff.

[30] *History of Greece* (see n.1 above), p. 186 ff. In the same sense, also Curtius, I, 372 ff., in particular 389 f.; and Andrewes, pp. 110 ff.

[31] *Athenian Constitution* (see n.1 above), pp. 122 f.

succinctly, "As great as Peisistratus was as statesman . . . he obtained his motivations not from a dedication to the country but from his personal wish to rule. For that reason does his work share the destiny which, according to a word of Aristotle, holds true for all rules of tyrants: the brief span of life." [32] It is true, of course, that we cannot probe but can only guess the motivations for a dictator's actions, but as to the predictable long-range consequences we may say that it makes little difference whether these aims are true or alleged, sincere or rationalized, or most likely a combination. In neither case do they justify dictatorial action.

These factors appear to be germane to the evaluation of a remarkable man and a remarkable specific system, in our context the intermediate system (B). In reviewing Peisistratus' achievements it is not possible to assign reforms precisely to each of his three administrations, though it is reasonable to assume that most of them fall into the period of the last and longest one, when his rule was most firmly entrenched. Neither is it possible to separate economic, political, and judicial reforms; they are all—and with them his dynamic foreign policy—much more closely related to the effort to perpetuate the regime than was true in Solon's administration. The extension of the economy of money instead of measures of oil and corn for the assessment of official duties and military service obligations blurred the division between classes and made for greater social mobility, clearly in the interest of the regime. The division of the estates of the tyrants' opponents in favor of landless workers, in particular the *hektemoroi,* served, as already noted, a twofold political and social purpose. The same seems to be true for the emphasis given to commerce and industry and the mining of gold and silver. All this was fully in line with the expansion and modernization of the national economy. At the same time it served quite well to reduce the status of the big landed estate owners, Peisistratus' most implacable enemies. In this sense the merger of tyrannis and state was symbolized effectively by the replacement of the family signs of the nobles with the head of the goddess Athena on the new coins.[33]

In gaining a foothold at the Hellespont by conquering the fortress of Sigeion from Mytilene and furthering the conquest of the far more extensive Thracian Chersonese the tyrant undoubtedly helped toward the colonial expansion of the future Athenian empire, and at the same time he diverted the interests of his aristocratic opponents and moved them in a

[32] *Solon* (see n.2 above), 148 f. (author's translation from the German).
[33] Hönn, pp. 136 ff.; Bury, pp. 186 ff.; Andrewes, pp. 110 ff.; Hignett, pp. 118 ff.

smooth and effective manner from the center to the outposts of the state.[34]

Peisistratus, like most dictators, was foremost the champion of the claims of the dissatisfied man. Inasmuch as such dissatisfaction coincided with the demands of the poor he was their advocate as well. In this respect he undoubtedly deserved credit for helping the small peasant, the landless agricultural workers, particularly the *hektemoroi.* Indeed, that class of people could change their status completely. They obtained title to the land and were pledged only to pay the land tax. This new, chief revenue of the country amounted to between 5 and 10 percent of the annual yield, which could not be considered excessive. Undoubtedly Peisistratus also improved agriculture, particularly the growth of oil trees, and he certainly supported industry, above all in the field of ceramics. That he drew money for such purposes by questionable means, such as the confiscation of the property of his banished opponents, has been noted. Nevertheless quite a few of his relief measures—loans in terms of agricultural tools, seeds, cattle; tax alleviations; and the replacement of patrimonial jurisdiction by a more independent village judiciary—went far beyond a policy of mere distribution of spoils by way of expropriation. Whether Peisistratus really liberated the peasants may still be open to question.[35] It may be doubted whether he had the means not only to improve but also to secure their economic status. Yet it is fairly certain that what he added in economic improvements was taken away in terms of political freedom. Over the long view this was bound to affect prosperity adversely as well.

Peisistratus did after all concentrate the principal offices of the state in his own hand and, as turned out to be worse, in those of the members of his family, who were consistently represented in the college of archons. He himself as a chief archon and commander in chief held supreme executive and, in a sense, judicial power as well.[36] In the imperfect Solonian system appointees to high office were frequently nominated by the popular assembly, and then selected by lot. Peisistratus' changeover to a straight appointive system reduced the power of the legislature further. As in any dictatorship the pursuit of power over all functions of government was related to the supreme objective of the regime to perpetuate itself. Aristotle perceived this also in the strong cultural interests of Peisis-

---

[34] Hönn, pp. 146 ff.; Hammond, *History of Greece,* pp. 165 ff.; Curtius, I, 383 ff.; Hignett, pp. 115, 329 f.

[35] Affirmed by Hönn, pp. 137 f.; Bury, pp. 186 f.; and with qualifications by Hignett, pp. 118 ff.

[36] Beloch, *Griechische Geschichte,* I, 329 f.; Andrewes, pp. 113 ff.; Bonner and Smith, *Administration of Justice,* I, 182 ff.

tratus, which were intended to serve Athens as well as the tyrant himself. This applied equally to the fields of literature and the formative arts and to improvements of the religious ritual.[37]

Peisistratus left the succession to his two sons. They were not his equals. The younger, Hipparchus, was murdered in 514, for personal reasons it seems, and the deed was only later glorified as allegedly struck for freedom. Now Hippias turned to outright despotism. As is usual with dictators, the new course seems to have been provoked primarily by fear. The façade of the Solonian system, skillfully preserved by the father, was now destroyed quite openly by the son.[38] His removal, initiated with the support of Sparta in 510 B.C., turned into a severe crisis for the state. The liberation movements led by the Spartan king Cleomenes soon became attempts to establish a kind of administration that might be called a Spartan puppet regime under an Athenian quisling, Isagoras. The vicor in the struggle, Cleisthenes, was a member of one of the old aristocratic families. He had been persecuted by Peisistratus, but he was acclaimed by the people after the fall of the tyrannis under the old dictator's lesser son. Again a leader from the ranks of the aristocracy had come to power, supported again by small peasants and craftsmen, but this time he was not a tyrant.[39]

Before we discuss the restored system under Cleisthenes' leadership, we must evaluate the intermediate system of Peisistratus and his sons. We have to acknowledge that the basic structure of the Solonian social and political reforms were preserved. What is more, in regard to the interests of the small peasant, agricultural worker, and craftsman, they were even extended. The formative arts and literature were furthered in a cultural climate that in some ways presaged the Periclean age. Peisistratus, who up to a point respected and preserved the traditions of his great predecessor Solon, restricted but did not destroy popular liberties completely. What condemns the *tyrannis* in spite of its advances is not primarily the sorry spectacle of its end in a wave of terror, mass executions, and many banishments under Hippias. Although Peisistratus was not directly responsible for the actions of his son, who in his earlier career according to all accounts seemed to be no less cultured than the father, in a deeper sense this development was inevitable. The deterioration of the dictator-

---

[37] Concerning the relationship between cultural achievements and political objectives see Aristotle's observations in *The Politics of Aristotle,* ed. Barker, p. 287; see further Hönn, pp. 138 ff.; Bury, pp. 190 ff.; Curtius, I, 392 ff.

[38] Beloch, I, 329, ff.; Rostovtzeff, *Greece,* pp. 93 ff.; Hönn, pp. 149 ff.; Hignett, pp. 124 f.; Bury, pp. 195 ff.

[39] Hignett, pp. 124 ff.; Hammond, pp. 185 ff.

ship into bloody despotism was likely to happen sooner or later as long as the framework and devices of the dictatorial system existed. Peisistratus has the full responsibility for its creation.

The significance of Cleisthenes' political philosophy and program are summed up rather well by Michael Rostovtzeff: "The work of Cleisthenes differs from that of Solon and Peisistratus in this respect: he . . . carried out a complete scheme which he had thought out in detail. His governing idea was to create a well-proportioned and completely co-ordinate state, based on the political equality of all the citizens, and on the participation of all in the working of the government machine. Existing institutions were neither destroyed nor abolished, but their life left them and entered into the new political bodies created by Cleisthenes." [40] In a sense he replaced the self-perpetuating practice of the tyrannis by the elective principles of the Solonian system, but important as this achievement was, it is only the basis of the new philosophy and practice of government.

Cleisthenes was as concerned as Solon with the reform of local and central government, though in regard to the former he had to overcome far greater resistance than Solon. The chief weakness of Solon's system had been the preservation of the power of the clans with its decisive influence on all further constitutional development. Cleisthenes was resolved to break up a system which encouraged factional strife on a local territorial and a social basis at the same time. [41] Thus he eliminated the old district organization, with its clannish, semireligious, semioccupational, but in any case restrictive, foundation. He replaced it with a new, more comprehensive one of several hundred small wards. They were based entirely on geographic and administrative expediency deriving from a natural partition into three main types of territories, city, coast, and inland. Each of the small districts or demes, not invented but reorganized by Cleisthenes, was subdivided further. He then formed groups of people from the three main regions, city, coast, and inland, into new administrative units, tribal in name only, each actually representing a cross section of the population as a whole, entirely devoid of the traditional clannish links. Every one of these new political bodies, ten altogether, was granted limited autonomy. Each had an assembly, elected its own officers, and could collect local taxes. They also kept the citizenship rolls, and the structure of the armed forces followed their pattern of local organization. The only concession to

[40] Rostovtzeff, *Greece*, p. 94; Curtius, I, 407 ff.; Hönn, pp. 153 f.
[41] *Politics of Aristotle*, pp. 266 ff., 273 ff.; Francotte, *"L'Organisation de la cité Athénienne"* (see n.3 above), pp. 60–68; Zimmern, *Greek Commonwealth* (see n. 2 above), pp. 144 ff.; Hignett, pp. 125 ff., 331 ff.; Bury, pp. 200 ff.

the system of old was the association of the demes with some specific religious or historic tradition and, more important, the provision that the
new demes organization would be hereditary. Thus eventually a new
clannish tradition might develop, but this possibility for the time being
could be considered remote.[42] The whole arrangement looked complicated, and it is difficult today to judge whether such elaborate organization was necessary in so small a state. Yet complexity was a small price to
pay for so momentous an achievement as the breakup of clannish segregation and its replacement by a better integrated society.

Related to the new tribal organization was the reorganization of the
council of four hundred, which had represented the four tribes of old; in
the new council, of five hundred, each of the ten new units sent fifty
members to a revamped council. Its powers were much greater and all
classes were now equally represented. This body was to be the deliberative
council of state and at the same time the supreme administrative authority. It exercised also a certain control over the judiciary; it could sit as
court itself in the impeachment of public officials; and it had the right of
legislative initiative. Naturally a large body of this kind could exercise its
manifold administrative and deliberative functions only in committees,
which required the participation of every member of the body for a tenth
part of the year.[43]

The popular assembly remained the legislative authority but—a notable
feature—it could exercise its main functions only after a bill had been de-
bated in the council of five hundred. The power to conclude treaties and
to declare war still rested with the assembly. These innovations indicated
an important step from direct to representative democracy and, what is
far more important, an expansion and entrenchment of democratic institutions.[44]

All this was not a sweeping change in the social structure of the Athenian governmental system. It provided the machinery to effect such
change in the future without violence and within the letter of the law.
Many foreigners and even freed slaves, it is true, obtained citizenship
rights.[45] Nevertheless, power was held by the same class of people, the
aristocracy, to which Solon, Peisistratus, and Cleisthenes all belonged,
though it was held no longer through privilege embedded in law but

[42] *Politics of Aristotle,* pp. 266 ff.; 312 f.; Francotte, pp. 68–101; Hignett, pp.
129 ff., 134 ff.; Zimmern, pp. 155–160; Hönn, pp. 153 ff.; Andrewes, pp. 114 f.

[43] Hignett, pp. 148 ff.; Bonner and Smith, I, 187 ff.

[44] Hignett, pp. 152 ff., 236 ff.; Zimmern, pp. 161–169.

[45] *Politics* of Aristotle, pp. 312 f.; Hignett, pp. 132 ff.

through gradually changing tradition. "The political reform of Cleisthenes, even though the order of demes lasted for two centuries, could not
erase the features of the old aristocratic republic completely. Members of
the nobility have always lead the state up to the times of Pericles," [46] two
generations later. Despite relatively minor interruptions evolutionary
democratic development in Athens was assured up to the advent of the
rule of the "Thirty Tyrants" at the beginning of the fifth century. Thus
only the impact and consequences of the horrible Peloponnesian war could
shake a system that for a full century remained in power as a genuine
restored system (C).

We cannot claim that democracy had become either complete or fully
secure. Measures such as the reduction of the position of the polemarch,
the commander in chief, to that of a simple administrative official, were a
big step in this direction, while the presumable introduction of *ostracism*,
the banishment of potential tyrants on political grounds by vote of the
political assembly, remained controversial in its effect. Yet the reforms
represented, all things considered, an advance toward true democracy, even
though the injured aristocratic class of Cleisthenes' times longed in later
days for the return to the golden days of their status under his regime.[47]

The study of Athenian development from Solon to Cleisthenes presents
an impressive example of the restoration process as understood in this
study. Inasmuch as the changes in Athens were less influenced by external
force than in the case of the deportation of the Jews to Babylonian exile,
the pattern to be studied here seems clearer. Similarities and differences
are obvious. The coincidence in time is amazing in such widely different
cultures. The original Jewish system was in full force under the king
Josiah in the last third of the seventh century; restoration was by and
large accomplished with the reconsecration of the Temple in about 516
B.C. The Solonian system in Athens—based on the institution of archonship initiated in the early seventh century—was established in the first
decade of the sixth century and the reforms of Cleisthenes in substance
presumably in the last decade of the century.[48] The intermediate system
of the Babylonian exile lasted not quite half a century, that of the Peisis-
tratidae in Athens to the flight of Hippias, just about half a century.

These comparative data indicate, for one thing, that people in different

---

[46] Hönn, p. 156 (author's translation).

[47] Beloch, I, 336 ff.; Hönn, pp. 157 f.; Zimmern, p. 169. It is not certain whether
ostracism was introduced at the end of Cleisthenes' administration or shortly after.
The former view is contested by Hignett, pp. 159 ff.

[48] Concerning the precise chronology, see Hignett, pp. 326 ff.

cultural settings with very little mutual contact may face similar problems. This does not in any way preclude the possibility that similarities may develop under the influence of one culture on another in phases of developments separated by centuries. On the other hand, the relative length of tenure of the intermediate system and the time required to establish a restored system for a long time to come are to be understood in less flexible terms. As we see it, they pertain to any time and place and should not be considered to be as subject to major change as to duration. Certainly, the two cases thus far discussed offer mutually corroborating evidence in this respect.

Even more important are analogies in regard to subject matter. Jewish development, not only related to the history in the Diaspora but even earlier under Persian overlordship and later in the Hellenistic period, was largely determined by the transition from the tribal organization to that of community life based on social and religious ritual bonds. The whole evolution of Athenian democracy and much of its ritual structure was equally shaped by the transition from the tribal order to the socially more inclusive community organization.

Obviously there are marked differences; the preservation of aristocratic privileges played a minor role in the Jewish case, an important one in the Athenian. On the issue of ethnic segregation the order of importance was reversed. There are numerous other disparities as well, embedded in religious and social traditions. The purpose of this study is not to hunt for artificial analogies but to point to those which are apparent. In the Jewish example the social regrouping brought about by the setting of the Babylonian exile under the intermediate system was recognized as inevitable and was part of the structure of the restored vassal state. In Athens we find that the emancipation of the skilled craftsman and above all of the small peasant and agricultural worker, prompted by the tyrannis of Peisistratus, was accepted and further developed under the restoration of Cleisthenes. In the case of the Jews we find a restoration in very tangible territorial terms, the return to the homeland and the rebuilding of a political body of limited sovereignty. In the Athens of Cleisthenes the return to principles of rotation in office and denial of self-perpetuating succession reestablished the premises—though by no means full achievement—of democratic government. From this point, at least partially representative government became the issue. In either case, restoration laid the groundwork for spiritual development on a higher plane than was previously in existence.

CHAPTER IX

Rome from the Imperial Republic to the Rise of Marius

An Inconclusive Case of Restoration

Chronology

201 B.C.	End of Second Punic War against Carthage
133 B.C.	Conquest of Spain nearly completed Tiberius Sempronius Gracchus (the elder Gracchus) elected tribune of the people. Contrary to law, he seeks reelection for the following year and is slain
132–129 B.C.	Modification of the reform legislation of the elder Gracchus
123 B.C.	Gaius Sempronius Gracchus (the younger Gracchus) elected tribune of the people
122 B.C.	Gaius Gracchus reelected for second term
121 B.C.	Death of Gaius Gracchus
121–111 B.C.	Modification of Gaius Gracchus' reform legislation
107 B.C	Gaius Marius consul and commander in chief
107–100 B.C.	Reforms of Marius
101 B.C.	Defeat of the Cimbri by Marius
100 B.C.	Marius reelected consul for the fifth time
91 B.C.	Reform legislation of Marcus Livius Drusus
91–88 B.C.	Social War
87 B.C.	Seventh consulate of Marius

82 B.C.   Beginning of counterrevolutionary dictatorship of Lucius Cornelius Sulla

Original system (A)   201–133 B.C.

Presumed intermedi-   133–121 B.C.
ate system (B)

Presumed incom-   121–100 or 91 B.C.
pletely restored sys-
tem (C)

This chapter deals in essence with the effect of the revolution of the two Gracchi brothers from 133 B.C. to 121 B.C. on the previous and following systems, if systems they can be called. The prerevolutionary era would be the period from the end of the second war against Carthage in 201 B.C. to the completion of the conquest of Spain in 133 B.C. and the suppression of the Sicilian slave-rising in the following year. This event coincides in fact with the beginning of the Gracchan revolt, which would correspond to the intermediate system, and ends quite clearly with the suicide of the younger Gracchus in 121 B.C.

The beginning of a restoration period could be determined easily enough, but not its durability in the face of new revolutions. This raises the question, At what time did the rule of the aristocratic senatorial republic really cease? When did the series of dictatorships begin, that terminated only when Augustus, a full century after the death of the older Gracchus, could establish a new regime of firm and stable power? Does the intervening dictatorial period commence with the military reforms of Marius between 107 and 105 B.C.? To be sure, the influence of the army was important before. From here to the end of the empire almost six centuries later it was a key force in domestic history. Legally, however, the full break with republican tradition was established only when Marius, after the defeat of the Cimbri and Teutones, was elected consul for the sixth time, for the year 100 B.C. Unlike his previous controversial reelections, this act could not be excused, let alone justified by reference to a state of emergency brought about by the threat of foreign invasion. And yet even Marius's deeds at that time were only a gross violation of republican tradition, not quite yet its open destruction. Here the assassination of the new champion of reform, tribune Marcus Lucius Drusus, which led directly to the so-called Social War against the Italian allies, marks the end of an era and, clearly, the beginning of a new one. By and large, the social ideas of these men were fully repudiated only with the coming dictatorship of Sulla, which was firmly established by the end of the year 82 B.C. Yet, although the regime of Sulla was in one way social restoration, it was also a counterrevolutionary dictatorship—in our terms the very antithesis of restoration.

Was there an end to a period of restoration with the turn to complete political and social dictatorship in 82 B.C.? With the erosion of republican institutions as early as the year 100 B.C.? or with the beginning of more than half a century of almost uninterrupted violence in 91 B.C.? The last assumption suggests a compromise between extremes, though in that case the period of restoration would be considerably shorter than the minimum time established previously as the premise for a successful restoration. Indeed, the proposition of a successful restoration after the death of the younger Gracchus in 121 will have to be very closely questioned, but this is true also for the intermediate period from 133 to 121, that of the Gracchan revolt. Here an intermediate regime, a revolutionary one at that, by no means held uninterrupted and complete sway. Thus it is a complex and interesting case we turn our attention to now.[1]

---

[1] The period under discussion offers only scanty primary source material for the specific problem of restoration. Even the more abundant sources pertaining to the end of the period are only tangential to the issue.

Regarding the expansion of the Roman Empire, the two main sources written by Greek historians are the histories of Posidonius (about 130–50 B.C.) and Polybius (about 204–122 B.C.). The former are lost, though they were used in several of the writings of Cicero, Sallust, Caesar, and Plutarch. The great history of Polybius covers only the background for the problems discussed here, that is, events just beyond the destruction of Carthage in 146. A fragmentary account of domestic history in late republican Rome was written in Greek by Appian of Alexandria in the second century A.D. Sallust's history of the war against Jugurtha gives some insight into the character of Marius, as do frequent references by Cicero. Plutarch's essays on the Gracchi and Marius, though written about two centuries after the events, are particularly valuable because of their apparent use of a number of lost sources.

On the historiography with particular regard to primary sources see Ernst Kornemann, *Zur Geschichte der Gracchenzeit, quellen kritische und chronologische Untersuchungen* (Aalen, 1963) reprint of the ed. of 1903; Howard H. Scullard, *From the Gracchi to Nero* (New York, 1959), pp. 203 ff., 382 ff., 388. In regard to a specific analysis of the presentations of Appian of Alexandria and Plutarch see Plinio Fraccaro, *Studi sull'età dei Gracchi* (Città di Castello, 1914).

A genuine standard history of the era is Gustave Bloch and Jerome Carcopino, *Histoire Romaine, La république Romaine de 133 a 44 avant J.C.* (Paris, 1935), one volume in two parts. Part I of this work, "Des Gracques à Sulla," was written chiefly by Carcopino, who is also the author of another notable publication on the subject, *Autour des Gracques* (Paris, 1928).

A good modern presentation of the period is to be found in Frank B. Marsh, *A History of the Roman World from 146 to 30 B.C.* 2d rev. ed. (London, 1953); see particularly chaps. 1–6; F. B. Marsh, *The Founding of the Roman Empire,* 2d rev. ed.

A profile of Rome in the second century B.C., during the period of transition from a middle-sized Italian state to a distinctly emerging world power shows some of the following basic features. Within the two generations from the end of the Second Punic War in 201 B.C. to the rise of the Gracchan movement after 134, the republic, in addition to its previous conquests of Sicily, Sardinia, and Corsica, had gained complete control of Spain, the Eastern coastal territories of the Adriatic, Cisalpine Gaul (the Po valley), Macedonia, and Greece, as well as Africa (roughly Tunisia and a long coastal stretch of Algiers). Unsolved domestic problems, which had existed for over a century, were aggravated rather than relieved by this rapid and incongruous growth.

One of the more obvious consequences was the rapid increase of money in circulation, of which a major share went to the senatorial aristocracy, in particular to the commanders in the field, who were part of it. Another effect was the large-scale import of slaves from the conquered territories, not only field hands in tremendous numbers but also educated Greeks, who were to shape the cultural values of the coming Augustan age.

The expansion of the money economy brought about a vast increase of consumer goods in the market and, because of the availability of slave labor, a corresponding increase in the purchasing power of the owners of big estates. The rising class of businessmen and contractors for public work—a misleading terminology generally refers to them as knights—benefited from either factor, but particularly from the latter. The major opportunity of this group, however, lay in the farming out of the right to collect taxes in the new provinces on a previously unheard-of scale. This scourge of the economic life of the provincial population was at the same time one of the chief reasons why liquid capital now became as unequally

(London, 1927), may well serve as continuation of this work. See chaps. 1 and 2. If not stated otherwise, references to Marsh in the following notes are to his first mentioned work, *History*. Joseph Vogt, *Römische Geschichte* (Freiburg, i.B., 1932), Vol. I, Part IV, chaps. 1–4, and Ernst Kornemann, *Römische Geschichte* (Stuttgart, 1938), Vol. I, Part V, present reliable surveys. References to Kornemann in the notes following are to this title. Enlightening also is Guglielmo Ferrero, *The Greatness and Decline of Rome,* Vol. I: *The Empire Builders* (New York, 1909), chaps. 2–4. See also Frank R. Cowell, *The Revolutions of Ancient Rome* (New York, 1963), pp. 77–128, and Lily Ross Taylor, *Party Politics in the Age of Caesar* (Berkeley and Los Angeles, 1949), chap. 1.

Theodor Mommsen's classic *History of Rome* is quoted here in the English translation by W. P. Dickson (London, 1867). See Vol. I, chaps. 2–6. While Mommsen's evaluation of the social problems involved in the Gracchan revolution may be considered somewhat antiquated at points, he has focused the restoration problem itself more clearly than any other historian.

distributed as landed estates had been for centuries.² Although the pressure of the new well-to-do business class for social advancement led indirectly to conflicts between old and new wealth and various forms of political corruption, the state of agriculture was far more directly affected by the double consequences of the war: devastation in southern and central Italy, and the influx of cheap slave labor. Here only the wealthy latifundia owners benefited, in particular the absentee landlords residing in the city of Rome, yet the small farmers were not less affected by the new conditions.

In a very different sense these became absentee owners too. Because of the military service obligation, which fell particularly hard on this class during the long periods of the campaigns against Carthage, the Macedonian wars, and the Syrian wars, small peasants were forced to neglect their agricultural work intermittently. They became heavily mortgaged, and since, unlike the aristocratic landowners, they could not afford slave labor, they were completely knocked out of the arena of economic competition. Import of cheaper and better grain from Sicily, then the granary of Italy, and grain speculations of the knights turned matters from bad to worse. Shift to other more complex branches of agriculture, such as cultivating vineyards, planting oil trees, or breeding cattle, provided no help. On the contrary, demands on labor, and therewith production costs, were higher. The small farmer all over Italy, heavily indebted already and completely priced out of the market, was driven from the land, and he joined now the landless but technically free proletariat of the discontented in Rome. Here the chances to make a living by work were smallest, but the opportunity to linger on, supported by doles, was greatest.³

All these problems must be perceived within the frame of the then existing political institutions. It may be presupposed that the student of the restoration problem is familiar with the constitutional order in its broadest outlines, as far as the powers of the magistracy, the consuls, praetors, aediles, quaestors, and in a different class, the tribunes of the people are concerned. Only the institution of these tribunes remained untouched. Otherwise the steady increase in the number of high officials, necessitated by imperial expansion, offered excellent opportunities for elected executive officials to block each other's administration. The political strength of the ten tribunes of the people lay not in administrative functions but mainly

² Bloch and Carcopino, pp. 72 ff.; Vogt, pp. 171 ff.; Mommsen, III, 77 ff.; Marsh, *History,* pp. 5 ff.; Scullard, pp. 8 ff., 13 ff.; Taylor, pp. 17 ff.
³ Bloch and Carcopino, pp. 85 ff., 98 ff.; Vogt, I, 169 ff.; Scullard, pp. 19 ff.; Ferrero, pp. I, 39 ff.; Marsh, *History,* pp. 9 ff.; Taylor, pp. 50 ff.

in the veto power exercised on behalf of the people in the Senate and the assembly. Since it was operative possibly even by a single tribune against nine others, this opportunity for political sabotage was especially dangerous.[4] It became, indeed, one of the chief devices of the opponents of the Gracchan reform legislation. Yet even before that period it was one of the means to keep supreme the power of the Senate, the deliberative body of the three hundred aristocratic officeholders and former officeholders. There were other ways to exercise power, of course. They all implied the supervision of officeholders from the consuls downward. They included the granting of an extension of tenure of office for a second year and beyond as provincial governors and—increasingly important—the control of appropriations and military contingents.[5]

Yet the chief strength of the Senate was exercised indirectly in regard to the very body that should have checked and in a wider sense directed its function, the popular assembly, the source of legislative power in the republic. The Senate's power in all its functions was wielded very largely on behalf of the interests of the landed aristocracy. To it belonged the members of the senatorial families with their curiously mixed tradition of courage, pride, and greed.

The patriotic devotion of this class, frequently proved in war, was hardly shown in domestic affairs. The control of the popular assembly is a strong case in point. As is generally known, the assembly consisted of a twofold organization, the assembly of centuries (hundredships) and the assembly of tribes, the former chiefly concerned with the election of high officials, the latter—far more important—with general legislation altogether. Only a few centuries, representing knights and the poorest classes, were probably added in the third century B.C. The tribe, unlike the Jewish and Greek patterns, was in the course of history determined primarily by territorial affiliation and only indirectly by descent. Of these tribes four lay within the city bounds, sixteen were in its immediate vicinity, and the remainder were scattered all over central and, increasingly, also southern Italy. Votes were taken by tribes, and although every Roman citizen residing within the thirty-five districts was eligible to vote, the rural population—still predominant in thirty-one of the thirty-five units, by distance as well as by occupation—was largely prevented from attending

[4] See Bloch and Carcopino, pp. 13 f.; Marsh, *Founding of the Roman Empire,* pp. 37 ff.; Taylor, pp. 14 ff.; Marsh, *History,* pp. 13 f.; Kornemann, I, 88 ff.; Mommsen, I, Bk. VI, chap. 2.

[5] Brilliantly discussed in Mommsen, II, chap. 11; see also Bloch and Carcopino, pp. 8 ff., 30 ff.; Vogt, I, 168 f.; Marsh, pp. 13 ff., 23 ff.

the assembly meetings.[6] Accordingly a rather small number of rural voters could generally outvote masses of city voters. The senatorial aristocracy, not as a body, to be sure, but as individuals, took advantage of this situation. Together with their clients—free peasants who committed themselves to allegiance in return for protection from powerful neighboring lords, and freed men, legally still dependent former slaves—they registered now in the rural wards. Therewith they could swing the vote in favor of the aristocratic establishment. This meant in turn that the vote of the dispossessed peasants who had flocked to Rome became that much less important.[7] Having lost his land because he could not compete with the slave labor used by the latifundia owner, many a dispossessed small peasant lost the weight of his vote as well. Not every one of them, to be sure. A substantial number of those who were driven from their land continued to be registered in their old tribal districts. Whereas the peasant formerly was prevented from voting by the demands of his hard tasks, he was at least free to exercise his political rights, and he could exercise them against the will of the aristocrats of senatorial rank. Whether the peasant was prevented from making his political weight felt in Rome or was prompted to fight for his rights against the lords and their retainers, political tension increased markedly. Winners in this unequal struggle between latifundia owners and landless peasants were to a degree the business class of knights, who wanted to sell their support to the old aristocracy in return for advancement of their social status. Yet they could not serve as mediators in the social conflict. When it came to a showdown, their interests were still much closer to the lords than to the peasants.[8]

In addition to the problems sketched thus far, that of Rome's Italian allies deserves foremost consideration. Those in Latium, in the immediate southern vicinity of Rome, by the middle of the second century B.C. had obtained limited citizenship rights approaching those of the Romans. The rights of citizens in the federated communities farther to the south and in central Italy, however, were still considered unsatisfactory. Although their sacrifices in the Carthagian, Macedonian, and Syrian wars were equal to those of the Roman citizens, they felt still discriminated against in the distribution of land and the opportunities to gain lucrative offices in the

---

[6] The division into *comitia centuriata* was based on social stratification into five classes according to wealth. See Bloch and Carcopino, pp. 16 ff.; Marsh, p. 20; Taylor, pp. 55 ff.; Mommsen, II, chap. 11.

[7] Mommsen, II, chap. 11; Bloch and Carcopino, pp. 21 ff., 102 f.; Kornemann, I, 101 ff.; Ferrero, I, 12 ff.; Marsh, pp. 18 ff.; Taylor, pp. 50 ff.

[8] Bloch and Carcopino, pp. 72 ff.; Marsh, pp. 28 ff.; Scullard, pp. 19 ff.

provinces. Yet extension of citizenship rights was blocked by the senatorial regime. Attempt to gain Roman citizenship by migration to the capital failed, on the whole, too. On the other hand, this movement increased dissatisfaction and tension in the core of the empire, the city of Rome. This city, through a truly unique set of historical circumstances, represented the structure of the empire itself.[9]

The facts and problems discussed in the foregoing characterize the original system (A). Subject to many changes brought about by territorial, agricultural, and industrial expansion, it represented a restless but not yet revolutionary social order. And this order was held together in the main by an evolutionary development of centuries-old political institutions. They were to be tested now by a genuine revolutionary movement under the leadership of the Gracchi.

It is not possible to retell here the story of this eventful phase of Roman history. A brief analysis of the main points at issue must suffice. Tiberius Gracchus and his brother Gaius—younger by about ten years—belonged to one of the great aristocratic families whose members had held consular rank.[10] This noble, or at least upper middle class, origin of revolutionary leaders was the rule rather than the exception in the social upheavals of the Roman republic. (Perhaps this is largely true in the history of social revolution and reform altogether.) An indirect census of education and wealth as a kind of social starting point was operative in the Roman system, where elective office was, at least nominally, purely honorary. The few exceptions—Marius, a generation after the Gracchan revolution, foremost among them—confirm this state of affairs. Marius was a professional soldier and a most successful one. Thus he made use of his military fame, which was, apart from noble descent, the most effective route to high civilian office.

Yet Tiberius Gracchus, who did not lack courage, was not a professional soldier, although he had distinguished himself in his youth in the campaigns in Spain. A man of caution and circumspection, he was a typical leader, yet not at all blind to the military commitments and challenges presented to the late republic.[11] Tiberius, a man of political

---

[9] Scullard, pp. 16 ff.; Vogt, I, 173 ff.

[10] See particularly the essay "Le Mariage de Cornélie" in Carcopino, *Autour des Gracques,* pp. 47 ff.

[11] Main ancient sources concerned with the activities of the two brothers are the biographical essays in Plutarch's *Lives,* to which a third comparative one, which evaluates their character, is added. There is also the Roman history of Appian of Alexandria, written in the second century B.C., presumably somewhat later than Plutarch's essays. Quotes are here from the English edition (London: Bell, 1899),

ambition as well as social compassion, was fully conscious of Roman tradition. As he saw it, the small peasants in central and southern Italy represented the historic foundation and keystone of Roman civic virtues. This was largely because the small peasantry, prior to Marius, served as the main pool for the recruiting of military forces under a system of selective conscription in case of war. Now this class was in numerical and social decline and was openly involved in the flight from the land. Tiberius, elected as only one tribune of the people among ten for the year 133, yet in every sense a *primus inter pares,* had a plan to fight these social evils.

Basically, it was an agricultural reform in which the portion of the conquered territories held by the government was to be distributed among the landless peasants or would-be peasants in small parcels of about twenty acres (thirty jugera) each. Much, perhaps most, of this land had been taken over in the course of several generations by the aristocratic landowners, who in some cases paid rent, in others not. Yet though they had never acquired clear title, they could claim possession in good faith, since the state—which they practically owned as a genuine ruling class—had never challenged their land-grab. These aristocrats were by no means to be completely dispossessed. They were to retain about three hundred acres (five hundred jugera) and once again that amount of land if the owner had at least two sons engaged in agriculture. Furthermore, limited indemnities were to be paid, probably for improvements, plantations, and buildings. Even more important, the old aristocratic landowners as well as the peasants with their thirty acres should now obtain unrestricted title of ownership to land that they had retained or gained. Judged by the undisputed needs for land, by the indemnities to be granted, and even by tradition, this bill could not be called radical in any sense. The new agrarian bill was, in fact, only the revised and improved draft of a law passed under the former tribune and later consul C.

Vol. II, Bk. I, chaps. 1–3. While Plutarch has probably used more sources than Appian, the latter's narrative seems to be less embellished, and thus perhaps less distorted by purely literary considerations. Marsh, pp. 378–380, offers an interesting comparative evaluation, weighted perhaps too heavily in favor of Appian. For the purpose of this study the differences between Plutarch and Appian are of minor significance. They are discussed at great length and with impressive discrimination in Fraccaro, pp. 11–188 *passim.* Concerning Plutarch and Appian as sources for the Gracchan revolts see also Kornemann, *Zur Geschichte der Gracchenzeit,* pp. 1–20 *passim.*

On the background of the Gracchi see Bloch and Carcopino, pp. 181 ff.; Carcopino, *Autour des Gracques,* pp. 47 ff.; and the stimulating essay by Theodor Birt, *Römische Charakterköpfe* (Leipzig, 1916), pp. 53 ff.

Licinius Stolo in the first part of the fourth century. In conceiving the draft of his bill Tiberius Gracchus stood indeed on solid ground.[12]

The same is true in principle for his endeavors to have the bill passed over the opposition of the senatorial aristocracy, their retainers, and the knights, whose business interests were closely interwoven with those of their aristocratic debtors. The Senate persuaded the tribune Octavius to veto the bill in the assembly. It is one of the characteristics of the aristocratic republic that this step, clearly in conflict with the popular will of the majority, was fully legal. An attempt by Tiberius to persuade the Senate to press Octavius to withdraw his veto was bound to fail. It may have been undertaken only as proof that the tribune wanted to fight as long as possible on legal grounds. Now apparently he deemed it no longer possible. A postponement of the vote until the following year, when new tribunes would be elected, offered little hope. The opponents of reform would then be even better prepared to thwart the popular will in the various wards, since the underprivileged supporters of Tiberius might be forced to leave the city, to be replaced by the retainers of the aristocrats.

The elder Gracchus saw no other course open to him but to propose the removal of Octavius from office because he had unmistakably defied the clearly expressed will of the majority of the people. The motion carried and Octavius was replaced by a faithful follower of the reform movement. Not even the Senate dared to intervene against this outright violation of Roman constitutional principles.

The suppression of opposition of any other official, from consul downward, by legal devices short of violence, might have been controversial in any case. Tampering with the sacred veto power of a tribune, even an abused veto power, was a far more serious matter. The veto of the tribune was perceived to be the very keystone of popular liberties. It should protect not so much the rights of the minority against the majority, but of the majority of the people, deprived of adequate representation, against the rule of an aristocratic oligarchy. As seen in retrospect, to have kept this right inviolate, even at the price of delaying reform for some time, would have served popular rights better than a struggle won by devious means. Such ambiguous triumph might compromise the status of the tribunes of the people for all time.[13]

[12] On the agrarian bill see Plutarch, Modern Library ed., pp. 997 ff.; Appian, Vol. II, chap. 1, 9–11; Mommsen, III, 90 ff.; Bloch and Carcopino, pp. 171 ff., 190 ff.; Vogt, I, 179 ff.; Ferrero, I, 51 ff.; Kornemann, pp. 412 ff.; Scullard, pp. 26 ff.; Marsh, pp. 34 ff., 378 f.

[13] On the history of the tribunate see Kornemann, I, 85 ff.; Vogt, I, 28 ff.; Marsh, *Founding of the Roman Empire*, pp. 37 f.; Mommsen, I, 274 ff.

Yet these are hindsight considerations. For the time being it seemed that Tiberius Gracchus had carried the day. An agricultural commission was appointed with the assigned task to distribute the land. Tiberius proposed to have the whole scheme of distribution and indemnities financed by a legacy of the Eastern satellite king of Pergamum. This device interested the creditors of many an indebted aristocrat, the knights in particular. A further move to get on the right side of the knights may have been a plan to put their representatives on the jury panels of the courts that dealt with malfeasance in office of provincial governors. Obviously, these opportunities to be opened to the knights, though seemingly modest, could become a means of exercising considerable pressure against those in power.

But all these stratagems were mere expedients. Tiberius could only hope to escape the vengeance of his senatorial opponents, and, indeed, enemies by the protection of his office. As soon as his term expired he would be an open target for the ruling Senate set to bring about his indictment by a packed assembly for his previous violation of constitutional procedures. The single way to fight this danger seemed to him to run for the office of tribune again and thus to gain immunity from prosecution through uninterrupted tenure. Whether such reelection was technically a clear violation of the law is doubtful. A statute of 151 B.C. dealt in this respect only with the position of the consul. Yet even the reelection of a tribune for a consecutive term was in conflict with a century-old tradition and in these terms truly revolutionary.

Tiberius' action enraged the Senate and split the assembly wide open. In the ensuing riots he was slain by a mob before the question of his reelection was decided, though it is not likely that he could have succeeded against well-organized senatorial resistance.[14] Such at least can be concluded from the prosecution and subsequent execution of several of the followers of the slain tribune. By no means, however, did all the signs point in the direction of reaction. The Senate did not dare to manipulate repeal of the agrarian law in the popular assembly. Even the agrarian commission was not openly interfered with, though its work was slowed down by the new members, who deferred as far as possible to the wishes of the Senate. Yet Gaius, the younger brother of the tribune, was elected chairman of the commission for the year 130, and he was more than eager to pursue the policies of his brother. Another setback followed. By a law initiated by the aristocracy in the assembly in 129, the judicial powers of

[14] On the death of Tiberius Gracchus see Appian, Vol. II, chap. 2, 16–17; Plutarch, pp. 1004 ff.

the commission were transferred to the consuls. This for all practical purposes stopped further distribution of land for some time. The commission was not formally dissolved, however, and the period between the stalling of its operation and further reform was so brief that we can hardly say the revolutionary period had ended by 129.[15]

A correct evaluation of the actions of Tiberius Gracchus in regard to restoration is possible only in conjunction with a survey of the deeds of his younger, far more dynamic brother. The reforms of the elder Gracchus had started something but settled nothing, though they had raised great expectations, which Gaius Gracchus, elected tribune for the year 123, hoped to fulfill. In addition to his qualifications as chairman of the agricultural commission and as previous quaestor in Sicily his biggest asset was the name he had inherited. Another advantage lay in the fact that his policy was not opposed by fellow tribunes. As Gaius probably saw it, he had the opportunity to tackle the reform problem on a much wider scale, through the creation of a political organization that could check senatorial power and at the same time secure a permanent majority for liberal reform. The independent city vote added to that of the retainers of the knights might work for such an objective.

Gaius took advantage of the fact that his brother had already weakened the tradition of nonconsecutive terms in the office of tribune. He served two terms, in 123 and 122, and was able to initiate a more comprehensive legal problem than Tiberius before him. He continued, or rather renewed, the work of the agrarian commission. At the same time he had something to offer to that part of the city proletariat in Rome which had never been engaged in farming and did not wish to turn to it now. Gaius instituted a corn law whereby Roman citizens could buy grain at prices considerably below production costs. The government and not the wealthy latifundia owners would be directly responsible for making up the difference. In any case, indirect burdens imposed on the rich from the operation of this law were not clearly visible. More important, Gaius probably felt that his program would not hurt the knights, whose support was important to him. He intended to meet their wishes in regard to two important issues. The first was a law which subjected the province of Asia (the western part of Asia Minor) to the infamous tax-farming system. Furthermore, the contracts to be let in Rome were not to require competitive bidding. These proposals offered opportunities for the enrichment of some enterprising knights at the expense of the vassal peoples. It will remain a black

---

[15] According to the estimate of Vogt, I, 184, the number of landed peasants in Italy increased between 130 and 125 B.C. from 318,000 to 394,000.

mark, for foul means used in a noble purpose, against Gaius' record. In his time only a very remarkable man might have been expected to think and act differently. But remarkable in more than one respect is exactly what Gaius Gracchus was.

Another law changed the jury system in the courts where former provincial governors were to be tried for corruption. The senatorial benches, which frequently acquitted defendants belonging to their own class, were to be replaced by a jury of knights. This device, probably drawn up by the older Gracchus, as noted above, increased the influence of the knights in dealing with their aristocratic betters. At the same time the social separation of jury and defendants in certain cases may also have served the interests of impartial justice, whether this was Gaius' intention or not.[16]

He probably cared as little for the knights as for the Asiatic provincials in his sorry tax-farming law. His prime, perhaps his only, interest continued to be the well-being of the Roman proletariat and of those depressed peasants migrating continuously to and from the city. This objective, like the court reform, required the weakening of the power of the Senate to deal with leaders of the reform movement. To this effect he had another bill passed by the assembly, which condemned any magistrate to banishment if he had ordered the execution of a citizen without the safeguard of an appeal to the people. A warning to the Senate was clearly implied.

Gaius added now to his corn law a road-building program. While the former measure was intended to mitigate the hardships of unemployment and as a side effect to gain voters, the second purported to create jobs and to expand commerce, particularly in southern Italy. More controversial, though not unreasonable, was a third plan, to establish colonies in southern Italy, in particular around the old and deteriorating towns of Capua and Tarent. Effectuation of this plan was expected to do for the urban population what the agrarian reform should do and partially had done already for the peasants. An esentially logical but politically ill-advised addition to this scheme was a plan to set up a third colony in Africa where Carthage had stood. Not only did this plan run counter to the nationalistic furor that had led to the annihilation of the city, but it also marked those destined to emigrate to Africa as second-class citizens.

Many reformers fail to understand the feelings of others. In regard to Gaius Gracchus there is a strange contradiction between a colonization measure that was bound to alienate sizeable sections of the Roman

---

[16] Marsh, pp. 56 ff., denies this possibility. See also Kornemann, I, 451 f. See further Bloch and Carcopino, pp. 246 ff.

proletariat and previous reforms which had heavily favored these groups. Whether other schemes by which Gaius wanted to win over the Italian allies were more acceptable in this respect is not clear. These included the granting of full Roman citizenship rights to the inhabitants of Latium and the elevation of the other Italian provincials to the relatively privileged status which the Latian provincials had enjoyed before.[17] Whether Gaius dealt with the top or the bottom strata of society, he could not ignore the existence of deeply rooted social differences, not only between the rich and the poor, but among the poor themselves. This patent social divisiveness is one of the major reasons for Gaius's failure.

In a sense it was this last issue which gave the opponents of the younger Gracchus their opening. The extension of citizenship rights and therewith franchise rights might establish a permanent majority that was anti-Senate and antiaristocrat. Plans like the establishment of the colonies furnished the means by which the hated objective could be foiled. Gaius's fellow tribune, Marcus Livius Drusus the elder, a representative of the interests of the Senate, though opposed to the extension of citizenship, proposed, in lieu of two petty colonies in Italy and one in Africa, the establishment of not less than twelve in Italy. If one gives Drusus all benefits of doubt, it is conceivable that he was in earnest with his proposals. In view of the fact that literally nothing of this plan was carried out after the fall of Gaius, it could well be argued, on the other hand, that this scheme was a brazen device of demagoguery right from the start, intended to confuse the masses in a critical situation. In the words of Plutarch, "The chief senators made their application, exhorting him [Drusus] to attack Caius and join in their confederacy against him; which they designed to carry on, not by using any force, or opposing the common people, but by gratifying and obliging them with such unreasonable things as otherwise they would have felt it honourable for them to incur the greatest unpopularity in resisting . . . , Drusus' . . . whole design being to outdo Caius in pleasing and cajoling the populace (as if it had been in some comedy), with obsequious flattery and every kind of gratifications . . ."[18]

---

[17] On the legislation and reform plans of Gaius Gracchus see Appian, Vol. II, chap. 3, 21–23; Plutarch, pp. 1010 ff.; Mommsen, III, 109 ff.; Bloch and Carcopino, pp. 239 ff.; Marsh, 55 ff.; Kornemann, I, 428 ff.; Vogt, I, 185 ff.; Ferrero, I, 58 ff.; Scullard, 33 ff.

[18] Plutarch, pp. 1012 f.; Appian, II, chap. 1, 23, neither subscribes to nor contradicts this interpretation, but practically the whole literature has followed Plutarch. See Mommsen, III, 125 ff.; Bloch and Carcopino, pp. 253 ff.; Marsh, pp. 65 f.; Kornemann, I, 432 ff.; Vogt, I, 188 ff.; Scullard, pp. 36 f.

The scheme worked and therewith the end of Gaius and his mission was in sight. He failed to be reelected as tribune for 121 B.C., and with the loss of the protection of his office he became a marked man. The issue of repeal of the law providing for the establishment of a colony on the grounds of Carthage led to riots on the part of Gaius Gracchus's followers, and this in turn led to the violence that terminated his life. Rather than be slain by the henchmen of the Senate or tried and executed on behalf of its pressure groups, he presumably either committed suicide or had himself killed by one of his slaves. There can be little doubt that neither a specific issue regarding this or that colony nor any gradation of citizenship rights but the overall attempt to transform the aristocratic republic to a socially more representative body was responsible for the death of the younger Gracchus.[19] Gaius's plans were in many ways contradictory. They did not establish equality in Italy, and they accentuated to a point even the tremendous social differences between the home country and the provinces around the shores of the Mediterranean. Like others before him, Gaius Gracchus failed to tackle and perhaps even to see the problem of worldwide empire. This in a sense was still based on the fictitious identification with the city government of Rome. Nevertheless, the fact remains that nobody else had gone or would go further to inject a measure of democratic principles into a political structure that had burst its seams. In this sense the regime of Gaius Gracchus was truly revolutionary, and inasmuch as some of his basic reforms tending to break up the class structure of the republic were initiated by his older brother Tiberius and resumed and only expanded by Gaius, we may well disregard the short break between their tenures and perceive their work as rolled into one truly revolutionary system.[20]

---

[19] Appian, III, chap. 3, 21–23; Plutarch, pp. 1010 ff.; Mommsen, II, 109 ff.; Bloch and Carcopino, pp. 258 ff.; Ferrero, I, 58 ff.; Kornemann, I, 428 ff.; Vogt, I, 189 ff.; Marsh pp. 63 ff.; Scullard, 36 ff.

[20] Historical doctrine supports this assumption, although with considerable modification.

Plutarch (pp. 1019 ff.) commends both Gracchi for their courage and spirit of self-sacrifice, but blames them for excessive ambition and dictatorial tendencies. He rates Tiberius much higher than Gaius, but in either case he has little understanding of the social issues involved.

Appian (II, chaps. 1–3) is more reserved in his judgment but certainly not more understanding than Plutarch in regard to the social issues and less so in his evaluation of the personalities.

Mommsen's overall evaluation (III, 119 ff.) is well known. He emphasizes the dictatorial aspects in the policy of the Gracchi and sees no social issues at the center of Roman history. Nevertheless, he does full justice to the personalities of the Gracchi, and rightly perceives Gaius as the far more important one.

Ferrero (I, 63 f.), who acknowledges the noble intentions of the Gracchi and

At this point it may be appropriate to present views from two different camps, one by Ernst Kornemann, who offers the most positive evaluation of the Gracchan policies, the other that of Theodor Mommsen, undoubtedly the highest authority among those who hold a negative view. Kornemann observes:

> The twelve years 133–121 are the most fateful years in the ever changing history of Rome. . . . It is the only period at the end of which the Roman state, strictly reorganized on an aristocratic basis, became for a short time a democracy under a strong leader, like the Attic state under Pericles. Gaius failed, like his brother, because of the hostility to reforms on the part of the ruling caste; he failed because of the impossibility to satisfy at the same time the needs of his urban supporters and the demands of the Latian-Italian allies. He failed above all because of the historic structure of his state. Its communal setup did not do justice to the new tasks. . . . Gaius Gracchus nevertheless was one of the greatest statesmen Rome has ever seen. In politics the new idea, the stubborn fight for it by all available means, must be honored, even if the promoter of the idea sometimes chose the wrong means. . . .

This last conclusion seems to be highly debatable and Kornemann himself admits that overpowering political personalities like Gaius Gracchus and Gaius Julius Caesar share the responsibility for the eventual development toward one-man government.[21]

And yet just at this point the Gracchan revolution is defended, strangely enough, by the far more conservative Mommsen, who was liberal in his time but would not be considered so in ours. Mommsen injects two new major ideas into the evaluation of the Gracchan revolution. First, he perceives the post-Gracchan era as a definite restoration period—to him a kind of natural corollary and consequence of revolution. Second, he sees in the reestablishment of an old system, filled with a spirit of vengeance rather than reconciliation, "the curse of restoration" in general.[22]

This is not, however, any condonation of a revolutionary system. "An

---

sees their course of action as inevitable, overemphasizes the harmful effect of Gaius' policies in regard to the provinces beyond the seas. Vogt (I, 189 f.) sees the same disintegrating effect in Italy.

Scullard (pp. 39 f.) sees both Gracchi as martyrs and true revolutionaries. The latter view in a more modified way is also that of Marsh (46 ff., 65 ff.). Birt (*Römische Charakterköpfe,* pp. 68 ff.) rates motivation and character of both brothers very high but perceives Gaius as the far more gifted and dynamic one. The same position is held by Bloch and Carcopino (p. 264). The Gracchi's methods are criticized in several ways. But both of them, particularly Gaius, are considered revolutionary champions of the interests of the masses against the selfish interests of the Senate party.

[21] *Römische Geschichte,* I, 437 f., 440 (author's translation).
[22] *History of Rome,* III, 137.

absolute monarchy is a great misfortune for a nation," he observes, "but it is less a misfortune than an absolute oligarchy; and history cannot censure one who imposes on a nation the lesser suffering instead of the greater, least of all in the case of a nature so vehemently earnest and so far aloof from all that is vulgar as was that of Gaius Gracchus." [23] All the same, he was

> a political incendiary. Not only was the hundred years' revolution which dates from him, so far as it was one man's work, the work of Gaius Gracchus, but he was above all the true founder of that terrible civic proletariat flattered and paid by the classes above it. And yet again, this greatest of political transgressors was the regenerator of his country. There is scarcely a fruitful idea in the Roman monarchy which is not traceable to Gaius Gracchus. . . . Right and wrong, fortune and misfortune were so inextricably blended in this singular man . . . , that it may well beseem history in this case—though it beseems her but seldom—to reserve her judgment.[24]

This may still be the best evaluation of an unusually complex historical constellation and personality. Yet no reservation is necessary for the opinion that the Gracchan era was a truly revolutionary one, an assertion supported also by the high authority of Jerome Carcopino.[25]

Kornemann observes further that the decade after the death of the two young leaders was as barren of ideas as the Gracchan period had been creative. "Yet at this time the Senate did not dare to tackle the lifework of the deceased greatest contemporary directly, but continued to rule on the basis of the Gracchan innovations." [26] It merely diluted them. In this Kornemann follows in principle the views of Mommsen, who saw in a very dim light what to him appeared to be a clear case of restoration.

> After the decease of Gaius Gracchus without heirs, the government of the senate . . . resumed its sway. . . . Yet we should greatly err, if we should discern in this restoration nothing further than a relapse of the state machine into the old track which had been beaten and worn out for centuries. Restoration is always revolution; and in this case it was not so much the old government as the old governor that was restored. The oligarchy made its appearance newly equipped in the armour of the *tyrannis* which had been overthrown. As the senate had beaten Gracchus from the field with its own weapons, so it continued in the most essential points to govern with the constitution of the Gracchi; though cer-

[23] *Ibid*, p. 120.
[24] *Ibid.*, pp. 122 f.
[25] Bloch and Carcopino, pp. 199 f., 264 f.
[26] *Römische Geschichte,* I, 441 (author's translation).

tainly with the secret intention, if not setting it aside entirely, at any rate of thoroughly purging it in due time from the elements really hostile to the ruling aristocracy.[27]

This evaluation of the injection of ideas and institutions of the revolutionary period into the restoration period ties in with the analysis of the restoration process offered in Part I. In one point Mommsen goes even beyond it. He apparently believes that tyrannical, dictatorial government was germane to the Gracchan period as well as to the restoration. This would mean in effect that the philosophy of the Gracchan period was in essential points preserved rather than that the philosophy of the preceding system was restored.

Here one may dare to differ with the deductions of a great man. His eyes were perhaps focused too intently on the domestic violence within the Roman world from the assassination of Tiberius Gracchus in 131 B.C. to the battle of Actium a century later, which initiated the domestic peace of the Augustan age. Although we must not underrate the importance of violence within the borders of the empire, neither must we overlook the decisive factor of substantive change brought about by the restoration.

All of the revolutionary and reform ideas of the Gracchi continued in the foreground of political thought and action or counteraction. The extension of citizenship rights was far more important than the distribution of public land and the court reforms, let alone the provision of doles by way of the corn laws. Even though these factors are interrelated, Mommsen himself testifies to the overriding importance of the first.

> All those measures which were devised by Gaius Gracchus for the promotion of the public welfare . . . were allowed by the aristocracy to drop. Nothing was so speedily and so successfully assailed as the noblest of his projects, viz., the scheme of introducing a legal equality first between the Roman burgesses and Italy, and thereafter between Italy and the provinces, and—in as much as the distinction between the merely ruling and consuming and the merely serving and working members of the state was thus done away—at the same time solving the social question by the most comprehensive and systematic emigration known in history. With all the determination and all the peevish obstinacy of dotage the restored oligarchy obtruded the principles of

[27] *History of Rome,* III, 131 ff., in the chapter "The Rule of the Restoration," pp. 131–165.

In a different way Hannah Arendt comes to the same conclusion when she reflects that the concept of revolution in the sixteenth and seventeenth centuries actually embodies the restoration of a previous state of affairs, unhampered by true or alleged tyranny. According to Arendt this process takes place primarily in the realm of ideologies. See Hannah Arendt, *On Revolution* (New York, 1963), pp. 36 ff.

deceased generations—that Italy ought to remain the ruling land and Rome the ruling city in Italy—afresh on the present.[28]

One might possibly question the immediate significance of the colonial project, though this idea too was emulated in diluted form by the establishment of at least one colony outside of Italy, in Narbo in southern France in 118 B.C. Yet, all in all, Mommsen's sublime evaluation as to the priority of substantive changes seems to be as correct as the less discriminating opinion on the factor of revolutionary change is doubtful.

Several major evnts in the Italian domestic crisis of the coming decades, as far as they can be studied separately from the foreign wars, should illustrate the point. The Senate, the primary factor, whose political and, indirectly, social power had to be restored, refrained in the early post-Gracchan period from an attempt to repeal either the corn laws or the court reform. The first action would have alienated the old as well as the recently immigrated city proletariat; the second would have strengthened rather than severed the unequal alliance between knights and lower strata of the city populace. The acquittal of the former consul Lucius Optimius, the man primarily responsible for the slaying of Gaius Gracchus, seems to have been a conspicuous turning point here. Unquestionably the Senate stood behind this verdict. It meant in essence that the executives under the control of the Senate could resort to emergency powers, even if these were in conflict with established law, if and when the powers of the Senate were threatened. In a sense this principle represented the ideas of the counterrevolution rather than of restoration. On the other hand, it cannot be maintained that further developments were entirely due to a shift in power brought about by renewed violence, provoked willfully by the opponents of reform. Thus it can be argued that the distortion of Gaius's African colonization program was shortsighted but fully in line with tradition. The founding of a colony in Narbo in southern Gaul was in this sense a genuine though inadequate compromise between such tradition and necessity.

The permission given to the new settlers shortly after Gaius's death to dispose of land which they were either not willing or not able to cultivate could not in itself be called unreasonable. Furthermore, in 111 B.C. even the limited distribution program of the agrarian commission was stopped by leaving the land in possession of those who had held it prior to the Gracchan reforms. At the same time the title of those who had since acquired it was recognized. This measure, too, was reactionary only in com-

[28] *History of Rome,* III, 133.

parison with the Gracchan period. It was only a standstill of reform legislation, by no means a return to the status quo of the pre-Gracchan period. In essence, the same holds true for modification rather than repeal of the corn laws three or four years after the death of Gaius Gracchus.

True, had it not been for the conflicts with king Jugurtha and the Numidian campaigns between 111 and 105 B.C. the policy of the Senate majority might have been more radically averse to the previous reforms.[29] Yet the initially mismanaged colonial war brought to the fore Marius, a peculiar representative of the lower classes. This released a chain of events which changed the whole constellation of power.

Broadly speaking, three main factors determined a course of history which checked further senatorial reaction. The first is the fact that Gaius Marius came from a small provincial family. True, this soldier, who had risen from the ranks, established business connections with the knights, and this served him well in his election as quaestor, tribune, and praetor. Still, he owed his first elevation to the office of consul primarily to his military proficiency and reputation. In any case, he was not committed to the maintenance of the senatorial establishment.

The second factor is that of Marius's military reforms, which proved to be of basic importance. Selective and general conscription in case of crisis was transformed into a mercenary service for soldiers of fortune with expectations of rewards in spoils and above all in land. A militia system of citizen soldiers, mostly of middle-class, agricultural background, would be gradually supplanted by a professional army with obligations of long service. It was to be composed chiefly of members of the landless and land-hungry proletariat. For better or worse it became attached to the fortunes of the leader to the extent that the commander himself was compelled to satisfy the need—or greed—of the soldiery. Leaving sweeping organizational changes entirely aside, a third force arose therewith in the empire, the power of which was never completely broken and in the following five centuries was even substantially increased. It would be impossible to identify such clearly profiled group claims under various leaders with basic progressive or reactionary interests. One thing is certain, these demands could never be associated with the defense of the status quo.

The third factor at issue is the repeated election of Marius to the consular position, which made a mockery of the republican legislation of the years 342 and 151 B.C. against self-perpetuation in office. Appointment at an early age to supreme military command by the popular assembly rather

[29] Bloch and Carcopino, pp. 266 ff.; Kornemann, I, 425 ff.; Marsh, pp. 68 f., 412 f.; Scullard, pp. 44 f. Altogether there were three land bills between 121 and 111 B.C.

than by the Senate had already violated established tradition more seriously than the Gracchan campaigns for reelection to the tribunate. As noted previously, it could possibly be argued, however, that Marius's earlier reelections were due to a supreme crisis in external affairs and were thus a bow to necessity. In retrospect the question seems to be a moot one. After the defeat of Jugurtha, the crushing of the second slave revolt in Sicily, and above all the defeat of the Cimbri and Teutones by 101 B.C., there was no need for Marius, the victorious commander, to engineer his election as consul for a sixth time. It was not his restraint but a complex combination of conflicting claims by latifundia owners and the interests of business and city proletariat and provincial peasants that delayed for almost twenty years the entrenchment of a more lasting dictatorship—Sulla's. Yet the idea of government by republican tradition and law was already hurt beyond recovery. What happened for the next ten years resembles an operation in a kind of ideological no man's land between restoration and dictatorship. It can hardly be definitely associated with either one alone.[30]

A case in point would be the court reorganization effected under the younger Gracchus in favor of the knights. Apparently this reform was voided in 106 B.C. but was reintroduced two years later.[31] The political course was clearly fluctuating. Far more decisive and even more erratic deviations from the republican course were to come. They were linked in part to the pressure of the soldiery for land and of the city proletariat in and around Rome for doles. Both forces were bound to drive Marius into the arms of the radicals. They were led by the tribune Saturninus, three times—contrary to legal constitutional tradition—elected tribune between 103 and 99. Another promoter of such developments was Gaius Servilius

---

[30] The still existing ancient source closest to the events of Marius's career is Gaius Sallustius Crispus, *Bellum Jugurthinum*. Sallustius himself, proconsul of the province of Africa in 46 B.C., perceives Marius as challenger of the corrupt senatorial establishment of old and—with the benefit of hindsight—of the coming dictatorship of Sulla as well. See Sallustius Crispus, *Bellum Jugurthinum*, in the edition by A. Scheindler (Vienna, 1907), particularly chaps. LXXXIII, XCIX, XCIV. See also the English translation by J. S. Watson (London, 1910). See further Karl Büchner, *Sallust* (Heidelberg, 1960), pp. 143 ff., 196 ff., 300 f. Plutarch (*Lives*, pp. 494 ff.) values Marius as a great soldier and at the same time as a revolutionary of despotic tendencies. Appian's perfunctory account in Vol. II, Bk. I, chaps. 3–5 is wholly negative.

Mommsen, III, 158 ff., 199 ff.; Bloch and Carcopino, pp. 305 ff.; Ferrero, I, 78 ff.; Marsh, *Founding of the Roman Empire*, pp. 41 ff.; Marsh, *History*, pp. 76 ff., 84 ff., 403, 413 ff.; Scullard, pp. 48 ff., 58 f., 392; Kornemann, I, 454 ff.; Vogt, I, 191 ff.; Cowell, *Revolutions of Ancient Rome*, pp. 109 ff.; Birt, pp. 77 ff.; Cowell, 110 ff., 117 ff.

[31] Marsh, pp. 69, 81, 89, 414; Scullard, pp. 57, 390.

Glaucia, praetor for the year 100 and, also in violation of the law, candidate for the consulate in 99.

First, Saturninus introduced or rather reintroduced a corn law that proposed considerable lowering of the price. It is not certain whether this bill was passed or whether it went much beyond the legislation of the younger Gracchus, but it surely followed the pattern of his reforms and appealed to the same strata of the urban population, for a time effectively.[32] Even more important was the legislation he initiated pertaining to distribution of land. An indirect means to break conservative opposition seems to have been the establishment of a court whose function was the adjudication of cases of high treason against the Roman people. Treason apparently was to be understood, though not defined, as opposition to the plans of Saturninus, Glaucia, and the man behind them, Marius.

It is important to realize that such an ambitious program could never have been introduced without the support of Marius, six-time consul and much admired commander in chief. Possibly he was, by this time, the captive of the armed forces rather than their true leader. For a while this could not change his commitments. One bill provided land for Roman as well as Italian veterans in southwestern (Transalpine) Gallia, the other, far more comprehensive one demanded the establishment of colonies for Roman and again also Italian citizens in Sicily, Greece, Macedonia, and possibly even in Africa. Some of the colonists were to be raised to the status of Roman citizens.[33]

With or without the colonial establishment in Africa the plan seemed already radical enough. It could be carried out only by means of a highly controversial legal device. This provided for the banishment of every senator who would refuse to comply with a law to the defense of which he was to be sworn. Marius—as chief magistrate apparently afraid to incur the passionate opposition of the senatorial establishment, threatened in its privileged position—refused at first to take the oath altogether. Later he took the oath but tacked to it a qualification that deprived it of any meaning. The Senate understood well enough that therewith the execu-

---

[32] Bloch and Carcopino, pp. 338 ff. Kornemann, I, 478; Scullard, pp. 56 ff., Marsh, pp. 89 ff.

[33] See Mommsen, III, 208 ff.; Ferrero, I, 69 f.; Scullard, pp. 60 f.; Marsh, pp. 90 f. All these authorities confirm the inclusion of Africa in the colonization plans. Kornemann (*Römische Geschichte*, I, 477 f.) does not state that African colonies were proposed at that time; Scullard is doubtful on that point. Plutarch (pp. 512 f.), who refers to Saturninus at some length, does not mention plans for colonial establishments in Africa.

tive forces that really counted had abandoned the radicals. At the behest of the Senate, Marius now dropped his burdensome allies, who were destroyed by the retaliatory violence of the senatorial and equestrian retainers. Marius, thoroughly compromised because of his dubious vacillations and subterfuges, withdrew from public life for almost twelve years. He was to return, only to lose his life at the time of the showdown with Sulla's dictatorship.

The fall of Marius and the destructions of his allies, relinquished by him, put the Senate establishment in control again for the last fairly peaceful years prior to a half century of uninterrupted civil war. The legislation of Saturninus, as far as it had been passed already, was repealed. Provincials were in large numbers driven from Rome; the hope for colonization and extension of citizenship rights was extinguished. Beyond this, new restrictive legislation made the passage of reform bills in the assembly extremely difficult in the future. It is likely that the administration could not have gone that far without the support of the knights. Apparently they were one with the Senate in their opposition to the extension of citizenship rights, land grants to the veterans of Marius's army, and the financing of further doles for the Roman city proletariat.

The one issue on which knights and Senate apparently differed seriously was the court system, which, in trials for malfeasance in political office, was again in control of the knights. It seems that the next and for a long time the last reform movement of at least halfway evolutionary character made use of this senatorial grievance to introduce a new set of bills. The third of the great reformers before Julius Caesar, the tribune for the year 91 B.C., M. Livius Drusus, the son of one of Gaius Gracchus's chief adversaries, proposed the admission of three hundred knights to the Senate. This move ought to have blurred economic differences between landed aristocracy of old and the business class. Juries should henceforth have been drawn from both classes. Apparently this compromise satisfied neither the senatorial majority of old nor the commercial senators, who were to be held retroactively responsible for genuine or trumped-up charges of corruption. It is thus not quite clear whether the overall purpose of this bill was to curb the senators of long standing, or the knights, or both; but it seems certain that Drusus wanted to use the proposal for the sake of new reforms in the interest of the underprivileged. Furthermore, according to an agrarian bill in favor of the landless citizens, particularly the veterans, the remaining public land was to be distributed in Italy proper and in Sicily. Another bill was to provide for the allotment of cheap or free grain at government expense in Rome.

According to the restrictive legislation passed after the fall of Marius, such a package of legislation was clearly unconstitutional and proved to be Drusus' undoing. At least a legal handle was found to move on grounds of a basically more deeply felt opposition. An overwhelming Senate majority, aroused already by the court reform, was doubled in face of the pending grain bill and particularly the agrarian bills. Here the well-to-do Italian provincials felt their property endangered as much as did the Roman aristocracy. Drusus hoped to meet their opposition by promises to extend Roman citizenship rights to the Italian allies. Presumably in perfectly good faith, he had given assurances in this respect which he was unable to honor. Yet the mere attempt to push forward on the citizenship question appeared to the Senate probably even more dangerous than the bulk of the illegally passed reform legislation. In a conflict with the protesting consul L. Marcius Philippus, Drusus initially still had the feeble support of a timid Senate behind him. He lost it when he raised the citizenship issue. Like the Gracchi and Marius before him, Drusus was not averse to the use of unlawful means for what seemed to him laudable aims. Again like his predecessors, but very much unlike the coming dictator Sulla, he shrank from large-scale open civil war. The outcome had only two alternatives, exile like that of Marius, or violent death, as was the fate of the Gracchi, Saturninus, and Glaucia. Judging by the precedents of the revolutionary period, the latter outcome was more likely. Violent death was, indeed, in store for Drusus.[34]

The death of Drusus may not have been the primary cause, but it certainly was the main signal for the outbreak of the so-called Social War, started by the frustrated Italian allies on the issue of citizenship rights. In a wider sense this was the beginning of the chain of revolutions which did not end even with Caesar's reform but only with Augustus' victory over Mark Antony and Cleopatra between 31 and 29 B.C. During this period, the most stormy and at the same time the most pregnant with new ideas in the history of the imperial republic, there were a number of factors that preserved and extended the Gracchan revolution. There were other, and major ones, which restored the pre-Gracchan institutions. Thus the Social War with the allies to the north and south led to the grant of Italian citizenship rights in a more comprehensive way than that envisioned by the Gracchi. The brutal vengeance of Marius after his brief comeback, and his death in 87, on the other hand, only promoted the dicta-

[34] Appian, II, Bk. I, chap. 5, 35–37. Mommsen, III, 220 ff.; Bloch and Carcopino, pp. 349 ff.; Marsh, pp. 94 ff., 417 f.; Scullard, pp. 64 ff., 392 f.; Kornemann, I, 487 ff.; Ferrero, I, 88 f.

torship of Sulla. The attempts by the consul Lucius Cornelius Cinna to push the citizenship question further, by irresponsible promises and violence against the senatorial establishment, had the same effect. It reestablished the senatorial social order around a full-fledged political dictatorship, which Mommsen, with his emphasis on political action, perceived as a new restoration.[35] The corn laws were rescinded entirely. Above all, the great powers of the tribune, the foundation of the Gracchan breakthrough into modern history, were voided. True enough, they were restored by Pompey and Crassus less than two years after the retirement of Sulla, one of the very few genuine dictators in Western history who did not die in his boots. Although Sulla's reform of the judicial system endured in regard to content and the procedure of civil and criminal law in general, the jury system in matters politic was now revised again by a compromise that favored the knights against the senatorial establishment. Altogether, under Pompey the knights increased their power, particularly because of the expansion of the tax-farming system in the provinces.[36] On the other hand, the distribution of land to the veterans was only resumed by Caesar under the First Triumvirate in the year 60 B.C. The whole reform program of Caesar in regard to the debt moratorium for small farmers, the establishment of new colonies in Italy, Gaul, Greece, and across the seas in Africa followed truly the Gracchan pattern. Even the reduction of the distribution of free corn in Rome—resumed on the Gracchan scale in 73 B.C.—does not contradict this.[37] In all likelihood this later curb is to be interpreted as gentle pressure to urge the landless city proletariat to become colonial farmers with citizenship rights. The transformation of the Senate into a broader, less class-conscious body should secure the passage of these reforms. Obviously Caesar's manifold plans and actions reach, in various fields of provincial administration and, indeed, in the overhauling of the whole governmental structure, far beyond the scope of the Gracchan designs. Yet most of these sweeping reforms were introduced only after Caesar had established an outright dictatorship in the last two years of his life, and they were revised, extended, and above all stabilized only in the following generation under the monarchical regime of Augustus.

[35] Mommsen, IV, 37–87; even on these grounds differences in degree of stringency as compared with the regime after the death of the younger Gracchus should be obvious.

[36] Scullard, pp. 88 ff.; Marsh, pp. 132 f., 149 ff., 336 f.; Mommsen, IV, 88 ff.; Taylor, *Party Politics in the Age of Caesar,* p. 103.

[37] Bloch and Carcopino, pp. 489 ff., 675 ff.; Scullard, p. 94; Marsh, pp. 141 ff.; Kornemann, I, 568 ff.

What does it all add up to? There is little disagreement that the original system (A) covers the period in which the Great Power position of the Roman republic was gradually but firmly established, that is, from the destruction of Carthage to the near domination of Greece and the completion of the conquest of Spain. Doubts begin to rise with the analysis of the Gracchan era as intermediate system (B). It could be held that the Gracchan revolts were neither comprehensive nor lasting enough to be classified as full-scale revolution. This argument, technically not without merit, does not seem quite convincing. Because of the peculiar status of Rome, which represented not only the core city of the republic but in more than one way the republic itself, the Gracchan insurrections might well be rated as a true revolution. In this respect the lasting effect of the uprisings outweighed by far their limited territorial sweep and their relatively brief duration.

Roman history, beginning with the Gracchan period, moved faster and faster through political and social change until the rise of the Augustan age a century later. If we take a long-range view over generations rather than decades or years, we can easily trace a development in the direction of the extension of citizenship rights, distribution of land, gradual social equalization, first between Rome and the provinces within Italy, then in Europe, outside the peninsula, and soon across the sea. These developments are accompanied by the transition of the aristocratic republic, with limited features of direct and representative democracy, to dictatorship and finally to a kind of bureaucratic monarchical system. Yet if we look at the same chain of events at short range, we see a rather confusing up-and-down of socially progressive and reactionary measures. The picture is not made clearer by the fact that dictatorial methods are more often than not related to the dynamics of a broadening social structure. Perhaps the one consistent trend conspicuous also for the short-range observer is the pattern of ever increasing violence.

Can this then be perceived as a genuine restoration period (C), which ought to be bound by the principles of preservation and reestablishment of the tradition of law? The case is not conclusive; it hinges on the interpretation of the events that took place between the death of Gaius Gracchus in 121 B.C. and of Marcus Livius Drusus in 91, just about a generation later. During that period the senatorial establishment undoubtedly was returned to power, though, owing to the greater influence of the knights, not quite to the same undivided power. Extension of citizenship rights to the Italian allies was impeded but not yet voided. Only the African colonization project fell through entirely. The same curb—not yet a reversal—holds true for the distribution of land, which, owing to the problem of the veterans that was created by the military reforms of Marius, gained even some new impetus. The corn laws, though restricted, seemed to be bound to stay, since no administration, whether reactionary or radical-progressive could do without support of at least part of the city masses. Sulla's dictatorship proved to be truly a transitory exception that confirmed the rule.

Thus on the basis of content of change one might well argue that the thirty years after the suppression of the Gracchan revolution restored much of the pre-Gracchan social and political situation. At the same time this period absorbed a measure of change, or perhaps more correctly a spirit of social change, brought about by the Gracchi. Such development would be fully in line with our previous analysis of the restoration pattern.

Yet, and this is the crux of the problem, did these changes and the restoration of previous institutions come about in an evolutionary way? If not, did they at least establish stable conditions of government by law after a violent counterrevolutionary transition period? One might hold that the latter assumption is by and large true until the year 100, when Marius, contrary to law, was elected consul for the sixth time, a fact which could not be excused any longer on the grounds of national emergency. It is more difficult to accept the interpretation of stable conditions for the following decade until the assassination of Drusus. Violations of established constitutional law, in terms of its Roman meaning, accumulated and accelerated now. The violations were curbed, however, and the radical leaders, Saturninus, Glaucia, and Drusus were destroyed —although destroyed only by new unlawful violence. Nevertheless, in extent it was limited violence on the part of the radicals of any persuasion. Peace was on the whole preserved; riots in Rome did not assume the proportion of civil wars.[38]

By stretching the point we may thus possibly assume the existence of a restoration period until the death of Drusus and the concomitant beginning of the Social War, which led straight into a whole series of military dictatorships from Sulla through Pompey to Caesar. According to our thesis this means only the destruction and in no way the restoration of tradition. This holds as true for a dictator of Caesar's stature as for his petty Italian imitator two thousand years later.

At the time when republican institutions were already destroyed and

[38] The slave revolt in Sicily between 103 and 99 was not considered an Italian affair any more than were the previous risings in Pergamum or Numidia.

the country was waiting for the man on horseback to choose his time and place, the controversial restoration period had lasted at best for one generation. The death of Drusus in 91 B.C. seems to us the last justifiable terminal date. The success of the restoration could perhaps be reasonably expected because the pre-Gracchan generation was still active in public affairs. As we see it, their expectations were to be disappointed but not because of any inherent contradiction in the pattern of the restoration process itself. The rapid expansion of the imperial republic created problems pertaining to aristocracy, business, small peasants, veterans, city proletariat, and provincials, which could not be predicted either by theory or by previous pragmatic experience. Accordingly the restoration period and its institutions had no chance to stand the full test of the time of at least two generations. Tradition could have been secure only if the re-established institutions had survived for at least a new generation after the pre-Gracchan one had passed from the scene. This was not to be. Civil war and dictatorship severed the pattern of development that otherwise might have been expected.

Whether the post-Gracchan development can thus be classified as a true system of restoration must remain doubtful. I do not feel that this confession invalidates previous deductions of this study. It has never been claimed here that life must conform to classifications; on the contrary, I feel deeply and without any misgivings that classification has to yield here as always to the innumerable varieties of life.

The Great Transition

RESTORATION SITUATIONS FROM THE DECLINE OF THE ANCIENT WORLD TO THE HIGH MIDDLE AGES

The case studies which are sketched in the following four chapters have one basic feature in common. The distinctions between the three systems, the original, the intermediate, and the restored, are seen far less clearly than in the cases studied thus far. This is apparent particularly in the shifts in social conditions brought about by the intermediate system. In all the contingencies of prerestoration orders to be surveyed here—the decline of the early Byzantine Empire prior to the reign of Justinian, the decline of the Holy Roman Empire under the last Carolingians and its rise under the Saxon rulers, England between the Plantagenet and Angevin kings, and again the empire during and after the interregnum between the death of Frederic II and the reign of the first Habsburg king —it is impossible to sharply delineate the intermediate systems. Profound as are the changes in the social and political order from the preceding and following systems, they cannot be focused clearly within the setting of revolutionary regimes as in the Greek and Roman cases, or of demographic change as in the Jewish one. Differences may be sweeping, but they become blurred in time and space.

This phenomenon is in all four cases almost equally significant for the millennium between the dissolution of the Western Roman Empire and the destruction of the Eastern one, yet the same reasons do not attach in all cases. The early Byzantine Empire began to evolve at the beginning of the era of migrations of Germanic and Mongolian tribes across Europe. The Holy Roman Empire under the Saxon dynasty was still fairly close to the end of this period. In the first instance political boundaries were becoming fluid, and in the second they were not yet quite rigid. The transitions in England from the Plantagenets to the Angevin kings and in Germany from the Ghibellines to the Habsburgs are largely determined by very different, even opposite forces. Here we face not so much the flexibility of political boundaries as the rigidity of feudal or semifeudal systems. The sameness of the order in particulars becomes far more important than the overall changes in countrywide government. Only the evolution of the national states creates conditions in which we may study cases fully comparable, though of course not parallel, to those in ancient history.

CHAPTER X

The Justinian Restoration Situation

Original system (A)   395–430's

Intermediate system   430's to period between accession of Justin I (518) and
(B)   beginnings of reconquest of Italy (535)

Questionable restored   From between 518 and 535 to the Lombard invasion
system (C)   of Italy up to 571

It has been rightly said that the three main features of the Byzantine
Empire manifested themselves from its very beginnings, namely, imperial
tradition, Christian orthodoxy, and Greek culture. These were the permanent directing forces of Byzantine government, religion, and literature.[1] But the time element in regard to these beginnings leaves room for
controversy. For example, in three classics in the field of Byzantine history
we find three interpretations at variance with each other. Charles Diehl
initiates his brilliant study, *Byzantium: Greatness and Decline,* with the
words, "On May 11, 330, the day Constantine founded Constantinople
and made it the second capital of the Roman Empire, the Byzantine
empire was born."[2] Indeed, from a cultural point of view it can be
argued that the division of the Roman Empire and the establishment of
the Eastern Roman Empire preceded the political partition by two
generations. Edward Gibbon in *Decline and Fall of the Roman Empire*
fully supported the traditional view that the Eastern Roman Empire was
established at the time of the death of Theodosius the Great, A.D. 395,
when his elder son Arcadius was made emperor (and Augustus) in the
East, and the younger, Honorius, was elevated to the same dignity in the
West. Gibbon asserts, "The division of the Roman world between the
sons of Theodosius marks the final establishment of the Empire of the
East which, from the reign of Arcadius to the taking of Constantinople
by the Turks, subsisted one thousand and fifty-eight years in a state of
premature and perpetual decay."[3] In this statement he makes two basic
assumptions. For one, he prejudged his case in the evaluation of the
Byzantine Empire in history; secondly, he saw a division as permanent
which indeed turned out to be lasting, but which was by no means perceived that way by contemporaries from the fourth to the sixth century

[1] Henry L. B. Moss, "The History of the Byzantine Empire," in *Byzantium: an
Introduction to East Roman Civilization,* ed. Norman H. Baynes and H. L. B. Moss
(Oxford, 1948), p. 3. This work will be referred to in the notes as Baynes and Moss.

[2] Charles Diehl, *Byzantium: Greatness and Decline,* trans. from the French, ed.
P. Charanis (New Brunswick, 1957), p. 5.

[3] Quotations from Edward Gibbon, *The Decline and Fall of the Roman Empire,*
are from the two-volume edition published by the Modern Library, New York. See
I, 1150.

B.C. The external facts support Gibbon in this instance to some extent, but they leave room for different views. John B. Bury, though he does not say so in so many words, indicates that he interpreted the partition at the death of Theodosius as a mere administrative division and that the concept of an undivided empire, with its center of gravity decidedly in the East, continued throughout the reign of Justinian.[4] This, to be sure, means only the preservation of the *idea* of an undivided empire, as distinguished from the undivided empire itself.

These divergences are of obvious importance for our purpose: to perceive a consecutive order of three systems culminating in the restoration of the empire under Justinian between 527 and 565. Bury does not question that the idea of a universal Roman empire as well as the political image of such an empire was reestablished under the great emperor. Whether emphasis should be on the idea of a reestablished unified empire or on the reality of a divided empire is controversial, however. In either case the question must be raised, Which events made Justinian's endeavors necessary? In other words, at what point of history was the established order really interrupted? In line with the approach of this study, which is based on political units rather than on socio-cultural orbits, the setting up of Constantinople as Constantine the Great's capital in A.D. 330 cannot be considered as the cutoff date of an original system. At that time merely the foundations for cultural prevalence of the Roman East over the West were laid. At the same time, for reasons of expediency and security, there was a shift of the center of gravity of political power and therewith, under existing conditions, the very contrary of a lasting political split. In this respect the orthodox division upheld by Gibbon is better substantiated than the views held by Diehl on the one side or Bury on the other. Does then the administrative partition in A.D. 395—rather than what might be called the mere gravitation toward the East indicated by the establishment of the Eastern capital in A.D. 330—determine the end of the original system (A) and the beginning of the intermediate one (B)? Certainly such an interpretation would be closer to political reality, yet not close enough to perceive three strictly divisible systems, the original, the intermediate, and the restored.

If we assume on a purely factual basis the emergence of the Byzantine Empire in 395 and the attempted reunification under Justinian with his accession as emperor in 527, the period of 127 years between would include the original as well as the intermediate system. It is, of course,

[4] John B. Bury, *History of the Later Roman Empire,* Dover edition, 2 vols. (New York, 1958). See I, 106 ff., 429 ff.; II, 25 ff.

conceivable to comprehend the Eastern Roman dominion, at least until the dissolution of the Western state in the late fifth century, as part of the disintegrating world empire. Yet such an interpretation, although defensible on the basis of tradition and institutions, would hardly take into account the realities of the political situation—in particular the perpetual crises in the East created by the invasions and settlements of Huns and Ostrogoths and by the Persian wars. If we see the years from 395 to the accession of Justinian in 527 rather as the initial phase of a new empire and even of a new civilization, these difficulties would not have to be faced, and we would be justified in assuming the rise of an original system in 395. Considering the fact that Justinian "played a very important part behind the throne during the reign of his uncle from the very beginning," that is, the rule under the emperor Justin from 518 to 527,[5] this period could be narrowed still further. Within that era the distinction, if not the break, between an original and an intermediate system must be perceived roughly between 430 and 460, on several grounds. The invasion of the Visigoths had been checked by Theodosius the Great shortly before his death, but under the feeble Arcadius they entered the Eastern Empire in force anew. Alaric's assault on Italy at the beginning of the fifth century from an Eastern Roman base meant presumably nothing more than temporary relief from a process of disintegration which had taken place since the death of Theodosius. Indeed, the previous incursions into the Balkans by the Visigoths were only the prelude for those of the Huns in the early thirties of the fifth century. By 441 they had crossed the Danube and threatened Constantinople and demanded tribute. Attila's invasion of Italy, about 450, after which the Huns returned to the Balkans, proved to be a lucky turn for the empire, insofar as it removed immediate danger. This event in no way indicated control or mastery of foreign invaders. At the beginning of the second half of the sixth century, the Ostrogoths claimed and secured the same rights and privileges in regard to land and tributes as the other conquerors before them.

Yet, Theodoric's invasion of Italy from the Balkans was in no way due to Byzantine pressure. This great ruler and his people were entrenched in the western Balkans as early as the 460's. His subsequent conquest and administration of Italy was presumably prompted very largely by the lure

[5] Alexander Vasiliev, *Justin the First* (Cambridge, Mass., 1950), pp. 92 ff.; Bury, II, 16 ff. Justinian held the dignity of consul as early as 521.

On Justinian's wars, see Procopius, in the edition by Henry B. Dewing, Greek text with English translation, 7 vols. (Cambridge, Mass., 1914-1940), Vols. I–V, *History of the Wars*. See Vol. I on the campaigns against Persia; Vol. II on the war against the Vandals; Vols. III–V chiefly on the Italian campaigns.

of spoils. In a sense his policy indicates also at the particular time that he favored the values of the Roman West. Except at the top level, the Roman institutions of the great days of the empire in the second and third centuries appeared to be more firmly preserved and entrenched in the West than in the East. Theodoric's westward move points in fact in more than one respect to the weakness of the Eastern Empire of his time. In conjunction with this must be seen the firm establishment of the Vandals in what is Libya today. It put an end to the Roman monopoly of naval supremacy in the eastern Mediterranean. The fortification of the ports, including the walling-in of Constantinople, was a consequence of these events.[6]

This weakening of the imperial body politic, which threatened dissolution between 430 and the 480's when Theodoric turned against Italy, shows, however, only the external aspects of the situation. Of equal importance are the disintegrating factors in matters ecclesiastic, which endangered not only the continued relationship to the Roman Church, but the domestic relations of state and church as well. The concept known as *Caesaropapismus* became a foremost issue. The whole problem of Arianism, only seemingly settled at the Council of Nicaea in 325, came in a different way to the fore again. Arianism was defeated once more at the Council of Constantinople in 381. Yet the first half of the fifth century, particularly the period between 430 and 450, was dominated by a passionate struggle over related issues of faith, church organization, and church and state relations. Nestorianism, the doctrine of the man born Christ who is only at his death elevated to divinity, originated in Constantinople and clashed with the Monophysitic views of the patriarchate of Alexandria, that is, of the nature of Christ as God and man merged into one. The Council of Chalcedon of 451 under the leadership of the Roman papacy rejected both views. The attempt to reconcile the views in the Eastern Church with Constantinople and Rome by the so-called Henoticon of 482 (the formula of unification) failed. The consequence was a schism between Rome and Byzantium that lasted technically until 579.[7] Yet the issue was not settled even then. At the fifth ecumenical council of Constantinople in 553, Justinian, formally in agreement with the Roman

---

[6] Charles Diehl, *History of the Byzantine Empire,* trans. from the French (Princeton, 1935), pp. 6 ff.; Bury, I, 213 ff., 240 ff., 265 ff., 488 ff.; Steven Runciman, *Byzantine Civilization* (Cambridge, 1956), pp. 25 ff.; see Procopius, Vol. II, Bk. III.

[7] See Vasiliev, pp. 132 ff.; Henri Gregoire, "The Byzantine Church," in Baynes and Moss, pp. 90 ff. See also Ernest Barker, ed., *Social and Political Thought in Byzantium* (Oxford, 1957), pp. 7 ff. See also John Barker, *Justinian and the later Roman Empire,* (Madison, 1966), pp. 53 f., 101 ff., 134 ff., 188 ff.

Church but actually working steadfastly for a compromise of his own choosing, admitted failure to end the struggle. The conflict between Monophysites, whose adherents included the empress Theodora, had not been resolved. Further attempts in the seventh century were no more successful, and in the eighth century the iconoclastic controversy accentuated the conflict. Religious conflict in the East and across the empire with Rome became, however, an issue of high politics as early as the mid-fifth century. In that sense we face here the second predominant issue of the intermediate period, allayed at times but not settled by Justin and Justinian.[8]

To major events in matters ecclesiastic and secular a great accomplishment should be added. We refer, of course, to the *Codex Theodosianus,* a legislative compilation in the 430's, the forerunner of the far greater legislative work under Justinian in the field of law.[9] But none of these factors, individually or combined, establishes a line of demarcation between the beginning of the Eastern Roman Empire under Arcadius (395–408) and the period of disintegration clearly visible under Theodosius II (408–450). Yet they indicate the introduction of a new transitory period of history. The empire, in its external aspects still firmly ruled by Theodosius the Great, showed ever more clearly the cracks in the walls, only superficially mended. This was even more conspicuous under Theodosius II's successors, particularly in the middle period of the fifth century. Afterward, external events alone, namely, the temptation of the disintegrating Western Empire for the so-called barbarian migratory people, offered temporary relief. The situation in the East was stabilized to a point. The real restoration, if restoration it can be called, commenced, however, only with Justinian's reign. The fact that the cultural and spiritual accomplishments of the preceding fifth century were much greater than the feeble political leadership would have led one to expect does not diminish Justinian's fame; it helps to explain his success in its positive and negative aspects.

The notion that the sweeping campaigns of Justinian in the West were not conquests for the sake of expansion but the restoration of an undivided Roman Empire, the partition of which was never acknowledged by the emperor, has been expressed by Charles Diehl. He in turn can refer to the authority of Procopius. "It was a principle of the Byzantine

---

[8] Gustav Krüger, *Handbuch der Kirchengeschichte,* 2d rev. ed. (Tübingen, 1923), pp. 234–250; Runciman, pp. 87–94; Gregoire, pp. 128 ff.; Bury, I, 348–359; Ernest Barker, pp. 36 ff.

[9] Bury, I, 231 ff.; see above all Constantin Hohenlohe, *Einfluss des Christentums auf das corpus civile* (Vienna, 1937), pp. 68 ff. and John Barker, pp. 166 ff.

chancellory never to admit the loss of any territory. . . . When in the second half of the fifth century, the Roman empire collapsed, Byzantium refused to regard the barbarian kings installed in Africa, Italy, and Gaul as anything but the Emperor's representatives: they were his deputies and servants. . . ." This tradition, preserved but by no means enforced by Justinian's predecessors, was now made real. "When the emperor judged the time ripe to reclaim [these territories] it was a matter not of conquest but of restitution. . . . Strangely enough the barbarians themselves accepted the principle. Eager to win the titles and insignia of Roman dignity and proud to govern their people as the Emperor's lieutenants, they bowed before the 'master,' received his commands and rebukes with humility, appealed to him as supreme judge and dazzled by the prestige of the Roman tradition, almost understood and acknowledged the legitimacy of the imperial claims." [10] Diehl rightly points to the successors of Theodoric as examples. He might have gone even further and pointed out that even the great Theodoric considered himself always a deputy of the emperor in the East. Despite his great power he refrained from such symbolic acts as dating official documents according to the years of his reign. He referred to his statutes merely as *edicta,* not as *leges,* since their issuance was the prerogative of the emperor. Furthermore, Theodoric had the head of the emperor, not his own, imprinted on his coins.[11] What had been true for the relationship between a regent of the stature of Theodoric and Justinian's relatively insignificant predecessors from Marcian to Justin became far more obvious under Justinian, and Diehl describes the situation aptly when he observes, "Constantinople was the capital of the universe, and the sovereign there enthroned was the universal emperor." [12] After the reconquest of North Africa, the twenty bitter years of eventually successful campaigns in Italy, and the victories on the Illyrian coasts and in southeastern Spain, all accomplished by the mid-fifties of the sixth century, Justinian could indeed believe "that in the reconquered provinces it would be easy to restore that perfect peace and good order which, in his eyes, were the mark of a truly civilized state, and that he could give to the inhabitants a replica of the Roman empire they had known in the past." [13]

It is easy to point out that this success was achieved at a higher price

---

[10] *Byzantium,* p. 177.

[11] Bury, II, 453 ff.; see also Berthold Rubin, *Theoderich und Justinian* (Munich, 1953), pp. 20 f. See also Joan M. Hussey, *The Byzantine World* (New York, 1961), pp. 19 f.

[12] Diehl, *Byzantium,* pp. 177 f.; Procopius, Vol. II, Bk. III, chap. 1. section 3.

[13] Diehl, *Byzantium,* p. 178; Moss, in Baynes and Moss, pp. 26 ff.

than could be justified politically by a prudent ruler. This appeared to be true in spite of the long-range cultural accomplishments in the West. Surely the great movements in the exarchate of Ravenna alone count on the positive side of the ledger. They do not alter the fact, though, that the Danube frontier was pierced under the onslaught of the Avars within two hundred miles of Constantinople, less than two decades after Justinian's death. The military frontiers of the empire were already in decay on all sides, but particularly in the north and east, at the time of his death. In an overall evaluation of Justinian's success and failure in foreign policy, even more critical, however, appears the situation in the East. Here we remember the indecisiveness of the first war against Persia until 532 and the failure of the second war, in which Syria, Armenia, and Mesopotamia were invaded by the enemy. The so-called fifty years' truce of 562 obliged Byzantium in fact to pay tribute to Persia. This may not have been decisive in itself, but it was the prelude to worse that would come. Syria in the early seventh century was first lost temporarily to Persia, and then by midcentury, together with Mesopotamia and the coast of Egypt and Libya (Carthage), it had to be surrendered to the Arabs.[14]

Important as these matters are for the destiny of the Byzantine Empire under Justinian and his successors, they are only indirectly related to the problem of restoration; it pertains primarily to the effort of the emperor to reestablish his authority in the West. Obviously this vast undertaking was severely hampered by the threat from the East, and in this sense the Eastern menace is part of the story in the West as well. The issue in the East was basically one of defense and preservation, under Emperor Heraclius I (610–641) one of temporary conquest, but it was never a matter of genuine restoration.

In the West the Huns had invaded the western Balkans as early as 540, and their forays came at times close to the capital itself. Slav tribes attacked the Adriatic coast of Illyria, and northern Greece was threatened. During the last years of Justinian's reign, new invasions of Huns and Avars shook the empire, though these were not yet permanent conquests. But three years after the emperor's death the Lombards marched into Italy from the north. "Byzantium was not capable of lasting resistance and confined itself to the defense of fortified places. . . . To be sure, it continued to hold important places [such as Ravenna, Naples, and in a sense, Rome] and could continue to exercise significant influence for centuries. Yet this could not obscure the fact that the heart area of West Rome was

[14] Diehl, *History of the Byzantine Empire,* pp. 26 ff., 40 ff.; Berthold Rubin, *Justinian* (Berlin, 1960), pp. 67 ff.; Hussey, pp. 24 ff.

held only for the sake of strategic key points and not for its own." [15] As
Gibbon summarizes the situation, "When the nephew of Justinian
ascended the throne, he proclaimed a new era of happiness and glory. The
annals of the second Justin are marked with disgrace abroad and misery
at home. In the West the Roman empire was afflicted by the loss of Italy,
the despoliation of Africa, and [at least indirectly] by the conquest of the
Persians." [16] Under Emperor Heraclius, Italy, except for the exarchate
of Ravenna, had to be considered as lost. The same was true for the
domains to the West and all the African possessions. Yet even the Balkan
territories of the empire were continuously exposed to attacks by Slavs,
Bulgars, and Arabs, as was Ravenna in Italy, by the Lombards. What is
more important, after the sixth century, when the efforts of Byzantium
were increasingly directed toward the defense against the Arab onrush
from the East, the traditional ties with the West were gradually weakened. The empire became fully hellenized and "although the Byzantine
Empire continued, until its last day, to call itself 'Empire of the Romans',
Latin was scarcely understood there, and the word Ρωμαῖοι meant
Greeks." Added to this must be the accentuation of the religious split
with Rome. All this helped "to drive the Byzantine Empire back toward
the East." Its main support became "Hellenism and the orthodox faith." [17]
The image of a united Roman Empire had withered away. The
restoration efforts of Justinian, as far as the reconquest of the West was
the issue, had barely lasted for two generations, from the death of the
emperor, at the very latest, to the latter phase of the reign of Heraclius.

Here we must bear in mind that a negative evaluation of Justinian's
conquests as a genuine movement toward restoration ignores the main
problem, which certainly is not the transitory duration of the emperor's
overall conquests. Not even the more specific issue of the conquest and
subsequent loss of Italy is the key proposition. The decisive factor is the
generally recognized motivation: reestablishment of the old undivided
empire within its historic boundaries. As long as this motive prevailed in
Byzantium—and this is generally affirmed—the restoration idea had to be
taken seriously. This holds true regardless of the question of its lasting
success.

There is agreement, by and large, on two counts; one is that Justinian's
foreign policy in its long-range effects was at best highly controversial.

[15] Rubin, *Theoderich und Justinian*, pp. 71 f. See also Diehl, *History*, pp. 26 f.
See also John Barker, pp. 215 f. and Kurth Groh, *Geschichte des oströmischen
Kaisers Justin II* (Leipzig, 1889), pp. 78 ff.

[16] Gibbon, *Decline and Fall*, II, 393. See also J. Barker, pp. 216 ff., Groh, pp. 87 ff.

[17] Diehl, *History*, pp. 49, 50.

His short success in the West had to be paid for by more serious setbacks in the East, or—as later in the case of the Arabs—defeat in the East led to disaster in the West as well. This negative evaluation leads to the second generally held conclusion, that the uncontested greatness of Justinian's achievements lay primarily in his domestic administration. This opinion suggests that the concept of a Justinian restoration can be based primarily on the domestic factor.

Such a view is not held in this study. The domestic administration of Justinian had its supreme achievements. At least some of them may be recalled here. Foremost is the compilation of the *Corpus Juris Civilis,* which spanned his whole reign from the convocation of Tribonian's commission in 528 to the publication of the *Novellae,* Justinian's own legislation, in 565 at the end of his rule. Equally spectacular though not equally important for this discussion were the monuments of art, particularly architecture, to wit the Hagia Sophia in Constantinople and the great churches in Ravenna. Notable also was a reform of the civil service which reestablished in the provinces the distinction between civil and military administration. The office of consul disappeared, having outlived its historic meaning and significance. Much of this reform work resulted from the consideration that defense needs required a more efficient administrative organization. Related to this was the building of extensive frontier fortifications and the improvement of communications. This did not preclude the promotion of civilian activities in the fields of industry and commerce.[18]

Least successful was the emperor's domestic reign in Church affairs, where he struggled vainly to maintain the unity of the Church in line with the doctrines of Rome. Attempts to check Monophysitism by outright suppression during the first part of his reign failed, as did later attempts to appease the Monophysites to win their favor and to arrive at the same time at a compromise on the issue with Rome. As Diehl puts it, this course "for more than twenty years (543-565) convulsed the empire and provoked schism in the Western Church, without bringing peace to the Orient." [19] Undoubtedly in matters ecclesiastic the emperor was less successful than some of his predecessors, in particular the emperors Zeno

[18] Diehl, *History,* pp. 28 ff.; Baynes and Moss, xxx ff.; Bury, II, 334 ff.; Gibbon, II, 341-382; Procopius, *Buildings,* Vol. VII, particularly Bk. I. See also M. Andreades, "The Economic Life of the Byzantine Empire," and "Public Finances," both in Baynes and Moss, pp. 51 ff., and pp. 71 ff. See also Wilhelm Ensslin, "The Emperor and the Imperial Administration," in Baynes and Moss, pp. 268 ff.

[19] Diehl, *History,* pp. 34 f. See also Gregoire, "Byzantine Church," in Baynes and Moss, pp. 94 ff., 100 ff.

and Anastasius I, or Constantine IV a century after him. The issue here is not so much what side the emperor took personally in matters of faith, but the extreme position of a Caesaropapistic attitude itself. According to this, he could determine doctrinal matters from the throne.[20]

A review of these remarkable feats, whether commendable or not, leads to clear-cut conclusions, provided we except religious matters. Justinian's great legislative reforms, which secure his place in history more than anything else, were by and large an act of preservation, having been initiated by Theodosius II a century before. They represent not the restoration of a broken tradition in the field of law but the successful attempt to maintain, guard, expand, and systemize the legal heritage of a thousand years. Within that treasure the last part of the *Corpus Juris,* Justinian's own legislation, the *Novellae,* is by no means the most important. We face here a sublime act of protection and further development of a great cultural heritage. Its significance as such was never challenged within the Roman civilization. In other cultural achievements of the reign, so eloquently, yet perhaps against his own volition, transmitted and exemplified by Procopius, originality rather than preservation seems to be the foremost trait, particularly in the formative arts. Justinian's primary administrative reform, the merger of civilian and military administration, indicates a more or less radical deviation from the established tradition rather than its revival. In questions of ecclesiastic policy and religion, the result seems inconclusive. After the emergence of Arianism in the fourth century, matters were in flux. It is true that Justinian upheld the Christian imperial tradition of two centuries, broken only by Julian "the Apostate" in the fourth century. Nevertheless, the results of his rule in this domain do not allow any unequivocal association with either Rome or the sectarian movements in the East. No case for restoration in domestic matters can be built on Justinian's reign.

Here we return to the key issue of the restoration problem, that of foreign policy, although Justinian naturally could not see it as anything but a problem of comprehensive imperial relations. There is widespread agreement in the literature that he wanted to reestablish the greatness of the Roman Empire. Yet little attention has been paid to whether he worked for a genuine restoration as defined in this study. Perhaps a psychological interpretation suggests an explanation. The Byzantine emperors after Arcadius did not rule the Western Empire *de facto,* but at the same time

[20] On the religious issue see Krüger, *Handbuch,* pp. 232 ff.; Diehl, *History,* pp. 33 f., 38 f., 45 f.; Gregoire, in Baynes and Moss, pp. 100 ff.; Bury, II, 360 ff.; Gibbon, II, 489 ff.

they were not quite aware of its actual loss. They believed themselves still to be sovereigns of a universal dominion; its administration happened to be vacant in the West. Justinian, the ruler who did most to reestablish this unified rule, was at the same time the one emperor who was keenly aware that the division between East and West meant something more than mere lack of law enforcement in the West by the East [21] Hence his genuine efforts for restoration, not because he did not realize the permanent character of the partition, but precisely because, recognizing it, he wanted to undo an apparently irreversible trend of history.[22]

If we take a long-range view, Justinian seems certainly to have failed, and in all probability where nobody else could have succeeded. Yet the emperor's daring and unstable attempts to achieve a controversial kind of restoration in the West, linked to his legal and administrative reforms and the cultural renaissance in the East, have secured his place in history. Restoration is only one path to greatness and by no means the most obvious. Failure to restore must not be equated with either the failure to preserve or the failure to achieve. This is illustrated by Justinian's genuine efforts and indifferent means to bring about restoration.

[21] See in this sense also Henri Pirenne, *A History of Europe,* trans. from the French (New York, 1936), 41 ff.

[22] The idea of restoration in Justinian's reign is touched upon briefly, and rejected, in Hans W. Hansing, *Kulturgeschichte von Byzanz* (Stuttgart, 1959), pp. 77 ff., and for insufficient reasons. Justinian, according to Hansing, was interested primarily in world politics and not merely in the rule of the Mediterranean area. As to the Roman image in Justinian's personality and reign, see Moss in Baynes and Moss, pp. 7 f.; Diehl, *History,* pp. 19 f.; Percy N. Ure, *Justinian and His Age (Harmondsworth,* 1951); Rubin, *Justinian,* pp. 3 ff.; Rubin, *Theoderich und Justinian,* pp. 63 ff.; Oskar Halecki, *The Millennium of Europe* (Notre Dame, 1963), pp. 37 f.; J. Barker, pp. 208 f., 241 f. Of these authors Rubin and Halecki stress the failure of Justinian's Western Great Roman policy as foregone conclusion.

CHAPTER XI

Ottonian Renovation and Restoration

CHRONOLOGY

(768) 771–814	Reign of Charlemagne
800	Charlemagne's coronation as emperor in Rome
843	Partition of the Carolingian empire by the treaty of Verdun
843–911	Steady weakening of the Eastern Carolingian empire under the later Carolingians. Brief rally under the reign of Arnulf of Carinthia (887–899). Decline continued to the election of Henry, Duke of Saxony, as king in 919
915	Berengar of Friuli crowned emperor in Rome
962	Otto the Great crowned emperor in Rome. Restoration of the Holy Roman Empire concept
Original system (A)	800–915, from the coronation of Charlemagne to the coronation of Berengar
Intermediate system (B)	915–962, from the coronation of Berengar to the coronation of Otto I
Restored system (C)	Beginning in 962, continued in political terms until 1806; but decline of idea of Christian world empire after tenth century

The problem of restoration in the Justinian era revealed a situation in which symbolic and traditional values were of high significance in the political power struggle between Christian East and West for the in-

186

heritage of the Roman Empire. Compared with these developments at the beginning of the period of Germanic and Mongolian invasions, we face a new problem of restoration soon after the end of the great migrations, when the importance of symbols and rituals of traditional power had increased even further. Because of a nostalgic look back to a truly imperial, more glorious, and in many ways more civilized past, a gulf gradually developed between the reality of power and the unreal semblance of its symbols. The less the former meant now in matters politic, the more weight seemed to be attached to its symbols as the paraphernalia of a divinely ordained sovereignty.

A very brief summary of these realities of power in the early Middle Ages in Central Europe, as seen by those who had looked to the reconstruction of the past, is in order. Charlemagne's reign (771–814) extended the rule of the Frankish empire to the Germanic territories east of the Rhine. Moreover, his regime continued and expanded a process of administrative centralization and judicial supervision initiated under his father, Pepin the Short (747–768). It furthered also a system of higher learning for an elite according to a pattern which has been followed by many a great conqueror. Whether these cultural changes went far enough to justify the term Carolingian renaissance is a question which does not have to be taken up here, for this rather limited renaissance has little connection with the problem of restoration to be discussed. Also of limited significance in Charlemagne's great reign is the famous coronation as Roman emperor of a renewed Christian empire by the pope, on Christmas day of the year A.D. 800, *if* the ceremony implies immediate political objectives.

No doubt about it, the coronation, to be surveyed here from the more important angle of ideology, helped to secure such political objectives as well. Charlemagne assured himself that the establishment of the papal states through the endorsement of Pepin—a strange confirmation of the apocryphal Constantine donation of the fourth century A.D.—would not seriously conflict with his own power in Italy. Yet these objectives, as well as the pacification of the Langobards, were secured by Charlemagne in the eighth decade of the eighth century and were merely confirmed now. Claims for the reunification of the empire in the West as directed against Byzantium, and a dedication to the principles of united Christian government, at least in the Occident, could certainly not be considered to be objectives of political reality.[1] Charlemagne's own, presumably sober

[1] See Heinrich Fichtenau, *Geschichte des Mittelalters* (Vienna, 1947), pp. 94 ff., and by the same author, *The Carolingian Empire: the Age of Charlemagne,* trans.

evaluation of the action is supported by the fact that in the summer of 813, one year before his death, he ordered his oldest son, Louis the Pious, to crown himself in the father's presence in the cathedral of Aix-la-Chapelle as co-regent and future heir to the imperial dignity. No commitment whatsoever to a future papal coronation in Rome was requested.

Nevertheless, the significance of Charlemagne's coronation should by no means be denied. It points as much to the future as to the past. Yet whatever may be its meaning in other than purely spiritual and ideological terms, there can be no question that the transaction had little relation to restoration as defined in this study. The Frankish empire of Charlemagne, it is true, strengthened and expanded the Roman tradition preserved by Syagrius, the late fifth century Roman administrator of Gaul in the north, after his defeat by Clovis. Yet the Merovingians and the Carolingians before Charlemagne did not preserve a pure Roman institutional order. They inherited domains in which Roman civilization was already thoroughly mixed with that of Frankish and Celtic tribes. Charlemagne could not restore a Roman civilization whose image, though not its remnants, had been lost for well over two centuries. The new emperor, Charlemagne, continued, however, to accelerate and extend the buildup of a new social and political order of mixed ethnic background.

Soon after his death its decline began and gathered momentum within a generation. Here we do not refer so much to the feeble reign of Louis the Pious and the subsequent treaty of Verdun of 843, which sanctioned the tripartition of the empire. This event might conceivably have helped toward the reorganization of its Eastern, purely Germanic part. The contrary was true. Pressure by Norsemen and by Slavic and, later, Turanian tribes, feeble rulers, and the concomitant emergence of the tribal duchies, saw the empire of Charlemagne virtually destroyed at the beginning of the tenth century when the Carolingian dynasty died out. The election of

from German (New York, 1957), pp. 47 ff.; Ferdinand Lot, *The End of the Ancient World and the Beginning of the Middle Ages* (New York, 1961), p. 253; Henri Pirenne, *Mohammed and Charlemagne,* trans. from French (New York, 1930), pp. 232 ff. The older interpretations, such as that by Wilhelm von Giesebrecht, *Geschichte der deutschen Kaiserzeit,* 4th ed. (Braunschweig, 1873), Vol. I, Part I, pp. 122 ff., in line with the national trends of the historiography of the early second German empire, perceive here a particularly great ideological and political significance. See also in *Universalstaat oder Nationalstaat, Macht und Ende des ersten deutschen Reiches,* ed. Friedrich Schneider, 2d ed. (Innsbruck, 1943), the introductory essay by the editor, pp. xi-xxxvi, which deals with the concepts of Heinrich von Sybel, Julius von Ficker, and Georg Waitz.

the most dynamic of the tribal dukes, Henry the Fowler, of Saxony, father of Otto the Great, as German king in 919, however, prepared the ground for change. By the end of Henry's reign in 936, a firm royal authority was reestablished, Magyars and Wends were checked in the east, and Lorraine in the west was regained for the Eastern Frankish kingdom.

Thus one might say that the authority of the state, as established by Charlemagne, was renewed after a generation of decline under Louis the Pious and after two subsequent generations of gradual but eventually checked disintegration. These developments represent restoration in our terms as little as does the renovation of the idea of empire under Charlemagne. Social changes during that period were neither radical enough nor sufficiently lasting in influence to allow us to speak of a genuine intermediate system. The profile of government under the later Carolingians was not clearly set off from that of the able earlier Carolingians. Furthermore, restoration should mean something more than return to power that has lapsed. If we refer to the political change that took place in the transition period between the rule of the Carolingian and the Saxon houses in Germany, it is in order, first, to trace the political setting germane to this discussion and, more important, to show that a restoration process of a very different kind, with politics on a very different level, may overlap and coincide with rather mundane changes like those sketched above.

This second process pertains to the idea of renovation of the Roman Empire, revived though not initiated in Germany by Charlemagne. If it appeared in a rather loose relationship to practical political objectives in the ninth century, it showed very real political, not merely symbolic spiritual, significance in the tenth century. As Gerhard B. Ladner puts it,

> Renovation of the empire, accompanied by age old tradition of ruler worship and of the eternal rejuvenation of Rome, became one aspect of Christian reform ideology. This imperial idea of Christian reform is inseparable from the Constantine Theodosian age. . . . The "Christian empire" was to live on as an important conception sui generis in the history of reform, of special significance also for the west in the Carolingian age and in the Ottonian-Salian age.
>
> In the Christian east the conception that the Christian empire by its very existence is close to the kingdom of God was most deeply ingrained. . . . The Christian king and emperor, in the east even more than in the west, was ipso facto considered as a minister of God on earth and . . . he saw himself and his actions in this light.[2]

[2] Gerhard B. Ladner, *The Idea of Reform* (Cambridge, Mass., 1959), pp. 118 f.

As Henri Pirenne observes, "There is no justification for doubting that the βασιλεύς who reigned in Constantinople still extended his theoretical authority over the whole Empire. . . . The Church above all, for which the Empire was a creation of Providence, could not dispense with him. The head of the Church in Rome and the city of Rome acknowledged him as the legitimate sovereign of the ecclesia."[3] This state of affairs was true as fully for the seventh century as for the Justinian age and, inasmuch as the exarch of Ravenna represented the Byzantine emperor, even for the first part of the eighth century.[4] Percy E. Schramm, following Paul Piur, Konrad Burdach's collaborator, perceives four main trends in this renovation issue: first, a religious evangelical one which demands individual as well as universal spiritual uplifting of man; second, a more practical trend working for ecclesiastic renovation, a renovation which still carries an apostolic message. The third tendency is messianic, directed toward the hope of a new world redeemer who will establish the kingdom of peace on earth. Here the idea of the state as the object of future transition and elevation moves gradually to the fore.

This idea definitely dominates the scene of the fourth trend, the Roman idea of renovation. It is linked to the image of the city of Rome and of those who consider themselves to be Roman. "This, however, was not a question of descent, but of political conviction. . . . What unites these people is the hope of renewing the Roman Empire." It may be perceived in ways of different breadth and depth, such as the recognition of Rome as head of the world, or just the universal recognition of Roman law. In any case, the messianic idea is the foundation of the Roman idea. It concerns such conflicting forces as the Romans and all those associated with the idea of a renovated Roman empire, above all "pope, emperor, and Byzantine basileus. Inasmuch as their objectives move in different directions, this means . . . that the history of these programs represents just as much a problem of political as of intellectual history of the Middle Ages." And here the further question arises whether this specific idea of renovation represents a continuous line of development, and if so, who supported it and how did political conditions determine the development of the idea in reality.[5]

It is this political emanation as product of a spiritual idea which concerns us here as pertinent to the problem of restoration. "The position of

[3] Pirenne, pp. 62 f.

[4] *Ibid.*, pp. 66 ff., 216 ff.

[5] Percy Ernst Schramm, *Kaiser, Rom und Renovation* . . . (Leipzig, Berlin, 1929), 2 parts in 1 vol. See Part I, pp. 4 ff., 6, 7. (This and the following quotations from Schramm were translated by the author).

Rome rested from the ninth to the eleventh century on the fact that all powers which included a universal tendency made claims on Rome and deduced from them their universal rights. Rome was not any longer the 'mistress of the world' . . . but the 'aurea Roma' was still the center of the earth," [6] the Christian earth, that is. "The oldest claims to Rome were held by the βασιλεύς τνῶ Ρομαίων, the Byzantine emperor. He was the successor to the Roman emperors, he was the heir to those rights restored by Justinian after the downfall of the Western Empire." Every territorial loss suffered since that time was merely tolerated as being transitory. "Yet since the Byzantines lacked the power for reconquest and the strength of the Carolingians to rule, and Italy had become exhausted by the middle of the ninth century, conflict between the two empires was no longer a dangerous possibility." [7] Signs of imperial renovation appeared and continued through the centuries: the re-emergence of the title of senator in the eighth, of *praefectus urbis* in the ninth, and above all, the reintro-duction of the dignity of *patricius* in the tenth. It was conferred "in the Orient successively and consecutively by the basileus, the pope, and by the Romans, and held by emperor, Romans, and southern Italians." [8] Renova-tion remained and increasingly became a renewable political reality, and to that extent it is a facet of the problem of restoration, which takes us back again to the Roman policy and within it to the coronation of Charlemagne. We must reexamine the action in the middle sphere between power politics and Christian rededication. This means renova-tion as the gradual and incomplete reintroduction of a genuine political idea. Inconsistencies and conflicting trends certainly played no small part. Colliding with the powerful idea of renovation of the empire was the continuing invasion of the rights of the basileus in Constantinople. Moreover, the image of the Roman and the Christian empires merged into one could be sustained to a point by the powerful personality of Charlemagne, conqueror, pacifier, and at the same time the creator of the Carolingian renaissance. The idea could not be upheld by his feeble successors. "Even the frequently observed wavering between the nomen-clatures imperator, Caesar, and rex is symptomatic of the fact that the empire was not yet deeply rooted in the Occident. It was not perceived as

[6] *Ibid.,* pp. 9, 29, 40; Lot, pp. 255 ff.; Fedor Schneider, *Mittelalter bis zur Mitte des dreizehnten Jahrhunderts* (Vienna, 1929), pp. 101 ff.

[7] Schramm, pp. 7 f. See also Wilhelm Ohnesorge, "Otto I und Byzanz," in *Fest-schrift zur Jahrtausendfeier der Kaiserkrönung Ottos des Grossen,* in *Mitteilungen des Instituts für österreichische Geschichtsforschung,* supplementary Vol. XXII, pp. 107 ff. (in the following quoted as MIÖG, XXII).

[8] Schramm, p. 63; see also pp. 57 ff.

an essential of a God-made world and historical order, either of the Christian as interpreted by the Church fathers, or of the Roman as comprehended by the Byzantines." [9]

Oscar Halecki sums up the situation brilliantly: "It must be remembered. . . that the Carolingian empire lasted only to the end of the ninth century, that is hardly one hundred years: the first restoration of the Roman empire failed even before the extinction of the Carolingian dynasty in the tenth century." [10] Although we do not consider Charlemagne's action in Rome as restoration in a political sense, we can fully agree with Halecki that it failed to have as yet the intended effect. "The conclusion seems clear . . . Charlemagne's coronation was indeed a significant precedent; but there is no continuity—only another crisis of the imperial tradition of the West—between the Carolingian empire, whose success"—and it was not even a success under Charlemagne—"depended on the outstanding personality of its founder, and the next restoration or *renovatio imperii,* which independent of the more or less prominent personalities of its rulers was to last for eight centuries and a half. The Carolingian age was, therefore, only the last phase of the preparation of the Christian community of Europe, a preparation which took a thousand years—the prologue of the second Christian millennium, the real millennium of Europe." [11]

This assumption of the emergence of a second millennium of Europe is a conclusion we will have to take issue with at a later point. Yet Halecki is certainly right that, in the short view, Charlemagne, realist that he was—though realist of imagination—did not think of a bellicose challenge to the Byzantine Empire. He probably was as fully aware as was Pope Leo III that the solemn transaction of the year 800 was fraught with the long-range potentialities of conflict between East and West and, closer home, between emperor and the Latin Church. "For all these reasons the establishment of the Carolingian empire, far from being a step in direction of the integration of Christian Europe, rather increased the multifold dualism which was such a permanent obstacle to that integration." [12]

In fact, after two major treaties of partition between the heirs of

---

[9] *Ibid.,* p. 15; see also pp. 12 f., 42 f.; Ohnesorge, MIÖG, XXII, pp. 108 f.

[10] Oskar Halecki, *The Millennium of Europe* (Notre Dame, 1963), pp. 51 f.

[11] *Ibid.* See also Fichtenau, *The Carolingian Empire,* pp. 60 ff.

[12] Fichtenau, pp. 53 f. See also Gibbon, *Decline and Fall of the Roman Empire,* Modern Library ed., II, 611 ff., who interprets the coronation as purely political from any angle and any power, pope and church alike. This rather extreme view, in line with Gibbon's general religious philosophy, is not accepted here.

Charlemagne, the concept of unity of the great Carolingian empire was definitely destroyed with the inglorious reign of Charles III, grandson of Louis the Pious. The following reign of Arnulf of Carinthia, a much abler man from the side lines of the dynasty, was restricted to the eastern part of Charlemagne's empire. Not unsuccessful in the defense against the Slavic Great Moravian empire from the east and the Norsemen from the west, he even secured the renewal of the tradition of a universal empire by his coronation in Rome in 896. Yet when he died in 899, every semblance of a claim to reunion under the leadership of the Eastern Frankish empire died with him. Moreover, the rule of the German branch of the house as witnessed by the following puppet king, Arnulf's son Louis the Child, was not secure east of the Rhine, let alone south of the Alps. This last Carolingian reign of a minor, who had ascended the throne at the age of six and died at eighteen, revealed the East Frankish state and its ruler as incapable of stemming the tide of Magyar, Slavic, and Norse invasions. Added to the unchecked external threat was the internal defiance against royal authority on the part of the rising stem duchies. The end of the Carolingian dynasty goes thus hand in hand with the paralysis of the Eastern empire manifest at the end of the ninth century and sealed by the death of the young king in 911.

Strangely enough, it was not the end, though, of the imperial line of Charlemagne. A grandson of the great emperor on the maternal side, the son of Louis the Pious's daughter Gisela, Berengar of Friuli, was to prolong it. His reign is in itself of limited significance. Involved in struggles for the domination of Italy against the Burgundian rulers, Louis from the Western Frankish Carolingian line and Rudolf of the house of Welf, Berengar died a defeated man, presumably by assassination in Verona, in 924.[13] Yet in 915 he could still prompt the pope to crown him emperor in Rome. Neither of the two German kings following Louis the Child—Konrad of Franconia (911–918) and the far more powerful founder of the Saxon imperial dynasty, Henry the Fowler (919–936)— managed to secure the coronation in Rome. Both were deeply involved— the latter more successfully than the former—in drives to reestablish some kind of German unity in the face of ducal rebellions and Magyar, Wendish, and Danish attacks. In fact, the necessity to defend Germany at home appertained also to the first part of the reign of Henry's great son, Otto I. Only during his second Roman campaign did he obtain the coronation as emperor by the pope in Rome, in 962. The lapse between

[13] Schneider, pp. 143 ff.

the imperial coronation of Berengar in 915 and that of Otto, to whose reign we will turn, is indeed the longest in the history of the empire until its dissolution in 1806.[14]

This fact, perhaps not too important in itself, assumes significance in the context of the restoration problem. As noted before, the coronation of Charlemagne, in its setting of time and place, cannot be considered as genuine restoration. Too long a period had elapsed since the disintegration of the Western Roman Empire, too different were the peoples and institutions involved, to make such an assumption feasible. Yet it is possible to consider the reign of Charlemagne, and particularly the renewal of the idea of a universal empire, as an original system in its own right. By the end of the ninth century this system had disintegrated. It was followed by an intermediate system, initiated by the coronation of Berengar in 915, and terminated by the new rise of the empire, culminating in the spectacular Roman coronation of Otto the Great in 962. In this sense we will have to consider a restoration process in which small men, such as most of the later Carolingians and Berengar of Friuli, played a part. And yet, inasmuch as the symbolic transactions related to Berengar and his forceful later successor, Otto I, show the rebirth of an idea as powerful in its future political implications as in its past spiritual meaning, a study of the problem appears justifiable.

The great reign of Otto I (936–973) had many facets, such as his successful enforcement of authority in the stem duchies, which now, to a large extent, came under the control of his family. Even more important was the defeat of the Wends and the final disposal of the Magyar danger by the middle of the tenth century. The enforcement of Otto's rule in Italy—never truly uncontested—and the control of the Roman Church by way of three campaigns between 951 and 972 were, from the point of *realpolitik,* not the most successful of his achievements, yet, culminating in the coronation of 962, certainly the most controversial and spectacular. If we take a long view, the situation looks rather different. In a genuine intermediate period in the first part of the tenth century, the imperial dignity not only had fallen into abeyance—it had been clearly denied to the German rulers. Its reestablishment is thus of great import. As Heinrich Mitteis points out, it was achieved by an empire which could not be called Frankish at that time. "The rule of the Italian kingdom and the incorporation of the curia

---

[14] The last imperial coronation in Rome took place in 1452 (Frederick III); the following, until 1531, were held in Aix-la-Chapelle, and then in Frankfurt. Yet at that time the symbolic act of coronation had lost its constitutive character entirely. The right to rule no longer depended on the ceremonial act of coronation.

into the imperial Church cannot be based any longer on the Carolingian Frankish rule by the Saxon emperors. The German empire needed for its legitimation a *renovatio Romani imperii,* a thought which Charlemagne had only taken up in a very transitory way in the first years of his rule as emperor."[15] In fact, we can justify the assumption that a seemingly transitory political initiative under Charlemagne was becoming a permanent establishment under Otto I. What is this then but restoration? "The renovatio of the year 962 pertained not to the Roman but to the Carolingian period; to restore the imperial dignity of Charlemagne was the leading thought of Saxonian policy in the coronation proceedings. The Roman imperial period played at the most an indirect part for Otto the Great as a prephase of the Carolingian era."[16] Numerous facts, however, point to the relation between Charlemagne's coronation and the revival of this Carolingian tradition by Otto. Unlike his father, Henry I, he had himself crowned king at the beginning of his reign, in Charlemagne's residence and residence cathedral in Aix-la-Chapelle. Pope John XIII, installed by Otto in 965 almost thirty years later, still referred to Charlemagne in a metaphoric sense as Otto's immediate predecessor.[17] There can be little doubt that Otto himself felt he had renewed the imperial dignity of the Carolingians, held in abeyance since 924. "Following the coronation he confirmed in relation to the pope in his name and that of his son and heir the pact" concluded with the Carolingian rulers since Pepin and Charlemagne, in particular Louis the Pious, Lothair I, and later from the western line, Charles the Bald.[18] This meant that in essence, until it was thrown out of balance by the investiture conflict in the eleventh century and the Hohenstaufen claims in the twelfth, a relationship existed between tiara and crown in the sense that "the emperor stood spiritualiter below the Pope but temporaliter above him."[19] Undoubtedly, this settlement was ruthlessly infringed upon by the repeated interference in papal elections on the part of Otto the Great, by his son,

[15] Heinrich Mitteis, *Deutsche Rechtsgeschichte,* revised by Heinrich Lieberich (Munich, 1960), p. 104 (author's translation). See also pp. 70 f., 83 f., 105 ff. See further Giesebrecht, *Geschichte der deutschen Kaiserzeit,* Vol, I, Part I, pp. 277 ff., 317 ff., 376 ff., 447 ff.; and recently, Percy Ernst Schramm, *Die Kaiser aus dem sächsischen Haus im Lichte der Staatssymbolik,* and Eugenio Dupre-Theseider, *Otto I und Italien,* both in MIÖG, XXII, 30 ff. and 53 ff., respectively.

[16] Schramm, *Kaiser, Rom und Renovatio,* p. 68; and by the same author, *Die Kaiser aus dem sächsischen Haus . . .* MIÖG, XXII, 33 ff.

[17] Schramm, *Kaiser, Rom . . . ,* pp. 68 f.; Schneider, pp. 185 f.; Giesebrecht, I; 2; 476 ff. Schramm, *Die Kaiser aus dem sächsischen Haus,* pp. 33 ff.

[18] Schramm, *Kaiser, Rom und Renovatio,* pp. 70 f., 21 ff.

[19] Mitteis, p. 105 (author's translation).

and in a different way by his grandson as well. Yet even without these distortions of the original agreement it is a fact that the concept of empire as reality (the *imperium merum*) stood now, and until the later Ghibelline period in the thirteenth century, as much in the foreground of political action as the idea of the universal empire, the *imperium mundi,* was intermittently in the foreground of political speculation.[20] In any case, whether universal or Central European empire, the concept was of a rule over many peoples, in part, of different national origins, though this factor was not fully realized. "When in 962 the occidental empire was refounded—though refounded to a more limited extent—it was this concept which acquired particular importance. . . . The emperor as lord over several, indeed many, peoples, was an image taken from historic reality, from which his uniqueness, his first rank among the princes of the Occident, resulted, as much as from the older claim to world rule, which had become devoid of meaning."[21]

As to the significance of this transaction in the general frame of European history it is not easy to find a middle ground between the sweeping ideological interpretation of Halecki and the purely political one of Bryce. Halecki sees in the coronation of 962 not "a return to the recent but disappointing experience of the ninth [century], but rather to the remote but unforgotten and much more inspiring tradition of the Roman empire of the first centuries A.D. It was this empire in its Christian form and interpretation, an empire much more universal than the Carolingian had ever been, and which was expected to last forever as the ultimate in the succession of world empires, that the representatives of the imperial idea in its Roman form wanted to restore."[22] From here, according to Halecki, proceeds the concept of a second Christian millennium inaugurating a Christian community of nations "to be based upon the close cooperation between emperors and popes, the latter being freely elected in Rome among candidates of various origin. . . ." This idea failed, of course, even in Otto I's own time, primarily because of the emperor's inordinate demand to control papal elections and therewith to become master of the Church. Yet this arbitrary action did not achieve the pacification even of Italy, let alone of the Christian world.[23] And it should be remembered in this context, and not quite in line with Halecki's deductions, that the empire of Otto I, though firmer in structure

---

[20] Schramm, *Kaiser, Rom und Renovatio,* pp. 74 f.; Mitteis, p. 104 f.

[21] Schramm, *Kaiser, Rom und Renovatio,* p. 76.

[22] *Millennium of Europe,* p. 79; see also O. Halecki, *The Limits and Divisions of European History* (Notre Dame, 1962), pp. 131 f.

[23] Halecki, *Millennium,* pp. 80 f.

than that of Charlemagne, was much narrower in extent than the Frankish one prior to the partition. Should we therefore accept the sober interpretation offered by Bryce?

> The Holy Roman empire, taking the name in the sense which it commonly bore in later centuries, as denoting the sovereignty of Germany and Italy, vested in a Germanic prince, is the creation of Otto the Great. Substantially, it is true, as well as technically it was a prolongation of the empire of Charles; and it rested . . . upon ideas essentially the same as those which brought about the coronation of A.D. 800. But a revival is always more or less a revolution: the one hundred and fifty years that had passed since the death of Charles had brought with them changes which made Otto's position [within a territorially narrower empire] in Germany and Europe less commanding and less autocratic than his predecessor's . . . [whom he followed not as] mere successor after an interregnum, but rather [as] a second founder of the imperial throne in the West.[24]

Thus a broad view, that of Halecki, based on a concept of empire derived predominantly from spiritual images, faces another one, Bryce's, which rests primarily on the German and Italian political union under a Germanic emperor. The significance of the idea of Christian universalism is by no means denied here, but the emphasis is clearly political. Before we can make a decision on this issue, we must ask: How long did the Ottonian restoration last in either terms? Only on the strength of an answer to that question is a satisfactory response to the more basic problem possible.

The ten-year reign of the great emperor's son Otto II (973-983), at a time when the so-called Ottonian cultural renaissance had already passed its high tide,[25] was filled with very real yet limited matters of internal and external aggression. A revolt by the Duke of Bavaria in the south was crushed, a French attack in the west checked, but a Danish invasion from the north was still under way when Otto died. Unsuccessful also were the emperor's attempts to dislodge the Saracens from southern Italy. Whatever the ambitions of Otto II, both the time and the opportunity were lacking to pursue the objectives of the idea of empire much further.

Whether external factors were in this respect more opportune during the following brief reign of his son, the young Otto III, may be open to serious question. Yet there can be little doubt that through the strength of

[24] James Bryce, *The Holy Roman Empire* (New York, 1914), pp. 80 f.; see also 77-140 *passim*. See further Geoffrey Barraclough, *The Origins of Modern Germany* (New York, 1963), pp. 44 ff.

[25] For a comparative evaluation of Carolingian and Ottonian renaissance, decidedly in favor of the latter, see Halecki, *The Limits and Divisions*, pp. 147 f.

an unusual personality and unusual circumstances, the idea of a universal empire stood, for a few hectic years, at the very core of history. There is no parallel in the happenings since the coronation of Charlemagne in A.D. 800 and little in the developments from the eleventh century onward. Otto III (983–1002), first under the tutelage of his Byzantine mother Theophano and, after her death, of his grandmother Adelheid, the widow of Otto the first, began his own reign only in 996. External events of this restless regime of a youth who felt himself to be a Greek and wanted to be a Roman, led to no promising beginnings, let alone permanent solutions. Considered a German, if not a German barbarian, by the Italians, he found greater resistance in Rome than had his father and grandfather. The two popes installed by him failed in their objectives. His cousin Bruno as Gregory V, the first German pope, did not succeed in driving the Cluniac reforms further. The second, the learned and astute Gerbert of Aurillac, former archbishop of Reims, as Pope Silvester II could not help his imperial friend in his schemes for a new universal Roman empire. A third companion, Adalbert, Bishop of Prague, who died a martyr's death in his attempts to convert the Prussians, as earlier the Magyars, was perhaps closest to Otto. All the same, Otto's Eastern policy remained a torso like his Western. What is decisive from our point of view, however, is the fact that this emperor had the idea of the universal East-West empire, the *imperium mundi,* steadily before him until his early death. He saw it in the plans of Charlemagne and paid homage to it when he had the tomb reopened in the year 1000. In the five-year reign of Otto III "the idea of Roman renovation had assumed a real significance for the whole empire and therewith indirectly for the whole of Europe. These matters . . . are differentiated by their dimensions and historical weight from everything else which during the two centuries from the end of the Carolingians to the investiture conflict pertains to the problems of emperor, Rome, and renovation." [26] The young mystic, the so-called *mirabile mundi,* by descent, tradition, and learning—imperial Roman and Byzantine—claimed that "Not to the Byzantines belongs the title 'emperor of the Romans,' but 'ours, ours is the Roman empire!' "

"Therewith the imperial court had decided to take a course from which the grandfather still had abstained. During the times of Otto I the official

[26] Schramm, *Kaiser, Rom und Renovatio,* pp. 87 ff. See also Schramm, *Die Kaiser aus dem sächsischen Haus,* in MIÖG, XXII, 46 ff.; Heinrich F. Schmid, *Otto I und der Osten,* in MIÖG, XXII, pp. 105 f.; Mitteis, pp. 104 ff.; Giesebrecht, I, 2, 670 ff.; Bryce, pp. 144 ff.; Halecki, *Limits and Divisions,* pp. 131 f., 147 f.

title was restricted to the word 'imperator.' . . . But now the Roman character of the occidental empire was fully affirmed. The Roman past . . . had become an essential part of the theory of justification [or perhaps legitimacy] according to which the imperium in the West stood for its claims." [27] In that truly ecumenical sense did the bull of 998 carry the imprint *Renovatio imperii Romanorum* supplemented by the title adopted in January, 1001, *Servus apostolorum*.[28] This means indeed the supreme union of secular and religious power under an emperor whose mystic and fervent dedication to his ideals and sweeping ambitions proved one thing clearly. Religious zeal did not mean here mere pretense for the sake of greater success in secular matters as it did among some of the outstanding rulers in the line of the Salian and Ghibelline emperors. Otto III's imperial religious exaltation and infatuation with a synthesis of the supreme powers under the cross and the orb was truly genuine. It has no full parallel in later German history. The reign of the Ghibelline Henry VI (1190–1197), it is true, brought once more the idea of the world empire to the fore, to perish again after his brief rule. Yet the great son of Barbarossa represented unequivocally the supremacy of secular rule. His world empire was distinctly meant to be of this world only. His Salian and Ghibelline predecessors as well as his Habsburg and Luxemburg successors, stood for the idea of a powerful Central European empire as the foremost but not the only empire in Christendom. Not even the empire of Charles V, on which the sun never set, is exempted from this statement. Wider in reality than any concept of empire that was ever materialized before or after, it owed its brief existence to specific historical contingencies and opportunities, not to a supreme idea like that promoted by Otto III.

Several interpretations are possible. Konrad Burdach, the great German literary historian whose views here represent many, believes that "The dream of a restoration of the imperium in its full ancient meaning was not materialized, but the idea on which it is based shone through the culture of the ages, moving it, alerting it, and seeding it." [29] In other words, there was a full revival of the concept of a universal Roman empire but in a Christian frame and with a Christian core. Achievement is doubtful but

[27] Schramm, *Kaiser, Rom und Renovatio,* p. 101; Karl T. Heigel, *Die deutschen Kaiser* (Stuttgart, 1880), pp. 67 ff.; Schneider, pp. 206 ff.

[28] Schramm, *Kaiser, Rom und Renovatio,* pp. 107 f., 147 ff., 157 ff.; *Die Kaiser aus dem sächsischen Haus,* pp. 47 ff.

[29] Konrad Burdach, *Die Entstehung des Romans,* quoted in Schramm, *Kaiser, Rom und Renovatio,* p. 187.

intent is clear. More mundane, in a comprehensive literature focused almost singularly on power politics pure and simple, is the interpretation of Geoffrey Barraclough:

> Even if contemporary letters and writings prove that Otto and his court were not unconscious of the glories of ancient Rome, such ideas did not directly influence Italian policy or imperial policy, which were dictated by events and circumstances calling for sober action.
>
> It is therefore credible enough, without having recourse to a legend of "Roma aurea," that Otto should, in 998, have set on his seal the famous inscription: *Renovatio imperii Romanorum,* and that a year later, in 999, we should find in his charters reference to the *restitutio rei publicae. Restitutio rei publicae* was, in the policy of the Ottonian government, the practical means leading directly to *renovatio imperii.* But *renovatio imperii* was neither more nor less than a revival and reform of Italian government. . . . The phrase *renovatio imperii Romanorum,* as used by Otto, was doubtless programmatic, but the programme it represented was not to restore the lost glories of ancient Rome, but to make the rights and powers of the ruler real and effective. [The phrase expressed Otto III's] policy and he was the first emperor from Charlemagne onwards . . . who set out to make his authority real. . . .
>
> There were therefore important differences between the imperial policy of Otto I and Otto III; but they were not . . . the difference between a "Saxon" and a "Roman" policy. . . . [Otto III's] imperial policy was more active than that of Otto I, but it was no less subordinate to German interests, and no less realistic. If it had been pursued to its logical conclusion over a period of years, it might have stabilized German government in Italy, and provided a firm foundation for the future.[30]

This evaluation is based on rather narrow grounds. First there is Otto's installation of two popes, the deposition of the *patricius* Crescentius—as more than merely honorary highest official in the city of Rome—on the emperor's first Italian expedition, and the cruel suppression of Crescentius and of the Roman nobles' revolt on his second. Such limited objectives should count little in a reign that intended not only to unite the Latin West and the Byzantine Southeast, but to convert the Northeast as well, and all this in a unique combination of Christian ascetic humility and imperial pride as the first servant of God, before pope and kings. Indeed, as Bryce observes correctly, "Short as was his life and few his acts, Otto III is in one respect more memorable than any who went before or came after him. None save he desired to make the seven-hilled city again the seat of dominion, reducing Germany and Lombardy and Greece to their rightful place of subject provinces. No one else so forgot the present to

[30] Barraclough, pp. 62 ff. See also Schmid, pp. 92 ff., 103 ff.

live in the light of the ancient order; no other soul was so possessed by that fervid mysticism and that reverence for the glories of the past, whereon rested the idea of the medieval Empire." [31]

In the reign of Otto III we face indeed the culmination and at the same time the termination of the drive for a world empire encompassing the secular and ecclesiastic institutions of Christianity. Ambition, determination to rule, desire for prestige, economic expansion, and what is commonly understood as plain imperialism may not have been lacking in this concept, but at the turn from the first to the second Christian millennium, they were surely secondary in nature. From here on, beginning with the reign of Otto's successor, Henry II, the situation is perceptibly reversed. The idea of the imperial Christian mission is not dead, but moves steadily, though at irregular intervals and speed, into the background.

Where does all this leave the concept of restoration? The Roman policy of Otto the Great, culminating in his coronation of 962, put the idea of the Christian Roman empire on a steady course. It had truly restored and strongly enforced the notion of the Christian Roman empire initiated by Charlemagne and continued with indifferent results by his successors until the great vacuum between the imperial coronation of Berengar of Friuli in 915 and that of Otto the Great in 962. A genuine intermediate system—genuine because it meant the true paralysis of the idea of a great Christian empire—had come to an end. Does the reign of Otto I, in particular his coronation, establish a genuine restoration? The answer is yes, as far as the emergence of a Christian world empire linked to the Roman tradition as *primus inter pares* of the nations of the earth is concerned. This concept, during its more than eight hundred years of uninterrupted history until 1806, began gradually to fade and decline in importance—particularly after the sixteenth century. Yet all this does not lessen either the original or the long-lasting significance of the idea. In this sense the policy of the first Otto had indeed established a genuine restoration. Yet there is the even more far-reaching idea of the universal Christian *imperium mundi,* not as the first among many but as the only one above the nations, above priest and laymen alike. Had Otto I really intended to establish such an empire? We do not know for certain; authoritative opinion attributes ambitious but less sweeping and speculative objectives to this powerful ruler and statesman who stood with his feet well grounded in reality. As to Otto II's short reign filled with internal and external conflicts, the issue is held in abeyance. For the reign of Otto III, prevailing opinion holds to the extensive, almost mystic and poetical

[31] Bryce, pp. 147 f.

interpretation which is generally rejected for the rule of his grandfather.

Hard and fast decisions based on fact are impossible here, of course. It must suffice when we say that according to even the most generous interpretation, the idea of a universal empire had a continuous reflection on earth, that is, in the Holy Roman Empire, not later than the beginning of the second millennium. It flares up from time to time, in particular at the end of the twelfth century, but it lacks steady, uninterrupted development. Thus one cannot proceed beyond the uncontested reality of the Holy Roman Empire as the foremost Christian state in principle, though not in fact. The more far-reaching, more sublime idea of the Christian world empire under the sign of Rome in Christ represents an incomplete case of restoration. It remains, however, a case superimposed upon a very real political body.

CHAPTER XII

The Transition from the Norman to the Angevin Kings

CHRONOLOGY

1066	Norman conquest of England
1135	Death of Henry I
1135–1154	Reign of Stephen
1154–1189	Reign of Henry II

Original system (A)	1066–1135, era of the Norman kings
Questionable intermediate system (B)	1135–1154
Restored system (C)	Beginning in 1154; accession of Henry II, first Plantagenet (Angevin) king

The notion that a feudal system in the High Middle Ages cannot be understood in terms of a state structure can hardly be considered valid. Carl Stephenson's incisive observation is to the point: "By 'feudalism' . . . we properly refer to the peculiar association of vassalage with fief holding that was developed in the Carolingian Empire and thence spread to other parts of Europe. Insofar as this association was effected for governmental purposes, feudalism was essentially political. It should not be thought of as a necessary, or even usual, stage in economic history. Although feudal institutions presupposed certain agrarian arrangements, the latter were not themselves feudal. The manorial system could prevail for centuries, as it did in Britain, without leading to the feudalization of any local state. Nor should feudalism be described as a sort of anarchical force because its growth coincided with the disintegration of the Carolingian Empire." [1]

Georg Dahm and Heinrich Mitteis have emphasized the different trends which in this respect pertain to developments in Central and Western Europe. Developments on the continent, in Germany and France in particular, shed much light on the contemporary or subsequent course of events which this case study is concerned with. "In Germany feudal law had a dissolving effect or at least one working against decentralization." Yet this is not in itself based on the character of feudal law. "In many another country of Europe, in the East as well, and particularly in the West, in France and England, in Normandy and Sicily, indeed even in some German territories, feudal law worked consecutively in the sense of moving toward the unitary state." [2] Depending on which aspect of feudal law is more emphasized—the right of the lord or of the vassal—we perceive trends on the one hand toward unification and on the other toward the mere aggregation of fiefs. Their affiliation is frequently determined by arbitrary action and not necessarily by a growing organic coherence. No doubt about it, in Germany in the High Middle Ages, and indeed before, as early as the ninth century, the vassal and his rights were in the forefront of institutional development. The institution of sub-infeudation found its fullest development and its most complex form in Germany. On the highest political level the issue played a prominent part in English and French relations as well. [3]

The development of feudal institutions in the West followed a different course in the latter part of the early Middle Ages and the early part of the High Middle Ages. In Germany the king could not add a vacated fief to the crown lands but had to confer it again on a vassal; in France the king could incorporate it into his domains. These crown domains were in decline in Germany and on the increase in France. "In the feudal law of Central Europe the rights of the vassal gained the upper hand; they developed along the pattern of rule by nobility. In Western Europe the

---

[1] Carl Stephenson, *Medieval Feudalism* (Ithaca, 1956), pp. 14, 96. Francois L. Ganshof, *Feudalism*, trans, from the French (New York, 1961); see particularly pp. xxi f., 144 ff.; Heinrich Fichtenau, *The Carolingian Empire: The Age of Charlemagne*, trans. from the German (New York, 1957), pp. 135 f.

[2] Georg Dahm, *Deutsches Recht* (Hamburg, 1944), pp. 133 f.; Heinrich Mitteis, *Deutsche Rechtsgeschichte*, pp. 52 ff., 79 f., 113 ff. (quotations from these sources were translated by the author).

[3] Stephenson, pp. 38 f.; Ganshof, pp. 144 ff.; see also Charles Petit-Dutaillis, *The Feudal Age in France and England from the Tenth to the Nineteenth Century* (London, 1936), pp. 51 ff.

royal claims of the king as supreme liege lord won out. Feudal law paved the way here for the unitary state." [4] Mitteis sees the roots of the French development in a greater awareness of the concept of state in Roman times; in Germany the rise of the stem duchies favored the vassalage. These developments, of course, had their ups and downs. In Germany, under Otto I as early as the tenth century, under Henry III in the eleventh, and under Frederick Barbarossa in the twelfth, the power of dynamic great liege lords rose considerably. In France, on the other hand, royal power in the tenth and eleventh centuries became practically non-existent with the decline of the western Frankish Carolingian empire. This does not change the main features of the picture. The rise of royal feudal power in Germany remained erratic and outside the stream of steady development; the kings from the Saxon dynasty onward could entrench themselves only through indirect control of the stem duchies by members of the royal house rather than through outright centralization. In France a well set up, though still small, feudal state based on solid royal power was established at the beginning of the twelfth century in the reign of Louis VI (1106–1137). This royal power, until its destruction nearly seven centuries later, was never to lose control completely; soon enough it was to entrench and expand. True, France "in the tenth century disintegrated in a loose federation of fiefs, but just this strong development of feudal law allowed royal power later on to centralize the state from the position of the supreme liege lordship. In Germany, on the other hand, feudal law became increasingly an instrument of the rule of nobility." [5] Indeed, "France in the tenth and eleventh centuries was roughly feudalized; but just this strong development of feudal law allowed the kings later to build up their position at the top of the feudal pyramid in a way that concentrated all the power on the lord's rights. Finally feudal law was defeated by its own devices. In Germany, on the other hand, it developed in the direction of the rights of the vassals. Accordingly, a more or less unified feudal law could not develop in Germany as it did in France and England." [6]

It developed indeed in England half a century earlier than in France, and by way of a firmly but more recently established feudal power of the supreme liege lord. It soon became so strong that we can almost speak of a unitary feudal state. This is indeed the English situation after the

[4] Mitteis, p. 53. See also Stephenson, pp. 134 f.

[5] Mitteis, p. 79. See also Stephenson, pp. 92 f.; Heinrich Brunner, *Deutsche Rechtsgeschichte* (Munich, 1927), pp. 95 f., 133 ff.

[6] Mitteis, pp. 113 f.

Norman Conquest under William the Conqueror. "To him . . . feudalism seemed quite compatible with strong monarchy—an opinion whose justification is surely to be found in the history of the kingdom for the next two hundred years. The Norman conquest established the legal principle that every bit of England, if not retained in the king's hand, was held of him, as part of some fief." [7] It is true that as the country advanced in the centuries that followed, centralization represented less a particularly strong power of the supreme liege lord than increasingly an institutionalized system of government quite independent of the king. This development reflects in a nutshell a basic feature of British history, with profound changes from the beginning of the twelfth century to its end, from the reign of the Conqueror's younger son, Henry I (1100–1135), to that of his great-grandson, Henry II (1154–1189).

The reign of the elder son of William I of Normandy, William Rufus, may be characterized as one of despotic feudalism, but that of Henry I may be called one of beginning "differentiation of function" in government, despite the king's obligation "to consult his tenants in chief." This combination—the centralization of governmental functions, linked to the improvement of the administration of justice and recognition of the representation of the barons—would be as "the seed out of which the liberties of England grew in the constitutional struggles of the Plantagenet epoch." [8]

Henry married a descendant of Alfred the Great, linking the Norman tradition to the Saxon, and attempted thus to establish a tradition of organic transition from one dynasty to another. This attempt at conciliation and merger by royal marriage was made by the first Tudor king three centuries later and was approximated again by the switch from the Stuarts to the Hanovers after another two centuries. In all these cases a bold new approach to government, together with a more prudent recognition of the forces of tradition, is characteristic of the pattern of transition. Yet in none is it more apparent than in the Norman type of political feudalism, which ruled England between the battle of Hastings and the death of Henry I, that is, for more than a century.

The main and generally known achievements of Henry's administration, inasmuch as they followed and adjusted the course set by the Conqueror, may be summarized here. The reform of the treasury as an

[7] Stephenson, p. 86. See also Petit-Dutaillis, pp. 60 ff.

[8] George M. Trevelyan, *History of England* (New York, 1953), I, 171 ff. Trevelyan stresses the last point and analyzes the others in different contexts. See also Petit-Dutaillis, pp. 61–75; Doris M. Stenton, *English Society in the Early Middle Ages (1066–1307)* (Baltimore, 1962), pp. 18 ff.

office of exchequer, before which the sheriffs appeared twice a year for general accounting, was initiated. Revenues, now faithfully accounted, were in general to be paid in cash rather than in kind (unlike continental customs). Yet the exchequer, important though it was, represented only part of a much larger design, the creation of the Curia Regis, or king's court. Its functions as supreme court were secondary to those of a kind of privy council, royal cabinet, and treasury. Three new chief executive officers of the crown—the justiciar (a kind of vice-regent), the chancellor (in charge of clerical and secretarial work), and the treasurer—were all part of this body.

The administration of justice was improved by a system of appointed circuit judges with extended royal jurisdiction. This and the selection of sheriffs on the basis of their ability, were halting steps in the direction of a centralized state, which was to rest on stronger foundations than the power of the king as supreme feudal lord and landholder.[9] Yet to go even as far as he did, the king had to make important concessions to the chief powers of the realm, the Church and the barons. The compromise of 1107 concluded with the famous Archbishop Anselm of Canterbury left the actual investiture of a bishop with the dignity, jurisdiction, and fiefs of his office to the Church. The king reserved for himself, however, the right to select the prelate and receive his oath of allegiance as liege lord.

Considering the great significance of symbols in the High Middle Ages, as reflected in the double ceremony of spiritual and secular investiture agreed upon in the Concordat of Worms in Germany in 1122, the waiver of these rights in England was a very real concession on the part of Henry I. Whether it influenced the more serious conflict between Henry II and Thomas à Becket two generations later is difficult to determine, but there should be little doubt that the compromise of 1107 did represent a victory for the king.

Undoubtedly the concessions which Henry at the beginning of his reign thought it wise to make to the barons were greater in the so-called Charter of Liberties. In regard to the ecclesiastic lords, the king waived his claims to benefit from vacancies in Church offices. The king's demands for feudal aid were sharply curtailed; and the right of the nobles to be consulted was to be respected, as evidenced in the creation of the Curia Regis. All things considered, England from the Norman Conquest

[9] H. W. C. Davis, *England Under the Normans and Angevins (1060–1272),* (New York and London, 1905), pp. 118 ff. See also Joseph R. Strayer, *Western Europe in the Middle Ages* (New York, 1955), pp. 113 f.; Petit-Dutaillis, pp. 65 f.; and Christopher Broke, *From Alfred to Henry III, 871–1272* (New York, 1966), pp. 159 ff., 220 ff.

to the death of Henry in 1135 had a system of a fairly well centralized, stable government. It still operated within the frame of political feudalism, but with a power and efficiency the like of which had not even faintly existed under the later Saxon kings. Firmly established and seemingly developing steadily toward a merger of feudal, centralized, bureaucratic, and still rudimentary representative institutions, Norman England from 1066 to 1135 may be considered a reasonably well established original system (A).

Matters changed clearly for the worse in the following decades during the unfortunate reign of Stephen, the son of Henry's sister. The conflict in which he stood against the king's daughter Matilda, widow of the Emperor Henry V and second wife of a French lord, Geoffrey of Anjou, represented, of course, a war of succession. The struggle set off English, French, and Scottish lords against one another, many of them changing sides frequently. This in itself sufficed to bring about the destruction of strongly centralized political feudalism established by powerful liege lords like William the Conqueror and his sons. Social, legal, and political consequences of the shift to an internecine conflict of feudal lords were inevitable. In fact, the establishment of Geoffrey de Mandeville as a kind of mayor of the palace, temporary though the institution was, created conditions of illegality and anarchy, which seemed to have been overcome by this time in France and Germany.[10]

Stephen's chaotic reign was in one way a struggle for the royal succession. This issue was settled by a compromise in 1153, the year before the king's death, when Matilda's son Henry was recognized as heir to the throne. Yet, two questions are in order. First, did not the anarchy of the nearly two decades of Stephen's sorry reign represent something more than the issue of succession? Second, how much of the achievements of the first three Norman kings survived these tragic times?

As to the first problem, we may assume that the struggles between 1135 and 1154, like the Wars of the Roses two centuries later, only gave release to existing social tensions. They began in a disorganized and confused pattern with peasant revolts and ended with the rise of the urban middle classes. These upheavals as background to the feuds under Stephen's reign represented a step in the direction of social progress. The discord among

[10] On the reign of Stephen see in particular R. H. C. Davis, *King Stephen, 1135–1154* (Berkeley and Los Angeles; University of California Press, 1967); specifically, on Geoffrey de Mandeville's role see pp. 59 ff., 79 ff.; on the chronicle sources, pp. 146 ff.; see further H. W. C. Davis, *England*, pp. 154 ff., 173 ff.; John H. Round, *Geoffrey de Mandeville: A Study of the Anarchy* (London, 1892), pp. 41 ff., 87 ff., 138 ff., 165 ff.; Petit-Dutaillis, pp. 99 ff.; Stenton, pp. 33 f.

the lords, on the other hand, looked backward to the entrenchment of feudal strife, following the still existing Norman French pattern prior to the reign of Louis VI of France (1108–1137). All the same, both movements, social conflicts and feudal rivalries, whether they were looking backward deliberately or groping forward without intent, represented very real social pressures among lords, townspeople, and peasants alike. Nobles and churchmen, in the earlier period as in the latter, were the protagonists of the fight; the peasants before Stephen and under him were losers. The urban burghers, although they had suffered under Stephen, began to emerge as a recognized element of stability and prosperity.[11]

As to the consequences of the war, with particular regard to the survival of previous institutions, Joseph R. Strayer's comment is very much to the point. "Yet everything was not lost. Stephen remained king . . . and the central government did not collapse completely. The Exchequer continued to function and some of Henry's administrators remained in the royal service. Most important of all, rear-vassals and knights could not forget the generation of peace which Henry had given them. As the war had dragged on they became unwilling to fight for either side or to aid their baronial overlords to gain powers which made them local tyrants. England had had too long a period of stable government to lapse into feudal anarchy like that of the tenth century. . . ."[12] It is an interesting fact that in this very period of political anarchy monasticism of a very practical kind—in particular by way of the immigration of well-disciplined members of the Cistercian order, trained in agricultural and industrial skills—began to play an increasingly important economic role. The stability of the Church organization and its relative rise in power during the political crisis served these new beginnings well.[13]

Thus the intermediate system (B) under Stephen, if system it can be called, had absorbed substantial remainders of the original one, and what is equally important, it had set the ground for the restored system (C). Far-reaching as economic destruction was in the two decades between the reigns of Henry I and Henry II, it had clearly become manifest now that

[11] Trevelyan, I, 188–191, 317 ff., 345 ff.; R. H. C. Davis, *King Stephen,* pp. 58 f.; H. W. C. Davis, *England,* pp. 157 ff., 175 ff.; Petit-Dutaillis, p. 125; Broke, pp. 166 ff.

[12] Joseph R. Strayer, *The Middle Ages* (New York, 1959), pp. 282 ff. See also Trevelyan, I, 207 f.; R. H. C. Davis, *King Stephen,* pp. 58 ff.; H. W. C. Davis, *England,* pp. 178 ff.

[13] R. H. C. Davis, *King Stephen,* pp. 98 ff.; see also pp. 126 ff.; H. W.C. Davis, *England,* pp. 195 ff.; Trevelyan, I, 207 f.; Petit-Dutaillis, p. 122; Stenton, pp. 215 ff.; Broke, pp. 169 ff.

the separatist feudalism of the German and French Norman pattern had outlived its *raison d'être*. This held true even for a regime which still depended heavily on the support of the aristocracy. The devastations of the civil war were mortgages of the reign of Henry II (1154–1189), which could be paid off fairly soon. A lasting asset, on the other hand, was the growing insight that law and order could be secured only by a firmly anchored, centralized royal power. Henry W. C. Davis aptly summarizes the situation at the accession of Henry II (1154–1189). "One purpose and that ignoble [Stephen] effectually served. His reign furnished a warning, never to be forgotten, against the evils of an uncurbed feudalism, and prepared public opinion to accept the drastic centralization of Henry II." [14] The achievements of Henry II in administrative and especially in judicial reforms went far beyond the objectives of his grandfather, and what counted more, they were far more enduring. This is well illustrated by the king's military reforms. The introduction of the payment of scutage, in lieu of short-term feudal aid rendered by the vassals, furnished the king with permanent military forces, which sufficed to check the worst transgressions of feudal nobles. The "assize of arms" of 1181, near the end of Henry's reign, which required every free man who was physically or financially able to contribute to the defense of the country, strengthened this policy in regard to foreign foes as well.[15] Furthermore, a somewhat more liberal rural policy raised substantial numbers of outright serfs to the rank of villein. The introduction of primogeniture, which frequently led to the marriage of younger sons of noble families with commoners, effectively loosened the rigidity of the feudal social structure on its higher levels as well. The office of the exchequer and the collection of revenue through a system of property taxes worked more smoothly than in Henry I's time.

The king's judicial reforms are generally rated as his greatest achievements, for two principal reasons quite apart from the extent of the reforms themselves. In the first place, judicial reform in a system not yet built on a separation of powers also means administrative reform, for they cannot be separated. Second, in an order which on the higher levels of government cannot even remotely be called representative, the develop-

---

[14] H. W. C. Davis, *England*, p. 180; R. H. C. Davis, *King Stephen*, pp. 111 ff.; see also Appendix 1 on "Earls and earldom," pp. 129 ff. See also Petit-Dutaillis, pp. 107 ff.; Stenton, pp. 33 ff.

[15] William Stubbs, ed., *Gesta Regis Henri Secundi, Benedicti Abbatis. The Chronicles of the Reigns of Henry II and Richard I, A.D. 1169–1192; Known Commonly Under the Name of Benedict of Peterborough*, 2 vols. (London, 1867), II, 149 ff.; Petit-Dutaillis, pp. 144 ff.; Broke, pp. 182 f.

ment of solid judicial institutions is the only bulwark of popular liberties. This truism, elaborated in Montesquieu's *Spirit of Laws,* has been proven and confirmed repeatedly in medieval history. The motivation of the king in this respect was, for the long-range effect of his action, as comparatively inconsequential as was the motivation behind King John's acceptance of the Magna Charta, in relation to modern English democracy.

The establishment of a permanent central court with professional judges on the bench, improvement of the system of circuit judges, a rapid evolution of the jury system with regard to civil cases, and a kind of grand jury of presentment in criminal law are here of particular importance. In regard to the determination of landownership—to take just one example—reform extends far into the domain of administration. But of greatest long-range significance in the judicial and administrative sphere is the evolution of the common law, which derived from the decisions of the king's central court. Apart from Anglo-Saxon and Danish folk laws, and the more recent feudal additions, it drew most heavily on Roman civil law and the laws of the Church.[16]

As to the Church, Henry's moral defeat in the conflict with Thomas à Becket as Archbishop of Canterbury must not obscure the fact that the Constitutions of Clarendon of 1164 represented a clear-cut secular victory for the comprehensive judicial power of government over all the king's subjects. Even the concessions forced upon Henry after Becket's assassination in 1170 did not impair the royal judicial power in civil law suits which involved the Church. Benefit of clergy was restricted to criminal cases. Royal authority in relation to the Church, though compromised by the deplorable actions of Henry II, was thus still stronger than at the time of the death of Henry I, let alone that of Stephen.[17]

Added to this must be the relatively far-reaching success of an ambitious but cautious foreign policy. Whatever seeds of further complications may have been sown by the conquest of Ireland and the sub-

---

[16] On the administration of Henry II, in particular on the reorganization of government, see H. W. C. Davis, *England,* pp. 201 ff., and Jacques Boussard, *Le Gouvernement d'Henri II Plantagenet* (Paris, 1956); on the establishment of royal supremacy, *ibid.,* pp. 436 ff.; and Petit-Dutaillis, pp. 126 ff.; on public finances, Boussard, pp. 444 ff., 527 ff.; and Petit-Dutaillis, pp. 140 ff.; on judicial reforms, Boussard, pp. 494 ff., 527 ff.; Petit-Dutaillis, pp. 134 ff.; and Stenton, pp. 91 ff. See also John T. Appleby, *Henry II, the Vanquished King* (New York, 1962), pp. 38 ff.; Trevelyan, I, 191 ff., 210 ff.; Joseph R. Strayer, *Western Europe in the Middle Ages* (New York, 1955), pp. 113 ff.; Broke, pp. 173 ff., 183 ff.

[17] Boussard, pp. 436 ff.; H. W. C. Davis, *England,* pp. 213 ff., 265 ff.; Petit-Dutaillis, pp. 116 ff.; Appleby, pp. 73 ff., 115 ff.; Trevelyan, I, 210 ff.; Stenton, pp. 214 ff.; Broke, pp. 24 ff., 176 ff.

ordination of Wales, these actions strengthened the royal power for some
time to come. The same applies to Henry's policy in regard to his substantial French fiefs and to his often minimized skillful intervention in
affairs of the Holy Roman Empire.[18] In spite of troubles in foreign and
domestic affairs that were in store for England in a not distant future,
Trevelyan's summary observations seem quite justified:

> Of all the monarchs, who had won the island crown, few have done
> such great and lasting work as Henry Plantagenet. . . . He found Eng-
> land exhausted by nearly twenty years of anarchy, with every cog in the
> Norman machine of state either broken or rusty with disuse, the people
> sick indeed with feudal misrule, but liable at any moment to slip back
> into it for want of means to preserve order. He left England with a judi-
> cial and administrative system and a habit of obedience to government
> which prevented the recurrence of anarchy, in spite of the long absences
> of King Richard and the malignant follies of King John. After the death
> of the First Henry, the outcome of bad government was anarchy; after
> the death of the Second Henry, the outcome of bad government was
> constitutional reform. And the difference is a measure of the work of the
> great Angevin.[19]

If any king, in spite of his personal shortcomings, restored an enduring
form of orderly government, it was Henry II, according to these conclusions, solidly supported by facts. Is this, then, a classical case of restoration? We hesitate to give a clear-cut positive answer. Surely the England
from the Norman Conquest to the death of Henry I, as witnessed in the
Domesday survey and directly or indirectly in the writings of Geoffrey
of Monmouth and Henry of Huntingdon, represented a sort of steadily
developing original system. Even more strongly anchored in the reality
of long-range historical developments is the new order, reestablished by
Henry II and continued throughout the reigns of Henry's sons and those
of the first three Edwards well beyond the beginnings of the Hundred
Years' War. The era commencing with the administration of Henry II
may thus be considered to be a restored system (C), successful on the
whole in spite of much adversity encountered, but successful also because
so much adversity had been overcome.

The weakness of England under the Norman and Plantagenet and
Angevin kings as an example of restoration lies in the middle era, the

---

[18] H. W. C. Davis, *England,* pp. 203 ff., 223 ff.; Boussard, pp. 458 ff., 569 ff.;
Appleby, pp. 183 ff. See also Friedrich Hardegen, *Imperialpolitik Königs Heinrich
II von England* in *Heidelberger Abhandlungen zur mittelalterlichen und neueren
Geschichte* (Heidelberg, 1915), Heft 12, pp. 17 ff., pp. 28 ff.; Petit-Dutaillis,
pp. 155 ff.
[19] Trevelyan, I, 192.

intermediate period under Stephen's more or less nominal reign from 1135 to 1154. This intermediate phase, of course, preserved some of the achievements of the earlier Norman rulers, yet it added little to these achievements bar the development of monasticism. This, however, is associated merely with the era, not with the regime. The significance of this period for our purpose as at least a questionable intermediate system (B) is certainly based neither on its modest positive achievements nor on any lasting direct influence. The importance of Stephen's reign lies in its indirect challenge to the next generation. Revolutionary in an almost wholly negative sense, it showed up the necessity for sweeping reforms in the whole body politic beyond any reasonable doubt. In this sense the era generated true restoration.

To sum up, the restored regime under Henry II indeed preserved and further developed the institutions in existence under Henry I. Yet, contrary to the course of events in a fully developed restoration process, the reign of Henry II could encompass little of an institutional development of the twenty years of crisis, simply because there had been very little of it, save a new strengthening of Church power. In this sense restoration under Henry II does not and can not represent the great compromise between two preceding systems, as is the case in genuine restoration. For this reason we will have to consider the present sample an imperfect illustration of the restoration process. This study does not intend to press such samples into artificial straitjackets of pseudo-perfection, true to systems rather than to nature. Evident imperfection, as illustrated by this case of the indirect but weighty impact of a questionable intermediate system on an unchallengeable restored system, may give us more insight into reality than a doctrinaire analyst might presume.

CHAPTER XIII

From Hohenstaufen to Habsburg

CHRONOLOGY

1215–1250	Reign of Emperor Frederick II
1250–1273	Great Interregnum (commences, according to some interpretations, with the death of Conrad IV in 1254 or with that of William of Holland in 1256)
1273	Election of Rudolf of Habsburg as king
1282	Rudolf's sons invested with the duchies of Austria and Styria
1291	Death of King Rudolf
Original system (A)	1250, death of Frederick II, ends gradually disintegrating system
Intermediate system (B)	Great Interregnum, 1250–1273
Restored system (C)	begins with election of Rudolf of Habsburg as king (1273) and outlasts his death

Some basic distinctions in the general trends of political feudalism in the High Middle Ages were noted at the beginning of the preceding chapter. In France and England the power of the supreme liege lord rose considerably. This transformation led to the overhaul and eventual disappearance of political feudalism altogether. In Germany, on the other hand, the autonomous rights of the vassals were increasingly enhanced. Patterns of change in the West differed, to be sure. In England we perceive at the beginning of the late Middle Ages, at the turn from the thirteenth to the fourteenth century, a broadening of representative institutions, which under Edward I initially strengthened the hand of the king against the feudal lords but gradually became a genuine separation of powers. In France at the same time, under Philip the Fair, we see a long-range development toward royal absolutism, which in its own way destroyed political feudalism.

In Germany, too, certain changes are obvious. Political feudalism had continued to have a disintegrating effect on the power of the emperor and of the empire. This trend offset the Ottonian achievements as early as the first half of the eleventh century, though as yet only in the domestic sphere. Within Christian Europe as a whole, imperial authority reached a new height under the great Salian emperor Henry III, who was as ambitious in his policy for the East as were Otto I and Otto II in theirs for the South. His political success was as short-lived as theirs, also. The following reigns of Henry IV and Henry V, both deeply involved in the investiture conflict between church and crown, gave the major feudal lords an opportunity to increase their power. With the ascent of the house of Hohenstaufen (Ghibelline party) the conflict between emperor and princes was raised to a higher plane as seen particularly in the struggle between Guelfs and Ghibellines. Here we no longer see a kind of feudal anarchy opposing, in a loose alliance, an emperor whose power lies in the hereditary fiefs of his house. We see a real clash between empire and states, both terms to be understood, of course, in their contemporary meaning.

The Guelfs at the height of their power in the second half of the twelfth century and at the beginning of the thirteenth stood for a kind of genuine sovereignty similar to that of the political feudalism of the early Norman rulers of England. But the king (or, after his coronation by the pope in Rome, the emperor), unlike those in Western Europe, had to invest new liege men with a vacant fief, unless it was by tradition (even then not by law) part of the domains of his house. In studying the lives of the most dynamic great Ghibelline rulers, Frederick Barbarossa and Henry VI in particular, one is apt to forget that their hereditary fiefs were very limited in size. Their power lay far more in their imperial prestige and claims, as well as in possessions beyond the Alps, than in their German domains. "Even when with the death of Henry the Lion the tribal duchy fell, it was not the crown but princely power that earned the fruits of victory." [1] Barraclough observes:

[1] Heinrich Brunner, *Deutsche Rechtsgeschichte,* 7th ed. (Munich, 1927), pp. 156 f. (author's translation).

It has been calculated that the demesne of the crown at the end of the Hohenstaufen period amounted in the aggregate to the equivalent of only three quarters of the margravate of Brandenburg; but they were scattered fragments, a weak basis for political power, which could not compare with the resources of the greater princes. Hence the allegiance of the princes was based no longer on respect for a monarch who was powerful enough to make his supreme authority felt, but rather on compromises, capitulations and promises. . . . Germany was condemned for centuries to decentralization and disunion and to the evils which went with decentralization and the unchecked conflicts of competing interests.[2]

One does not have to subscribe to these sweeping conclusions to accept the premise of waning imperial power, which for the reign of Frederick II is fully supported by the high authority of Oswald Redlich and Ernst Kantorowicz.[3] Yet when the Ghibelline rule in Germany approached its end in the mid-thirteenth century, neither tribal duchies nor vassalage, whether of lesser or major import, characterized Germany any longer. Instead, there was the sovereignty, the *Landeshoheit* or *Landesherrlichkeit,* of the major princes. To be sure, it was not a uniform concept of sovereignty which in modern terms existed neither in national nor international relations. Sovereignty under the feudal system was one of degree of special privilege for individual princes and domains. At the same time the *Landeshoheit* of the major princes we are concerned with here could, in political practice, stand for princely powers that in domestic affairs advanced gradually to a stage of practical independence. In relation to other princes within or outside of the empire, they frequently led to arbitrary actions which more often than not had to be condoned by the wearer of the crown. In this sense the issue of sovereignty was no longer one of king versus feudal lords, but of emperor versus state.[4] Minor vassals or *ministeriales* no longer played a major part in high politics, if we exempt local, though frequently quite serious, political conflicts. Two imperial laws of the thirteenth century, the *confoederatio cum principibus ecclesiasticis* of 1220, supplemented and extended for the secular princes by the *statutum in favorem principum* of 1231/32, granted major sover-

[2] Geoffrey Barraclough, *The Origin of Modern Germany* (New York, 1963), p. 246; H. Brunner, pp. 155 ff. See also Georg Dahm, *Deutsches Recht* (Hamburg, 1944), p. 131.

[3] Oswald Redlich, *Rudolf von Habsburg, Das deutsche Reich nach dem Untergange des alten Kaisertums* (Innsbruck, 1903), pp. 47 f.; Ernst Kantorowicz, *Kaiser Friedrich II* (Berlin, 1928), pp. 348 ff.

[4] H. Brunner, pp. 155 ff., 160 ff.; Dahm, pp. 133 ff.; see also Theodor Lindner, *Deutsche Geschichte unter den Habsburgern und Luxemburgern* (Stuttgart, 1890), Vol. I, pp. 5–19.

eign rights in jurisdiction, immunity from imperial interference, levying of customs, minting of coinage. A civil service was developing rapidly within the principalities and was paralleled by the gradual rise of the estates in each land.[5]

Compared with this centralization of the state within a decentralization of the empire we face on the supreme level of government far less conspicuous trends toward a new order. It is a moot question, from our point of view, whether the developments in Germany leading to the decline of imperial power were due to the ambivalent genius of the last Ghibelline Emperor, Frederick II (1212-1250), or in spite of it.

This statement is not meant to be paradoxical. Was the emperor's brilliant performance as regent in Sicily the precondition for his failure in Germany? The question oversimplifies the facts. The rise of princely power in Germany certainly had preceded Frederick's reign; the progress of centralized institutions, on the other hand, benefited from the emperor's experience in Sicily. Yet the newly established offices of supreme imperial judge (*justiciarius curiae*) and of *notarius curiae* were, as representatives of feudal interests, but a feeble copy of the Sicilian supreme court created by the emperor: a bench of learned judges, well versed in Roman and canon law. The attempts to establish general *constitutiones pacis*— above all the famous Moguntina, the *Landfrieden* of Mayence of 1235— were vain attempts to exert imperial authority in the empire in principle. The enforcement of law and order in the principalities and even between them was at the same time left largely to the princes.[6] The Moguntina failed in its general aim to serve as a kind of constitutional chart for the empire as a whole, as well as in its specific objectives to reclaim imperial rights to tax and to offer to the towns a measure of protection against the princes.[7]

Kantorowicz believes that Frederick II had neither opportunity nor intention to convert Germany into a monarchy with a civil service system

[5] H. Brunner, pp. 155 ff.; Heinrich Mitteis, *Deutsche Rechtsgeschichte* (Munich, 1960), 86 ff., 90 ff., 152 ff. One of the best discussions of state institutions and state rights in medieval times is to be found in Otto Brunner, *Land and Herrschaft,* 4th ed. (Vienna, 1959), pp. 111 ff., 133 ff., 146 ff., 357 ff.; see further, Kantorowicz, pp. 349 f.; Barraclough, pp. 236 f.

[6] The term *Landfrieden* in its general meaning may be translated as *public peace;* as a legal term, it means *constitutio pacis.* If reference is made to a specific state act like that of Mayence in 1235 (the Moguntina), the latter meaning is the appropriate one.

[7] Mitteis, pp. 92, 116 f.; H. Brunner, pp. 106 ff.; Redlich, pp. 429 f.; Fedor Schneider, *Das Mittelalter bis zur Mitte des dreizehnten Jahrhunderts* (Vienna, 1929), pp. 416 ff.; Kantorowicz, pp. 376 ff.

on the Sicilian pattern. "He never thought to absorb German feudal power in the wide and diversified Germany and to rule through servants without the intermediate link of the princes." [8] This, of course, does not preclude the notion that specific reforms on the Sicilian pattern were attempted, but the great ideas of the Ghibelline empire under Frederick have little foundation in German reality. The dream envisaged

> a strong emperor, strong princes, as ultimate perfection of the old empire, the hoped-for return of which revived the visions of shallow centuries. . . . At that time Germany as "imperium" was a genuine simile and mirror of the great idea of the Roman Empire, which should unite all peoples and tribes. . . . It was a reflection of the great Christian world empire. It was both at the same time and should remain so. . . . Just as the ideal world empire of the Middle Ages pointed not toward the suppression of the peoples under the rule of one people but to the community of all kings, princes, lands, and peoples of Christianity under the one Roman emperor, who should belong to all nations and to none, who . . . should reside in the one eternal city . . . only thus should one perceive the perfect Germany . . . : Roman imperium and yet nation.[9]

Such may have been the dreams of the mysterious emperor Frederick II. The reality in Germany showed a quite different trend, namely, a progressive weakening of the imperial power, but also the gradual replacement of political feudalism on the state level by a halting, yet clearly perceptible rise of partly bureaucratic states. This new concept replaced the stem duchies and pushed the incongruous vassalage system of old into the background for a time. This was the order which in this analysis represents the original system (A) prior to the Great Interregnum.

The dramatic period from the death of Frederick II in 1250 to the election of Rudolf of Habsburg as king in 1273—for our purpose the intermediate system (B) can be interpreted in several ways. In a purely formal approach the objection seems quite justified that an interregnum never existed, in a legal sense. Conrad IV, the son of Frederick II, elected Roman king as early as 1237 though not recognized as such by the papacy, was undoubtedly the legitimate heir to his father and, by tradition, to the imperial crown as well. After his early death the counter king, William of Holland, elected in 1247 as candidate of the papal and Guelf party, had strong claims to the rule of the empire until his death in 1256. In 1257 within short intervals the empire witnessed the elections of two

---

[8] Kantorowicz, p. 348 (author's translation).

[9] Kantorowicz, p. 303. Omissions beginning with the second sentence in the quotation are by the author as translator.

kings, both of whom, like William, maintained their claims until their deaths—of the English prince, Richard of Cornwall, in 1272, and of the Spanish pretender, Alfonso X of Castile, in 1282, nine years after the election of Rudolf of Habsburg. The election of the British and Castilian kings, or rather counter kings, is not without significance, for therewith the tradition of election of the German ruler by the major princely electors was initiated, though it was legalized only by the Golden Bull of Emperor Charles IV in 1356.[10] Leaving this issue aside, the main point is that of these imperial claimants only Conrad exercised a contested authority, in Italy but not in Germany. The other three could not claim even that much *de facto* sovereignty. This point did not preclude a mighty ruler like Ottokar II of Bohemia from basing his claim to the rule of Austria and Styria on the investiture by the shadowy authority of Richard of Cornwall.

As to the very essence of the nature of the interregnum, of an era not legally but practically without supreme imperial authority, two basic interpretations are possible. Barraclough offers one. He perceives the core of the crisis "in the collapse of the royal authority, the wholesale transfer of royal rights and properties and the practical consummation of the tendencies licensed by the *Statutum in favorem principum* of 1232. But these results and the regime of anarchy and violence which set in were the corollary of the failure to unite on a successor to Frederick II. . . ."[11] As he sees it, "The result of the period 1215-1272 was thus to throw Germany back, to check its development by comparison with England and France. The functions carried out elsewhere by a strong monarchy . . . were in Germany either carried out by private associations within limited areas or limited purposes, or were not carried out at all. The centralized machinery of administration and law enforcement, which in England was in formation in the days of Henry II, had no parallel in Germany, and it was only later and haltingly that a similar organization was formed in the principalities. In 1250 the whole organization of German government was extraordinarily retrograde. . . ."[12] Barraclough places the responsibility for this development plainly at the door of Frederick II's unsuccessful reign in Germany. "The result was to place political power in the princes' hand."[13]

[10] On the precedents of the election procedure see Bernhard Schmeidler, *Das spätere Mittelalter* (Vienna, 1937), pp. 49 ff.; Mitteis, pp. 97, 141.

[11] Barraclough, *Origin of Modern Germany*, p. 244.

[12] Barraclough, pp. 245 f. See also O. Brunner, *Land und Herrschaft*, 165 ff.; Josef Hirn, *Rudolf von Habsburg* (Vienna, 1874), pp. 11 ff.

[13] Barraclough, p. 246.

There is much to be questioned in these views. While the interregnum was, of course, closely related to Frederick's chief concern with interests south of the Alps, to inconsistencies and neglect in his German policies, and above all to the emperor's break with the papacy, every future untoward development cannot be deduced from these facts. Even more questionable is the lumping together of the reign of the emperor and the interregnum as one great period of disintegration. The evolution of princely sovereignty to a somewhat advanced stage of direct governmental power precedes the reign of Frederick II by at least half a century; indeed, it goes even further back than the reign of Frederick Barbarossa. Full of seeds of future conflict though these developments may have been, complex and full of frictions though relations between the German princes were, princely autocracy—and this holds true for the Ghibelline rulers from Conrad III to Frederick II—did not stand for anarchy and lawlessness.[14] The suspension of imperial power alone and its poor replacement by foreign shadow kings does not suffice to explain the state of affairs during the interregnum, well characterized by James Bryce:

> Every floodgate of anarchy was opened: prelates and barons extended their domains by war: robber knights infested the highways and the rivers: the misery of the weak, the tyranny and violence of the strong, were such as had not been seen for centuries. Things were worse than they had ever been under the Saxonian and Franconian emperors; for the petty nobles who had then been in some measure controlled by their dukes, were now after the extinction of several of the great houses, left without any feudal superior. Only in the cities were shelter or peace to be found. Those of the Rhine had already leagued themselves for mutual defense. . . . The Pope himself, having now sufficiently improved the weakness of his enemy, found the disorganization of Germany beginning to tell upon his revenues, and threatened that if the electors did not appoint an emperor, he would.[15]

Transgressions on the part of princes and estates directed against imperial power and domain were involved here only to a limited degree. The arbitrary seizure of fiefs by imperialist princes like the last Babenberg duke, Frederick II, Louis II of Bavaria, and above all, Ottokar II of Bohemia, was partly responsible for the state of affairs during the interregnum, after the death of Frederick II. The expansionist objectives were nothing new; but, revived after centuries and therefore seemingly new was the lawlessness, in Bryce's terms, of the "petty nobles," the

[14] H. Brunner, pp. 155 ff.; O. Brunner, pp. 387 ff.; Heinrich Fichtenau, *Geschichte des Mittelalters* (Vienna, 1947), pp. 249 f.

[15] James Bryce, *The Holy Roman Empire* (New York, 1914), pp. 214 f.

knights, whose economic position had deteriorated when the princes rose in power and when the impotence of the empire in foreign relations barred the possibility of new territorial gains, essential for a primitive agricultural economy. Here we find a major source of the lawlessness of the interregnum. The aggressiveness, motivated by the urge to defend a declining social status, was directed primarily against the force weakest by military standards but strongest in economic strength and potential development, the chartered towns.[16] The Rhenish federation of cities of 1254 and also, in a sense, the Swabian league of 1276, after the tide of lawlessness had come to recede gradually, offered unmistakable signs that the institutions of a slowly rising new order were bound to stay. Surely "Christian European universalism was destroyed"[17] and could never be regained in the sense that it had existed more as an idea than as reality, but still as a vigorous ideal in bygone centuries. But this does not mean at all that in the interregnum there was only lawlessness and violence, only a vacuum like the reign of Stephen in England between that of the Norman Henry and the Angevin Henry. "[It] was for Germany a time full of storms, yet also penetrated by the vigorous motions and shaping up of new conditions. . . . The old ideal of the ruler has to yield in heavy battles. It is replaced by the princes striving for full territorial sovereignty. . . . The leading estate thus far, the landed nobility, struggles with economic crises which not rarely lead to its doom in debts, poverty, and pressure into the activities of robber knights. But a new stratum of the people coalesces . . . and advances strongly, the burghers. Princes and cities, territories and city states begin to give the German imperial body a new character.

"All this took place during ceaseless fighting. . . ." If public safety left much to be desired before, all the previously discussed factors merged now "in these middle decades of the thirteenth century to give them the image of a period full of conflicts, feuds, and violence. And if princes and the Great [nobles] did not want to concede to the weakened royal power otherwise new strength and significance, they learned after all one thing in these times of the interregnum; the king needed at least the strength and means to secure peace and law in the empire."[18]

Surely, the interregnum stood for something more than the mere desire to reestablish and to improve law and order, though even this was a major task. It injected new social forces and expectations into the middle

---

[16] Redlich, *Rudolf von Habsburg,* pp. 47 ff., 55 ff., 63; H. Brunner, pp. 164 ff.
[17] Mitteis, p. 142.
[18] Redlich, pp. 76 f. The quotes from Redlich were translated by the author.

period between the outgoing Ghibelline rule and the coming Habsburg power. Above all, it manifested the need for political and social change beyond any reasonable doubt. In a very real sense the interregnum is a genuine intermediate system which, despite all violence, preserved some of the institutions of the past, changed them, and added new ones and transmitted them to a new era.

The new era commenced with the rise of Rudolf of Habsburg, a feudal lord endowed with rich fiefs in southwestern Germany and in Switzerland. He was duly elected king by the electors, with the exception of the king of Bohemia, and crowned in Aix-la-Chapelle in 1273. "Thus Rudolf took over the crown, so to speak, as mandate from the princes. He was supposed to reconstitute a lawful royal power, recognized by the Church as well," [19] in contradiction to the state of affairs under the Ghibelline rulers. Restoration of royal power—after a fashion—was also "in the interest of the princes, who wanted their whole domains" including the recently acquired ones "as far as possible legitimized by royal authority. The new king should again establish peace, law, and order in the empire. . . . The new king should restore the imperial domains as well. They were to establish the material foundations essential for the accomplishment of his task. At the same time a merger of the imperial domains with the king's hereditary fiefs was not foreseen. Lastly, it was Rudolf's objective to check the rapidly expanding power of Ottokar II of Bohemia and to enforce against him the empire's claims to the Austrian hereditary lands." [20] This did not mean that in a legal sense the new king, who was never to be crowned emperor in Rome, would have to incorporate these Austrian lands into the hereditary domains of his own house. When he did so, the rise of the new great eastern power with Bohemia as nucleus was successfully checked by the rise of the Habsburgs.

"King Rudolf did accomplish all this. . . . With ceaseless care he worked for public peace (Landfrieden) in the empire; in Swabia, in the Alsace, on the Middle Rhine, and in Thuringia he intervened energetically. With the help of the territorial forces he created organizations for the protection of public peace, which, as in Bavaria and Thuringia,

---

[19] Redlich, pp. 734 f., 509 f.; Mitteis, pp. 140, 93 ff. For the historiography of Rudolf's reign, with particular emphasis on Austria, see Karl and Mathilde Uhlirz, *Handbuch der Geschichte Österreichs* (Graz-Cologne, 1963), I, 266–278. For Rudolf's ecclesiastic policy in Germany see Karl Klutz, *Der Einfluss Rudolfs von Habsburg auf die Vergebung geistlicher Stellen in Deutschland* (Berlin, 1936), pp. 134 ff.

[20] Redlich, pp. 734 f. See also Hirn, *Rudolf von Habsburg,* pp. 15 ff.; M. Plischke, *Das Rechtsverfahren Rudolfs von Habsburg gegen Ottokar von Böhmen* (Bonn, 1885), pp. 8 ff.

assumed a character of lasting exemplary significance." [21] The princes were pledged to maintain peace in their territories, a peace whose provisions for preservation of the *Treuga Dei* and jurisdiction of state agencies, relationship between liege lords and liege men, were minutely determined in solemn acts of state. Concerning the imperial administration, "the developments of imperial bailiwicks *(Reichslandvogteien)*, the renovation of imperial castles, the evolution of imperial taxation, all this is the work of Rudolf" and its success is shown in the reestablishment of the imperial domains and in the tax returns from the cities. Notwithstanding new investitures with fiefs, royal power gained substantially in economic matters in all these proceedings.

> But king Rudolf accomplished even more. He went far beyond the intentions of his princely clients. . . . The universal designs of Frederick II could not seduce him any longer [in his time and place]. He considered the kingdom of Sicily as lost right from the beginning, and he saw no chance to establish genuine rule over an imperial Italy; he saw clearly that understanding with the papacy was essential for order in Germany. But to restore royal power in this very Germany soon dominated the new king's aims. The rule over [the princely] territory served, after the course of events of the last fifty years, as the only means by which genuine royal power could now be established.[22]

In this sense the acquisition of the Habsburg hereditary power in Austria and the reduction of that of the Bohemian crown performed a dual purpose. It strengthened the status of the king in the only sense in which this was still possible in the second half of the thirteenth century: by the establishment of sovereignty over sizeable territories. This in turn led to the rise of a particular dynasty, which took advantage of existing conditions to surge ahead mightily at the proper time and place. Not only hereditary power in general but hereditary power in the southeast part of the empire, the new center of gravity, became gradually a prerequisite of successful kingship.[23]

Most important in all these actions were Rudolf's earnest and on the whole successful endeavors to base his revival of royal authority in imperial affairs as far as possible on the consent and cooperation of the princes, particularly in the reconquest of imperial domains lost since the

---

[21] Redlich, pp. 735, 436 ff., 447 ff. See also Hirn, pp. 35 ff.; W. Wyneken, *Die Landfrieden in Deutschland von Rudolf von Habsburg bis Heinrich VII* (Göttingen, Naumburg, n.d.), pp. 5–14.

[22] Redlich, pp. 735 ff. See also Uhlirz, pp. 265 ff.; O. Brunner, pp. 180 ff., 197 ff.; H. Brunner, pp. 155 ff.; Hirn, pp. 88 ff., 120 ff.

[23] Barraclough, *Origin of Modern Germany,* p. 280.

latter part of Frederick II's reign. It gave Rudolf's otherwise ambiguous policy against Ottokar, beginning with the Reichstag of Nürnberg in 1274, some kind of legitimacy.[24] It may seem natural that most of the major princes endorsed the general objectives of the new king's domestic policy: reestablishment of law and order by way of princely rather than royal power. Yet Rudolf's alliance with the free cities, based on the grant of charters of royal autonomy in matters of commerce in exchange for extraordinary subsidies and taxes, introduced a new force in support of the crown.[25] Unquestionably Rudolf's enlightened self-interest served here the common welfare. In a sense the hub of the overall domestic policy was still the enforcement of the Moguntina of 1235 as applied, modified, and frequently strengthened in regard to specific territories. Armed feuds and self-help by violence had to be prohibited or at least restricted. Arbitrary seizure of property and illegal levying of customs and tolls, and various abuses of the privilege of coinage, had to be fought. The jurisdiction of the courts—and of newly appointed royal judges in particular—in all these matters had to be instituted, supervised, and as in the case of the robber knights, ruthlessly enforced.[26]

In foreign affairs relations with the papacy were hardly less important than in the times of the Ghibelline rulers. Rudolf wanted very much to be crowned emperor by the pope in Rome, though the universalist aspects of the venerable imperial idea were alien to his down-to-earth philosophy. This coronation, which he failed to secure largely because of his continued preoccupation with domestic conflicts, meant to him above all a further legitimization of his rule in Germany.

After the fall of the Ghibelline dynasty in a collision with the combined forces of papacy and princes, a new ruler was indeed badly in need of such confirmation by the most exalted power in Christendom. Rudolf was fully ready to pay a high price for conciliation between ecclesiastic and secular authority. In the empire this meant recognition of at least limited princely sovereignty and sweeping autonomy. In regard to the papacy an implied waiver of the imperial claims in Italy was necessary. The Pope on the other hand, was just as much interested in the reestablishment of order in a truly Christian Germany. Furthermore, he was in need of peace

[24] Schmeidler, *Das spätere Mittelalter,* p. 57; Barraclough, p. 302; Redlich, pp. 211 ff.; Theodor Görlitz, *Rudolf von Habsburg* (Vienna, 1961), p. 93; Hirn, pp. 27 ff.; Plischke, pp. 8 ff.

[25] Hellmuth Rössler, *Ein König für Deutschland* (Munich, 1960), pp. 78 ff.; Görlitz, pp. 150 ff.; Barraclough, p. 282; Hirn, pp. 93 ff.

[26] Redlich, pp. 429 ff., 444 ff.; in regard to Austria see particularly pp. 335 ff.; Görlitz, pp. 144 ff.; Hirn, pp. 127 ff.; Wyneken, pp. 8 ff.

with the emperor because of the church and state conflict with France. Accordingly an understanding was reached. Although he was not crowned emperor in Rome, Rudolf reached his limited objective: recognition of his rule by the supreme spiritual power, not in the sense of Christian universalism but within the territories where he could enforce his authority. As Barraclough sees it:

> The Pope was prepared to work for a restoration of stable conditions in Germany, and in particular to countenance the substitution of hereditary, for elective monarchy; in this way he hoped to create in Germany an effective counterweight to France and the house of Anjou. Such a policy could only be of advantage to the house of Habsburg . . . and Rudolf . . . therefore worked in close alliance with the Pope. Provided that continuity of succession was maintained, and . . . the friendship of the other European powers . . . was assured, the Habsburgs had reasonable prospect of establishing sound rule in Germany; and they were therefore willing to negotiate for the redrawing of the map of Europe, which would enable them to exchange their imperial burdens for greater control within Germany.[27]

With Rudolf's defeat of King Ottokar of Bohemia and the acquisition of Austria as hereditary fief of his house, the center of gravity of his interests shifted to the East. His interests in the problems of the empire beyond the Rhine valley and across the Alps declined markedly. Hence Rudolf's surrender or rather nonenforcement of Italian and possibly Sicilian claims and the withdrawal of the empire from the advanced position of the kingdom of Arelat (the territories around Arles).[28] Rudolf maintained his claims in principle, as he did in Burgundy, and as most Habsburg rulers continued to do with most of their claims ever since. Görlitz is probably right when he assumes Rudolf would have been quite satisfied with a purely German hereditary empire for his successors. He would, or perhaps more cautiously, he might "not have grudged a competitor the crown of a second southern empire. He was chiefly concerned with the order and restoration of Germany. Since he had little imperial ambition compared to the Hohenstaufens, the non-German states of the old empire could be a matter of indifference to him if he could at least secure for centuries the success of his administration in the wide area from Austria to the Rhine." [29]

Did he succeed in this? The early death of Pope Nicolas III—his chief

---

[27] Barraclough, pp. 294 ff. See also Görlitz, pp. 66 ff., 136 ff., 182 ff.; Redlich, pp. 170 ff.; Hirn, pp. 100 ff.

[28] Barraclough, pp. 292 ff.; Redlich, pp. 405 ff.; 594 ff., 627 f.

[29] Görlitz, p. 142. See also pp. 131–43 *passim* (author's translation).

counterpart in the negotiations for a French and German compromise in Burgundy, the Arelat and Italy—certainly worked against him. Further-more, the Aragonese-supported "Sicilian Vespers" and the overthrow of the power of the house of Anjou in Italy created an instability in foreign affairs which did not allow Rudolf to resume plans for a Roman corona-tion.[30] Still these events did not disturb the king's pacification of Germany decisively. Who is to say that a more fortunate Italo-French policy of Rudolf, culminating in the imperial coronation in Rome, might not have revived sweeping imperial ambitions as well? All this could have led conceivably to new conflicts in the empire and between emperor and papacy, similar to those between Ghibellines, Guelfs, and church, but with odds even more unfavorable to the crown. Rudolf, the head of a new dynasty of far less imperial grandeur than that of the Hohenstaufen rulers before him, was faced with solidly entrenched princely powers. They continued to rise steadily. The king was therefore in a poor position to resume ambitious imperial designs abroad. Lack of both opportunity and volition may have played a part here. Neither one is the supreme test of the success or failure of Rudolf's reign. As Dante will have it, Rudolf sits in Purgatory as one of those who has "left undone what he ought to have done, and who moves not his lips with the others' songs, . . . Ru-dolph the Emperor, who might have healed the wounds that were the death of Italy, so that too late through another she is succoured."[31] This evaluation may well be true from the point of Ghibelline universalism, but from that of the restoration problem we have to look in other direc-tions.

Lacking the powerful imperial tradition and the universalist appeal of the Hohenstaufen dynasty, and facing the rising sovereignty of the princely states, Rudolf acted largely as trustee of princely interests.[32] In that sense, and in some contradiction to Barraclough's view, the king represented and championed the hereditary power of his princely house among other leading princes far more than any hereditary claims of his dynasty to royal power. "He was to establish again a lawful royal power recognized also by the Church,"[33] but he did so on behalf not only of the

[30] Franz X. Seppelt, *Papstgeschichte* (Munich, 1940), pp. 150 ff.; Redlich, pp. 385 ff., 591 ff.; Hirn, pp. 101 ff.; Augustin Demski, *Rudolf von Habsburg und die römische Kaiserkrone während des Pontifikates Nikolaus II* (diss. Breslau-München, 1906), pp. 56 ff.

[31] *The Divine Comedy, Purgatorio,* Canto VII, Modern Library edition, pp. 232 ff. "The other" refers to Ottokar II of Bohemia. See also Bryce, *Holy Roman Empire,* pp. 272 f.; Görlitz, pp. 196 f.; Hirn, pp. 186 ff.

[32] Redlich, p. 734; O. Brunner, pp. 146 ff.; Hirn, pp. 185 f.; Klutz, pp. 10 ff.

[33] Redlich, p. 737.

major princes in general but of his own claims. These were to be legitimated by royal authority as royal authority in turn was sanctioned by Rudolf's princely status, anchored in his newly acquired domains. The new king had to reestablish law and order in the empire and to restore and expand the imperial domains as well. He did so, skillfully and bravely against the exorbitant power of a sovereign like Ottokar II of Bohemia, without destroying the idea of princely power itself and without losing the confidence of his peers.

But "the attempt of Rudolf and of his son Albrecht to create a new strong royal power" concurrently with the stormy process of the formation of princely territories, set strong counterforces into motion. "They wanted to defeat the territorial state by means of the territorial state. They had come close to the goal. But the separatist powers in the empire, representing . . . the institutions of the electors, opposed Rudolf's endeavors at the last moment. After his death princes and lords, towns and peasants . . . rose in defense of their separate existence against the Habsburg regime, which wanted to absorb everything. This whole opposition and its first victory is represented decisively in the election of Adolf of Nassau. . . ."[34]

Other similar victories are apparent in the events that led to the assassination of Albrecht I, and the rival elections of Louis of Bavaria and Frederick the Handsome. "Then the crisis had passed. The attempt of a rise of centralized power, of the foundation of a *de facto,* later perhaps *de jure,* hereditary royal power had failed. The result was ratified by the Golden Bull of Charles IV . . ." of Luxemburg in 1356.[35] "Thus the acquisition of the Austrian lands and the considerable expansion of the southwestern territory remained the lasting success of Rudolf's life. Therewith he had opened far-reaching objectives to his house. . . ."[36] Indeed, "Rudolf gave up completely any continuation of Ghibelline policy, any claim to Sicily, even to the Romagna." He did "all that to preserve the urgently needed harmony in the relations to the Curia." He hoped therewith to secure "the imperial crown as premise to the accomplishment of his final objective, the succession of his son in the empire."[37] In this Rudolf seems to have failed, only if one takes a short view of the success of his dynasty. Within one hundred and fifty years its success was obvious to everyone. Yet Rudolf failed in a wider and deeper

[34] Redlich, pp. 737 f.
[35] Redlich, p. 737
[36] Redlich, pp. 737 f. See also Bryce, pp. 229 ff.; H. Brunner, pp. 136 f., 150 ff.; Lindner, *Deutsche Geschichte unter den Habsburgern und Luxemburgern,* pp. 84 ff.
[37] Redlich, p. 739; Hirn, pp. 176 ff.

sense, if the issue is the rise of imperial power by way of centralized institutions and not merely through princely might. While the Habsburg power for all practical purposes was to establish its *de facto* hereditary rule in the empire, it never succeeded in establishing an empire comparable to the firm structure of the late medieval princely states.

Nevertheless, there are solid accomplishments which in their lasting effect transcend in importance Rudolf's initial contribution to the greatness of his house. Public disorder, particularly the threat of a new interregnum, disappeared from the German scene. And undoubtedly Rudolf's moderation in his foreign policy in regard to Tuscany, Lombardy, Sicily, Burgundy, and the Arelat made it possible to enforce some kind of order in Germany.[38]

May we therefore perceive Rudolf's regime as a successful restoration? Is the whole process of transition from the Holy Roman Empire under Frederick II through the interregnum to the reign of Rudolf a genuine change from an original system through an intermediate one to a truly restored one? In our opinion it comes much closer to genuine restoration than any of the three restoration situations discussed in the preceding chapters. The original system of Ghibelline Germany under Frederick II was more clearly accentuated than that of an Eastern Roman Empire after the death of Theodosius the Great. While the Holy Roman Empire was undoubtedly disintegrating during Frederick's reign, a strong unifying effect of the imperial crown was undisputed ideologically. Prospective centralization did not yet lack a foundation. The intermediate situation in the Eastern Roman Empire, the crisis in the mid-fifth century, was hazy in its political character. This was even more true for England under Stephen. In Germany under the interregnum the revolutionary rise of new forces, particularly in regard to princely states and chartered towns, was patent in its political impact. This becomes clear in comparison with the German situation that existed between the imperial coronations of the last Carolingian descendant, Berengar of Friuli, and Otto the Great. There an intermediate system was only dimly recognizable in the ideological sphere. During the Great Interregnum, on the other hand, there emerged quite clearly a new alignment of social and political forces with a lasting effect for many centuries. This took place in spite of the crisis of executive and judicial power, and largely even because of it. The further expansion of city autonomy, culture, and the future rise of princely sovereignty versus the crown—on the whole, in orderly fashion—were inconceivable without the experience and challenge of the Great Interregnum.

[38] See also Görlitz, pp. 195 f.; Lindner, pp. 84 f.

To sum up: The chief difficulty with the Byzantine case—apart from the religious issue—centers on original and intermediate systems. Distinctions in regard to Germany under the Carolingian and Saxon emperors pertain chiefly to the ideological sphere and only indirectly, though not indistinctly, to the political one. In Plantagenet-Angevin England, the middle period under Stephen raises the main problem.

In thirteenth century Germany clear-cut original and intermediate systems may easily be discerned. Here the problem hinges on the restored system. What did Rudolf really restore? Certainly not uncontested imperial elections. His reign was in fact followed by the era of the so-called *springende Wahlen,* between the houses of Nassau, Habsburg, Luxemburg, and Wittelsbach. When Habsburg supremacy was definitely established in the fifteenth century, the idea and reality of empire were more feeble than prior to the interregnum. Princely authority in the larger states, particularly those under the rule of the electors, had become much stronger. So had, on the whole, law and order, and they remained so until the political crisis brought about by the Turkish wars and Reformation created new situations of civil strife, though not full anarchy any longer. Credit for these developments of the future goes to princely, not to imperial power.

Such transition may be called genuine restoration only if chief emphasis is put on the concept of law and order, whether it was founded on princely executive force or on direct imperial authority. Rudolf and those of his successors who exercised this authority did so by strength of their own princely sovereign power, a power which was new, not restored. This is particularly true of the Habsburgs in Austria. Those emperors from other dynasties who did not possess such power failed lamentably, such as Adolf of Nassau (1292–1298) and the able and noble Henry VII of Luxemburg (1308–1313). Rudolf, on the other hand, succeeded to a large measure because he strove, by means of a policy of enlightened self-interest, for more modest goals.

The situation which commenced with the reign of the first Habsburg ruler in Germany can indeed be understood as genuine restoration only if the reestablishment and strengthening of the public peace stands for two things: public peace as value in itself, and also as historical value deeply rooted in the German soil. The first assumption is easier to make than the second. In view of Germany's sad history, not only during the interregnum but also under the last Ghibelline rulers, the latter issue certainly appears debatable. On the other hand, if we see a genuine restored system in the fact that the ideas and innovations of an intermediate one—here the interregnum—exercised a distinct influence and challenge under the new era initiated by Rudolf, then we tread on much safer ground. We then could—and should—agree that the transition from the Hohenstaufens to the Habsburgs truly represents a genuine restoration process. The Christian ideals of peace and justice, even if materialized by imperfect means and in an imperfect manner, rate higher than the shadowy concept of Christian imperial universalism. Tolerable reality precedes noble dreams.

CHAPTER XIV

Reformation and Counter Reformation in Austria

CHRONOLOGY

1564–1576	Maximilian II emperor
1568	Grant of free exercise of Lutheran creed to the noble estates in Upper and Lower Austria
1572	Similar concessions made to Protestants in Inner Austria
1576–1612	Rudolf II emperor
1578	Further concessions to Protestants in Inner Austria at general diet in Bruck/Mur
1578	Beginning of Counter Reformation measures in Upper and Lower Austria
1580	Beginning of Counter Reformation measures in Inner Austria
1596	Ferdinand III (as emperor subsequently, Ferdinand II) begins rule in Inner Austria in his own right
1607	Archduke Matthias becomes head of dynasty
1608	Pact of Lieben between emperor and archduke Matthias, who secures rule in Upper and Lower Austria, Hungary, and Moravia, and succession to Bohemian crown
1609	Emperor Rudolf II's Letter of Majesty grants religious liberty in Bohemia
1611	Matthias crowned king of Bohemia
1612–1619	Matthias emperor
1614	General diet of Linz
1615	General diet of Prague
1617	Ferdinand crowned king of Bohemia
1618	Ferdinand crowned king of Hungary
1618	Beginning of Thirty Years' War
1619–1637	Ferdinand emperor, second of his name
1621	In his will Ferdinand determines succession in favor of oldest line of dynasty; asserts the principle of indivisibility of Austrian Hereditary Lands (*Erblande*)
1624–1627	Counter Reformation and peasant war in Upper Austria
1628	Reconversion decree for Protestant nobles in Inner Austria

1629	Imperial Edict of Restitution favors Catholic side
1637–1657	Ferdinand III emperor
1648	Westphalian Peace Treaty
1665	Complete merger of all ruling Habsburg lines under emperor Leopold I
Original system (A)	1490–1521, from the reunification of the Habsburg lands to the beginning of Ferdinand I's administration in the Hereditary Lands
Intermediate system (B)	1521–1576, to death of emperor Maximilian II
Restored system (C)	1576, initiated; between 1620's and 1648, firmly established

THE GERMAN (AUSTRIAN) HABSBURGS IN THE 16TH AND 17TH CENTURIES
(Simplified genealogical table)

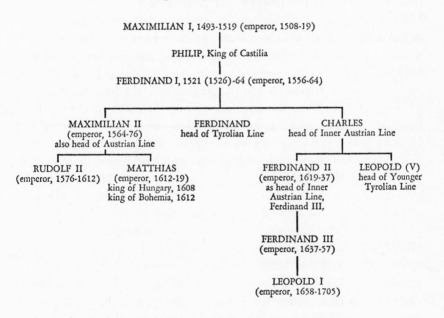

MAXIMILIAN I, 1493-1519 (emperor, 1508-19)

PHILIP, King of Castilia

FERDINAND I, 1521 (1526)-64 (emperor, 1556-64)

MAXIMILIAN II (emperor, 1564-76) also head of Austrian Line   FERDINAND head of Tyrolian Line   CHARLES head of Inner Austrian Line

RUDOLF II (emperor, 1576-1612)   MATTHIAS (emperor, 1612-19) king of Hungary, 1608 king of Bohemia, 1612   FERDINAND II (emperor, 1619-37) as head of Inner Austrian Line, Ferdinand III.   LEOPOLD (V) head of Younger Tyrolian Line

FERDINAND III (emperor, 1637-57)

LEOPOLD I (emperor, 1658-1705)

ALL GERMAN (AUSTRIAN) LINES MERGED IN 1665

REFORMATION

The phase of Austrian history discussed in this chapter adds a new dimension to our problem: development of a strictly ideological restoration process in clearly limited political entities. The analysis is complicated by the fact that the Austrian hereditary lands, for the best part of the period surveyed here, were partitioned and governed by three separate administrations. Therefore, we will have to discuss the three systems in three different theaters before we can summarize. Some data of political history are inevitably complex; this is preferable to misleading over-simplification.

Austria in geographic terms is to be understood in this chapter as "broadly speaking, the so-called *Erblande* or Hereditary Lands, . . . the Alpine domains from the spurs of the Alps in the north to the shores of the Adriatic in the south, from the Bavarian frontier in the west to the Hungarian plains in the east, predominantly German, but of Slav character in the south." [1] At the beginning of the period we are concerned with, the middle and latter part of the reign of emperor Maximilian I, the so-called "last knight" (1493–1519), the administrative organization of the country was as follows: Lower Austria, which comprised then the two archduchies, Austria below and Austria above the river Enns, in addition to Styria, Carinthia, and Carniola; and Upper Austria, which included the so-called Windisch mark, Austrian Istria with Trieste, Tyrol, Vorarlberg; and Vorder Austria, the Habsburg possession in southern and southwestern Germany, Swabia and the Alsace. This political arrangement did not correspond well to the geographic and ethnic conditions of all these lands and was therefore not of long duration. At the death of Ferdinand I, the second grandson of Maximilian, who succeeded his brother Charles V as emperor only in 1556 but who had actually ruled the Erblande since 1521 or 1522, an important and long-lasting division took place. Unlike the administrative apportionment under Maximilian I, in 1564 it was an actual partition between the sons of Ferdinand. The new division reflected to some extent the tradition of the Alpine–Danube lands. Ferdinand's oldest son, Maximilian, who as Maximilian II succeeded his father as emperor and king of Bohemia and Hungary, obtained the archduchies above and below the Enns, henceforward and until today referred to as Lower and Upper Austria. The second son, named Ferdinand like his father, inherited Tyrol, Vorarlberg, and the possessions in south and west Germany, and the third, Charles, received Styria, Carinthia, Carniola, Gorizia, Trieste, and Istria. While there was no strong ethnic bond between Tyrol and the domains in southern Germany, or between the Alpine and Adriatic lands and Upper and Lower Austria, a significant cohesion between the principal other domains did exist. Our analysis will be focused on Lower and Upper Austria in the modern sense, then on

[1] Robert A. Kann, *The Multinational Empire* (New York, 1950), I, 4.

the Inner Austrian lands Styria, Carinthia, and Carniola, and lastly on Tyrol. Of the three ruling lines of the house of Habsburg, the one in Tyrol, which had little political power, became extinct in 1595. After long-drawn-out negotiations within the Habsburg dynasty the Inner Austrian line of Emperor Ferdinand II (1619–37) eventually became heir to these domains. According to the emperor's will of 1621, the Erblande were never to be divided again. Like many of the resolves of this ruler, who was obdurate only in religious matters, this one failed to materialize fully. The complete merger of all lands of the German Habsburgs under the Styrian main branch of the family took place only in 1665. The last division of the Habsburg lands had thus lasted for just over a century, and in view of the extraordinary stormy events during that century it left diverse but distinct and lasting marks on the history of the three groups of lands.[2]

The common destiny in the century of Protestant Reformation, Catholic Reformation, and Counter Reformation, experienced in different political settings and under different conditions, is not the only reason why these political entities have to be defined.[3] It must be made clear that we are dealing here not with all the lands under the rule of the house of Austria, the gradually emerging Habsburg empire comprising the kingdoms of the Bohemian and Hungarian crowns, but in essence only with the predominantly German Erblande. The eminent German historian Karl Brandi observes, "The Bohemian restoration was the most incisive and at the same time most enduring kind of Counter Reformation."[4] If that is so, why then are we not dealing rather with the process of Reformation

---

[2] Alfons Huber and Alfons Dopsch, *Österreichische Reichsgeschichte* (Vienna, 1901), pp. 174 ff.; Ernst C. Hellbling, *Österreichische Verfassungs- und Verwaltungsgeschichte* (Vienna, 1956), pp. 270 ff.; Franz von Krones, *Handbuch der Geschichte Österreichs,* 5 vols. (Berlin, 1880–1881), III, 258 ff.

The independent archbishopric of Salzburg, under imperial rule but not under that one of the Austrian three lines, was during the period under discussion most closely related to Upper Austria.

[3] Concerning the obvious distinction between the concepts of Catholic Reformation as a primarily ideological movement and Counter Reformation as a primarily political movement, see Karl Eder, *Die Kirche im Zeitalter des konfessionellen Absolutismus (1555–1648)* (Vienna, 1949), pp. 8-10; Robert A. Kann, *A Study in Austrian Intellectual History* (New York, 1960), pp. 1 ff., 23 ff.; Grete Mecenseffy, *Geschichte des Protestantismus in Österreich* (Graz, Köln, 1956), p. 71; Friedrich Heer, *Die dritte Kraft. Der europäische Humanismus zwischen den Fronten des konfessionellen Zeitalters* (Frankfurt am Main, 1960), pp. 434 ff. See also chap. 1 in this study.

[4] Karl Brandi, *Deutsche Reformation und Gegenreformation,* 2 vols. (Leipzig, 1927), II, 214. All the passages quoted from German works in this chapter were translated by the author.

and Counter Reformation in Bohemia? There, after the Albigensian and Waldensian revolts, anti-Catholic heresies of various kinds had succeeded earlier than in any other part of continental Europe. Accordingly, after the battle of the White Mountain in 1620, Protestantism was more drastically suppressed than anywhere else.

Precisely so. Hus and his followers in the early fifteenth century had indeed in a sense largely succeeded for generations before Luther. At the time when the Counter Reformation in Central Europe was in full swing, between the Religious Peace of Augsburg and the death of Emperor Maximilian II (1576), a benevolent would-be arbiter in the religious struggle, sovereign and Church seemed to be still in retreat before the advance of the Reformation—Lutherans, Calvinists of various kinds, and Bohemian Brethren.[5] At the time of the outbreak of the Thirty Years' War the estates, representing these denominations and their social and religious interests, were almost in full control of the government. Yet all this means that the religious upheavals in Bohemia and the concomitant changes in government had a history of some two centuries. In terms of this study this could not, of course, be considered an intermediate system (B) that could be superseded or absorbed within the course of two generations by a restored system (C). A system, in this case a chaotic one, that has lasted for two centuries can be suppressed, as has frequently been done, but it can hardly be fully uprooted and, in a psychological sense, undone. Indeed, the whole Czech history after the battle of the White Mountain, its relations to the Habsburg monarchy until 1918, and its tragic fate afterward has been largely and consistently determined by the reaction to the full sweep of the Counter Reformation in Bohemia under Ferdinand II. This is a clear sample of an original system, harshly suppressed by a subsequent order, but never merged with it; paralyzed in its external manifestations for a long time to come, but never destroyed and never truly reconverted.

[5] Eder perceives the turning point from Reformation to—what he refers to as "konfessioneller Absolutismus"—the complete subjection of religious freedom of the individual to the state, in the Peace of Augsburg in 1555. See Eder, pp. 2 ff. Hugo Hantsch in *Die Geschichte Österreichs,* 2d enlarged ed., 2 vols. (Graz, 1947), I, 270 f., focuses his attention in this respect on the termination of the Council of Trent in December, 1563. Both views, with some justification, are primarily concerned with the transition of an ideological movement into political action. Considering the slow system of communication in these times, it might be suggestive to point to a later date namely, the significance of the transition of government from Maximilian II to his son Rudolf II in 1576, from a pro-Protestant sovereign to a ruler who was in clear sympathy with the Counter Reformation.

The situation was very different in the Erblande. Here the success of the Reformation, especially within the governmental sphere, was never as sweeping as in Bohemia. Neither was it even remotely as lasting, over the long view. The influence of Protestantism in these lands does not begin before 1521, the year when Luther was outlawed at the Reichstag of Worms. It has not ended completely to this day, though it was in retreat, by and large, after the death of the emperor Maximilian II in 1576, despite the fact that the conflict between the Habsburg princes, the emperor Rudolf II and his brother and successor Matthias, gave the Protestant estates for a few years the chance for a new advance.[6] Within the first years of the reign of the new emperor Matthias (1612–1619), erroneously considered for some time to be a friend of Protestantism and rightly for all times to be a weakling, this fallacy became obvious. Under Ferdinand II (as emperor 1619–1637) the rout of Protestantism was already fully apparent. By 1628 it had for all practical purposes lost the last residues of its legal standing in Austria. It is thus fair to say that the rise of Protestantism in the German Austrian lands, and in substance its decline, had taken place within the period of two generations which we have allowed as the maximum for an intermediate system. It never became permanently established, though it came close to such establishment.

Thus from the chronological angle the selection of the example in this chapter can be defended. Another objection can be disposed of equally well. As set forth in the first part of this study, the cases should pertain primarily to the restoration processes of sociopolitical systems within clearly circumscribed political units. Primarily ideological movements—with only the partial exception of the Ottonian renovation—were ruled out because they can hardly be linked to definite political systems.[7] There seems to be more substance to the argument that the Habsburg Erblande, for the best part of the period under discussion here, formed not one but three political units: Lower and Upper Austria, Tyrol and the German possessions (the *Vorlande*), and Inner Austria. Yet the Erblande had been divided before (1379–1470), reunited by Maximilian I, partitioned again in the mid-sixteenth century, and merged for good after the mid-seventeenth century. Even during the intervening period they were under the rule of the same dynasty and in a sense subordinated to the head of the dynasty in his capacity as emperor of the Holy Roman Em-

[6] See Mecenseffy, pp. 140 ff.; Krones, III, 313 ff.; Franz M. Mayer, *Geschichte Österreichs mit besonderer Rücksicht auf das Kulturleben*, 3rd rev. ed. (Vienna, 1909), Vol. II, pp. 100 ff.

[7] See chap. 1, section on basic limitations of the value of historical analogies.

pire.[8] It should be permissible to stretch the point somewhat and to perceive the Erblande in a wider sense as one political though not one administrative power structure.

Another objection, namely, that the Protestant Reformation, the Catholic Reformation, and in a sense even the Counter Reformation, were primarily ideological, not political, movements, has more substance. In this context it seems of particular interest to argue a rare case where a predominantly ideological movement of the widest possible range can be studied within clearly established political lines. Within Central Europe it is indeed a unique case: a territory firmly attached to one ideology, which in the course of one generation falls under the sway of another, to be restored within a third generation to the original. In other comparable cases, such as Saxony, Brandenburg, Hungary, Bavaria, we observe either the complete victory of the new faith (Brandenburg, Saxony), a partial defeat of both the old and the new doctrine (Hungary), or the reentrenchment of the ancient creed into which the new one has never made substantial inroads (Bavaria). The Austrian case, on the other hand, reveals a far-reaching victory of the new faith, followed by almost complete and, what is even more important, genuine reconversion. This is not contradicted by the obvious use of political pressure by the victorious Counter Reformation. Such pressure, exercised on the Protestant side as much as on the Catholic, has been consistently an ugly concomitant of sweeping ideological movements. In no way must it be confounded, however, with their religious essence.

One important question is still open. To what extent have the Erblande become Protestant in the century between Luther's defiance of the emperor and empire and the battle of the White Mountain, which decided the issue not only in Bohemia but in the German-speaking Alpine-Danube lands as well? Varying criteria, such as baptism, profession of faith, church membership, and church attendance, make religious statistics unreliable and controversial, even today—and how much more true for the sixteenth century! Yet the century of denominational absolutism (Karl Eder's term) gives us at least a firm, though unhappy, guideline, the principle of the Religious Peace of Augsburg of 1555, *cuius regio eius religio*. Therewith, if not free and voluntary profession of faith, at least nominal church affiliation was clearly established. In the Habsburg lands a generation before, when the Reformation was advancing strongly, it is difficult to perceive even a formal distinction between the devout fol-

---

[8] Except for the last years of Rudolf II's reign during the conflict with his brother and successor, Matthias.

lowers of the old faith and the numerous adherents or sympathizers of the new creed.

How numerous were these? Catholic and Protestant sources abound in references to the spread of Protestantism in the Erblande.[9] They pertain almost equally to the better part of the sixteenth century after 1521. Except for a brief period in the latter part of Rudolf II's reign in Lower and Upper Austria, rights to Protestant worship and education in all the Erblande were guaranteed only for the two noble estates, lords and knights.[10] Similar rights did not exist legally for the burghers in markets and towns nor for the peasants in the villages. The latter were not represented in the estate diets at all. To be sure, burghers, then the fourth estate,[11] and peasants benefited in many ways from the privileges of the nobles to attend services in the chapels of the castles. In the villages they frequently took part in the instruction provided by the lord's personal predicants or preachers. Even substantial Protestant estate schools of fine quality were set up by the burghers in the major towns, clearly against the letter of the law, by mere sufferance of the sovereign, not by right. The number of students in these schools—by no means secret but still only semilegal—is uncertain. It is even more difficult to estimate the number of Protestants among the vast majority of the population, urban burghers and, above all, peasants. The fact that the bulk of the nobility was affiliated with Protestantism does not allow more than tentative conclusions in regard to free and unfree commoners, despite a large number of data available concerning individuals.[12] Yet these data too are reliable

[9] See, for instance, Krones, III, 538 f.; Josef Wodka, *Kirche in Österreich* (Vienna, 1959), pp. 215 f.; Mayer, II, 51 ff.; Mecenseffy, pp. 50 ff., 140 ff.; Georg Loesche, *Geschichte des Protestantismus im vormaligen und neuen Österreich* (Leipzig, 1930), pp. 17 ff.

[10] Mayer, II, 107 f.; Mecenseffy, pp. 132 f. Even in the early part of Rudolf's administration, which was more or less favorably disposed toward Protestantism, rights of Protestants in towns and markets were only in a vague way safeguarded and by no mean fully secured.

The most comprehensive work on Ferdinand I is still Franz B. von Bucholtz, *Geschichte der Regierung Ferdinand des Ersten,* 9 vols. (Vienna, 1831–1838). Although Bucholtz emphasizes foreign affairs, a useful survey of the religious conflicts can be found in Vol. VIII, pp. 123 ff.

[11] The high ecclesiastic dignitaries, the prelates generally, represented the first estate; the lords and knights, the second and third.

[12] See particularly Johann Loserth, ed., *Akten und Correspondenzen zur Geschichte der Gegenreformation in Innerösterreich unter Erzherzog Karl II (1578–90)* (Vienna, 1898), *Fontes rerum Austriacarum,* sec. 2, *Diplomataria et acta,* Vol. L; and by the same editor, *Akten und Korrespondenzen zur Geschichte der Gegenreformation in Innerösterreich unter Ferdinand II,* Part I, 1590–1600, and Part II, 1600–1637 (Vienna, 1906–1907), *Fontes rerum Austriacarum,* sec. 1, *Diplomataria et acta,* Vols. LVIII and

only for the privileged Lutheran Augsburg denomination. Data concerning Calvinism, or former Lutherans with Calvinist tendencies, Anabaptists, and adherents of the strange Flacian heresy with its emphasis on original sin, are even more vague.[13]

Most important is another related problem, namely, that during the reign of Ferdinand I, differences between the old and the new faith were not clearly marked at all. Celibacy began to be strictly enforced again only under the influence of the Council of Trent. Marriage of priests, communion of both kinds, that is, including the cup for the laity, was in the first half of the sixteenth century by no means considered evidence of heresy. As faithful a Catholic sovereign as Ferdinand I had asked Pope Pius IV to grant the cup for the laity to his subjects, and the papal adherence to this request was promulgated solemnly from the pulpit of the cathedral of St. Stephen in Vienna, hardly a month prior to the emperor's death.[14]

The supreme aim of his oldest son and successor, Maximilian II, was the "general Christian Reformation and blessed reconciliation of religion in the German nation." [15] This meant to him the merger of the new creed with the ancient in one indivisible reformed religion, but one still based on Catholic tenets. Granted that Maximilian was not as devout a Catholic as his father, the issue here is that the final break between the Church and Protestantism in Germany was established neither by the

---

LX. Specific references to these most important collections of documents will be made in the following notes. See further various monographs in *Jahrbücher des Protestantismus* (Vienna, 1880–   ). For the reign of Ferdinand I, the collection of documents in Vol. IX of Bucholtz is still useful.

[13] Concerning Calvinism in Austria, see Irmtraut Lindeck, "Der Einfluss der staatsrechtlichen und bekenntnismässigen Anschauungen auf die Auseinandersetzung zwischen Landesfürstentum und Städten in Österreich während der Gegenreformation," *Jahrbuch der Gesellschaft für die Geschichte des Protestantismus*, Vol. 60 (1939), pp. 81–104; Vol. 61 (1940), pp. 15–38; see particularly pp. 15 ff., 32 f.; see further Hans Sturmberger, *Georg Erasmus Tschernembl* (Graz, Cologne, 1953), with particular regard to Upper Austria, pp. 36 ff., 407 f.; Hantsch, *op cit.,* (see n. 5 above), I, 327 f., 344.

Concerning the Flacians, the doctrine of the former Lutheran theologian from Istria, Vlacich, with the pseudonyms Flacius or Matthias F. Illyricus, see Eder, *op. cit.* (see n. 3 above), pp. 217 f.; Mayer, II, 60 ff., 157 f.; Johann Loserth, *Die Reformation und Gegenreformation in den innerösterreichischen Ländern im XVI. Jahrhundert* (Stuttgart, 1898), pp. 279 f., 372 f.; Hantsch, I, 283 f.; Loesche, 82 f.

Concerning the Anabaptists, see Mayer, II, 30 ff.; Mecenseffy, pp. 35 ff.; Adam Wolf, *Geschichtliche Bilder aus Österreich* (Vienna, 1878), Vol. I, pp. 67–112; Bucholtz, V, 568 ff.

[14] Hantsch, I, 271 ff.; see also 240 f., 267 f.

[15] Hantsch, I, 285.

Schmalkaldic war of Charles V nor by the Peace of Augsburg. It was caused by the reformulation of Catholic doctrines at the Council of Trent and their spread, largely by Jesuit mission to the north, not before the middle of the 1560's at the earliest. Before this time a clear dogmatic distinction is not feasible; afterward political division based on enforced religious conformism, up to then traceable only by approximation, becomes distinct. Yet even this tells us only who should be considered a Protestant, on the strength of data which are often not available in regard to commoners. Barring the not infrequent open revolt and widespread violence between different groups on a social and religious basis, such as the peasant wars in Upper Austria, knowledge of numbers is here primarily an educated guess. We do know, however, that the noble estates, who exercised secular power, were predominantly Protestant. Their influence on the religious affiliation of the unfree peasants was often prevalent; on free burghers in towns it was considerable. Therefore, we are justified in assuming that the Erblande throughout the better part of the sixteenth century and at least the first decade of the seventeenth century were largely Protestant. And this assumption gives special interest to the case of religious restoration with its social connotation in a strictly limited political sphere.

The Original System under Maximilian I

The onset of the original system (A) in the Erblande may be perceived around the year 1490, when all the Habsburg domains were reunited in the hands of the old and undistinguished Emperor Frederick III (1440–1493) and his young heir, the Roman King Maximilian I, who then governed in the Erblande in the place of his father. Because of the spiritual unity of the prereformatory era, the beginnings of the original system could be traced back much farther than the year 1490. Yet, inasmuch as our ideological analysis lies within definite political confines, it is reasonable to commence with the year 1490 when, after the death of king Matthias Corvinus of Hungary, the Magyars were forced to withdraw from the Erblande. The original system ended when the Reformation began to make serious inroads in the Erblande, roughly when, after Luther's return from exile to Wittenberg, the Reformation received a new uplift in Germany. These events coincided approximately with the beginnings, in 1521, of the administration of Ferdinand I in Austria.

The relationship between ideological change and political partition should be noted here. The partition period of the Erblande following the death of Ferdinand I in 1564 may be considered to have terminated in 1621, when the emperor Ferdinand II reasserted in his then valid will the

indivisibility of the Erblande by strength of the primogeniture successions. It is notable that prior divisions of the Habsburg lands were not
related to religious conflict. This is obvious for the division of 1379, but
even the division in 1564 into three lines, based on Ferdinand I's domestic
ordinance of 1554, did not refer to the religious crisis.[16] What then, is the
strange connection, if any, between the facts that the Habsburg Erblande
were united at the time the Reformation started, and were reunited rather
firmly when the Counter Reformation was fully successful? I believe that
at least an indirect relationship with the religious issue can be assumed.
The division of the Habsburg lands strengthened the powers of the
estates versus the sovereign in the individual domains. The more centralized governmental power was, the more easily could the estates be controlled—regardless of any ideological issues in the process of centralization.

Since the two noble secular estates in the individual Erblande fell in
general under the influence of Protestantism, the fourth, the princely
towns and markets, was linked fairly closely to the two socially superior
secular estates and by commercial and cultural affiliations to Protestant
German cities as well. This clearly benefited the spread of Protestantism,
and all the more so since even the first estate, the Catholic ecclesiastic
lords, in questions of administrative and judicial autonomy versus the
sovereign, sided quite frequently with the secular lords.[17] Under Lutheran influence this meant at the most an assertion of legal and political
rights by petition and interposition with the sovereign. Under the
influence of Calvinism, which under certain conditions authorized resistance by force of arms against what it considered religious tyranny, rule
by the estates might have meant open revolt. The late sixteenth and early
seventeenth century risings in Upper Austria illustrate the point particu-

[16] Even though the complete enforcement of this policy of unification was materialized only by 1665, the principle itself as a guideline for Habsburg administration was already clearly established by Maximilian I, but defied at the time the
Reformation reached its high tide. Huber and Dopsch, op. cit., pp. 174 ff.; Hellbling,
op. cit., p. 268; Krones, op. cit., III, 258 ff. (for these see n. 2 above); Mayer, II, 57 f.
The well-established concern of Ferdinand I regarding the religious views of his
oldest son, Maximilian II, is not expressed in this document, but only later in his
will and in a pledge by Maximilian in 1562 to live and die within the Catholic
Church. See also Bucholtz, VIII, 753 ff.

[17] On the estates system in the Erblande in the late fifteenth and early sixteenth
centuries see Bucholtz, VIII, 26 ff.; Huber and Dopsch, pp. 212 ff.; Hellbling, pp.
111 ff., 134 ff.; Krones, II, 586 f., III, 47 ff.; Karl and Mathilde Uhlirz, Handbuch der
Geschichte Österreichs, 2d rev. ed. (Graz, Cologne, 1963), Vol. I, pp. 460 ff.

larly well. According to Calvin, the justification of resistance against tyranny is to be deduced, however, not directly from popular sovereignty but from the power of the magistrates, and only in extreme cases.[18] They in turn are responsible to spiritual authority. Only if it was held that the sovereign had violated God's law was the estates' resistance against him sanctioned by Calvinist doctrine. What counted in practice, however, was far less alleged Lutheran cooperation with secular authority of any persuasion or any conceivable Calvinist opposition to it, but the nobles' claims to autonomy. These were based primarily on the old demands of the liege men and vassals and were naturally strengthened by appeal to principles of faith. In this sense the reasoning of the Protestant nobles was sincerely meant but conveniently used.

The colorful reign of Maximilian I was largely dedicated to the strengthening of the power of central government. He intended also to weaken the power of the estates, which, unknown to him, was to further so mightily the task of the Reformation in the Erblande. This objective of centralized power versus pluralistic estates' rights was a major reason, though not the only one, for linking his regime with the victorious Counter Reformation a century after his death. It pursued in this respect the same objectives, though on different ideological grounds. Yet the community of important political interests should suffice to perceive Maximilian's reign as the original system (A) in our terms.

Maximilian I, the imaginative ruler whose reign initiated the ambitious marriage policy [19] that led to the expansion of his house in the East and West, had two major ambitions in the administrative field, empire reform and reforms in his own Erblande. In neither was he completely successful, though in the latter more than in the former. As for the empire, a permanent *Treuga Dei* (*Landfrieden*), could not be fully enforced in the emperor's lifetime, and even less in the following stormy period. A division of the empire into districts (*Reichskreise*), under sovereign princes as imperial deputies, could be only partially effected. Consequently, taxes to

[18] On the distinction between Lutheran and Calvinist political doctrine in this respect see Irmtraut Lindeck, *op. cit.* (see n. 13 above), Vol. 60 (1939), pp. 92 ff.; Vol. 61 (1940), pp. 19 f., 30 f., who erroneously assumes a direct relationship between the concepts of popular sovereignty and resistance against tyranny as doctrine of orthodox Calvinism. See further George H. Sabine, *A History of Political Theory,* rev. ed. (New York, 1958), pp. 358 ff., 366 ff.; Heer, *op cit.* (see n. 3 above), pp. 271 f.

[19] On the early life and the Burgundian marriage of Maximilian, see Heinrich Fichtenau, *Der junge Maximilian* (Vienna, 1959), pp. 5 f., 19 ff. On the Burgundian and Jagellonian marriage policy in general, see Maximilian Jansen, *Kaiser, Maximilian I* (Munich, 1905), pp. 37 ff.; Krones, II, 496 ff.; Uhlirz, I, 457 ff.

maintain troops of the empire could only rarely be collected. A supreme imperial court, the *Reichskammergericht*, was established; much against Maximilian's wishes it became an instrument of the imperial estates, rather than of the emperor himself.[20]

He was somewhat more successful in integrating the Habsburg lands with the empire. The plan to transform the Erblande into a full-fledged *Reichskreis* failed. Yet Maximilian's attempt to create agencies for the joint administrative and particularly the joint financial agenda of empire and Erblande, the Aulic Council and the Court Chamber, served as foundation for more efficient reforms under his grandson Ferdinand I. Finally, the convocation of a general diet of all the Erblande in Innsbruck in 1518, only a few months before the emperor's death, was only a failure in its immediate effect as far as centralization was concerned. Maximilian visualized here an objective that was largely fulfilled within a century.

More specific reforms were effectuated within the emperor's lifetime, namely, the division of the Erblande into two major administrative units, the Lower Austrian and the Upper Austrian groups. Each of these two main units of lands was to be governed by a well-organized system with appropriate administrative subdivisions and corresponding judicial organizations. Most important, each of these administrations was controlled by officials, appointed by the sovereign and responsible to him. This innovation, though not fully put through, meant not only the abolition of political feudalism by delegated power, but also the curtailment of the participation of the estates in government.[21]

Although the emperor's reign was touched upon by the unfolding German Reformation only at its very end and not yet with any decisive effect, it already felt the full effect of the Renaissance and specifically of Humanism. The emperor's court in Vienna and Innsbruck became the center of manifold cultural activities. Literature, history, geography, and the formative arts benefited from Maximilian's interests. Even though this Austrian Humanism did not spread to the cities as cultural centers independent of courtly culture, this did not in any way mean the deliberate exclusion of commoners. It merely indicated that the Austrian Renaissance and Humanism had not yet arrived at a stage where bourgeois culture independent of courtly patronage had sufficient time to

[20] See Heinrich Brunner, *Grundzüge der deutschen Rechtsgeschichte* (Munich, 1927), pp. 282 ff., 287 ff.; Hellmuth Rössler, *Europa im Zeitalter von Renaissance, Reformation und Gegenreformation* (Munich, 1956), pp. 189 ff. The plan for the creation of Reichskreise actually goes back to the emperor Albrecht II in 1438.

[21] Hantsch, *op. cit.* (see n. 5 above), I, 206 ff., 209 ff.; Krones, II, 507 ff., 575 ff.; Uhlirz, I, 460 ff.; Rössler, pp. 200 ff.; Jansen, pp. 72 ff.

develop.[22] Such spread might well have taken place—as in other countries to the south and west—if the age of religious conflict and the victory of the Counter Reformation had not put a stop to further development in this direction. It is possible also, that a victory of the Reformation, particularly under Calvinist Puritan influence, would have led to similar delay. In any case, although the cultural activities under Maximilian I were a major and distinctive feature and accomplishment of his reign, they were not reflected in the restored system (C) under Ferdinand II. The line of development we must pursue from initial to restored system is concentrated primarily on the political conflict between some kind of civil service system and political feudalism, between princely sovereign might and power of the estates.

THE INTERMEDIATE SYSTEM UNDER FERDINAND I

The intermediate period (B) in the history of the Austrian restoration process covers, roughly speaking, the reigns of Ferdinand I in Austria from 1521–1564, under whom the Reformation spread, and of his son Maximilian II (1564–1576), under whom it was more or less fully sustained. After that it was forced to yield gradually and with increasing momentum, despite a short flare-up at the end of Rudolf II's reign and at the beginning of that of Matthias. The latter part of the second and the third decade of the seventeenth century sealed the fate of Protestantism in the Erblande in a way hardly less radical than in Bohemia. Thus we have to deal here with a half century of stormy development, of which the greater part covers the reign of Ferdinand I.

This younger brother of Charles V, born and raised in Spain but destined to become the head of the German line of the Habsburgs, was installed by the emperor in 1521 as regent of the five Lower Austrian duchies (Austria below and Austria above the Enns,[23] Styria, Carinthia and Carniola). The formal investiture with the Erblande including Tyrol, Vorarlberg, and the possessions in south and southwest Germany, the Vorlande, was followed the next year by the treaty of Brussels.[24]

[22] On Renaissance and Humanism under Maximilian's patronage see Rössler, pp. 206 ff.; Jansen, pp. 91 ff.; Hantsch, I, 211 ff.; Mayer, I, 556 ff.; Otto Rommel, ed., *Wiener Renaissance* (Vienna, 1947), pp. 245 ff.; 321 ff.; Hans Ankwicz-Kleehoven, *Der Wiener Humanist Johannes Cuspinian* (Graz, Cologne, 1959), pp. 78–135; Kurt Adel, ed., *Konrad Celtis, Poeta laureatus* (Graz, 1960), pp. 17 ff.

[23] Later, as will be remembered, constantly referred to as Lower and Upper Austria.

[24] See Wilhelm Bauer, *Die Anfänge Ferdinands I.* (Vienna, 1907), pp. 100 ff., 121 ff., 149 ff.; Bucholtz, *op cit.* (see n. 10 above), I, 141 ff.

Through the policy initiated by his grandfather Maximilian I, Ferdinand, married to a princess from the originally Polish house of Jagello, became in 1526 king of Hungary and Bohemia and in 1527 king of Croatia. Nominal though the possession of the major part of Hungary remained for a long time, owing to the Hungarian rebellions and Turkish wars, Ferdinand was actually the first ruler of the emerging multinational Habsburg empire. In 1531 he was elected Roman king and therewith the declared successor and representative of his imperial brother in Germany. After Charles's abdication in 1556, Ferdinand succeeded him finally as emperor as well.

There can be little doubt that this able and humane ruler was sincerely devoted to his brother Charles V, despite the fact that Charles would have preferred to transmit the imperial mantle to his son Philip II, and that Ferdinand in the fight against the Protestant Reformation took a more realistic, more moderate line. As to the loyalty to the faith of the devout but not bigoted Ferdinand, no more convincing proof is needed than the passage in his will in which he implored his oldest son and heir, whose Protestant tendencies were known: "God knows that on this earth nothing could hurt me more than that you, Maximilian, my oldest son, who will have to rule over so much, should leave our faith." [25]

Ferdinand's far-reaching administrative reforms in the empire as well as in the Erblande were in no way controversial. They were far more practical and successful than those of his grandfather. Maintaining in broad principles the administrative division of Maximilian I during his reign, he created in the Aulic Council a supreme administrative and judicial agency for all the Erblande. It was later transformed into the Imperial Council, in which the empire was represented by a deputy of the imperial chancellor, the Archbishop of Mayence. Of lasting importance, particularly in foreign affairs, was the creation of the Privy Council, of the General Court Chancellery as one of the overall supreme administrative agencies, and of the Court Chamber, which was primarily concerned with major financial administrative agenda. Furthermore, the Aulic War

[25] Brandi, *op. cit.* (see n. 4 above), II, 60 f.; I, 221, 320 f. See further Wilhelm Bauer and Robert Lacroix, eds., *Die Korrespondenz Ferdinands I.* (Veröffentlichungen der Kommission der neueren Geschichte der Akademie der Wissenschaften in Wien) (Vienna, 1937–38), Bd. II, Part I. *Familienkorrespondenz 1527 und 1528;* see particularly the letter of April 9, 1524, pp. 58 f., in which Ferdinand admonishes his sister, Queen Maria of Hungary, known for her Protestant leanings, to remain loyal to the faith; see also Part II, *Familienkorrespondenz 1529 und 1530,* letter of May 22, 1529, pp. 414 f., warning the queen about a heretical preacher. See also Bucholtz, VIII, 700 ff.; and family correspondence of 1527 and 1552 with Queen Maria of Hungary, IX, 8 ff., 535 ff., 544 ff.

Council, a collegiate body, was to become one of the most important but, by the nature of its combined strategic and administrative functions, least effective institutions. The overall utilitarian effect of the reforms, however, remains uncontested.[26]

A strict distinction in early modern times between executive and legislative power in the sense that one derives from the sovereign, the other from the estates cannot be justified historically. Yet it is correct to acknowledge the existence of two power systems which combined executive and legislative functions; in one the sovereign gives equal emphasis to both functions, in the other the estates exercise legislative functions, though not exclusively. In this sense Ferdinand's efforts toward centralization impinge on the power of the estates, and since the estates were the champions of the Reformation, they impinge heavily. This does not mean necessarily that these estates—in this case the noble estates—were selfless champions. As Franz M. Mayer puts it aptly: "In addition to the sovereign, the estates held great power in the last centuries of the Middle Ages. Then they became concerned with the movement of the Reformation and opposed the Catholic princes. In this conflict, the burghers attempted to side as equals with the nobles, and nobility favored these endeavors, since the nobles could expect to gain in strength if they could rely on broad strata of the population. The estates asked in the diets for religious liberties and made the grant of appropriations dependent on their acceptance. . . . The sovereigns were led to believe that the existence of the monarchy was threatened by the power of the Protestant estates. Consequently, they desired religious unity, which according to existing conditions could be achieved only by the elimination of Protestantism." [27]

This does not mean that administrative reform was motivated primarily by Ferdinand's stand against Protestantism; it means that the reforms had a decided and eventually an adverse effect on the Reformation in the Erblande. Its first stage was not fought by bigotry and intolerance. Admittedly, it was checked by firmness, but quite frequently

---

[26] Huber and Dopsch, 180 ff.; Hellbling, *op. cit.* (see n. 2 above), pp. 229 ff., 239 ff.; Erich Zöllner, *Geschichte Österreichs* (Vienna, 1961), pp. 187 f.; Hermann I, Bidermann, *Geschichte der österreichischen Gesamtstaatsidee 1526–1804* (Innsbruck, 1867), Abt. I, pp. 29 ff.; Mayer, II, 269 ff.; Hantsch, I, 277 ff.; Kann, *A Study in Austrian Intellectual History,* pp. 19 ff.

See also Bucholtz, VIII, 4 ff., on the administration in the Lower Austrian lands, and 313 ff. on the administration in the Upper Austrian lands, Tyrol and the Vorlande. On the administration in Bohemia see IV, 414 f.

[27] Mayer, II, 264 f. and passim to 270. The interpretation of Hantsch, I, 277 f., differs as to the effect of centralization or decentralization on the estates. See also Bucholtz, VIII, 26 ff., 123 ff.

by constructive reasoning as well. Ferdinand was sincerely concerned with the improvement of education and with the misconduct of the clergy, whose low state prior to the reforms of Trent has been aptly and vividly pictured by Catholic and Protestant authorities alike.[28] The sovereign was even somewhat aware of the close connection between economic and religious grievances in the Austrian peasant revolts in the mid-twenties of the sixteenth century, as evidenced by the discussion of the peasant demands in the so-called Meran articles at the diet of Innsbruck in 1525. Suppression by force of the ensuing upheavals, under the peasant leader Michael Geissmayer, without any general alleviation of the existing hardship, is another matter.[29] Ferdinand's attempt, on the other hand, to take advantage of the Catholic Reformation, particularly of the Jesuit mission in the field of higher education, was only natural for a devout Catholic regent.[30] So was the introduction of the visitation commissions in the service of the Catholic Reformation. Originally these were intended to improve religious services rather than to impose reconversion by force, as was done after 1596 by Ferdinand II. The conciliatory attitude of Ferdinand I in such matters as the communion cup for the laity has been noted. The same holds true for his readiness to condone the marriage of priests and his toleration of Protestant services outside the castles.[31] Even an extreme Protestant interpretation could recognize Ferdinand's conciliatory effort toward Lutheranism. His harsher policy concerning various sects considered as outright dissident is another matter.[32]

Incidents of oppression by force, though not lacking, remained isolated in the sphere of Lower Austria (in modern terms) and Vienna, and religious concessions were relatively far-reaching.[33] Religious privileges of the nobles were generally respected and this includes private education.

[28] Hantsch, I, 242 ff., 254 ff.; Mayer, II, 21 ff.; Mecenseffy, *op. cit.* (see n. 3 above), pp. 6 f. For conditions at the University of Vienna and higher education in the Lower Austrian lands in general, see Bucholtz, VIII, 218 ff., 226 ff.

[29] Mayer, I, 428 f., 507 ff.; Krones, *op. cit.* (see n. 2 above), II, 644 ff.; Hantsch, I, 249 ff. See also Bucholtz, VIII, 342 ff.; for the so-called Landesordnung of Geissmayer, see IX, 651 ff.

[30] Bucholtz, VIII, 183 ff.; Mayer, II, 51 ff.; Karl von Otto, "Die Anfänge der Reformation im Erzherzogtum Österreich," *Jahrbuch der Gesellschaft für die Geschichte des Protestantismus,* Vol. 1 (1880), pp. 18 f.

[31] Otto, pp. 19 ff.; Bucholtz, VIII, 170 ff., 195 ff.

[32] Loesche, *op. cit.* (see n. 9 above), pp. 17 ff.; Bauer, *op. cit.* (see n. 23 above), pp. 181 ff.

[33] Mayer, II, 21 ff.; Otto, pp. 24 ff.; see also Georg Ernst Waldau, *Geschichte der Protestanten in Österreich, Steiermark, Kärnten und Krain vom Jahre 1520 bis auf die neueste Zeit,* 2 vols. (Anspach, 1784), Protestant account. See Vol. I, chaps. 4, 5, 13, 19, 22, 23.

As for the burghers in the towns and particularly in Vienna, Lutheran religious services and schools were tolerated, though there was occasional harassment. The burghers in markets and towns, the fourth estate, operated in a gray area, one not expressly sanctioned by governmental authority.

In Inner Austria, particularly in Styria, but also in Carinthia and in (predominantly Slovene) Carniola, Lutheranism was even more firmly entrenched among the nobles and in towns and markets. Nor should the Protestant impact on the monasteries be forgotten. The affiliation with Protestant doctrines, not merely with general ideas and tendencies, seems to have been more direct than in Lower Austria. Sectarian dissidents, however, particularly Anabaptists, were persecuted here as there, and in the Tyrol as well.[34]

Of all the Erblande, "Upper Austria developed as the center of the Augsburg Confession and became the firmest bastion of Austrian Protestantism."[35] It might be added that Calvinism, largely under the influence of Georg Erasmus von Tschernembl more than a generation after Ferdinand I's death, played an important part in the Upper Austrian Reformation, too. Hugo Hantsch believes that an especially unsatisfactory relationship between the diocese of Passau and the clergy in Upper Austria was largely responsible for the development of resistance, organized and unorganized, against the traditional authority of church and state, that was more violent, frequent, and lasting than in any other of the German-speaking Habsburg domains. This may well be an important factor, to which others should be added, such as the proximity to the German and Bohemian centers of Protestantism and rebellion. There is also an economic issue worthy of consideration. The markets and the peasant holdings in fertile Upper Austria were more prosperous than those in the Alpine Inner Austrian lands and at the same time were farther removed from the seat of governmental authority than Lower Austria and, within it, Vienna. To be sure, there was reason enough for social dissatisfaction linked to the religious demands, but there existed also more economic power for concerted resistance, which there, as anywhere in the Erblande, was only temporarily contained at the time of Ferdinand's death in 1564. He had centralized government in his lands to

[34] J. Loserth, *Die Reformation und Gegenreformation* (see n. 13 above), pp. 13-286 *passim;* Otto, pp. 12 ff.; Mayer, II, 25 ff., 46 f.; Theodor Elze, "Die Anfänge des Protestantismus in Krain," *Jahrbuch der Gesellschaft für die Geschichte des Protestantismus,* Vol. 1, pp. 21 ff.; J. Loserth, "Truberiana," *ibid.,* Vol. 24 (1903), pp. 1–10.

[35] Hantsch, I, 258. Concerning the Anabaptists, see also Bucholtz, V. 568 ff.

a large extent. He could not achieve even a measure of unity among the peoples.

THE INTERMEDIATE SYSTEM UNDER MAXIMILIAN II

The next phase of the Reformation process in the Erblande is clearly marked by the reign of Maximilian II (1564–1576). Largely because of his pro-Protestant inclination or, according to some, outright Protestant affiliation, the period is generally referred to as the high tide of Austrian Protestantism. That is correct, inasmuch as there was legal consideration for a time. Yet one can hardly speak of a further spread of the Reformation. In Maximilian's time and realms, this was already checked to some extent by the decisions of the Council of Trent and thus by the advance of the Catholic Reformation. Maximilian II, after the division of Ferdinand's realms, emperor, king of Hungary and Bohemia, and archduke in Lower and Upper Austria, was a most interesting personality, though as Hantsch rightly points out, probably not quite the mysterious character which his biographer Viktor Bibl sees in him.[36]

There is conclusive evidence that the emperor belonged to the none too rare type of sixteenth century statesmen, intellectuals, and, specifically, theologians—often referred to as Irenicists—who believed in a merger between Catholic and Protestant doctrines, brought about by peaceful compromise and conciliation. This meant to give some ground to the doctrines of the new faith; but this had been true up to a point for Maximilian's father, Ferdinand, whose devotion to the Roman Catholic Church was never in doubt. The difference between the two rulers in religious questions is externally a matter of degree; in a more personal sense the problem may have been quite different. Ferdinand clearly yielded to necessity in his concessions to Lutheranism; Maximilian just as clearly sympathized with it. But on the basis of the idea of reconciliation this does not mean a formal break with the old faith and a solemn acceptance of the new. Either step presumably would have defeated the emperor's purpose. After all, Maximilian had promised his father, at his request in 1562, to live and die within the Church. Accordingly, he had dismissed his Protestant court preacher, Sebastian Pfauser, prior to this pledge, and from that time on he always professed himself officially to be a Catholic. The fact that extreme unction apparently was not adminis-

[36] Hantsch, I, 397, 275 f.; Viktor Bibl, *Maximilian I, Der rätselhafte Kaiser* (Hellerau, 1929); Bucholtz, VIII, 700 ff., IX, 689 ff. (reports by Maximilian to Ferdinand I in 1563).

tered to him before his death is, in terms of his time, no proof to the contrary.[37]

Maximilian's overall attitude is perhaps best expressed in a letter of November 20, 1569, to Philip II of Spain, in which he defends himself against a polite insinuation by the king of laxity in religious matters: "Often, it is true, have I preferred the path of counseling to that of severity. I have avoided the shedding of the blood of my subjects, so that the unrest and the misfortunes of these times will not be increased. In this, Señor, I have always followed the example of my father. . . . I declare, in short, that I think of nothing else but to live and die a Catholic prince." [38]

The major legislative actions of this frequently indecisive, irresolute, but always humane and, as far as possible, peaceful reign bear out the conclusion that the emperor's religious policy was directed at reform and conciliation, not at outright conversion. In 1567 and 1568 he introduced a new order of improved conduct and education for the clergy in the Lower and Upper Austrian monasteries. In 1568 he made religious exercises for the noble estates in these two lands fully lawful; thus he moved clearly beyond mere toleration. In 1571 he endorsed this policy by a solemn declaration, though it still was not extended to the fourth estate of burghers in markets and towns. In 1572 the ruler of the Inner Austrian

[37] Mayer, II, 56 ff., 58 ff.; Krones *op cit.* (see n. 2 above), III, 266 ff.; Irmtraut Lindeck, *op. cit.* (see n. 13 above), Vol. 60 (1939), pp. 87 f.; Waldau, I, 128 ff., 196 f.; Loesche, pp. 21 ff.; Mecenseffy, *op. cit.* (see n. 3 above), pp. 48 ff. None of these three last-mentioned Protestant sources claims that the emperor had ever become a Protestant. Maximilian in his correspondence refers to himself consistently as a good Catholic and defender of the faith. Although obvious political considerations enter here as well, particularly in the relationship to his cousin Philip II of Spain, this evidence cannot be taken lightly. See Viktor Bibl, ed., *Die Korrespondenz Maximilian II,* Vol. I. *Familienkorrespondenz,* Juli 1564 bis August 1566 (Vienna, 1916), Kommission für neuere Geschichte Österreichs. See in particular Maximilian's letter to the Spanish ambassador of May 20, 1565, pp. 162 ff. See further Vol. II, correspondence 1566–1567 (Vienna, 1921), letters of August 31, 1566, September 21, 1566, March 7, 1567, and September 30, 1567, to Philip II of Spain, in which the emperor consistently counsels moderation in the Netherlands. The reason given is always that thus the faith could be defended better, foreign complications could be checked. After all, Calvinism is perceived as a worse danger even than Lutheranism.

See Mathias Koch, ed., *Quellen zur Geschichte des Kaisers Maximilian II,* 2 vols. (Leipzig, 1857–1861), II, 101–107, the report of the Spanish ambassador, Marquis D'Almazan, about the death of Maximilian. It is inconclusive concerning the question whether Maximilian died before extreme unction could be administered or whether he did not care to receive it.

[38] Otto, pp. 37 f., in answer to a letter by the king of October 26, 1569. For the text of this exchange of letters see further M. Koch, ed., II, 92–100.

lands, the emperor's brother, the archduke Charles, followed this with the religious pacification of Graz, which in substance equals the imperial concessions for Upper and Lower Austria. Further concessions were made by the emperor as king of Bohemia to the Bohemian estates in 1575, one year before his death.

Specifically, this meant that during Maximilian's reign services were also tolerated in the diet buildings in Vienna and in Linz, and general religious instruction was given as well, clearly for the benefit of the burghers. Similar arrangements existed in smaller towns in Lower and Upper Austria. The question arises: Why did Maximilian steadfastly refuse to extend religious privileges to the fourth estate of the urban burghers as well, by something more than mere sufferance? Otto assumes that "the emperor presumably wanted to prevent the Protestants from gaining preponderance because this would make the desired merger of the two religious parties more difficult." [39] This may indeed have been a factor, though probably more in Maximilian's thought than in his actions. Although he sincerely wished for conciliation, he did not actually fight for it. Fighting for a cause was not the emperor's strong point, witness his irresolute conduct of the Turkish war. Maximilian went only as far as he did perhaps because he was consistently pressed by the noble estates, on whose support he was dependent in more ways than one. This is not to say that they pressed consistently very hard in religious matters. In this respect they shared some feelings of solidarity with the towns and, particularly in Upper Austria, with the peasants as well. On the other hand, they had strong common interests with the prelates, the ecclesiastic lords in the social field, and they did not look with favor on an advance in status of the burghers, an advance that surely could not have been confined for long to the religious question. This was doubly true for their relationship to the peasants. [40]

In a brief review of the situation in the other units of the Erblande, Tyrol and the Vorlande, and Inner Austria—the one under the emperor's brother Ferdinand, the other under his brother Charles—we deal with entirely different entities. The two archdukes did not necessarily have to follow the emperor's policy in detail, though the imperial policy may have

[39] Otto, pp. 18 f.; see also Loserth, *Die Reformation und Gegenreformation,* pp. 287 ff.

[40] Brandi, *op cit.* (see n. 4 above), II, 153 ff.; Karl Völker, "Die Stände Augsburgischen Bekenntnisses auf den niederösterreichischen Landtagen," *Jahrbuch der Gesellschaft für die Geschichte des Protestantismus,* Vol. 58 (1937), pp. 6 ff.; Lindeck, *op. cit.* (see n. 13 above), Vol. 60 (1939), pp. 93 ff.; Otto, pp. 22 ff.; Mayer, II, 62 f.; Hantsch, I, 288 f.

served as a guideline, at least in Inner Austria, which was contiguous to Maximilian's own domains, Lower and Upper Austria. The brothers were far stricter Catholics than Maximilian. Ferdinand introduced aggressive counterreformatory measures, which could already be distinguished from Catholic reformatory missionary measures in the 1560's. They were directed partly against Anabaptist sectarianism, but also partly against Lutheranism. Pressure on Protestants to leave the land, and other hardships, were initiated in Tyrol long before similar measures were begun in the other Erblande.[41]

The archduke Charles was more moderate and certainly more under the influence of the emperor. Only at the end of Maximilian's reign, and more markedly under Rudolf II's, did he turn to a counterreformatory policy. During the early part of his reign and Maximilian's he was in particular need of support by the estates. This was largely because his lands were fully exposed to the Turkish threat. Beyond his assurances to the noble estates of Styria in 1572, Charles tolerated Protestant services and educational establishments in Graz and smaller towns, though, like the emperor, he strictly refused to concede religious liberty by law to the fourth estate. Yet at the diet of Bruck, convoked for the estates of all his lands in 1578, the archduke, badly in need of financial support, was forced to extend to Carinthia and Carniola his previous pledges to the Styrian estates. The Protestant interpretation, that Charles had actually issued a Magna Charta for all the Protestants in Inner Austria, is exaggerated. Like Maximilian, he neither tolerated non-Lutheran sects nor more than tolerated—but did not sanction—religious liberties of Lutherans in markets and towns. As for toleration, the estates in Inner Austria had secured and coordinated their privileges to a wider degree than the nobles in the other Habsburg Erblande.

In view of the increasing Turkish threat, the estates might have gone one decisive step farther. They might have secured religious liberties for the burghers. Because of the nobles' influence on the unfree peasants, this would have meant full victory for the Protestant Reformation in the largest area of the Erblande. Charles, who had called the Jesuits to Graz and had established a college there, which in 1585 became a full-fledged Jesuit university, certainly was able to prevent this against feeble opposition. Hantsch is right when he notes: "It was all too clear that the

[41] Mayer, II, 64 ff.; Krones, III, 251 ff.; Loserth, *Die Reformation und Gegenreformation,* pp. 287-360 *passim;* Mecenseffy, pp. 66 ff.; see also, on conditions in Tyrol, Georg Kirchmair's memoirs, edited by Th. G. v. Karajan (Vienna, 1865), particularly pp. 452, 458, 465, 513, 521.

last position of princely territorial power was involved here. No hope would remain if the towns were drawn completely into the camp of nobility and Protestantism. The noble estates did not succeed beyond this boundary of their influence and that was the beginning of their defeat." [42]

But why did the estates not put up a stiffer fight? A conflict between the solidarity of Protestant and Catholic estates as nobles and of Protestant nobles and burghers as co-religionists became apparent. The former bond proved stronger at the time. As Hantsch sees it: "If we remember the important role the democratic burghers . . . played in the history of the Reformation, particularly in Germany, then we cannot wonder too much that the isolation of the burghers . . . opened welcome gates to the Counter Reformation. This could happen because the burghers had not reached the level of Germany either politically or economically." [43] The issue of conflicting powers does not explain the motivations of the Protestant Reformation in Inner Austria, though it does help us to understand how the course of the Reformation was channeled. [44]

THE RESTORED SYSTEM

COUNTER REFORMATION UNDER RUDOLF II AND MATTHIAS

The following period, until the outbreak of the Thirty Years' War, or perhaps more precisely, to the election in 1619 of Ferdinand III of Styria, as emperor Ferdinand II, is perhaps the most confusing in Austrian history. This confusion arose from several sources, above all the spread of the Counter Reformation. At the time of the conflict between the Emperor Rudolf II (1576–1612) and his brother Matthias (1612–1619) in the first decade of the seventeenth century, it led in turn to a last flare-up of the Protestant Reformation in the Erblande. The Protestant estates, whose support Matthias desired for a time, began a new political offensive. Further complicating factors were the war in Hungary against the Turks and the revolts in Transylvania and Bohemia, the former largely supported by external forces, the latter more domestic in character.

Confusion in the actions of the government during the whole period from the death of Maximilian II to the election of Ferdinand II is largely explained by the simple fact that the imperial lands, the Habsburg

---

[42] Hantsch, I, 290; Loserth, *Die Reformation und Gegenreformation,* pp. 478 ff.

[43] Hantsch, I, 303 f. See also Lindeck, *op. cit.,* Vol. 60 (1939), pp. 82 ff.; Loesche, pp. 66 ff.

[44] On the Reformation in Inner Austria, see further: Loserth, *Die Reformation und Gegenreformation,* pp. 13–286 *passim;* Mayer, II, 68 ff.; Hellbling, *op. cit.* (see n.2 above), pp. 248 f., 263 ff.; Mecenseffy, pp. 61 ff., 66 ff.; Krones, III, 266 ff.

domains including Hungary and Bohemia and specifically the Erblande, were ruled during these four decades by two brothers of rare incompetence. Rudolf II was by mental disposition and character completely unfit to rule, but his personality as a whole, because of his intellectual interest in the arts and sciences, including the pseudoscience of astrology, commands a certain respectful interest. The same does not hold true for Matthias, who was as deficient in character as in intellectual ability. The situation becomes clarified with the reign of Ferdinand II, the great simplificator. Conspicuous in the man are not only his religious zeal and devotion but also his limitations, a tendency to comprehend, or more often misapprehend, complex problems at their lowest intellectual level. Although the emperor's sincerity cannot be doubted, this frequently was bound to look like a low moral level as well.

With the succession of Ferdinand, events in Inner Austria moved at a faster speed than in the other Habsburg realms. There the situation remained, until 1619, less than clear. The Counter Reformation in Inner Austria might well be treated in conjunction with Ferdinand's rule as emperor, that is, after 1619. Undoubtedly he had already been, for more than two decades, the most determined foe of Protestantism in Inner Austria. Yet during the best part of that period he was also its most influential enemy in all the Habsburg lands and the empire as well. Accordingly, the earlier phase of his activities and their consequences may well be discussed in connection with the reigns of Rudolf and Matthias.

Within the limits of our problem the main theaters of action in the Habsburg realms from 1576 to 1619 were not in the Erblande but rather in Hungary and Bohemia. The outcome of these conflicts were unpredictable at the time. Yet it was already clear that Ferdinand's radical policy in Inner Austria was a weighty factor in provoking the violent action of the Bohemian estates and then again the new Habsburg emperor's even more violent response. Combined, they contributed to the outbreak of the Thirty Years' War. The restoration process in the Erblande merges thus with wider issues across Central Europe and accordingly must be comprehended in this context. Before going into these matters it is necessary to review a few skeleton facts.

The Counter Reformation began in Lower and Upper Austria under the regency of Rudolf's devout and energetic brother Ernest in 1578, and in Inner Austria under the Archduke Charles. Following the tendencies of the regime under the new Emperor Rudolf II, Charles wanted to annul the concessions made at the general diet of Bruck in the same year. Rudolf II and his brothers were, at that time of crisis and quarrels with the estates at home, seriously and unsuccessfully involved in the fight for the succession to the Polish throne. In 1593 the war against the Turks was resumed and was conducted as inefficiently and unsuccessfully as under Maximilian II. Whether these operations were initiated to deflect attention from the problems at home is questionable. The extinction of the Tyrolian line in 1595, to which the imperial line (Lower and Upper Austria) and the Inner Austrian line fell heir, increased the influence of the latter. Here the future Emperor Ferdinand II, a former student of the Jesuit college in Ingolstadt became, in 1596 at the age of eighteen, a ruler in his own right. This meant the acceleration of the Counter Reformation. The same held true in an only slightly more moderate sense for Tyrol and the Vorlande under the regency of Rudolf's brother Maximilian and Ferdinand's brother Leopold. The latter ruled these lands between 1626 and 1632 in his own right. While the revolt in Transylvania against the Habsburg rule continued, an inglorious peace with the Turks was concluded in 1606, and the dissatisfaction of the princes of the imperial house, manifest at least since 1605, came to a head.

Matthias was recognized in 1607 as chief of the dynasty in lieu of the emperor, whose mental condition deteriorated rapidly. In 1608 the Protestant estates of the Bohemian, Moravian, and Lower and Upper Austrian lands concluded an agreement with Matthias, in which they promised to support him in return for the extension of the rights of estates, in practice primarily Protestant estates. Two months later, in the treaty of Lieben, Rudolf yielded to Matthias, Lower and Upper Austria, Moravia, and Hungary, as far as it was still under imperial control. His succession in Bohemia was now likewise recognized. Disappointed by Matthias's attitude, which was promoted only by ambition and not by genuine tolerance or any sincere intention to share power, the Protestant estates of the two Austrian lands separated from Matthias in the fall of 1608. The conflict was patched up by new concessions obviously deriving not from Matthias's conviction but from his weakness. Meanwhile the emperor had issued the famous Letter of Majesty of 1609 to the estates of Bohemia, which established religious liberties for the principal denominations there to an extent never secured in the Erblande. At the same time Rudolf's influence in German affairs, apparent in his non-alignment with the Catholic League of Princes, was dwindling. Weak and yielding in so many respects, the emperor tried now to force a decision by the strength of arms against his brother. When he failed, he left the crown of Bohemia to Matthias in 1611, only half a year before his death.

Elected emperor in June 1612, Matthias reverted to the course of the Counter Reformation and attempted to revoke Rudolf's concessions to the

Bohemian estates. At the time when the conflict in Bohemia about the validity of the Letter of Majesty was in full swing, Ferdinand as Matthias's declared heir was in command already to a wide extent. Two months after the Defenestration of Prague, in July 1618, Ferdinand would dare to have Matthias's chief adviser, Cardinal Khlesl, a spiritual leader of the Catholic Reformation, arrested, confined, and banished because he counseled a course of relative moderation. The death of Matthias in April, 1619, and the election of Ferdinand as emperor the following August confirmed only in external matters a transfer of power which had been obvious for some years.

Why would a weak and irresolute ruler like Rudolf II initiate, right from the start of his reign, Counter Reformation measures such as the edict of 1578 according to which Protestant preachers in Lower Austrian markets and towns would have to cease their activities and either reconvert to the old faith or leave the country? Why should citizenship rights from here on be granted only to individuals who could satisfy the authorities concerning their loyalty to the Church? According to Hantsch, the emperor in his policy at the beginning of his reign meant merely to stop further concessions to Protestantism. Counteraction fostered by the spirit of the vigorous Catholic Reformation developed only slowly and gradually. Viktor Bibl, on the other hand, assumes that Rudolf was forced to act because Protestantism threatened to gain the upper hand to a degree which a Catholic could not condone if he intended to rule at all.[45] Bibl is probably right in this respect. The measures referred to here may serve as small examples of other more radical ones soon to come. Not only do they reveal a missionary tendency but they already present the unholy choice of forced reconversion or expulsion. Protestant affiliation barred townspeople now not only from the right to religious exercises but from citizenship itself. No ruler, however strong in his Catholic convictions, would have challenged a still powerful opposition at that time without any real necessity to do so. Religious devotion and zeal was, of course, a general motivating issue for a sovereign like Rudolf, raised at the court of Philip II of Spain.[46] But the specific cause

---

[45] V. Bibl, "Das österreichische Reformationsedikt vom Jahre 1578," *Jahrbuch der Gesellschaft für die Geschichte des Protestantismus,* Vol. 23 (1902), pp. 2 f.; Hantsch, I, 297 ff.

[46] Concerning Rudolf's character see Brandi, II, 122 ff.; Gertrude von Schwarzenfeld, *Rudolf II: Der saturnische Kaiser* (Munich, 1961), pp. 7 ff. This full-length biography is disappointing, however, as to factual material. See further Mayer, II, 77 ff.; Zöllner, *op. cit.* (see n. 26 above), pp. 199 ff.; Krones, III, 289 ff. See also Anton Gindely, *Rudolf und seine Zeit 1600–1612,* 2d ed., 2 vols. (Prag, 1868), I, 27 ff.; II, 331 ff.

which mobilized the forces of the Counter Reformation has to be sought on social and political grounds. Here the estates issue presents itself again in full force all throughout the reign of the imperial brothers Rudolf and Matthias.

Some observations by Irmtraut Lindeck are very much to the point. "With the grant of the 'Religionsassekuration,' [by Maximilian II in 1568 for Lower and Upper Austria, formalized three years later and with similar action by his brother Charles in Inner Austria in 1572 and 1578] religious freedom had become part of the liberties and privileges of the estates. The fight for it was no longer a purely ideological religious matter, but a political one also. Every violation of the concession, every restriction of religious freedom, was at the same time a violation of the freedom of the lands [to be understood as the autonomous rights of the country] which the estates were entitled and obliged to defend." [47] One may go even farther and question whether the ideas of the Protestant Reformation in Austrian lands had ever been a purely religious issue separated from politics; if it ever was, the author is certainly right to assume that it had gradually ceased to be one. She perceives two principal reasons for this change: the rise of Calvinist ideas among the Austrian Protestants, and the religious authorization of resistance against the government. As has been noted, this interpretation of Calvinist doctrine can be accepted only with modification. This problem, however, pertains in the Habsburg lands primarily to Bohemia.

More important is the point that the Protestant estates, on any question that involved social issues, represented a kind of split personality. Here they stood on common ground either with the ecclesiastic lords or with the sovereign himself. "It is a distortion of facts . . . [to claim that] the Counter Reformation was only necessary in the interest of the authority and rule of the princely sovereign as a consequence of the Protestant subjects' disobedience. It is true, though, that the mistaken policy of the noble estates paved the way for the Counter Reformation. Instead of joining the peasants in the defense of their religion and to alleviate social matters, they joined sovereign and governor and suppressed the revolt [meaning the various peasant revolts, particularly in Upper Austria]. The feeling of solidarity of the lords triumphed over the community which ought to have been formed by religion. . . ." Suppression of revolts was then inevitably enforced by the traveling princely commissions with their policy of reconversion or expulsion. "The estates had not yet arrived at the

[47] Lindeck, *op. cit.,* Vol. 60 (1939), pp. 91 ff.; Loserth, *Die Reformation und Gegenreformation*, pp. 369–572 *passim*.

notion of religious war. They still believed they could put their conscience at ease if they shifted the whole issue from the religious to the political sphere." [48]

It is true that the estates in Upper Austria during the late stages of the peasant revolts there decided to support burghers and peasants more actively, though allegedly against armed bands and not against the government. It is further true that in the negotiations with the vacillating and unscrupulous Matthias in 1608/09 the question of religious liberties for the fourth estate (markets and towns in Upper and Lower Austria) was seriously raised and some temporary success secured.[49] Yet this success was primarily due to the political opportunism of a Matthias desperately in need of estates support. To the estates in the Austrian lands the question whether their rights were part of a permanent covenant with the sovereign rather than a revocable unilateral promise was in general far more important than the achievement of religious and social liberties for others. Matthias, as might have been expected, went back on his promises as soon as he felt himself to be secure in power. It seems that the peasants were not unaware of the hopeless choice between vague princely promises and estates' reluctance to support them. Hence, one sees, particularly in Upper Austria, the increasing though hopeless tendency toward self-help. The peasants and also the burghers had to learn that the noble estates were not willing to pay the price in social concessions which the extension of religious liberties to markets and towns, and in the end to the peasantry, would have entailed.[50]

Regular missionary endeavors at reconversion and improvement of ecclesiastic standards were quite successful in Lower Austria, and within it, in Vienna, though considerably less so in Upper Austria. Here the able Cardinal Khlesl—in his various capacities as vicar of the diocese of Passau in Vienna, episcopal administrator of the bishopric of Wiener Neustadt, chancellor of the University of Vienna, but above all as head of princely reform commissions—played an important role. It would be unjust to ascribe the results of these endeavors only or perhaps even mainly to the activities of the reform commissions which stood behind the missionary work with their cruel alternative of conversion or expulsion. Still, it can

[48] Lindeck, *op. cit.,* Vol. 61 (1940), pp. 23 ff., 31 ff. See also Hantsch, I, 327 ff., 344.

[49] Viktor Bibl, *Die Religionsreformation Kaiser Rudolfs II in Oberösterreich* (Vienna, 1921), pp. 55 ff., 60 f.

[50] Mayer, II, 100 ff., 112 ff.; Hantsch, I, 303 ff., 328 ff. On Matthias's character, *ibid.,* pp. 334 f.; Rössler, *op. cit.* (see n. 20 above), pp. 576 ff.; Mecenseffy, *op. cit.* (see n. 3 above), pp. 71 ff., 82 ff., 89 ff., 123 ff., 135 ff.

hardly be denied that the religious restoration went back to a combination of sincerely religious reformatory action and forced suppression with the threat of police measures in the background. In short, we face a combination of Catholic Reformation and Counter Reformation measures. The mixture of these two factors varies often from place to place, and certainly from land to land.[51]

As noted above, Counter Reformation measures were initiated in Lower Austria in 1578 by the emperor's brother as vice-regent, the rigorous and devout Archduke Ernest. The prohibition of Protestant religious services in Vienna followed. At the time, when the sad state of affairs in the administration of the Church and the conduct of the clergy had been markedly improved the moral effect of these reforms was partly offset in the 1580's by a determined policy of harassment of Protestants and in particular of expulsions at short notice. Temporary relief was found only during the last years of Rudolf's reign when Matthias was anxious to please the estates and seemed even positively inclined to the religious claims of towns and markets. This policy was reversed shortly after the death of Emperor Rudolf, but matters went from bad to worse when Archduke Ferdinand of Inner Austria succeeded Matthias in March, 1619. It is true that the Lower and Upper Austrian estates had been in close contact with their colleagues in the Bohemian diet who were soon to be considered rebels. Yet general diets intended for all the Habsburg lands, such as those of Linz in 1614 and Prague in 1615, had been convoked by Emperor Matthias previously. Indeed, this latter general diet attempted, though unsuccessfully, to arrive at a kind of federation of all the Habsburg lands. In the light of these events, the famous audience of the Austrian noble estates with Ferdinand in June, 1619, was by no means as mutinous as it appeared to him after the open break with the Bohemian estates. Neither the insistence on reconciliation with Bohemia nor the subsequent alliance between Bohemian and Austrian (Lower and Upper) estates in August of the same year were in themselves treasonable. The Counter Reformation had been in full swing long before that time. After all, Cardinal Khlesl, a priest of considerable spiritual zeal, had been arrested as early as July, 1618, by orders of Ferdinand because he favored some conciliation. The arrest of Khlesl, who by intervention of the curia regained his freedom after some years, but never his former

---

[51] On Khlesl's activities, see Brandi, II, 154 f.; Bibl, *Das österr. Reformationsedikt,* pp. 16 ff.; Mayer, II, 96 ff.; Waldau, *op. cit.* (see n. 33 above), Vol. I, chap. 74, pp. 322 ff.; Vol. II, chap. 25, pp. 191 ff.; Loserth, *Die Reformation,* pp. 521 ff.

influence, indicates the clear victory of the Counter Reformation over the Catholic Reformation in the Erblande.[52]

Even more radical were the developments in Upper Austria where forced counterreformatory efforts in the 1580's met such violent resistance that Emperor Rudolf had advised his brother and deputy, Matthias, to proceed cautiously and step by step. Caution was no strong point with the Upper Austrian people, for in 1595 widespread riots started and soon the major part of the country revolted against the government. This rebellion was fully suppressed only by intervention of troops sent by the Archbishop of Salzburg in 1602. Here again the demands of cities and towns to share the religious privileges granted to the noble estates were steadfastly refused. Yet there is no doubt that social unrest among the peasants played an important role. If social and religious demands are closely intermingled, it is usually an oversimplification to emphasize the materialistic aspects and to play down the religious. The only proper deduction that can be drawn is that emotions become more passionate in social crises. These passions served all the claims of the peasants equally, though badly at times—those against the lords and those for the pure gospel. The peasants probably saw them as one issue.

Illuminating here again is the policy of the noble estates, which in Upper Austria was more homogeneously Protestant than in any other of the Erblande. Nevertheless, "The Protestant nobility, which represented the power of the estates, played an ambiguous role. As far as the revolt was directed against the Catholic Reformation, they sympathized with it, even at points supported it. As far as economic and social conditions were concerned, the peasants stressed the drive for their ancient rights . . . the feeling of the lords turned against the rebellion and supported the power of the state."[53] Considering the violence of the reaction of some of the nobles—the Protestant Count Gottfried Starhemberg, the cruel commander of a mounted estates force against the peasants, to wit—one might even say that the socially homogeneous character of the Upper Austrian estates made its negative response to the social demands of the peasants much more certain. It is true that in later times, during the negotiations between the Archduke Matthias and the Austrian estates in 1608 and 1609, this attitude changed somewhat because of the influence of

[52] Brandi, II, 206 f.; Mayer, II, 112 ff., 121 ff.; Lindeck, Vol. 61 (1940), pp. 26 ff.; Bibl, *Das österr. Reformationsedikt,* pp. 9–21; Waldau, Vol. II, chaps. 34, 35, 37, pp. 253 ff., 261 ff., 279 ff.

[53] Hantsch, I, 309 ff. See also Mayer, II, 96 f.; Sturmberger, *Georg Erasmus Tschernembl,* pp. 77 f.; see also 48–79 *passim.*

such men as the Upper Austrian Calvinist estates leader, Tschernembl, who remained constantly friendly to the peasants. But Tschernembl died in exile. His political influence ended with the beginning of the Thirty Years' War, and by that time the estates, Protestant and Catholic alike, represented a lost cause. The estates in Upper Austria may have had greater opportunities than those in other Erblande; they did not make any better use of them.[54]

The introduction of the Counter Reformation in Upper Austria was accompanied by more violence on either side than in any other of the Habsburg lands. One-sided radical and swift suppression and oppression by the Counter Reformation was most conspicuous, however, in Inner Austria, and here we have to turn again to the personality of the later Emperor Ferdinand II, ruler of these lands. Devout Catholic scholars have the highest opinion of Ferdinand's character, for all his actions were purely motivated to bring about complete religious unity, which means the elimination of Protestantism, in view of the spirit of the time, by pardonably harsh means. Such views do not approve of cruelty, but they perceive a scale of values in which religious zeal comes first, efforts to centralize administration, next, and the means to either end, last. The intellectual faculties of Ferdinand are not rated highly, nor are they deemed to be very important.

Religious determination, the vow to free his lands from heresy, was certainly the overriding motivation in the life of Ferdinand, an authoritarian but by no means dictatorial personality. Powerful ideologies, however, have prompted the rise and actions of some of the most powerful dictatorships of all times. Accordingly, Ferdinand's submission to a strong idea rather than to mere imperialist aims—though the latter were by no means alien to him—may not in itself rate high in a moral sense. Yet if one perceives the idea as sublime and beyond the need of justification of its defense and promotion by force, the interpretation will be entirely different. Value judgments are involved here which may be respected but can hardly be reasoned.

Non-Catholic scholars are frequently more critical of the consequences of the emperor's intolerance, though a lack of malice in his character is generally admitted. His intellectual limitation and his indecisiveness in any but religious questions are frequently judged more severely. A significant feature of Ferdinand's character in this respect is perhaps his stolid,

---

[54] Brandi, II, 154 ff.; Lindeck, *op. cit.,* Vol. 61 (1940), pp. 26 ff.; Waldau, Vol. I, chap. 26, pp. 329 ff.; Vol. II, chap. 35, pp. 261 ff.; Sturmberger, *Tschernembl,* pp. 36 ff., 167 ff.; 407 ff.; Mecenseffy, pp. 89 ff.

religiously animated equanimity in adversity and, unfortunately, a complete lack of moderation in success. His Edict of Restitution of 1629 is an outstanding example. Here we find a strange similarity of character with his grandson Leopold I and his great-grandsons Joseph I and Charles VI, who, by inordinate zeal, lost Austria's chance in the fight for the Spanish succession. Perhaps Karl Brandi's evaluation of Ferdinand comes closest to what may be called a cross section of historical opinion. "One usually represents the former archduke of Styria as a moderately gifted, basically soft-hearted, and zealously Catholic lord. . . . The archduke was never leading but always led. Yet now and later, even in difficult and dangerous situations, he revealed unshakable consistency and stamina." [55]

It would be easy but pointless to cite unfavorable opinions coming in particular from radical Protestant and German national sources.[56] Far more interesting is the question raised by Brandi concerning the general historical significance of Ferdinand's personality. There should be little doubt that it consists primarily in the promotion of a new kind of princely absolutism, in which are submerged the ideas of limited representative government by the estates, territorial autonomy, and above all, religious freedom. Their place is filled by a new complacent conformism. Tired out by a century of passionate conflict, this conformism is bound to submit to the sovereign. Lacking the artificial, pseudodemocratic stimulus of a state-controlled mass movement, this means not totalitarian, but certainly intolerant, government. We will follow it first in the sphere of Inner Austria.

Ferdinand had "in Styria, Carinthia, and Carniola the whole ecclesiastic order of the Reformation eliminated, although his father, the archduke Charles, had bestowed privileges there in 1572 and 1578, similar to those granted by Emperor Maximilian in Austria. Every tendency to resistance was suppressed with strong force; the removed predicants were expelled and in some places hunted like game. Bishop Martin Brenner von Seckau, the 'Ketzerhammer,' with government protection and supreme energy had undertaken the job of leading the nobles, burghers, and peasants back." [57]

The restrictive policy had already started in the latter part of the reign of Ferdinand's father, the Archduke Charles, by way of strict enforcement

[55] Brandi, II, 206 ff. See also Hantsch, I, 304 f.; Rössler, 594 f.; Krones, *op. cit.* (see n. 2 above), III, 338 ff.; Mayer, II, 91 ff.; Hans Sturmberger, *Kaiser Ferdinand II und das Problem des Absolutismus* (Munich, 1957), pp. 9 ff., 45 ff.

[56] One example of many would be the distorted portrait in Loesche, *op. cit.* (see n. 9 above), pp. 29 ff.

[57] Brandi, II, 206 f.

of existing laws, without any tolerance, against burghers and peasants, who were not covered by the privileges of 1572 and 1578. The burgher oath which prescribed submission to the old faith had been enforced since 1590. Still, under Charles and under the archdukes Ernest and Maximilian as successive regents for the minor Ferdinand, reconversion was primarily based on the spirit of the Catholic Reformation, in particular the Jesuit mission. Under Ferdinand after 1596, unmitigated force became the order of the day, and the governmental strength employed was so compact that widespread organized resistance was not even attempted. Therefore, large-scale terror and executions like those in Upper Austria could be avoided.

We face here for the first time one of the characteristic features of Ferdinand's counterreformatory activities. In his efforts toward reconversion he was entirely satisfied with submission to the Church by lip service alone. That more might have been necessary for the true propagation of the faith did not seem to dawn on this mediocre mind. Yet this narrow-minded satisfaction with superficial results led to the curbing and eventually to the termination of the attempt at reconversion and thus to the alleviation of oppression. A Ferdinand would not have understood the motivations of the Inquisition to make sure of genuine conversion and penitence by more subtle and often more painful means, and consequently he had no need for them. Expulsion of Protestant preachers and educated burghers unwilling to submit was ordered, frequently at short notice. Protestant churches, churchyards, and heretical books were destroyed, but compliance with governmental decrees was in the end nearly complete. Protestant nobles were not expelled, but their right to religious services was restricted and their personal preachers were ousted, against the clear letter of the law. "But the Inner Austrian lands lost, through the Counter Reformation, many prosperous and educated burghers. It was even more important that 'the close relationship to Germany, the rich intellectual and personal contact with the empire' was severed through the destruction of Protestantism. At that time began the intellectual separation of Austria from Germany, followed eventually by the political." [58]

These observations by Franz Mayer and Alfons Huber are certainly to the point, though they don't take account of two other consequences of the Counter Reformation in Inner Austria. One is the overall effect on Austria and the Austrians of the future, which transcends in importance even the effect on the relationship to Germany. We will return to this

[58] Mayer, II, 94, 88 ff. The quotes in quotes are from Alfons Huber, *Geschichte Österreichs*, Vol. IV, p. 354.

problem in a wider context at the end of this chapter. The other, immediate effect was of considerable importance, too. Ferdinand in a tense political, social, and cultural situation showed to his peers, the princes and the then emperor, that the simplest way was also the most effective. Smashing through by brutal force led to better results, from his point of view, than a carefully laid plan of mission and education. By administration of drastic force, Ferdinand had initiated a policy which inevitably was followed by others in all camps, and cruelty increased far beyond the imagination of the emperor. Against his volition and comprehension the basically good-natured Ferdinand had retarded moral and intellectual development in Central Europe.[59]

[59] Hantsch, I, 358 ff. (by no means uncritical of the counterreformatory measures). Mecenseffy, 71 ff.; Krones, III, 334 ff., who stresses particularly the superficial character of the reconversion; Zöllner, *op. cit.* (see n. 26 above), pp. 202 f.; further, J. Loserth, ed., *Akten und Correspondenzen zur Geschichte der Gegenreformation in Innerösterreich unter Erzherzog Carl II (1578-1590)* (Vienna, 1898), *Diplomataria et acta,* Vol. L., which deals with events in Styria, Carniola, and Carinthia. See Introduction, pp. v, vii, and in particular the following documents listed by number: 6, letter of December 18, 1578, Archduke Charles to his brother, Archduke Ferdinand of Tyrol; 7, answer of January 11, 1579, by Ferdinand; 10, records of the conference in Munich concerning the enforcement of counterreformatory measures (October, 1579); 55, report of the Emperor Rudolf II of December, 1580, concerning the impact of the Counter Reformation in Styrian markets and towns; 90, petition of the Styrian estates of 1581 to the archduke concerning their privileges; 116, report by the Styrian Jesuit provincial of 1581 concerning the state of affairs and further proposals; 139, negative reply of archduke to noble estates in March, 1582.

See further J. Loserth, ed., *Akten und Korrespondenzen zur Geschichte der Gegenreformation in Innerösterreich unter Ferdinand II; I. Teil, Die Zeiten der Regentschaft und die Auflösung des protestantischen Cabinets und Kirchenministeriums in Innerösterreich 1590-1600* (Vienna, 1906), Vol. LVIII; see Introduction, pp. vii ff., xi-xxx, xliv-lx concerning the long-range planning of counterreformatory measures. Document 297, petition of Styrian estates to Archduke Ferdinand prior to his investiture as sovereign. Request to accede to complaints in religious matters (December, 1596); 298, negative answer in the name of archduke. No connection between religious matters and his obligations as ruler (December, 1596); 456, estates petition to archduke to remain unmolested in church and school matters (September, 1598); 457, rejection by archduke (September, 1598); 649, the Styrian diet and representatives from Carinthia and Carniola petition archduke to have ever-increasing religious persecutions halted (February, 1599); 670, negative answer by archduke, the complaint is not really an estates complaint; since prelates, towns and markets are not cosigners, he cannot deal with requests of individuals in the context of this petition (February, 1599); 787, rejection by the archduke of another Styrian estates petition. Motivation of this action is the zeal to help the seduced non-Catholic peasants (July, 1599); 842, Ferdinand's ordinance resulting from frequent requests of Catholic priests that the Protestant preachers in the country should be immediately expelled by sanction of severe punishment for them and those who shelter them (November, 1599); 844, prohibition to sell and keep heretic books. They must be destroyed. Barrels and chests containing books must be opened in

COUNTER REFORMATION UNDER FERDINAND II AS EMPEROR

The following are the principal facts of the last phase of the Counter Reformation in the Erblande which directly affect our problem. In 1621 the new emperor's brother, archduke Leopold, became regent in Tyrol and the Vorlande. Since Ferdinand, the sovereign in Inner Austria, with the death of Matthias had become heir to Lower and Upper Austria as well, counterreformatory measures were now almost completely coordinated in all the Erblande. In 1620 the new emperor introduced administrative reforms which moved the Austrian lands farther in the direction of centralized absolutism. Upper Austria, between 1624 and 1627, became the theater of a great rising against Counter Reformation and peasant oppression. In 1627 the privileges granted to Protestant nobles were formally rescinded in Lower Austria; in 1628 similar legislation was imposed in Inner Austria. In 1629, at the onetime height of the emperor's

presence of a priest (November, 1599); 946, urgent petition of estates from Styria, Carinthia, and Carniola to end religious persecutions. They deny that they are heretics (February, 1600).

See further J. Loserth, ed., *Akten und Korrespondenzen zur Geschichte der Gegenreformation in Innerösterreich unter Ferdinand II,* Part II, *Von der Auflösung des protestantischen Schul und Kirchenministeriums bis zum Tode Ferdinands II 1600–1637* (Vienna, 1907), Vol. LX; see the Introduction, particularly pp. xxvii-xxxii, on the crisis of 1609; pp. lvii-lxxv, on the Counter Reformation and the burghers; pp. lxxv-lxxxii, on the Counter Reformation and the peasants. On the superficial character of reconversion, see particularly pp. cx f. and cxii. See further: documents 1262, general mandate by Ferdinand that all Protestant preachers, preceptors, scribes, and teachers should be expelled from his lands and their religious services should be immediately halted (March, 1601); 1527, complaint by the estates of Styria, Carinthia, and Carniola that the nobles of the three lands are not even allowed to hold religious services outside of their lands. They are ready to leave if properly indemnified for their estates (October, 1603); 1528, Ferdinand censures the estates for a joint meeting and forbids it strictly for the future (October, 1603); 1548, the Lutheran nobles of the three lands ask the electors and princes of the empire for intercession on grounds of religious persecutions inflicted on them (January, 1604); 1734, complaint of the estates of Carniola against the Counter Reformation visiting commissions, defense against accusations (August, 1607); 1895, complaint by Catholic prelates and nobles transmitted to their Protestant colleagues in the estates, that Catholics should have equal claim to estates offices (April, 1610); 2121, report by the governor of Carinthia to archduke how the Counter Reformation should proceed in Carinthia, clerics should not be allowed to have wives or mistresses, the sons of Protestant nobles must be educated as Catholics. The reconversion of burghers and peasants is deemed equally necessary; 1616, general mandate by Emperor Ferdinand II in which the expulsion of Protestant lords and nobles from Styria, Carinthia, and Carniola is ordered (August 1, 1628).

Concerning Tyrol, where the Counter Reformation, except against so-called sectarians, in particular Anabaptists, proceeded until 1618 somewhat less abruptly under the regency of Rudolf II's brother Maximilian, see Mayer, II, 123 f.; Krones, III, 321 ff.; Loesche, pp. 351 ff.

military success against Protestantism in the Thirty Years' War, the Edict of Restitution was issued, which was in two respects, at least in theory, of importance for the Erblande. The forced reconversions and expulsions of Protestants were retroactively fully legalized. Even more important, ecclesiastic estates, secularized since the treaty of Passau in 1552, had to be restored to the Church on request. Non-Lutheran sects were declared to be illegal without exception. This refers in particular to Calvinists, but also to Anabaptists. In view of the sweeping success of the Counter Reformation in Austria up to that point, most of the changes now authorized had already been put through.

The death of Ferdinand II and the succession of his son Ferdinand III in 1637 did not change the counterreformatory policy in principle, but it slightly softened the manner of its execution. The Westphalian peace treaty (1648), which confirmed the Convention of Passau (1552) and the Religious Peace of Augsburg (1555), changed the key date of transfer of ecclesiastic property from 1552 to 1624. Yet—a symptom for the forced Austrian separation from the empire—the Erblande were expressly excluded from this modification in favor of Protestantism. The recognition of Calvinism as not only the *de facto* but the *de jure* recognized faith in Germany was by now of neither legal nor practical consequences for the Habsburg lands. In 1655 the extinction of the new Tyrolian line led to the permanent unification of the Habsburg domains in the head of the house, who was generally also the emperor.

Some remarks by the knowledgeable and moderate Franz Krones are still of great significance almost a century after they were written. "It is true, we have to distinguish between the principle of the Catholic Reformation of Ferdinand II and the manner of its realization as much as between the intent and the final results of the conversion of faith . . . desired by this Habsburg. The henchmen of this restoration frequently gave free rein to their own passions, their intolerance, their hatred, not seldom their greed. Thus they made the orders of the sovereign arbitrarily more severe. . . . Let us not forget, either, the pressure of the policy of the Catholic Church on the measures of the sovereign." Here Krones points to a basic distinction between Ferdinand II and Philip II of Spain. In relation to the Church Philip's will proved just as supreme in matters ecclesiastic as in secular matters, if either was related to politics. Ferdinand proved always to be completely subservient to the Church when faced by similar problems.

> But [here Krones approaches the core of the matter] it would be wrong to deny that Ferdinand perceived in the Catholic Restoration at the same time the victory of monarchy. After all, opposition of the es-

tates had gone hand in hand with the Protestant Reformation. This point of view made it easier for the Roman See, the high clergy, and the ecclesiastic court party to influence the ruler. . . .

The estates movement, defeated so decisively, had moved toward anarchy, for it was incapable of regenerating the state, incapable of materializing its own program by unity and moderation. To intervene in this anarchy was the task of the victorious monarchy, and despite all serious aberrations, transgressions, and sins of omission, it reestablished respect for the law and stopped the inner dissolution, the permanent scheming, and the conspiracies which had reached the point of betraying the country.[60]

One modification of this keen observation is in order. The regime did not reestablish respect for the law which it had frequently and grossly violated. This is true from the point of the estates state and even from that of the authoritarian state, which claims to be bound by its own principles. The regime merely reestablished respect for the authority of government, irrespective of its changing policies. This is quite another matter and more controversial.

In regard to the strengthening of princely authority, which is only indirectly though strongly related to the purpose of the Counter Reformation, we can point to the setting up of an Austrian court chancery. It could be considered a central agency for the Erblande in the main fields of foreign, general administrative, and judicial affairs, although the chancery was entrusted with Bohemian and Hungarian agenda as well. Undoubtedly in this respect the rise of the Erblande as the nucleus of an Austria as a future Great Power was closely related to Ferdinand's counterreformatory regime.[61]

As to the Counter Reformation itself in its external aspects during the Thirty Years' War, reference has already been made to the harmful effect of the Edict of Restitution of 1629. Because of its immoderation, the imperial policy weakened rather than strengthened the Catholic cause throughout Europe. The insensitivity of Ferdinand to the needs and possibilities of the hour was instrumental, no doubt, in bringing about the Swedish intervention and with it a widening of the war. On the other hand, the accession in 1637 of Ferdinand III with his greater moderation might in the long run have helped rather than hurt the imperial cause, despite repeated military setbacks.

Ferdinand III may have learned this lesson among others from his

[60] Krones, III, 433–436 *passim.*
[61] Huber and Dopsch, *op. cit.* (see n. 2 above), pp. 198 f.; Hellbling, *op. cit.* (see n. 2 above), pp. 241 ff.; Hantsch, I, 354 f.

father's unhappy reign. "In spite of all his strictly Catholic convictions and attitude as ruler . . . he realized the necessity not to put ecclesiastic interests above political ones. After all, the Roman See, too, managed to practice this self-denial, whenever issues of power were at stake." [62] Thus, although the new emperor did not accept any formal obligation in regard to religious privileges in the Westphalian peace treaty, he promised not to force the emigration of the Protestant nobles remaining in Lower Austria, and he permitted the return of emigrants, provided they had submitted to reconversion. Furthermore, concessions in regard to the return of property were limited to those who had lost it since 1630. More liberal were only the concessions made in the Silesian principalities.[63]

The last victorious stages of the Counter Reformation in the Erblande changed little in principle but somewhat in the manner of enforcement. In Lower Austria and Vienna, the general expulsions of 1627 were modified only on behalf of seventy-five noble families in 1648 in regard to freedom of conscience but not to religious exercise or eligibility to office. Thus reconversions continued, although after 1627 indirect pressure would frequently suffice where outright compulsion had previously been necessary. However, in the latter part of the seventeenth century, particularly under the influence of mercantilist reforms, not only some Protestant nobles but also substantial numbers of Protestant merchants and industrialists lived unharmed in Lower Austria, including Vienna. Even prior to the promulgation of the *Toleranzpatent* of Joseph II in 1782, this held true in the eighteenth century for Protestant professional men to a fairly wide extent. This state of affairs was based on mere toleration and not on recognized rights to religious exercise.[64]

The Counter Reformation in Inner Austria was practically completed with the decree of expulsion in 1628 concerning the Protestant nobles. The cause of Protestantism was eradicated more thoroughly than in Lower

[62] Krones, III, 537, on the character of Ferdinand III. See also Hantsch, II, 19 f.; Loesche, 34 f.

[63] Mayer, II, 182 ff.; Hantsch, II, 20 f.; Hellbling, pp. 222 ff.; Mecenseffy, pp. 177 ff.; Loesche, pp. 467 ff. As to the approximate numbers of nobles who had left the Hereditary Lands, see Krones, III, 538 ff.

[64] See Mayer, II, 137 ff.; Otto Brunner, *Adeliges Landleben und europäischer Geist, Leben und Werk Wolf Helmhards von Hohberg 1612–1688* (Salzburg, 1959), pp. 51 ff., 314 ff.; Kann, *A Study in Austrian Intellectual History,* pp. 23 ff., 31 ff.; Völker, *op. cit.* (see n. 40 above), pp. 12 ff.; Ignaz Hübel, "Die Ächtung von Evangelischen und die Konfiskationen protestantischen Besitzes im Jahre 1620 in Niederösterreich und Oberösterreich," *Jahrbuch der Gesellschaft für die Geschichte des Protestantismus,* Vol. 58 (1937), 17 ff.; Waldau, *op. cit.* (see n. 33 above), Vol. II, chap. 34, pp. 253 ff.; chap. 35, 36, pp. 261 ff.; chap. 39, pp. 294 ff.; chap. 42, pp. 318 ff; Mecenseffy, pp. 161 ff.

Austria. This may perhaps have been because the Catholic Reformation was more active here, as shown by the Jesuit missions, the activities of the new Jesuit university in Graz, and the establishment of numerous new monasteries. Archduke Leopold, the emperor's brother, succeeded in keeping the progress in the religious purification of Tyrol abreast with that in Inner Austrian lands.[65]

Most dramatic and tragic, though not any more decisive, were the events in Upper Austria during this last major phase of the Counter Reformation in the Erblande. Here, two decrees had a revolutionary effect—one in 1624 ordered the expulsion of Protestant predicants, and an even more sweeping one in 1625, reconversion for all Protestants. Much explosive material had already been piled up. The land had been pawned since 1620 to the duke of Bavaria as security for imperial war debts. Taxes were now imposed by a foreign sovereign who was no more popular than the future Bavarian regime in Tyrol between 1806 and 1813. Visitation commissions of the Counter Reformation deposed Protestant mayors, aldermen, and state officials even before 1624. Foreign soldiers were quartered in villages at the expense of the peasants. The disorders of the war, the increased taxation, and the suppression of religious freedoms led here to the heightening of passion brought about by a combination of social and religious factors. Riots in Frankenburg were cruelly and cynically suppressed by mass executions in which captured peasants had to gamble for their lives, but soon the revolt spread all over the country. The issuance of the general reconversion decree, a few months after the outrage of Frankenburg, was a particular challenge. Peasant troops under the leadership of Stephan Fadinger now occupied a number of towns and successfully fought the Bavarian troops. After Fadinger was killed in battle imperial troops entered the country and a truce might have been feasible. Some assurances concerning reprieve to the rebels, but no binding commitments regarding religious liberties, were made to the peasants. When Bavarian troops reentered the land the fight flared up again and the Bavarian general Pappenheim's cavalry joined with imperial troops to put down the revolt in the fall of 1627. Atrocities equal in some ways to those of the South German Peasants' War in the 1520's had been committed on both sides. They were followed now by mass executions and

<hr/>

[65] Mayer, II, 141 f.; Krones, III, 538 f.; see also 456; Mecenseffy, pp. 169 ff. See also Erich Winkelmann, "Zur Geschichte des Luthertums im untersteirischen Mur und Draugebiet," *Jahrbuch der Gesellschaft für die Geschichte des Protestantismus,* Vol. 58 (1937), 35 ff., and *ibid.,* Paul Dedic, "Der Kärtner Protestantismus vom Abschluss der 'Hauptreformation' bis zur Adelsemigration 1600–1629/30," pp. 70 ff.

mass conversions practically at the point of a bayonet. As was to be expected, underground Protestantism among the peasantry could not be wiped out by such means.

A few facts stand out. The overriding cause of the revolt between 1625 and 1627 unquestionably was Ferdinand's radical Counter Reformation policy, initiated by his own express orders. The Bavarian stadholder Count Herbersdorff, a converted former Protestant, was only instrumental in the execution of imperial policy. Foreign troops and foreign taxation undoubtedly were factors that aggravated the situation further. Yet the possibility of a peaceful reconciliation lay with the emperor. At one point even Herbersdorff was ready to intercede with him in support of some limited religious liberties for the peasants. Because of the punitive taxes for those who wanted to leave the country, emigration frequently offered no solution. The situation called for some kind of compromise, however limited. The emperor refused, however, to make the slightest concession on the religious issue.

This is the first salient main point in the Upper Austrian tragedy. The second is that the noble estates had again deserted the peasants. A number left the country, it is true, but most of them submitted to the reconversion decree of 1627. Although at the time the cause of the peasants might rightly have been thought to be lost anyway, it is notable that the nobles did not offer appreciable resistance in the two preceding years either, when the situation was still fluctuating. They were obviously scared by the possible social implications of the revolts, far more than the burghers in towns. Here the noble estates had failed their countrymen and, perhaps, history.[66]

REFORMATION AND COUNTER REFORMATION

Before we evaluate the Counter Reformation in the Erblande in relation to the problem of restoration, it may be advisable to review a few important facts. In the first place, a movement which in its later stages under Ferdinand II relied to such a high degree on force can hardly be called primarily religious. To say this does not in any way deny the possibility, indeed the actuality, of true reconversion. But such a process takes a long time; to perceive its immediate success in the fast work of the police-supported commissions of visitation in the Alpine lands would be

[66] Krones, II, 446 ff.; Mayer, II, 137 ff.; Hantsch, I, 356 ff.; Mecenseffy, pp. 163 ff.; Brandi, I, 239 f.; Sturmberger, *Tschernembl,* pp. 371 ff.; on Herberstorff, Eder, *op. cit.* (see n. 3 above), pp. 344 ff.; Josef Wodka, *Kirche in Österreich* (Vienna, 1959), pp. 239 f.; Waldau, Vol. II, chaps. 37–39, pp. 279 ff.

worse than naïve. Johann Loserth emphasizes the superficiality of Ferdinand's policy in regard to genuine mission as follows: "The hope for a
restoration of the old [that is, Protestant] religious conditions had not
been extinguished in the circles of lords, burghers, and peasants at the end
of Ferdinand II's reign. Only the development in the next and the following generations brought it about, that the Protestants in all strata of
population except for small minorities gradually adjusted to the new
conditions." [67] Even this gradually changing situation left equal opportunities for genuine reconversion and opportunistic conformism. Both
undoubtedly existed in many instances. No attempt will be made to
determine here which eventually proved stronger, but the failure of immediate genuine reconversion seems evident. What then were the more
tangible results of the Counter Reformation beyond formal reconversion?

Two interpretations are of interest here. Hans Sturmberger perceives
the Counter Reformation as a final phase of the conflict between princely
and popular sovereignty, the latter in the restricted medieval sense presented by the estates. In sixteenth century Austria this meant primarily
the Protestant estates. Here in the Erblande they appeared to be successful
but not fully victorious. "Because the estates constitution was not destroyed in Austria—at least not fully in the seventeenth century—and because the Austrian princes of this time deviated from positive law only in
an emergency, it was said no real absolutism had developed in seventeenth century Austria. Austria got stuck in mere centralism." [68] This, in-
cidentally, is not the view of Sturmberger himself, who believes that
Ferdinand introduced a very real though moderate form of princely
absolutism, and his views in this respect are supported by facts, insofar as
the estates system from these times onward lost much of its significance.[69]
This seems to be the opinion also of Hantsch concerning Ferdinand's
success, which is even more positive than the very favorable one of
Sturmberger. In an overall survey of the results of the Counter Reformation, he observes:

> The important success of this tremendously difficult and fateful fight
> about Austria consists in the establishment of the political and spiritual
> unity of the Hereditary Lands, the strengthening of the position of the

---

[67] J. Loserth, *Akten . . . zur Geschichte der Gegenreformation . . . unter Ferdinand II,* annual LX, CX, CXII; Mecenseffy, pp. 186 ff.

[68] Sturmberger, *Kaiser Ferdinand II,* p. 7; with reference to H. Rössler, *Sachwörter-
buch,* p. 8; see also Sturmberger, p. 5 *passim.*

[69] Huber and Dopsch, pp. 212 ff.; Hellbling, pp. 262 ff.; Sturmberger, pp. 45 f.

sovereign . . . and of the real foundation of power of the imperial position, of the preservation of the boundaries of Germandom in the East, of the expansion of the field of activities of the German spirit in the Slavic lands. Austria as the greatest power of the Catholic South stood against the Protestant North. . . . In Austria the universal perception of the world (*Welterlebnis*) triumphed over national understanding; bonds between people, over separation of people. This was the premise of the growth of the multinational state, which in closer affiliation of the various nations, in the exchange of cultural and spiritual character put its peculiar mark on each group of peoples. The comprehensive state (*Gesamtstaat*) emerged from the Catholic Reformation. Vienna became the dominant city in a comprehensive political transformation (*politischen Gesamtgestaltung*) of the Danube area. Austrian character was formed in people and landscape.[70]

An accomplishment indeed, and if true, greater than any brought about by other periods of Austrian history.

As seen from the angle of the restoration problem, events look somewhat different. We have perceived the reign of Maximilian I and the brief period that followed, up to the beginnings of Ferdinand I's administration in the Erblande, as the original system (A) and as such it may be considered a fairly homogeneous one. The Erblande were again under one ruler, and administrative reforms had gone far to transform the feudal administration by new institutions approximating an incipient officialism in government. The influence of the estates on such government, though by no means negligible, was held in manageable bounds. The Austrian lands were, in the matter of religion, completely homogeneous except for the very last years of Maximilian I's reign. This is not quite as obvious as it may seem, for the doctrines of the Bohemian Brethren, linked to residues of Waldensian heresies, might well have spread to Austrian lands as to some extent they spread to German territories adjacent to Bohemia in the north. If Maximilian's Erblande thus represented a fairly unified political entity, at the same time, under the influence of the Renaissance and Humanism, they moved only slowly toward a society which had clearly begun to shift from the medieval unity in theology, philosophy, the sciences, and the arts to far more pluralistic patterns.

At this point the Reformation and the Counter Reformation had almost simultaneous impact on the Erblande. Counter Reformation measures, partly clearly political, partly religious or spiritual, or, most frequently, both, were initiated immediately following the sudden impact

[70] Hantsch, I, 360 f.

of the Reformation. It was one of the most characteristic features of the intermediate system (B)—roughly from the beginning of the regency of Ferdinand I in the Erblande to the death of Maximilian II, more than half a century—that these forces balanced each other fairly evenly. In an age that did not recognize the problematical theory of mutual deterrence of armaments, this did not make for civil peace. The sweeping innovations and important changes brought about by this intermediate system were, of course, the religious division of the Erblande, which in turn led to some extent to a social division as well. By and large, Protestantism penetrated in particular the upper strata of society and also the lowest, to a greater extent than other social groups. This means nobles and in certain places peasants as well. Towns were of course affected, too, but in Austria the burghers were not as strongly represented as in more urbanized Germany. Social relations within society became more strained and less cohesive. By and large, the sixteenth century after the sudden end of the Maximilian renaissance was no era of marked and widespread cultural progress in the Erblande, despite notable exceptions, particularly in education and the fine arts,[71] which pertained to Catholics and Protestants alike. Considering the intensity of conflicting passions aroused on both sides, such positive factors helped very little, unfortunately, to establish a better integrated society.

The rise of the noble estates brought about more obvious changes in religious freedom, and in territorial autonomy and preservation of social privileges. In the first they were opposed by the Catholic prelates, the first estate; in the latter they were often supported by them. Markets and towns, the fourth estate, and the peasants were frequently and grievously disappointed by the egocentric attitude of the lords and knights. This disappointment on the strength of bitter experience arose slowly, however, and time and time again the urban burghers and peasants hoped in vain for the support of the noble estate, which they only occasionally received. Yet during this whole period the idea of estates as a concept of an eventual representation of all the people was still vigorous, nurtured in the minds of large groups of people in all walks of life. This, too, is a most important factor, for it makes the intermediate system (B), though not especially alert culturally, appear truly pluralistic politically. Even though this intermediate system never took full governmental control, it spanned an era which, politically as well as ideologically, can be separated from the preceding and the following periods. This holds true for a clearly marked territorial entity, the Erblande.

[71] Hantsch, I, 256.

Roughly speaking, the restored system (C), with some ups and downs during the last years of Rudolf II's reign, began with the death of Maximilian II and within half a century was fully victorious. We certainly do not have to worry about whether this system, according to our theory of the restoration process, outlasted two full generations. In its ideological aspects it changed very little, at least until the reign of Maria Theresa two centuries later, and in many respects not even afterward as much as is commonly assumed. In fact, the victory of the Counter Reformation was so sweeping and lasting that we face quite a different problem here. Was not the Protestant Reformation and with it the whole interplay of conflicting spiritual forces so completely erased that the essential synthesis between the ideas of the intermediate system (B) and the restored system (C) is here lacking entirely? [72] We have attempted to show that without such synthesis no restored system has a chance to last. It obviously did last for a long time. May we assume therefore that it inherited some concepts or institutions from the intermediate system and if so, precisely which ones?

It is easy enough to determine first the nature of the restoration process from the original to the restored system without regard to the intermediate system. Obviously, religious unity was restored, but here a very important point suggests itself immediately. It is one thing to have religious unity in a country—for instance, the Erblande under Maximilian I—where extensive division had not existed before. It is quite another to have unity restored after widespread and lasting division had to be overcome by force. This should be particularly true if a new and now suppressed faith was supported in many places at one time by the majority of the people.

The second main issue is the further centralization of government in the sovereign, the incipient princely absolutism, and the corollary reduction of the significance of the estate system. Because of the strong sense of tradition in most of the Habsburg rulers, there was not even in Bohemia a formal elimination of the estates. Just the same, the drastic curtailment of their actual powers in all the Habsburg lands except Hungary was of lasting importance. The complete reunification of the Erblande by the restored system is another factor which symbolized the power of princely absolutism.

[72] Protestant underground activities in the second part of the seventeenth and the first part of the eighteenth centuries, while in themselves not without significance, may be properly disregarded here. They had no appreciable influence on public opinion, nor could they have any. See Mayer, II, 308 ff.; Mecenseffy, pp. 186 ff.

Hantsch is fully correct in saying that changes of such kind had the most profound influence on the further course of Austrian history, though one may differ from him considerably in regard to the effect of these changes. One thing should be made clear from the outset: If we speak of the lasting and, in our opinion, unfortunate effect of the suppression of Protestantism, we do not imply a superiority of Protestant over Catholic religious affiliation in either a moral or a cultural sense. It seems to us decisive that a widely held and sincerely believed system of ideas was intentionally and almost completely eradicated, to some extent by persuasion but largely by force. Those who held to the new faith were expelled and punished; those who reconverted—relatively speaking—were rewarded. Reconversion was in many instances undoubtedly sincere but, inasmuch as it clearly coincided with social interests, under moral suspicion. The long-lasting complete subordination of conviction and freedom of expression—even in the limited sense recognized by the estates—under the order of governmental authority had a most harmful effect on Austrian intellectual development. The striking discrepancy between the spectacular achievements of the Austrian baroque in the formative arts and the relatively meager ones in the intellectual disciplines illustrates the point.[73] A pluralistic society was transformed in an intellectually barren, strictly conformist one. The results were obvious. Yet the problem is not primarily an intellectual but rather a moral one. The choice—reconversion with its social advantages, or their rejection at the price of discrimination and persecution—influenced not only public but also private morale for the worse. Widespread rationalization that the expedient course was also the right one was only human.

The same in a different sense has to be deduced on the political side of the ledger. The policy of the Austrian noble estates prior to the victory of the Counter Reformation may have been complex in many details, but it was clear in principle. To put it simply, these estates—in the period under discussion, predominantly Protestant estates—let the urban burghers and peasants down. They did so not only in isolated instances but throughout three generations in several lands, Upper Austria only foremost amongst them. The lesson could hardly be lost on the Austrian commoners, urban burghers and peasants alike. Their faith in the estates as a force which, as in many another country, could be converted eventually into truly representative institutions anchored in genuine popular sovereignty, was destroyed. They could hardly be blamed for this negative attitude. The limited influence which the Austrian noble estates exercised after Ferdi-

[73] See, for instance, Kann, *op. cit.* (see n. 3 above), pp. 42–49 *passim*.

nand II was used primarily, if not exclusively, to defend their own social status, not for the common welfare. The enlightened reforms of Maria Theresa and Joseph II were introduced not because of but in spite of the estates. Even the difficulty with the introduction and operation of constitutional government under Francis Joseph was largely due not to national conflict but to the lack of a virile democratic tradition within the country. Liberalism had to focus attention continuously on the models of Western countries, whose social stratification and tradition appeared alien to the majority of the Austrian people. On the home grounds, attention was called only to isolated instances of estate rebellion at various times in various Habsburg lands. Yet this association of democracy with revolt, whether in Hungary, Bohemia, Tyrol, or Upper Austria, could be only harmful to the development of an organic democratic tradition. It is also difficult to see how the Counter Reformation with its permanent, damaging effect on the relationship between Czechs and Germans, and partly on that between Germans and Calvinist Magyars, helped appreciably to build up and strengthen the multinational empire of the future.

Other factors might well be examined here, some of which may be considered harmful only to a point, some in a measure even beneficial. The cultural separation of the Erblande from Germany as a lasting aftereffect of the Counter Reformation was undoubtedly damaging in many ways, but not in all ways and not at all times. The administrative centralization arrested the development toward truly representative institutions, but in its gradual elimination of feudal administrative procedures it proved to be beneficial. The greatest progress in this respect was made neither by the original system under Maximilian I nor by the restored one under Ferdinand II, but throughout the intermediate one under Ferdinand I. Here we have a very real impact of the intermediate system on the restored one. It is suggestive that this intermediate system worked quite well because in the time of Ferdinand I differences within society, and in particular between estates and sovereign, were still adjustable. This includes specifically religious issues.

As to these religious issues, one may well imagine that a less drastic, more humane approach of the Catholic Reformation and above all of the Counter Reformation might have led eventually to the same overall results, without, however, the most detrimental aftereffects. Undoubtedly, the execution of a conciliatory policy during the Thirty Years' War would have been very difficult, but conciliation in time might have avoided the necessity for the war altogether. There were other possibilities. The two faiths might have learned to exist peacefully together under a system devoid of the detrimental effects of a majority–minority relationship. On the other hand, a victorious Protestant Reformation in the Erblande might have led to precisely the same kind of intolerance and harassment as that shown by the Catholic Counter Reformation. Political experience with isolated Protestant successes makes such an alternative by no means unlikely.

To sum up: Spiritual movements, even within an already defined political territory, naturally coincide only by approximation with the span of a princely sovereign's administration. Still, this division by princely reigns in a given area seems to us the best there is in this complex case to facilitate the understanding of the sequence of the restoration process. This much is highly suggestive: The intermediate system had a measurable effect on the structure of government in the restored system. It had also an immeasurable but presumably profound psychological effect resulting from the restriction and suppression of convictions and institutions. There is no good reason to assume that the negative effect of oppression is less distinct than the positive one of preservation and evolution of any kind of establishments and ideas.

All this confirms what has been said before; the detrimental impact of the Counter Reformation has little to do with the influence of Catholic or Protestant ascendancy, but it is in every way related to the catastrophic result of sweeping—though not totalitarian—*Gleichschaltung*. It took centuries to overcome that.

The Classical Cases: Stuart and Bourbon Restoration Problems

Students of history associate political restoration in the broadest sense primarily with the transformation of England after the end of Cromwell's Commonwealth in the second half of the seventeenth century and the reestablishment of the Bourbons in France in the nineteenth century after the fall of Napoleon. Traditionally restoration is equated with the reestablishment of a specific dynasty identified with a not less specific ideology. Yet if we probe more deeply, the situation looks quite different. Dissimilar as the English and French cases are in many respects, these two restorations, as understood in the traditional sense, have one most important feature in common: they did not last. Each was overthrown within a span of time shorter than one generation. The reasons for failure were different, however, in each case.

We shall assume that the English and French "Restorations"—we use the terms advisedly in quotation marks at this point—are, as far as the principal political data are concerned, more familiar to the reader than any of the historical situations surveyed thus far, and consequently we shall focus our attention more on historical analysis than on the narrative itself.

CHAPTER XV

The English Restoration

CHRONOLOGY

1558–1603	Reign of Elizabeth I
1603–1625	Reign of James I
1625	Accession of Charles I
1628	Petition of Rights
1640, Nov.	Long Parliament convenes
1641, May	Triennial Act
1641, July	Abolition of the courts of Star Chamber and High Commission
1641, Oct.	Grand Remonstrance
1642–1646	First Civil War
1643	Solemn League and Covenant
1647	King surrendered by Scotch to British Parliament
1648	Second Civil War
1649	Trial and execution of king
1653, April	Dissolution of Rump Parliament by Oliver Cromwell
1653, July	Barebone's Parliament convenes
1653, Dec.	Oliver Cromwell Lord Protector
1654	Parliament dissolved
1656–1658	Cromwell's Third Parliament
1658, Sept.	Death of Oliver Cromwell. Richard Cromwell installed as Lord Protector

1660, April	Declaration of Breda by Charles II
1660–1685	Reign of Charles II
1660, Dec.	Dissolution of Convention Parliament
1661–1679	"Cavalier Parliament"
1661	Clarendon Code
1661, August	Act of Uniformity
1672	Declaration of Indulgence
1673	Test Act
1679–1680	First and second Exclusion Bills
1685	Accession of James II
1687	Declaration of Liberty of Conscience
1689–1702	William III and Mary (to 1694)
1689, January	Convention Parliament
1689, February	Declaration of Rights
1689, December	Bill of Rights
Original system (A)	1558–1625, reigns of Elizabeth I and James I
Intermediate system (B)	1625–1660, revolution, civil war period, and protectorate
Restored system (C)	1660– , Restoration period commences with reign of Charles II, definitely established with reign of William and Mary.

In seventeenth century England, in the sequence of original, intermediate, and restored systems, several possibilities suggest themselves. They are discussed here not in order to classify terminology but to gain better insight into the meaning of the historical process under discussion. The most elementary division would be, of course, to perceive the reign of Charles I from 1625 to the outbreak of the Civil War in 1642 as the last phase of the original system, with the Civil War and Cromwell's Commonwealth as an intermediate, revolutionary system, terminated by the reestablishment of the monarchy under Charles II in 1660. This restored system would then last up to the outbreak of the revolution of 1688, commonly referred to as the Glorious Revolution. Therewith a new historical epoch commenced, which from a strictly constitutional point of view has developed as a parliamentary monarchy in an evolutionary way to this day.

Serious difficulties arise if we accept this simple view. For one thing, further subdivisions may be in order. Thus the Civil War might be divided into two very distinct phases, the first until 1647, to which Cecily Wedgwood rightly refers as "the King's war," the second between 1647 and 1649, a by no means clear-cut conflict between England and Scotland, royalists and parliamentary army, Presbyterians and rather radical sectarian Independents.[1]

Secondly, are we justified in lumping together the Civil War and Cromwell's Commonwealth—a revolution and a semiauthoritarian system established by revolution? No doubt about it, from the point not of legitimacy but of law and order, Cromwell's administration had a more solid foundation than Charles I's regime could ever claim.

Thirdly, can the reigns of Charles II and James II from 1660–1688 be perceived as one undivided period of Restoration altogether? This contention could be challenged from two opposite grounds. According to one, the Restoration period in question would have to be subdivided further; according to the other, it would have to be extended in time. According to some views, the actual Restoration period ends not with the overthrow of James II's disastrous reign in 1688 but with the dissolution in 1679 of Charles II's first and most successful parliament, the so-called Cavalier Parliament of 1661. The four consecutive parliaments, each of short tenure, the fight for and against the bill to exclude the Catholic heir to the throne, the republican Rye House Plot of 1683, and perhaps the so-called Popish Plot of 1678 and the ensuing oppressive measures in the political and religious fields certainly do not convey any longer the notion of evolutionary constitutional government. This holds even more true, of course, for the clearly unconstitutional, only slightly camouflaged legislation against the established Anglican Church under James II. Foremost facts to be considered here are his arbitrary action against the protesting Anglican bishops and the Bloody Assizes following the Monmouth insurrection, which ran so much counter to the ideas of British justice. A clear attempt to undo the British Reformation was indeed in the making, and the point is certainly arguable that the peaceful evolutionary Restoration had come to an end in 1678/79 followed by an arbitrary revolt from above.[2]

---

[1] The fact that King Charles I surrendered to the Scotch as early as May, 1645 makes no difference here, since at least until 1647 the issue at stake was predominantly that between crown and parliament. No such generalization of one predominant issue holds true for the so-called second Civil War from 1647 to 1650, when Charles II fled to France.

[2] George M. Trevelyan, *England Under the Stuarts* (London, 1930), pp. 331 ff., 378 ff., perceives the Restoration period to be between 1660 and 1678 and refers to

Whether we limit the Restoration period to less than the two first decades of Charles II's reign and separate it from a decade of arbitrary government to the fall of James II, or whether we perceive the era from 1660 to 1688 as one historical unit, the restored system will not have lasted for even one generation. Yet we have argued that a restored system can be considered successful only if it has lasted throughout at least two generations, one still active under the restored system and instrumental in setting it up, a second to which the tenets of restoration are transmitted by tradition, not any longer by direct contact.

A suggestive answer to this argument might be that the substance of restoration lay not in the reestablishment of a particular type of limited constitutional monarchy under Charles II, transformed by a new revolution into a kind of parliamentary monarchy, but in the restoration of monarchical government itself. If one takes this position, the restored system would not end with the Glorious Revolution, nor even with the succession from the Stuart dynasty to the house of Hanover in 1714. For all practical purposes the restored system, including, to be sure, numerous evolutionary adaptations in the course of time, would be perceived as still in power today.

At this point we approach the basic issue at the very core of the divisions between the three systems and their subdivisions. What actually was the essence of the restoration in seventeenth century England? What essential features of the original system (A) were restored, separately or combined—monarchy? legitimacy? law and order? religious establishment? invested property rights and privileges? or any other? Equally important, to what extent if any were the institutions of the intermediate system (B) partially absorbed by the restored system in the political, social, and religious fields? We have taken the position that successful restoration requires an absorption of some of the ideas and institutions of the intermediate system.

the last seven years of Charles II's reign as one of "terror." He may overstate his case, but even a modern standard work on the reign of Charles II, by David Ogg, *England in the Reign of Charles II*, 2 vols. (Oxford, 1963), singles out the last four years of Charles II's, reign as an era of tyranny. See *ibid.*, II, 656 ff. See also in D. Ogg, *England in the Reigns of James II and William III* (Oxford, 1955), pp. 139 ff., the same interpretation concerning the reign of James II. See further Maurice Ashley, *England in the Seventeenth Century (1603–1714)* (Baltimore, 1961), pp. 144 ff., where again the sharp dividing line in Charles II's reign is seen in 1678/79.

Thomas B. Macaulay in his classic *History of England from the Accession of James II*, 5 vols. (New York, 1880), sees the decisive break in continuity only in the accession of James II. See particularly I, 364 ff.

The chart of comparative dates in politics, religious, social, economic matters, etc. in G. E. Aylmer, *A Short History of Seventeenth Century England* (New York, 1963), pp. 232–244 is very useful for our purpose.

The answer to these decisive questions requires but a brief analysis of the main events which formed the three systems. To begin with the original system, according to our theory we do not have to trace the history of such system back through several centuries. We are required to show only that it lasted unchallenged for at least two generations. Yet beginning with the Reformation in England and certainly after the passage of the Act of Supremacy of 1534, which made the king protector and supreme head of church and clergy of England, British history had been in a continuous, rapid, and at times revolutionary flux. This pertains as much to the religious issues of separation from Rome and the Reformation as to the social ones of enclosures or poor laws and the strictly political one of the rise of parliament in opposition to the crown. Should we then assume that the original system (A) had ended with the reign of Henry VII, the first Tudor king and last prerevolutionary ruler? It might well be argued that this reign of twenty-four years (1485–1509) was from a dynastic viewpoint certainly of doubtful legitimacy. More important, it presented only a brief breathing spell between the revolutionary situations of the fourteenth century, British peasant revolts and Wyclif's reform movement, followed by the civil Wars of the Roses in the fifteenth century and the struggle of Reformation and Counter Reformation under Henry VIII, Edward VI, and Mary Tudor, up to the Elizabethan Compromise in 1563. To gauge the comparative depth of revolutionary movements, however, seems to be well nigh impossible. This means that we cannot place a system in its proper historical context without the support of less controversial criteria.

I believe these can be found by examining the opposition to a system. If a regime, in spite of strong and widespread opposition, has maintained itself in power for at least two generations without manifest violation of its legitimate foundations, we can speak in our terms of a truly original system. In this sense we may say that the English government under the Tudors as well as under the first Stuart king, James I, could claim a legitimate base of authority. Arbitrary royal actions were as a rule sanctioned by an obedient Parliament, even though under James I with increased difficulty. Yet this is not the issue here. It is rather one of overall consent of the parties which, in terms of time and place, have a legitimate voice in the affairs of government, as far as its principles of operation are concerned. To be sure, James was at times in serious trouble—with Puritan trends within the clergy concerning episcopal church organization, with Parliament concerning taxes. Furthermore, public opinion was opposed to an alleged pro-Catholic appeasement policy in foreign affairs.

Still, there is no sufficient evidence to assume as yet the existence of a serious threat to the foundation of a limited constitutional monarchy.[3] To stretch the point considerably, even if one assumes that the unhappy counterreformatory reign of Mary Tudor (1553–1558) represented at the same time a revolutionary break with the policies of the two previous Protestant Tudor rulers, the legal continuity was certainly not interrupted throughout the reigns of Elizabeth (1558–1603) and James I (1603–1625), that is, for sixty-seven years.[4]

We contend in this study that the original system (A) ended with the reign of James I. The reign of King Charles I, even before the outbreak of the Civil War, must be considered part of an intermediate revolutionary system in any but a formal sense. We start from the simple premise that the government of England is not the rule of a counter revolutionary king who is opposed by a revolutionary parliament, that English government comprises king and parliament as equal, coordinate factors. Open or slightly camouflaged breaks with constitutional legitimacy occurred with increased frequency and seriousness on both sides. It would be impossible to say that those on the part of the crown, in spite of its basic defensive position, were but a response to revolutionary action by the parliament, as would be true in a genuine counterrevolutionary situation. Crown and parliament were involved rather in a struggle in which initiative and response were interlocked on both sides in revolutionary action. An inner unity of the revolutionary intermediate system (B)—whether we perceive its life-span to be from the beginning of the Civil War in 1642, or the execution of the king in 1649, to the submission of Richard Cromwell in

[3] Ashley, pp. 43 ff.; Joseph R. Tanner, *English Constitutional Conflicts of the Seventeenth Century, 1603–1689* (Cambridge, 1961), pp. 17 ff.; Frederick W. Maitland *The Constitutional History of England,* ed. Herbert A. Fisher (Cambridge, 1963), pp. 238 f., 250 ff., 260 ff., though rather critical of the constitutionality of James I's conduct of government, does not suggest a revolutionary breach with tradition. Neither does Albert F. Pollard. See his *Factors in Modern History* (Boston, 1960), pp. 141 ff. See also Margaret A. Judson, *The Crisis of the Constitution: An Essay in Constitutional and Political Thought in England, 1603–1645* (New Brunswick, 1949), pp. 50 ff., 225 ff.

[4] Maitland, p. 267, points merely to irregularities in the judicial sphere under Mary. Preserved Smith, *The Age of the Reformation* (New York, 1920), pp. 319 ff. emphasizes the constitutional legality of the religious repeal legislation, notwithstanding the uncontested cruelty of religious persecutions which took place. See also James A. Froude, *History of England from the Fall of Wolsey to the Death of Elizabeth* (New York, 1873), Vol. VI, p. 277; Godfrey Davies, *The Early Stuarts, 1603–1660* (Oxford, 1952), pp. 28 ff. See also Samuel R. Gardiner, *History of England from the Accession of James I to the Outbreak of the Civil War, 1603–1642,* 10 Vols. (New York, 1883), V, 314 ff.; Pollard, 100 ff.; Judson, pp. 17 ff.

1660—existed only in the sense of concerted opposition to establish authority. It was first directed against the prerogatives of the crown, then against the crown itself, but also against the claims of parliament. Thereupon the forces of army and parliament contested each other's authority. Finally and broadly speaking, the battleground lay between the Protector and the elusive forces of legitimacy and true freedom of conscience. Beyond this a whole era of English history, unique in its wealth of ideological issues, reforms, and new policies, abounds in political, social, and religious conflicts. They can hardly be perceived under one common political denominator.

Cecily Wedgwood makes the point, and it appears to be well taken, that the major causes of the Civil War were administrative, economic, and religious. "The first was the problem of administration: what services was the state to give its subjects, how were they to be organized and who was to pay for them? The second was the problem of financial control: could actual wealth be divided indefinitely from political power? The third was the problem of religion: was the land to be united in a single Church and in *what* Church?"[5]

All three of these broad complexes of issues were as much unsolved under the Commonwealth of Cromwell as under the Stuart monarchy of Charles I. This appears obvious, despite all the important differences in the approach to these problems in the operation of government and the resulting consequences of domestic and foreign policies. The regime of Charles I, almost as much as that of Cromwell, was one of continuous revolutionary flux. If one dares to make a sweeping generalization, the chief difference lay perhaps in the fact that in the first case the head of government wanted to check revolutionary changes to a large extent but not fully, and, in the second he supported them, but by no means to as large an extent as is commonly assumed. In either case the political initiative changed intermittently from one of the conflicting parties to the other.

The specific main events in the political domain until the outbreak of the first civil war in 1642, are generally known to be roughly the following. The passage of the Petition of Rights of 1628 was the first milestone on the road to the ascendancy of the parliament. This landmark statute dealt with the prohibition of the collection of taxes and benevolences (free gifts of money from subjects) without parliamentary consent,

[5] Cecily V. Wedgwood, *Oliver Cromwell* (London, 1939), p. 28. See also by the same author, *The King's Peace, 1637–41* (London, 1955), pp. 64 f. Godfrey Davies, pp. 79 f. concurs largely with Miss Wedgwood.

prohibition of arrests without specific charges and the arbitrary billeting of soldiers and sailors in private homes, as well as the suppression of proceedings of martial law in peacetime. There followed in 1629 the passage by the House of Commons of resolutions introduced by one of the opposition leaders, Sir John Eliot. They condemned High Church practices allegedly moving in the direction of Roman Catholicism. Those who advised the levying of taxes without parliamentary consent, as well as others who cooperated in their collection, were ostracized as enemies of the kingdom. To be sure, Eliot's resolutions had not the constitutional significance of the Petition of Right, but they were as indicative of the rift between crown and parliament. There followed the so-called "eleven years tyranny" from 1629 to 1640 to which Cecily Wedgwood refers as "the eleven years of the King's benevolent, aspiring and insolvent despotism, absurdly miscalled the 'Tyranny.'" [6] Yet, whether the spirit of royal government during that period was tyrannical in substance is really not the issue: it clearly operated against the constitutional tradition of the country. In the royal writ of 1634 that extended the levying of ship-money from the coastal towns to the whole country, the regime acted against the letter of the law as well. Inasmuch as the king was at complete liberty to call for new elections to the House of Commons, serious financial straits could serve here merely as an excuse, not as justification.

After the reestablishment of parliamentary government under pressure of necessity in 1640, the passage of the Triennial Act of 1641 weakened the royal cause further. According to it Parliament, then the famous Long Parliament, had to be summoned into session within three years from the dissolution of the preceding Parliament. Charles was presumably no more inclined to assent to this act than to the Petition of Rights, although he probably gave it far less attention. On the very day of the signing of the Triennial Act he assented to the bill of attainder against his chief minister, Lord Strafford, for the latter's unconstitutional actions. The manner of proceedings against Strafford and the king's helpless surrender to unlawful parliamentary pressure was revolutionary. The same year witnessed the long overdue abolition of the courts of Star Chamber and of High Commission, which terminated royal influence on judicial proceedings in matters politic and voided the powers of the ecclesiastic courts. Added to this was the outright repeal or radical modification of the royal writs in matters of taxation during the "eleven years tyranny." Above all, there was the Grand Remonstrance passed by the House of Commons in November, 1641, which summarized all the grievances of Parliament ac-

[6] Wedgwood, *Cromwell*, p. 21; Tanner, pp. 68 ff.; Judson, pp. 295 ff.

cumulated during Charles's reign. Inasmuch as this declaration was meant to appeal to the people and announced furthermore a new reformation in church and state relations far beyond the Elizabethan Compromise, it may be called a truly revolutionary act.[7]

It is, of course, impossible to separate religious matters clearly from political ones in regard to either English or Scotch ecclesiastic conditions. Yet religion primarily motivated the king in his attempts to introduce the High Church liturgy in Presbyterian Scotland in 1637 and the ensuing Scotch Covenant for the protection of the Kirk of Scotland. It was still dominant in the English-Scotch quasi-parliamentary Solemn League and Covenant of 1643 for the preservation of the Kirk of Scotland. Religion primarily motivated also the curbing of semi-Catholic High Church practices in England and the attempt to unify liturgy and creed in the three kingdoms. In their most radical form, prior to the outbreak of the Civil War, these religious motives were expressed in the British Root and Branch Bill of 1641, which asked for the outright abolition of the episcopal system. Here again religious and political motivations and actions were as closely interwoven as the revolutionary character of streamlined reforms on both sides. They appeared in the frame of enforced High Church practices on the part of the king, in the direction of still unorthodox Presbyterianism on the part of Parliament. Soon that body itself became torn by serious sectarian religious and social conflicts.[8] All of these actions, including some of equal and many of lesser importance, were in substance taken prior to the open outbreak of the Civil War.[9]

We have dealt here primarily with parliamentary actions, partly of an arbitrary nature, like the bill of attainder against Strafford. We observe, on the other hand, a procedure of government which frequently circumvented constitutional traditions and in a number of cases violated them

[7] Davies, pp. 79 ff.; Trevelyan, pp. 156 ff.; Wedgwood, *King's Peace,* pp. 135 ff.; Gardiner, Vol. IX (London, 1884), pp. 218 ff., 257 ff.; Tanner, pp. 68 ff., 83 ff. See also Samuel R. Gardiner, ed., *The Constitutional Documents of the Puritan Revolution, 1628–1660* (Oxford, 1889), the documents referred to here: Petition of Rights, pp. 1 ff.; Remonstrance against Tonnage and Poundage, pp. 5 ff.; Triennial Act, pp. 74 ff.; Tonnage and Poundage Act, pp. 88 ff.; Act of the Attainder of the Earl of Strafford, pp. 85 ff.; Grand Remonstrance, pp. 127 ff. See also Judson, pp. 295 ff., 349 ff.

[8] Davies, pp. 66 ff., 188 ff.; Trevelyan, pp. 166 ff.; Wedgwood, *King's Peace, pp.* 173 ff.; Gardiner, *History,* IX, 373 ff.; Tanner, pp. 83 ff.; Gardiner, ed., *Constitutional Documents:* Root and Branch Petition, pp. 67 ff., Solemn League and Covenant of 1643, pp. 187 ff.

[9] Obviously in a technical sense this would not hold true for the Solemn League of Covenant of 1643, as far as the extension and adaptation of its principles to England and Ireland is concerned. In substance, however, the core of the matter, the defense of Scotch Presbyterianism, was agreed upon in 1637.

outright. On neither side, court or parliament, was there yet open violence. All the same, and regardless of responsibility, the operation of government under Charles I, even before the outbreak of civil war, entirely lacked an essential consensus on basic issues between crown and parliament.

As to the major expansion of constitutional government, Petition of Rights, Triennial Act, and abolition of the high courts, the king yielded under duress; as to the "eleven years tyranny," the outgoing Parliament acquiesced temporarily only under compulsion. Stretching of the law and its spirit by mere technicalities or even by an open break of legal continuity was to be observed on both sides, crown and parliament. Weighty factors of tradition, financial necessity, social pressures, and religious convictions can easily by adduced to explain motivations of the forces locked in conflict, soon to be in combat.

Decisive from the point of this study, however, is the fact that the changes in the structure of government between 1625 and 1641 were so weighty in content and either so questionable as to their legality or so clear-cut in their illegality that we have to perceive them as truly revolutionary in character. The original system, disintegrating in its structure even under James I, had become revolutionary under Charles I. This took place irrespective of the king's passionate and vain opposition to change, which seemed to him to head in the wrong direction. Yet this makes no difference in the revolutionary character of the actions taken by king and parliament during the pre-civil war reign of the second Stuart king in England. From its very beginnings to its tragic end this reign was, in our opinion, fully encompassed within the revolutionary intermediate system.

If we were to look at the history of the civil wars up to the surrender of the king by the Scotch to the British Parliament in 1647, and perhaps beyond to the end of parliamentary negotiations with the royal prisoner in December, 1648, we might come to a closely related conclusion. The distinctions between the pseudolegal but in substance largely revolutionary actions until 1641 and the openly revolutionary actions between 1642 and 1648 (which still included, however, the concept of continued negotiations between crown and Parliament) were not as radical as they might seem.

There is little difference in substance and spirit between the Grand Remonstrance, passed during the last weeks of the pre-civil war era, and the Nineteen Propositions of Parliament concerning further abridgments of royal power communicated to the king a few months afterward. Although this proposal for a settlement preceded the outbreak of open hostilities by a few weeks, it followed the break between parliament and crown, Charles's attempt to arrest members of Parliament in the House of Commons, his withdrawal to military headquarters, and the issue of parliamentary ordinances without formal sanction by the royal seal. The execution of the Archbishop of Canterbury, Laud, in 1645 by a bill of attainder passed by a Puritan Parliament in 1644 differs little from the proceeding against Strafford in 1641. Even the settlement submitted to the king after he had become the prisoner of parliament, the so-called "Newcastle proposals" of July, 1646, and "the four bills" of late December of the same year, radical as they were, follow closely the spirit of the Grand Remonstrance. Parliamentary control of the militia, the rescinding of the tenure of the members of the House of Lords appointed since 1642, convocation and adjournment of Parliament independent of royal pleasure, and adherence to the Solemn Covenant would have in effect only sanctioned a relationship between crown and parliament which was well in the making since 1625.

In the context of this study it is pointless to argue whether it was wise or unwise for the king to reject these proposals and to put his hopes on the Scotch-British conflict. What counts here is the fact that the legislative measures taken and reforms proposed during the civil wars were neither more nor less revolutionary than those before 1642.[10]

There is, of course, a difference between revolution and civil war, two terms which may overlap or may, on the other hand, signify entirely different concepts. A revolution in the limited technical sense used in this study will always mean the break of legitimacy and usually, but not inevitably, the resort to physical violence. Yet such violence does not necessarily mean full-scale warfare by organized military forces within a country, though such possibilities are of course, inherent, in every revolution. On the other hand, civil war does not inevitably signify revolutionary action on both sides, though this possibility exists here, too.

The examples are obvious. Neither the eighteenth century American nor the French Revolutions were connected with civil war. Although the French Revolution revealed the most terrible kind of violence, military actions by the warring parties within the countries, such as the peasant risings in 1789, the fight within the Vendeé in spring, and the siege of

---

[10] Cecily Wedgwood, *King's War, 1641–1647* (London, 1958), pp. 22 ff., 47 ff., 384 f., 400 ff., 565 f.; Trevelyan, pp. 272 ff.; Gardiner, ed., *Constitutional Documents:* Newcastle Propositions, pp. 208 ff.; The King's Answers, pp. 223 ff.; The Four Bills, and the King's Answers, pp. 248 ff., 265 ff.

Lyons in the fall of 1793, were neither sufficiently widespread nor continuous in time to be considered as phases of a civil war. The American Civil War was certainly not revolutionary in a technical sense on the part of the North, which defended the existing legal institutions and the lawful process of change; as for the South, the case is more controversial. The Spanish Civil War from 1936 to 1938, which followed a revolution, became on the other hand clearly revolutionary on both sides, since neither party wanted merely to restore the status quo.

The English Civil War as a whole represented the middle period of a revolutionary era which began with the accession of Charles I and ended with that of Charles II a generation later. During this period there were revolutionary acts on both sides, crown as well as parliament. Charles I was not satisfied to defend the status quo; he wished to return the power of Parliament to the limited status which it had held under the Tudor monarchy. The revolutionary character of the actions of Parliament between 1625 and 1641 was, of course, even more obvious. Thus a two-sided revolutionary situation existed throughout Charles I's reign. Although a fratricidal civil war is important in any country's history, this does not change the fact that the revolutionary intermediate system commenced long before this war started and ended only with the Stuart Restoration eighteen years after its outbreak.

There are those who hold quite legitimately that the trial and execution of the king in 1649 made all the difference. Since the Restoration centered at least externally on the reestablishment of the crown, its destruction also represented, according to this opinion, the very core of the revolution. To others the trial of the king was only its beginning and what had happened before a mere prelude. Such view is at least arguable, since up to barely a month before the king's death it would have been within his power to agree to a compromise which might have restored him to a throne, though one of drastically cut royal powers. It is an unanswerable question whether the course of English history would have been very different if the king at the most critical moment had submitted instead of deciding to engage in political maneuvers by which he played unwittingly into the hands of the new republicans. It may well be that if Charles I during the last months of his life had acted with prudent moderation instead of, first, with insincere cleverness and then with reckless courage, the course of events might have been entirely different. England, Ireland, and Scotland would possibly have been spared further suffering, and the results of the Glorious Revolution could have come about a generation earlier.

On the other hand, there is overwhelming evidence that Cromwell, at least until November, 1648, tried to avoid the elimination of the crown, let alone the execution of the king. During his whole tenure of high offices he was seriously though vainly concerned with the problem of legitimacy of government under his leadership. Until the late fall of 1648, a severely limited parliamentary monarchy offered a better basis for a solution of this intricate problem than the stillborn constitutional experiments between 1649 and 1659.[11] From this angle the destruction of the monarchy, though of the highest and most conspicuous symbolic significance, seems neither more nor less revolutionary than some actions taken before and afterward.

This holds true, indeed, for the whole era from 1649—particularly for 1653, the establishment of the Protectorate—until the Restoration. The basic difference between the period from the outbreak to the end of the civil wars and from the parliamentary regime to the end of the Commonwealth under a Lord Protector consists in a shift not so much in revolutionary emphasis as in revolutionary objectives. Until 1649/50 the revolutionary forces were concentrated primarily on the destruction of the old order; after that the chief efforts could be directed to the building of a new one. This new order, evolving out of continuing conflicts between Parliament, army, Presbyterians, radical sectaries, and the domestic underground forces of royalists and Catholics, was to be viewed as the result of increasing radicalism and gradually strengthened stabilizing forces. Two remarks by Cecily Wedgwood appear again in this context to be very much to the point. Cromwell in the Civil War "had himself fought for principles which were directly contravened by the establishment of his own rule," and balancing this statement at a later point, "There is, however, a distinction between a tyranny which is an end in itself and one which is but a means to another end. . . . His autocracy did not increase in severity as time went on. After those bad months in 1655—the months after he had dissolved the first Puritan parliament of the Protectorate and had set up military districts under Major generals—it gradually lessened."[12] By the beginning of 1657 the system of military administration was abolished. There can be little doubt that Cromwell's endeavors, from the malfunction of the Puritan Rump Parliament in existence until 1653,

[11] Wedgwood, *Cromwell*, pp. 74, 81 ff., 89, 98 f.; Wedgwood, *A Coffin for King Charles I: The Trial and Execution of Charles I* (New York, 1964), pp. 103 ff.; Sir Charles Firth, *Oliver Cromwell and the Rule of the Puritans in England* (London, 1958), pp. 203 ff.; Davies, pp. 145 f.; Maurice Ashley, *Oliver Cromwell* (London, 1937), pp. 150 ff.

[12] Wedgwood, *Cromwell*, pp. 14, 115.

the token Little Parliament with its radical Puritan character, and the following two anti-army parliaments until 1658, were meant to establish legislatures of restricted power which were, however, by no means submissive. For much of this time Cromwell might have governed with the support of the army, a council of state partially controlled by the army and supported by the religious and socially radical sectarian movements, largely following utopian semisocialist ideas like those of John Lilburne. As Maurice Ashley points out, Cromwell's search for a constitutional foundation of government was based on the idea that only thus could law and order be preserved, only thus could the military source of his power be sufficiently broadened to give his rule full respectability. Such respectability implied respect for traditional institutions.[13]

Other issues in which the stabilizing aspects of Cromwell's regime became increasingly conspicuous were his stand against social radicalism and for religious tolerance. Cromwell, as is generally known, was a strict advocate of political rights based to a large extent on property. In this respect, to give the squirearchy, the landed propertied classes, greater influence in governmental affairs, he went even farther than the royal regime. Qualifications for electors were based on much stiffer property requirements than under the previous Stuart regime. Ideas of political and economic equality were completely alien to him. Cromwell steadily and consistently opposed the sociopolitical doctrines of radicals during the whole revolutionary period.[14] This pertained to the Levellers, the followers of Lilburne, as well as to various independent sectaries such as the Fifth Monarchy Men, the believers in a universal kingdom to come after the Roman Empire.

Yet Cromwell's rigid position toward the radicals in the social and political sphere did not extend to the overlapping religious one. Here his well-known ideas of liberty of conscience as viewed by the standards of his times were notable indeed. Not only did he extend far-reaching protection in the truly religious sphere to those whose social tenets he rejected,

[13] Ashley, *England in the Seventeenth Century,* pp. 99 f.; Firth, pp. 419 f.; Wedgwood, *Cromwell,* pp. 98 f. See also Wedgwood, *A Coffin,* pp. 58 ff.

[14] Wedgwood, *Cromwell,* pp. 35 f., 62, 70, 75, 81 f.; Firth, pp. 156 ff., 240 ff., 406; Ashley, *England in the Seventeenth Century,* pp. 91 f., 112 ff.; Ashley, *Cromwell,* pp. 119 f., 160 f.; Trevelyan, pp. 282 ff.; Judson, pp. 415 ff.

Three monographs are of specific interest in this context: George P. Gooch, *English Democratic Ideas in the Seventeenth Century* (Cambridge, 1927), in particular pp. 118–140, 239–257; Margaret James, *Social Problems and Policy During the Puritan Revolution, 1640–1660* (London, 1930), pp. 145 ff., 224 ff., and from a Marxian point of view, Eduard Bernstein, *Sozialismus und Demokratie in der grossen englischen Revolution* (Stuttgart, 1908), pp. 63–206, *passim.*

such as those of the Quakers; he also went much farther in the toleration of non-Christians (Jews) than any contemporary ruler. On politically more dangerous religious issues, Cromwell's treatment of Anglicans, whose liturgy had been forbidden since 1645, was actually less strict than a majority of members in his parliaments wished it to be; his dealings with the Catholics, while harsh enough, were less arbitrary than during the civil wars. All these effects were marred, unfortunately, by a Puritan self-righteousness based on the assumption that decisions made after personal communion with God in prayers could never be wrong.[15]

In a sense this could be called the counterpart of a divine-right theory, though on a personal rather than a hereditary basis. That this conviction motivated constructive, moderate, and humanitarian acts in such fields as higher education, particularly that of the clergy, the courts, criminal law reform, and commercial legislation, is undeniable. This applied even to the relatively moderate enforcement of Puritan mores. Furthermore, the notably undoctrinaire character of Cromwell's French and Dutch foreign policy followed rationally sounder principles than those of the Stuart regimes before and after him. At least in relation to the Dutch the Protector pursued morally less controverial ones as well. Against all this must be held the weighty failure to solve the constitutional issue, plus the ruthlessness of the Lord Protector's Irish policy. The latter can be partially explained, but certainly not justified, by reference to ancient and barbarian military customs.

The evaluation of Cromwell's rule in either a positive or negative sense is important, but it is not the basic issue. For the purpose of this study the conclusion must suffice that his regime as part of the intermediate system was not more revolutionary from the point of legitimacy than the foremost actions on the side of both parliament and crown under Charles I's reign. From the spiritual angle the Puritan revolution was as clearly manifest between 1625 and 1641 as during the Civil War and the parliamentary and commonwealth phases of the administration afterward. At what point the revolutionary spirit was strongest here would be difficult if not impossible to assess, inasmuch as ideological movements cannot be measured in strictly political terms. Yet if revolutionary force is to be de-

---

[15] Wedgwood, *Cromwell*, pp. 60 f., 64 f., 105 f., 133; Firth, pp. 353 ff.; Samuel R. Gardiner, *Cromwell's Place in History* (London, 1899), pp. 102 ff.; Trevelyan, pp. 312 ff.; Davies, *Early Stuarts*, pp. 208 ff.; Gooch, pp. 220 ff.; James, pp. 15 ff. Concerning Baptists and Quakers, see also Richard Schlatter, *The Social Ideas of Religious Leaders, 1660–1688* (London, 1940), pp. 233 ff.; Bernstein, pp. 242 ff., 291 ff.; Gardiner, ed., *Documents:* Act of 1650, repealing several clauses in statutes imposing penalties for not coming to church, pp. 300 ff.

termined by success in the maintenance of law and order, then the Commonwealth was certainly less revolutionary than the era from 1625 to 1648. What we call in modern terms police-state methods were not infequently employed in either period and on either side, under the king, during the Civil War, under parliamentary rule, and under the Protectorate. Accordingly, it is hardly possible to make a determination on the strength of motivation. As far as effectiveness goes, the decision should be easy.

Let it be noted again that the tremendous significance of trial and execution of the king, as the ideological foundation of the restoration process cannot be denied. But here we are not concerned with its origins but with the comparative character of the regimes from 1625 to the outbreak of the civil wars, the civil wars themselves, and the Commonwealth. We have to distinguish only between revolutionary accomplishments and revolution without them.

Eventually these accomplishments failed. When Oliver Cromwell died in September, 1658, he was barely fifty-nine years old. He installed his son Richard, a weakwilled man of limited competence, as his successor as Lord Protector. The younger Cromwell could not settle the conflict between the army and Parliament, the fourth after his father had turned out, in 1653, the remnants of the Long Parliament of 1640. He could not prevent the recall of this Rump Parliament in May, 1659, which practically put an end to the Protectorate. When General Monck, one of Cromwell's most faithful and capable lieutenants, moved into the ensuing vacuum of power, a new Parliament, the last convoked without royal summons until 1689, met in April, 1660. Yet at the behest of Monck it included all peers eligible to seats in the former House of Lords and the former and new royalists in the new House of Commons. Charles II's Declaration of Breda promised a somewhat restricted amnesty, liberty of conscience, title by and large to property of the confiscated estates to the present holders, but above all, recognition of the legislation passed prior to the civil wars. It was accepted by the Convention Parliament on May 1, 1660. The king entered English soil shortly afterward. The restored system was thus installed owing largely to the skill of Monck. The question whether one can speak of a successful restoration as well, will engage us in the following pages. Yet it may be noted that great care had been taken by Monck, the leading parliamentarians, the clever young king, and his most capable adviser and subsequent lord chancellor, Edward Hyde (soon to be Earl of Clarendon), to arrange for a transition that would be not only orderly but constitutionally irreproachable as well.

To what extent the contracting parties succeeded in this purpose is a highly complex and controversial matter which does not have to be argued here. The most remarkable aspect of the problem, however, is the fact that both sides by deeds rather than words attempted to link the Restoration not only to the pre-civil war reign of Charles I but by clear implication to the Cromwellian intermediate system as well. This was done regardless of the fact that the bodies of the regicides were exhumed and displayed on the gallows.[16] This in itself would prove the obvious, that expediency and nothing else motivated either side. The facts themselves are uncontestable. The Convention Parliament represented, for all practical purposes, according to the new eligibility requirements, an enlargement, not a replacement, of the Rump Parliament, which in turn had been strongly linked to the original and revolutionary systems. The amnesty and the generous guarantee of property rights acquired during the revolutionary period, as well as the solemnly proclaimed liberty of conscience, were constitutional links to the revolutionary intermediate system, not solely to the original one. By its actions, the restored system had acknowledged, to an extent rarely paralleled in the history of previous restoration movements, that no restoration was feasible without a bow, albeit a most reluctant bow, to the strength and virility of the revolutionary intermediate system.

At this point another question, not unlike the one previously posed seems justified: whether without the execution of the king in 1649 a peaceful transition to the parliamentary monarchy might have been feasible. Could the Restoration have been avoided if Cromwell had selected his abler, younger son, Henry, or either of the generals Monck or Fairfax as his successors in the Protectorate rather than Richard Cromwell?

Considering the fact that the Puritan revolution as ideology had run its course, that many of its mores and thoughts were incorporated imperceptibly for all time into English history, though few could remain effective under the label of the revolutionary period, such is not likely. Evidence in this direction may be seen also in Cromwell's response to the parliamentary request made in the famous "Humble Petition and Advice of spring 1658 to accept the title of king." [17] He was too experienced and farseeing a statesman not to realize that whatever might happen, a regime

---

[16] Tanner, *English Constitutional Conflicts,* pp. 201 ff.; David Ogg, *England in the Reign of Charles II,* 2 vols. (Oxford, 1963); see I, 12–34; Davies *op. cit.,* pp. 235 ff. See also Godfrey Davies, *Essays on the Later Stuarts* (San Marino, California, 1958), pp. 9 ff.; Gardiner, ed., *Documents:* Declaration of Breda, pp. 351 ff.

[17] Gardiner, ed., *Documents:* Humble Petition and Advice, pp. 334 ff.; Davies, *Early Stuarts,* pp. 180 ff.; Trevelyan, pp. 309 f.; Pollard *Factors in Modern History,* pp. 193 ff.

could not change its *raison d'être* on its own. This does not necessarily mean that Puritanism could not have continued to thrive *in abstracto* under a monarchy. It does mean, however, that those who had promoted or were bound to promote it in a more radical way could not effect the change, even assuming but by no means granting that they wanted to do so. According to this view, the royal Restoration as Stuart Restoration was bound to come one way or another and at some time or another, most likely after the great Protector's death.

Maurice Ashley in a masterly summary surveys the very essence of the Restoration of 1660.

> What did the Restoration of Charles II in 1660 in fact restore? First of all of course it restored the monarchy. But it was not the Elizabethan monarchy. All the acts to which King Charles I gave his assent before he left his capital retained their full validity. Consequently many of the devices which until that time had been perfectly legally used by the King to uphold his prerogative and to enable him to govern and raise money without parliament's aid were abolished for all time. The prerogative courts were not reconstituted. [Star Chamber and High Commission.] Unparliamentary taxation, such as ship money and forced loans, stood condemned. The criminal jurisdiction of the Privy Council had vanished. The King could no longer order the arrest of members of Parliament without showing cause. In fact, . . . the monarchy had become "constitutional." Secondly, Parliament was restored, but on the old basis [that is, of the era before 1642]. . . . Thirdly, the Church of England was restored with its full panoply of bishops and deans, but it was no more a comprehensive Church, for many of the Puritans were driven from it. On the other hand, the Church, like the country, never entirely lost its puritan undertone. Thus in spite of the Restoration being, in theory at least, "unconstitutional" neither King nor Parliament nor Church was left unscathed by the fire of revolution. And both the monarch and his ministers were aware that they dare not take the road back to the old Tudor methods of government. Their policies were always tempered by the knowledge that behind them lay the precedent of a civil war and an anointed monarch's execution. . . . [Ashley adds a most important point:] Clarendon's triumph had been to procure the Restoration without the assistance of foreign arms. The price he had to pay was to persuade the King to promise in his Declaration of Breda to leave to Parliament the settlement of all the knotty points arising out of the recent upheaval.[18]

This was, of course, the amnesty, which went far, though probably not far enough. It made possible the peaceful disbanding of the army, but it did not prevent a new, though relatively small-scale, revolutionary rising

---

[18] Ashley, *England in the Seventeenth Century,* pp. 121 f., 123 f.

in 1661. The land settlement on the whole favored those who had obtained estates after 1641, except by outright confiscation. The determination of the king's income, so complex an issue under the first Stuart kings, was again in the hands of Parliament. Altogether, according to Ashley's viewpoint, the synthesis between restored, intermediate, and original systems would have to be considered quite successful.

The view of George M. Trevelyan is quite different. He distinguishes between a first successful restoration in 1660, brought about chiefly by the Convention Parliament and the skill of Monck, and a second one in 1661, which by way of the Anglican-Cavalier Parliament from 1661 to 1679 ushered in reaction. According to this view, "First in 1660 were restored Parliament and King, the non-military state, and the dominance of the hereditary upper class; secondly [a harsh indictment] in 1661 was restored the persecuting Anglican Church. The first Restoration was made by the Presbyterians, the second by the Cavaliers. The political and social restoration has fixed its roots apparently forever in the character and institutions of the English. The religious restoration, though substantially modified in 1689, has formed the religious and political character of the various strata of our society." [19]

This view perceives a much earlier break in the restoration process than is commonly assumed. The change, which undoubtedly cast a long shadow on the troubles to come, is usually associated with such events as the election of the three Whig parliaments of Charles II in quick succession after 1678, the evolution of party movements in a modern parliamentary sense, the introduction of the Exclusion Bill concerning the succession of the Catholic Duke of York, the spurious so-called Titus Oates or Popish Plot of 1678, and the genuine republican Rye House Plot of 1683. With the unfortunate reign of James II, all these speedily evolving crises came to a head.

Trevelyan is ertainly right in his assumptions that irrespective of the merits of the issue, restoration in ecclesiastic matters prompted the first and ever continuing problems of the regime. This must not be construed as either affirmation or rejection of the frequently voiced opinion that the Restoration must be understood as primarily a consequence of oversaturation with the Puritan ideology. This is as it may be. Far more obvious is the fact that political doctrines were generally founded on religious grounds. By strength of this deeply imbedded historical tradition and conviction, political allegiance and loyalty were measured in terms of church affiliation and church and state relations. The ecclesiastic legislation known as the Clarendon Code (1661–1665), with its severe

[19] Trevelyan, p. 332.

measures—unenforceable even by a police state—against independent sectaries as well as Presbyterians, is again quite rightly referred to by Trevelyan as "persecution under a Cavalier parliament . . . more thorough than persecution under the vexed and straitened monarchy of Charles I. . . . The present under Clarendon [though by no means entirely of Clarendon's own choosing] was worse than the past under Laud." [20] The obvious class conflict associated with it was based far more on the differences between democratic and semifeudal church organizations than on distinctions of wealth. This is particularly clear in the revolts of the Scotch Covenanters in 1666 and again in 1679. It is still evident in the Test Act of 1673, a bill aimed at further solidifying the supremacy of the Church of England against Puritans as well as Catholics. Here we can already observe an evolving Protestant alliance of Anglicans and Presbyterians against the undisputed Catholic proclivities of the king and, strengthened by the Disabling Act of 1678, even more so against Catholics. Naturally, the political hysteria following the alleged Popish Plot played an important part.[21]

The Catholic issue dominated almost completely the last years of Charles II's reign, inasmuch as the Exclusion Bill, aimed at eliminating the succession of the Catholic Duke of York, became now the foremost problem of domestic and foreign policy. The social balance of domestic government and foreign policy was involved here. Charles's internal administration in the latter part of his reign made an open alliance between his Anglican supporters and Puritan adversaries a distinct possibility. This largely accounted also for the opposition to his substantially pro-French policy, though just here he came much closer to Cromwell's policy than most of the king's opponents wanted to admit. That Cromwell's rather unorthodox foreign policy was motivated by the national interest as he saw it, is rarely denied. How far personal motives played a part in the rather subtle policy of Charles II is difficult to determine. As far as the effectiveness of the restoration movement is concerned, both the succession question and foreign policy had an unfavorable short-range effect on the standing of the king in public opinion.[22]

[20] Trevelyan, p. 344.

[21] Ashley, *England*, pp. 125 ff.; Ogg, *England in the Reign of Charles II*, I, 200 ff., II, 559 ff.; Trevelyan, pp. 342 ff., 383 ff., 426; Macaulay, I, 138 ff., 336 ff.; Tanner, pp. 227 ff.; Pollard, pp. 171 f. That Charles II must be considered a Catholic when he received extreme unction on his deathbed, is certain. Whether he was a practicing Catholic before, and if so, when he became one, is not clear.

[22] On the exclusion issue, see Ashley, *England*, p. 150; Ogg, II, 584 ff.; Macaulay, I, 202 ff.; Tanner, pp. 233 ff. On foreign policy in relation to domestic policies, Ashley, pp. 121 ff.; Ogg, I, 322 ff., 354 ff. See also Dennis T. Witcombe, *Charles II*

The royal endeavors to mitigate the harshness of the Clarendon Code in the Declaration of Indulgence of 1672 could be referred to as counter-argument. Certainly this unsuccessful attempt, to a large extent motivated by Charles's thinly camouflaged Catholic preference, represented in a devious way tolerance against the Puritan bigotry of the parliamentary opposition. So did the Habeas Corpus Act of 1679, which must be considered a lasting achievement of his reign, irrespective of the motives behind the royal assent. It should be remembered also that the royal administration honored the concessions made in the Declaration of Breda in 1660 to a rather wide extent. This pertains to relations between crown and parliament for the better part of Charles II's reign. In the controversial sphere of liberty of conscience the faults were by no means all on the king's side. Above all, England at the end of Charles II's reign in the socio-economic sphere, in military defense, and in international relations, was in a more favorable position than at the beginning of the Civil War. In this respect the abolition of the standing army after the Restoration strengthened the power of Parliament; the subsequent gradual, small-scale buildup of the army together with that of the navy did hardly hurt it and was not devoid of long-range benefits in the future. Again the strengthening of the English position as compared with that under Charles I's reign was undeniable.[23]

Nor can we deny the complete failure of James II's reign, which in less than four years, by a combination of ignorance, illegality, and immorality, led to the collapse of the order established at great pains and, all things considered, with great skill in 1660. Although the interpretation of Charles II's complex personality and his diffuse administration is controversial, that of the slow-witted and brutal James II is clear-cut.

There can be little doubt that the Catholic succession by itself was not the primary cause of the rallying of an overwhelming majority of Anglicans and Presbyterians against the new king. As Ashley observes correctly: "The doctrine of the inviolability of hereditary monarchy had many rigid defenders who even argued that to dispose or exclude a ruler for his religion was a 'Popish' and not a 'Protestant' doctrine. The king 'whom God in wrath' might give us 'is not in our power to change,' explained Leoline Jenkins," the learned Anglican lawyer and leader of the fight against the Exclusion Bill.[24] Only the birth of a son to the aging

[23] Macaulay, I, 116 ff., 220 ff.; Trevelyan, pp. 337 f.; Pollard, p. 196.

[24] Ashley, *England*, p. 150.

James II in 1687, which threatened to perpetuate the Catholic succession, brought the issue again directly to the fore. Yet this happened only after, but not before, the king had violated the provisions of the religious establishment of liberty of conscience and of judicial safeguards for the protection of the individual in various ways. Indeed for many years after the revolution of 1688/89 the notion of the so-called Jacobite succession, that is, the Catholic succession, in the male Stuart line, was still widely entertained in England by Tory opinion. It was by no means exclusively associated with pro-Catholic proclivities.

The dismal failure of James II was originally not due to unwillingness of his first Parliament to support him. It was the cumulative effect of a reign which gradually subverted and distorted ancient traditions of constitutional government and religious truce as well as those acquired and revised within the last two generations. This regime did so by what in modern terms might be called a rather clumsy application of the "salami tactics" of undermining the institutions of the constitutional monarchy step by step rather than by an outright assault on them. A belated and bungling attempt to appease the rising opposition failed, an opposition held together equally by the outrages of the new reign and by the scarcely healed wounds of previous conflicts, which were now reopened. Only this combination of factors made the Catholic succession count heavily against the king.

What weighed even more heavily were the distortions of justice in the trial of the great Puritan theologian Richard Baxter and in the infamous Bloody Assizes following the Monmouth and Argyle revolts in 1685. Continuous appointment of Catholic officers in the army, contrary to a law however unjust in itself, and the attempts to set up a large standing army beyond the control of Parliament weakened the regime further.

Interference with the university establishment at Oxford showed an especial insensitivity to that part of public opinion which counted most. Charles II's endeavors to revise the religious establishment of 1660–1661 in favor of all dissenters were received with suspicion by Parliament and the public as underhand attempts to strengthen the Catholic cause. Still, the motivation of Charles's policy concerning liberty of conscience could be considered debatable. The same was not true for similar actions on James's part. His declarations of Liberty of Conscience of 1687 and 1688, though formally pertaining to all dissenters, were perceived as outright efforts to no less an undertaking than to undo the English Reformation. The king's clumsy attempt in 1687 to interfere with the election of a Parliament that according to his will should repeal the Test Act of 1673, and the infamous trial of the bishops who opposed this policy, strengthened suspicions concerning James II's motives. His endeavors to bolster his position by resort to legal authorities were of little avail in the face of public opinion.

The birth of a male royal heir offered justification or at least rationalization to the opposition in its resolve to put an end to the regime and ask for the intervention of William of Orange, the consort of the king's elder daughter, Mary. At this time a large part even of Catholic public opinion in England was concerned with the danger of royal absolutism and its indifference to French dominance on the Continent. This opposition must be added to the more obvious opposition of orthodox Church of England and Puritan followers. In particular, a majority of the Parliament of 1685–1687 was aroused by the domestic situation and the status of foreign affairs. This pertained especially to the royal disregard for the dangers which the Dutch had to face from the hereditary French enemy.[25]

At this point, after a review of significant aspects of the course of events between 1625 and 1688, we return to the questions raised at the beginning of this chapter, the success or failure of the restoration movement between 1660 and 1688. Based on that evaluation it will be necessary to turn to the even more important question whether the Glorious Revolution of 1688/ 89 represented a decisive break in historical development. Did it signify the failure of a previous restoration movement which had never become a full restoration or did it stand merely for the revision of the restoration process? If that latter assumption should be correct, we would face a restoration which has not come to an end in three centuries, to this very day. It would be indeed the most successful example of restoration in Western history.

Unquestionably the Stuart Restoration had to face great difficulties, which arose not only from the opposition of the defeated Puritan cause but from all political sides. Thus, to take just one conspicuous example, as early as 1667 Clarendon's fall appeared to be due to such conflicting causes as opposition to the Catholic Portuguese marriage of the king, and the alleged harshness of the Clarendon Code against Presbyterianism. Yet to the royal court Clarendon himself appeared to be an advocate of Puritan mores. The king saw in him the leader of an obstreperous Parliament, unwilling to ameliorate the status of the Catholics. As Trevelyan rightly

---

[25] David Ogg, *England in the Reigns of James II and William III* (Oxford, 1955), pp. 139 ff., 195 ff.; Francis C. Turner, *James II* (London, 1948), pp. 233 ff., 266 ff.; Davies, *Essays on the Later Stuarts* (San Marino, California, 1958), pp. 41 ff.; Ashley, *England*, pp. 167 ff.; Macaulay, I, 348 ff., 375 ff., 385 ff., 506 ff.; II, 9 ff., 33 ff.

points out, "By representing King against Parliament in matters of religion, Clarendon incurred the hostility of both and fell between the two stools on which it was his constitutional theory that every minister should sit." [26]

Trevelyan believes also that the idea "of the Second or Catholic Stuart despotism" preceded the reign of James II and originated actually from Charles who "though he afterwards abandoned it . . . handed it on to his less able brother. It was based on Catholicism, toleration, a standing army and the French alliance." [27] This may be an extreme view, though one not entirely out of line with the classical interpretation of Macaulay. Certainly the king's pro-French attitude and his leanings toward dissenters in name but Catholic dissenters in fact, played an increasingly decisive role, beginning at least in the early 1670's. The Popish Plot of 1678, the dissolution of the Cavalier Parliament in 1679 and its rapid succession by three Whig opposition parliaments ending with four years of nonparliamentary rule, shook the stability of the regime probably as much as the issue of the Exclusion Bill itself and the republican plot of 1683.

There can be little doubt, however, that the damage resulting from Charles II's arbitrariness and from parliamentary fractiousness could still be repaired. In every major respect, in the economic, social, and cultural spheres, the position of England was strong in 1685. The critical transition of government to a declared Catholic ruler proceeded smoothly, and in the honeymoon of James's reign a Parliament responsive to the new king's wishes was elected. Surely had it not been for the disastrous further actions of James II the difficulties of the latter part of Charles II's reign might have been passed over easily and hardly anyone would question the success of the restoration process until 1685. Only the total failure of James's rule led to the understandable assumption that his political bankruptcy had its direct causes in an alleged maladministration of his older brother. Allowing for a close historical relationship between the transactions of both reigns, such interpretation is still only hindsight after the event. If we speak of a failure of the restoration process we must lay it directly at the door of James II's reign. That it represented pure and unmitigated failure cannot be denied. Whether it represented mere interruption or a termination of the restoration process has to be investigated.

The bare facts are clear enough. On September 30, 1688, William of Orange accepted the invitation, rendered to him in June of the same year

[26] Trevelyan, pp. 361 f.; Ogg, *England in the Reign of Charles II*, I, 205 ff.; Aylmer, *Short History* (see n. 3 above), pp. 173 f.; Witcombe, pp. 61 ff.

[27] Trevelyan, pp. 365 f.; Macaulay, I, 130 ff.; Ogg, II, 559 ff.

by outstanding spokesmen for Tory and Whig views, to put an end to tyranny in England. While this acceptance and avowed declaration of intent to come to England as a regent, though not necessarily as king, was of little legal consequence, it undoubtedly gave the prince important assurances for the success of his daring expedition. The famous landing at Torbay followed on November 5. After some hesitation James turned to flight on December 11, a factor of some consequence in the interpretation of the legality of the subsequent events.

The period from December 11, 1688, to February 12, 1689, is frequently referred to as that of the interregnum, when James II had allegedly abandoned the throne, but his son-in-law William had not yet been proclaimed king. In that period was the convocation of the new Convention Parliament by the end of January, 1689, in composition far closer to the last parliaments of Charles II than to that of King James. On February 13, William and Mary were proclaimed jointly as royal rulers; the actual administration, however, was settled on William. This decisive provision was never challenged by his consort queen, Mary, who, as daughter of James, was actually the heir to the succession, though from the strictly dynastic viewpoint, one of doubtful legality. The—from here on—exclusively Protestant succession was settled on the potential heirs of the royal couple; in default of them, on those of the queen's sister, Anne. In default of these—from the point of legitimacy, strangely enough—William's offspring from a future marriage would have succeeded, even though the Prince of Orange was not a descendant of the royal line.

Major provisions of the Declaration of Rights, enacted with minor changes as the Bill of Rights by Parliament in December, 1689, will be summarized briefly here. They provided royal assent to provisions that the king without consent of Parliament could neither make nor suspend law. The dispensing power of the sovereign in regard to duly passed laws was abolished, levying of money without parliamentary consent was again declared to be illegal, as was the right to maintain a standing army without parliamentary approval. Freedom of parliamentary elections, parliamentary debate, and right of petition were affirmed, jury trials were upheld, and the confiscation of estates prior to conviction was declared to be unlawful. Parliament was to convene frequently, a somewhat vague clause substantiated by a new Triennial Act of 1694, according to which, unlike the previous Triennial legislation, not only should Parliament meet at least every three years but its tenure should not exceed three years.

Most of this basic legislation, with the foremost exception of the succession issue, was, of course, reaffirmation and clarification of existing constituitional principles. Even the often-voiced assumption that this declaration and its subsequent parliamentary enactment put the crown in a far weaker position than the one reestablished in 1660/61 is fully valid only insofar as the Bill of Rights had a stronger constitutional standing than the Declaration of Breda a generation before. David Ogg is probably right when he states that the purpose of the legislation was not "to enunciate abstract principles of government but to provide safeguards against royal wrongdoings. The legislators of 1689 did not even try to make monarchy foolproof; all that they were concerned with was that certain evils within their own experience should not recur." [28] In fact, as another historian points out, the precarious Whig-Tory unity between the propertied classes could not have been brought about and maintained at all during a critical transition period if this fundamental legislation had concentrated on still controversial principles of the settlement of religious establishments and the question of indemnity for supporters of the previous regime.[29]

The Convention Parliament had passed the legislation concerning the establishment of a new ruler easily enough as far as the deposition of King James as "popish" ruler was concerned. Yet a further resolution, more doubtful in its legal reasoning, that the king had violated a controversial contract theory and had vacated the throne, was passed only by a narrow majority in the new House of Lords. Through James II's attempt to regain his crown by his landing in Ireland in March, 1689, the theory that the king had vacated the throne or even that he had abdicated, according to some, received a further blow.

Because of the wise and firm policy of William of Orange as king—in some ways perhaps England's greatest—these cracks in the armor of legitimacy mattered little. By the new sovereign's dissolution of the Convention Parliament of 1689 and the almost immediate free election of another one more in line with William's wishes, the passage of a Corporation Bill was prevented. This would have perpetuated the exclusion of dissenters from municipal offices as punishment for their yielding to Charles II's Corporation Act of 1661. The memory of previous persecutions made the Puritan attitude understandable, but politically it was most unwise. Had it not been checked, the conflict between Whigs and Tories would certainly have been exacerbated and perhaps—even more

---

[28] David Ogg, *England in the Reigns of James II and William III*, pp. 242 f.; see also Stephen S. Baxter, *William III* (London, 1966), pp. 221 ff.

[29] Christopher Hill, *The Century of Revolution, 1603–1714* (Edinburgh, 1961), pp. 276 f.

important—the one between Anglicans and Presbyterians as well. The new Tory Parliament, which met as early as March, 1690, passed an Act of Grace for the former but no longer active supporters of the various ideologies in conflict since the beginnings of Charles I's reign.

The Act of Grace in turn would not have been possible without two previous important pieces of legislation which combined firmness with forbearance. First there was the Mutiny Act of March, 1689, which proclaimed military revolt against the new regime to be treasonable activity. On the other side of the ledger, the Act of Toleration, passed in May of the same year, exempted religious dissenters, except Catholics and Unitarians, from the enforcement of the penal statutes against nonconformists. This toleration was still a far cry from religious equality, and the unjust disabilities concerning the right to hold public office were not removed. The new Calvinist king had obtained the very minimum of concessions essential for a peaceful pursuit of government. In this sense and particularly in view of the alliance with the Catholic Habsburgs against France, of which England became a part now, on the side of Holland, the enforcement of the anti-Catholic legislation was considerably modified. Still, the case of the hundreds of members of the unbeneficed high clergy who refused to take the oath of allegiance to William and Mary on the theory of nonresistance to established authority—the authority of James II —proves how deeply the revolutionary rift of these anxious years was felt, by no means only in conflicts between Anglicans and Catholics, but within the High Church itself as well as between Anglicanism, Calvinism, and the various sectaries. It took all the skill of a ruler as firm in the execution of his policies as he was moderate in his design to overcome these difficulties. Had it not been for the general fear of new predictable conflicts on religious grounds and, above all, of the increasing importance of the struggle with France, which practically ended only with the peace of Utrecht in 1713, even a leader of William III's ingenuity and honesty might have failed. The association of James II, in exile in the Bourbon castle of St. Germain, with French politics is perhaps the most important single factor which rallied the English people of all persuasions around the new king.

The death of James II in the fall of 1701, barely six months before that of William, did not change the legal situation. Yet the association of legitimacy was not as firmly established in the minds of the people with the young pretender, who had left England as an infant, as with the anointed king, James II, despite his reprehensible character. Even prior to this event the healing element of time became evident. The Act of Settlement of June, 1701, which gave the royal succession after the death of the future Queen Anne to the German descendants of the Stuarts in the female line, the house of Hanover, did not encounter the same difficulties as the revolutionary succession of William and Mary, although legally nothing had changed.[30]

In a technical legal sense there can be little doubt, indeed, about the revolutionary character of the revolution of 1688/89. Even if one accepted the questionable proposition that King James had vacated his throne, this would not have impaired the claims of his infant son. The theory of forfeiture of the right to rule by the king's arbitrary actions, as declared by the Scotch Parliament, on the other hand, was based on a theory of contract which had no uncontested legal foundation in constitutional law. The right of armed resistance against a tyrant was founded on natural law, not on traditional precedent or statutes. Perhaps the best summary of the legal situation is that of Frederick W. Maitland. "Those who conducted the revolution sought, and we may well say were wise in seeking, to make revolution look as small as possible, to make it as like a legal proceeding as by any stretch of ingenuity it could be made. But to make it out to be a perfect legal case is impossible. Had it failed, those who attempted it would have suffered as traitors, and I do not think that any lawyer can maintain that their execution would have been unlawful. . . ." Between December, 1688, and February 1689, England was without a king. "It is difficult . . . to regard the Convention Parliament as a lawfully constituted Assembly. By whom was it summoned? Not by a King of England, but by a Prince of Orange. . . . The act which declares it to be a parliament depends for its validity on the assent of William and Mary. The validity of that assent depends on their being king and queen; but how do they come being king and queen . . . ?" Maitland expressly declares that he does not by any means intend to argue the justness of the Jacobite cause, but he adds, "It seems to me that we must treat the Revolution as a revolution, a very necessary revolution, but still a revolution. We cannot work it into our constitutional law."[31]

Of course, legal authorities like Maitland and Tanner necessarily argue

[30] For the legislative acts of William III's reign referred to here, see E. Neville Williams, ed., *The Eighteenth Century Constitution, 1688-1815* (Cambridge, 1960), pp. 10-50; Baxter, pp. 248 ff.

For a discussion of the pertinent aspects of the revolution and the early parts of his reign, see Ogg, *England in the Reigns of James II and William III,* pp. 222 ff., 491 ff.; Trevelyan, pp. 446 ff.; Hill, pp. 275 ff., 308 ff.; Baxter, pp. 221-242 *passim,* 248 ff.; Macaulay, II, 126 ff., 141 ff., 509 ff.; III, 35 ff., 55 ff., 164 ff.

[31] Maitland, *Constitutional History of England* (see n. 3 above), pp. 284 f.; see also in the same sense Tanner, *English Constitutional Conflicts* (see n. 3 above), pp. 250 ff.

the case of the revolutionary change on relatively narrow legal constitutional grounds, irrespective of their sympathy for what is generally considered a proud chapter of English history. It may be assumed that the association of the events of 1688/89 with the unimpeded development henceforward of a tradition of parliamentary supremacy leads the majority of political historians, even more unhesitatingly than the constitutional historians, to assert the existence of a "glorious" revolution.

The views of Maurice Ashley, Christopher Hill, G. M. Trevelyan, and David Ogg are typical in that respect.[32] They stand here only as examples for those of many others. Most definite in this matter is Ogg. He defends the revolution not only on moral grounds. "As David Ogg has pointed out, if consistency had been pressed, the revolution could not have been bloodless. . . ."[33] ". . . once James had left the country, there was no alternative but submission to his successor. Not perhaps a very consistent attitude. Other revolutions have been more consistent, and therefore more violent."[34] This is, of course, a defensible political interpretation, although if drawn to its final conclusion it may put illegitimate government without bloodshed in a doubtful juxtaposition to perversion of justice, the axe of the headsman and the threat of royal arm as legitimate means of widespread shedding of the blood of innocent victims by order of the rightful ruler. In this sense the pragmatic view of E. Neville Williams, which questions the revolutionary character of the events, is perhaps more convincing when he argues that "The men of 1688 . . . were not Founding Fathers enunciating general principles of constitutional law, but empiricists coping with practical difficulties. And in this . . . spirit they tackled the . . . problem . . . of settling 'the religion, laws and liberties of this kingdom, so that the same for the future might not be in danger of being subverted.'" This reference to the Bill of Rights means that "they regarded themselves not as revolutionaries demolishing the power of the crown, but as conservatives correcting revolutionary tendencies on the part of previous monarchs."[35]

This view goes in substance back to the history of the Great Old Man of the later Restoration period, the revolution, and the reign of William III, Thomas Macaulay. He does not shrink from the term "revolution," but he minimizes its revolutionary character. He perceives its glory in the

[32] Hill, pp. 275 ff.; Ashley, *England* pp. 178 ff.; Trevelyan, pp. 468 f.; Ogg, pp. 222 f.

[33] Williams, p. 3 (with reference to Ogg, p. 211).

[34] Ogg, p. 211.

[35] Williams, p. 3.

maximum of benefit for the public good, brought about by a minimum not only of violence but, above all, of illegality. On the Declaration of Rights he observes:

> The change seems small. Not a single flower of the crown was touched. Not a single new right was given to the people. The whole English law . . . was in the judgment of the greatest lawyers . . . exactly the same after the Revolution as before it . . . there had been a slight deviation from the ordinary course of succession. This was all and this was enough. . . . Both the English parties agreed in treating with solemn respect the ancient constitutional traditions of the state. The only question was, in what sense those traditions were to be understood. [And further] The Declaration of Rights, though it made nothing law which had not been law before, contained the germ of . . . every good law which may hereafter, in the course of the ages, be found necessary to promote the public weal, and to satisfy the demands of public opinion. . . . [And finally] If it be asked what has made us to differ from others, the answer is that we never lost what others are wildly and blindly seeking to regain. It is because we had a preserving revolution in the seventeenth century that we have not had a destroying revolution in the nineteenth. It is because we had freedom in the midst of servitude that we have order in the midst of anarchy. For the authority of law, for the security of property, for the peace of our streets, for the happiness of our homes our gratitude is due under Him who raises and pulls down nations at His pleasure, to the Long Parliament, to the Convention and to William of Orange.[36]

These somewhat lengthy quotations may be excused not only for the beauty of their style but even more for the weight of their content. There is, of course, much of the Glorious Revolution pictured in too rosy a light. Much is seen from the standpoint of a historian who does not really try to put himself in the shoes of the protagonists of political action but who interprets events from the vantage of a Whig of the early Victorian period. Shortcomings are obvious, especially in his social interpretation of events. Nevertheless, Macaulay's view appears to me correct in essence. It does not seem substantially impaired even by the high credit given to the activities of the Long Parliament and the minimizing of the controversial constitutional issues of 1688/89.

No question about it, the revolution of 1688/89 preserved legitimacy to the largest extent compatible with inevitable change, strengthened existent guarantees of constitutional government instead of creating new ones, held to the absolutely necessary minimum revolutionary change in royal succession while preserving the main facts of monarchical reign, and

[36] Macaulay, II, from 516, 517, 518, 519, 520.

Stuart reign at that. On the other hand, there is no question that the revolution fell woefully short of solving (did not in fact even attempt to solve) the social conflicts of English society and moderated the religious ones only to a point.

Yet Macaulay is substantially correct in the two main points, that the revolution preserved and strengthened the weakened constitutional heritage of England and in this sense it was part of a true regeneration. He is correct also when he states that every reform ever since was based on this accomplishment. In a sense Macaulay was even more right than he could be aware of in his own lifetime. When he wrote, with but little exaggeration as to cause and effect, more than a hundred years ago, "It is because we had a preserving revolution in the seventeenth century we have not had a destroying revolution in the nineteenth," he could not know that this statement would stand unchallenged in the second half of the twentieth century, despite world revolutions and world wars.

We little hesitate to endorse the view that the revolution of 1688/89, in spite of its technical break with legitimacy, is part of the restored system that commenced with the breakdown of Cromwell's Commonwealth. In spite of its honest endeavors, Cromwell's regime could never lead to legitimacy. It failed to do so not on account of illegal technicalities, not even primarily because of the abolition of the monarchy, but because of the inherent failure to base government on overall agreement between executive and legislative powers of government. With all obvious extenuating factors of historical time and place freely granted, this meant the lack of some indispensable basis of consent of the governed. Such coordination and consent could never be established by a dictatorship, whether it would have accepted the royal mantle or not. Because of its legitimacy, the Stuart Restoration, with all its shortcomings, offered at least limited chances for such cooperation, as events were to prove.

Its relationship to the revolution of 1688/89 could be interpreted in a threefold way. First, it could be argued—correctly, on merely technical grounds—that the revolution put an end to the restoration process going on since 1660 and that therefore this process never became a full-fledged restoration. In the preceding pages we have taken issue with this main argument and have maintained the position that the Glorious Revolution was part of a great restoration process. What part? There may be still room here for considerable disagreement. It could be argued that it was but a brief episode, a revolutionary ripple in the restoration process, a minor flaw of legitimacy. It could be held, on the other hand, that this revolution did not impair the restoration process, that on the contrary, on all but minor technical grounds, it mightily furthered and strengthened restoration.

The historian should, of course, look at history as an observer of the contemporary scene, who is thus enabled to understand the views of the past as seen in the past. Yet this does not mean that he should deprive himself of the advantage of looking at history from the standpoint also of almost three centuries of historical experience. In availing oneself of both these approaches it is not difficult to deduce from the first that the revolution of 1688/89 gave England domestic peace. Moreover, it secured peace at a time when it was most urgently needed, in the early eighteenth century conflagration in Europe, from which England emerged as a world power. From the vantage of historical retrospect, it is also easy to comprehend that the revolution, as Macaulay saw it, assured the evolutionary development of English institutions. On the strength of these two main considerations we perceive the revolution of 1688/89 not only as an episode in the restoration process but as a major phase of events which made restoration successful. Let us go one step farther. This restoration system, which has not yet come to an end and, it may be hoped, never will, is the most successful case of restoration known to us in modern times.

CHAPTER XVI

The Problem of the French Restoration of 1814/1815

1830, July 26	The Five July Ordinances
1830, July 30	Abdication of Charles X
1830, August 7	Louis Philippe proclaimed king of the French by the Chamber of Deputies
1830, August 7	Revised *charte constitutionelle* passed by Chamber
1848, February 22	Beginning of workers' riots in Paris
1848, February 24	Abdication of King Louis Philippe; Beginning of revolution
1848	Revolution

Original system (A)	to summer 1789, ancient regime
Intermediate system (B)	1789 to June, 1814, era of revolution and revolutionary change
Restored system (C)	June, 1814 to February, 1848, efforts toward restoration

The French case represents the second conspicuous example of a historical action referred to generally as restoration. Although the English seventeenth century and the French nineteenth century cases differ greatly, we may assume that in both cases the basic facts we have to deal with will be familiar to the reader. Yet the differences in these facts in themselves are striking. The English civil wars, Cromwell's Commonwealth, and the Stuart Restoration represented national issues, in which problems of international relations played a limited part. The French Restoration was of course a national issue, but it was at the same time a late stage of a European and, in the terms of the times, even of a worldwide upheaval in all fields of social activity. The second phase of the French Restoration, the new return of the Bourbons after the collapse of Napoleon's Hundred Days regime in 1815, is often contemptibly referred to as the return in the baggage vans of the victorious Allies. This is compared unfavorably with the Stuart Restoration, where General Monck, Edward Hyde (the Earl of Clarendon), and the young king himself took great pains to bring about the reestablishment of the Stuart rule at least without conspicuous foreign intervention. Yet the close relationship of the French Restoration with the counsel and active support of foreign powers was not due to a lack of national pride. It was perhaps not even primarily due to the defeat in the "wars of liberation." The continued foreign intervention was rather a consequence of the simple fact that it was the destiny of France to remain an international problem—which she had become with the outbreak of the revolution in 1789—until the vestiges of the revolutionary period were liquidated. In a sense, these expectations were never fulfilled.

The extent, speed, and complexity of politial and social changes brought about within a quarter of a century present, of course, very specific difficulties. There is little disagreement that what is generally referred to as the ancient regime ended in 1789. It makes little difference whether one believes with Ferrero that this period ended with the storming of the Bastille on July 13 of the year 1789 or according to others, with the "tennis court oath" of the third estate some three weeks before.[1] Day to day data are not the issue where not only political movements but sweeping intellectual and social transformations are involved. More important for our purpose is the question: When did the great French revolution end, and when did the process of restoration begin?

A number of possibilites are at least arguable. One fairly obvious one would be to see the break in the events of the 9th of Thermidor (July 27), 1794, that is, the beginning of what is generally called Thermidorian reaction. Undoubtedly on that day the high tide of revolutionary radicalism had, so to speak, officially passed, but the events were legalized only by the acceptance of the new constitution by plebiscite in the summer of 1795 and its promulgation as the law of the land the following September. In foreign policy the establishment of the Directory meant, of course, anything but the end of the revolutionary course, while in the domestic sphere the case was less clear. The momentum of events had slowed down, but risings like the rightist Vendémiairan insurrection of October, 1795, and the stillborn leftist plot of François Babeuf's followers in the spring of 1796 proved that social stability had not yet been achieved. The revolutionary drive had been stopped, but whether the revolution itself had been stopped for good appeared to be still doubtful.

The situation did become clearer with the famous coup d'état of the 18th of Brumaire of the year VIII (November 9, 1799), which swept away the Directory and its legislature and ushered in the Consulate and with it Bonapartism for nearly fifteen years. To be sure, radical change had taken place; but did this change mean the initiation of a genuine restorative process? Was not Napoleon's acceptance of the title of emperor and the establishment of a new monarchy, rather than the founding of the

[1] Guglielmo Ferrero, *The Principles of Power,* pp. 82 ff. Concerning the terminology of the specific restoration process discussed in this chapter, see particularly Ernst R. Huber, *Deutsche Verfassungsgeschichte seit 1789* (Stuttgart, 1957), Vol. I. pp. 531 ff.; and Louis Madelin, *La Contre Révolution sous la Révolution, 1789–1815* (Paris, 1935), pp. 353 ff.

Consulate, the decisive issue? Surely, in a study of the restoration problem the establishment of a new hereditary monarchical system cannot be dismissed lightly.

Accordingly we must seriously consider four conceivable interpretations, namely that the intermediate revolutionary system ended with the fall of Robespierre in 1794, with the establishment of the constitution of the Directory in 1795, with the Consulate in 1799, or with the establishment of the First Empire in 1804. The acceptance of any one of these four alternatives would rule out the possibility that a successful restoration was inaugurated in 1814/15.

Here the preliminary question arises: To what extent were the institutions of the ancient regime related to any of the following regimes? This means in particular—before we move to the events from 1814 to 1848—the relationship of the ancient regime to Thermidorian reaction, the Directory, the Consulate, and the Empire. Alexis de Tocqueville's masterpiece, *L'ancien régime et la révolution,* can still teach us very much in this respect. This holds true for the verifiable theory that basic trends during the revolution, above all the centralization of the administration, derived directly from a century-old tradition of royal administration. Feudal powers and the limited provincial estates institutions, on the other hand, had become increasingly feeble prior to the outbreak of the revolution. Minimizing somewhat the ideological impact of the revolution, Tocqueville deduces revolutionary fervor less from the strength than from the weakness of feudalism. In a famous phrase he observes, "Reduced tax . . . it excited much greater hatred: it can be said with truth that the destruction of a part of the institutions of the Middle Ages has rendered a hundred times more hateful that part which remained." [2] This theory is supported by a wealth of material pertaining to administrative organization and justice, economic prosperity and reform under the old regime. While Tocqueville's truly enlightened conservatism was based on a highly critical but on the whole not negative evaluation of the old regime, that of Hippolyte Taine two decades later was determined primarily by his condemnation of the revolutionary regime without any corresponding praise of the monarchy. [3] The ancient regime appeared only relatively speaking

[2] Alexis de Tocqueville, *L'Ancien Régime et la révolution,* trans. M. W. Patterson, with the title *De Tocqueville's L'Ancien Régime* (Oxford, 1947), pp. 36, 220 ff.; see also Henry E. See, *Economic and Social Conditions in France During the Eighteenth Century,* trans. E. Zeidel (New York, 1927), pp. 222 ff.; Jacques Godechot, *Les Révolutions, 1770–1799* (Paris, 1965), pp. 114 f.

[3] Hippolyte Taine, *The Ancient Regime,* trans. J. Durand (New York, 1931); see particularly pp. 13 ff., 60 ff., 170 ff., 329 ff.

in a more favorable light because of the rejection of the revolution and in particular what appeared to Taine as the Jacobin conspiracy. Both he and Tocqueville were, in a sense, students of Edmund Burke, who in his *Reflections on the French Revolution* had held that the ancient regime was a system which could have been saved by moderate reforms since it was sanctioned by a deeply rooted national tradition. Such possibilities were denied later on by the liberal historians François Aulard and Albert Sorel, the radical Albert Mathiez, and even by those in a very moderate center position, like Georges Lefebvre.[4]

The interpretation of the older classics, Tocqueville and Taine, though they differ otherwise, are separated from more modern interpretations by their stress on the factor of continuity in historical events. Tocqueville saw here a substantially positive process and Taine a progressively negative and destructive one. As to continuity itself, these views come closer to that of the interrelationship of consecutive systems discussed in this study than most of the outstanding contributions to the history of the revolutions made within the last two generations. The skeleton of a rigid division between ancient regime, revolution, and restoration became increasingly accepted and remained substantially unchallenged. Perhaps we have even reached a dead end in this respect. At least two recent remarks of Robert Palmer, which I would heartily concur with, point in this direction. "That the revolutionary movement was renewed in 1830, 1848 and 1870, confirmed and gave new life to these old feelings. The revolution remained a continuing movement, spasmodically reappearing; counterrevolution remained a continuing movement also."[5] And furthermore, ". . . Conservatism and counterrevolution were no 'reactions' against revolution, but eighteenth century forces against which revolution was itself a reaction."[6]

It is not suggested here that the distinctions between various systems could be meaningless. Yet within the rapid course of dynamic change in French history from 1789 to 1852 it would be a mistake to departmentalize history chronologically in revolutions and counterrevolutions without acknowledging underlying continuous thought and institutional

[4] Georges Lefebvre, *The Coming of the French Revolution,* trans. and ed. Robert R. Palmer (New York, 1957); see particularly pp. 35 ff., 133 ff., 157 ff., 177 ff. See also Karl Griewank, *Die französische Revolution,* 2d ed. (Graz, Cologne, 1958), pp. 9 ff., 113 ff. See Edmund Burke, *Reflections on the French Revolution.* Everyman's Library ed. (London, 1935), pp. 201 ff.

[5] R. R. Palmer in the preface to Lefebvre, p. vii.

[6] Robert R. Palmer, *The Age of the Democratic Revolution,* Vol. I, *The Challenge* (Princeton, 1959), p. 22; see also the literature referred to in n. 15 on the same page.

trends. Blindness to their existence—stronger or weaker at times, yet continuously visible—would amount to the conversion of history into mere histories. In any analysis of the ancient system within the context of this study, we must first look for the connection with subsequent regimes, as much as for their separation from them.

It is true, of course, that the period from summer, 1789, to the 9th of Thermidor of the year II (July 27, 1794) represents a rapidly moving yet clearly distinguishable revolutionary system, with the transition from the absolute monarchy through the constitutional monarchy to the parliamentary republic and eventually to the dictatorship by parliamentary committee. It includes the abolition of economic feudalism and the guild system, the complete administrative reorganization of France, in principle the introduction of general conscription, the initiation of comprehensive new legal codifications, in fact the introduction of a new legal order itself. The system included furthermore the expropriation and subordination of the Church by the state and finally the abolition of Christianity and the establishment of a new religion of reason. All these tremendous domestc changes are part of the mighty crescendo of the revolutionary movement from 1789 to 1794. To be sure, varied and radical as these changes were, those of 1791 could not be fully envisaged in 1789 and those of 1793 not even in 1792. All the same, there is no question that the course of history moved throughout these hectic five years in one direction.

This direction was radically reversed by the "Thermidorian reaction" from summer, 1794, to the establishment of the Directory in the fall of 1795. Did the victory of the moderates, the destruction of the Jacobins, the termination of the economic emergency legislation, and the establishment of a far more conservative bicameral legislature signify the end of the revolution? If so, could this mean then the beginning of a restoration? Could the new regime, in such fields as administrative reorganization, elimination of feudalism in the rural sphere and of the guild system in the urban, sweeping educational reforms, a new judicial system in operation, and drafts of new codification, establish a link with the modest reform legislation during the earlier part of Louis XVI's reign?

We do not think so, for several reasons. In the first place the reversal of policies after 1794 was obvious only in the domestic sphere and not at all in international relations. The period of warfare that had started in 1792 continued unabated, not only in a military but in an ideological sense as well. Yet even in domestic matters violence had by no means ceased. That pertains both to the activities of the radical Left, the remainder of the Jacobins in the spring of 1795 (year II), and on a larger scale to the rightist White Terror in the south and west of France, culminating in the abortive rightist coup of Vendémiaire of the year III (October 5, 1795). If one perceives the French Revolution primarily as the struggle of the urban middle class, then one might even go so far as to say that during the period of 1794/95, when the economic emergency legislation was largely repealed, the supremacy of the most successful force during the revolution, the bourgeoisie, was actually stronger than ever before and for a long time afterward. However, the instability of the political structure during that genuine transition period, in which constitutional, religious, and military issues remained as unsettled as the spirit of revolutionary violence remained unbroken, makes us reject the two diametrically opposed alternative interpretations, namely, that the revolution continued, or that it had ceased to exist. The events in 1794/95 had reversed the course of history since 1789. In this sense the revolution had indeed ceased in the domestic sphere, even though revolutionary violence and instability continued. This means that revolutionary changes were to persist, for even though the Thermidorian reaction was not any more part of the same revolution, it was still very much part of a period of revolutionary change in France. Restoration was by no means around the corner.[7]

In our opinion the four years from the installation of the Directory to the coup of the 18th of Brumaire of the year VIII (November 9, 1799) was just as much a period of revolutionary change as was that of the Thermidorian reaction and just as little part of the great revolution. It is true that in foreign policy the conclusion of the peace of Basel with Prussia in 1795 had a dampening effect on the pursuit of ideological warfare. On the other hand, Bonaparte's famous campaign in Italy in 1797 and the events leading to the peace treaty of Campo Formio with Austria revived the expansionist, proselytizing ideology again. Obviously the outbreak of the war of the Second Coalition strengthened these ideas still further, its original defensive character in a military sense to the contrary notwithstanding. The establishment of the Parthenopean republic in Janu-

[7] A moderate interpretation like that of R. R. Palmer agrees with that of a radical like Albert Mathiez that the revolution continued under the Thermidorian reaction. Palmer, *Age of Democratic Revolution,* II, 129 ff.; Mathiez, *La Révolution Française,* continued by G. Lefebvre, Paris, 1922–1946, Vol. II, part IV. Emphasis in both cases is based on the idea that the oneness of one revolution was preserved by the continued and indeed strengthened supremacy of the bourgeoisie and the continuation of revolutionary tactics. See also Godechot, *Les Révolutions,* pp. 171 ff., who perceives the period from 1795 to 1799 as that of the bourgeois republic. See finally L. Madelin, *La Contre Révolution sous la Révolution, 1789–1815,* pp. 59 ff. and 113 ff. Madelin distinguishes between Thermidorian reaction and reaction under the Consulate.

ary, 1799, in the former kingdom of Naples may serve here as an obvious example.

More important, however, is evidence deriving from domestic events, to which the causes for the Egyptian expedition of Bonaparte must be added. Yet disregarding even the motivation to remove a potential man on horseback from the political scene, disregarding even the fantastic and, if not revolutionary, certainly not traditional objectives of Bonaparte's strategy for the Orient, there remains an abundance of evidence to show the revolutionary instability of the Directory. Two of the main problems inherited from the great revolution, economic inflation and religious anarchy, remained unsettled, despite halfhearted, feeble, and frequently bungling attempts to solve them. Political stability was completely lacking; representative democracy seemed to be unworkable. The leftist attempt of Babeuf and his followers in the spring of 1796 was followed in the fall of 1797 by the better prepared and thus more serious rightist Fructidor coup. Both these attempts to overthrow the government were defeated. They implicated only the stamina of the government and its dubious popular appeal, but not directly its representative democratic character. The governmental manipulations in Floreal of the year VI (May, 1798) to deprive a number of radical republican members of the *corps législatif* of their seats and the likewise unconstitutional complementary move in Prairial of the year VII (June, 1799) against the rightist members of the Directory clearly showed the unlawful practices of the administration. Lack of popular support, illegal machinations in domestic policies, and the critical stage of the war opened the way for the coup d'état of the returning general Bonaparte and thus for a much more clearly marked chapter in the history of the great French transitions from 1789 to 1852. The period between 1795 and 1799 represents no such chapter in history any more than does that from 1794 to 1795. Neither period, unlike the ancient regime and unlike the great revolution, had established a distinctive system. What could be restored were the features of strength and weakness of the ancient regime as changed and molded by the revolution of 1789 and the Napoleonic era. The blurred transition periods of Thermidorian reaction and the Directory had no image capable of restoration.[8]

The situation was entirely different concerning the chain of tremendous events initiated by the successful coup d'etat of November 9, 1799 (18

[8] Mathiez, Vol. III, Part V; Palmer II, 211 ff.; François A. M. Mignet, *Histoire de la Révolution Française* (Paris, 1930), II, 199 ff.; Griewank, pp. 99 ff.; Godechot, pp. 177 ff.

Brumaire of the year VIII). Within six weeks the authoritarian constitution of the Consulate was established; in August, 1802, Napoleon at his behest was given the lifetime consulate, in which the dictatorial features were hardly camouflaged any longer. Within three additional years the empire was established. Undoubtedly the Consulate had given France a considerable measure of domestic stability. The situation in international relations was in this respect more controversial. On the other hand, the strengthening of the authoritarian features in the constitution of the year 1802, as compared with that of 1799, may not have changed the picture substantially as far as the question of restoration is concerned. It could well be held, though, that the reestablishment of a monarchy in 1804 introduced constitutional and political change amounting to a restorative process. It could then be further deduced, either that this process was stopped by the forced abdication of Napoleon in 1814 and the ensuing return of the Bourbons, or that the old dynasty brought it actually to fulfillment. The Hundred Days of 1815, the return and short rule of Napoleon, would in either case be considered merely a highly dramatic episode. The key issue remained, of course, whether the turn of events between 1799 and 1805 established a regime capable of bringing about genuine restoration of the ancient regime.

Even the briefest evaluation of the Napoleonic rule from the point of our problem makes a two-faced approach necessary: the assessment of the period either as a stabilization of the revolutionary era or as a restoration of basic features of the ancient regime. In any case we must differentiate between domestic and foreign policy. To begin with the former, the situation appears as follows. The uncontested establishment of law and order did not in itself represent restoration. The pacification of domestic conflicts was under way, though it was by no means fully accomplished throughout the whole period after the fall of Robespierre. The tapering off of revolutionary zeal after 1794 would in all probability have brought about this particular accomplishment in the course of time under any postrevolutionary regime. As it happened it came about within a few weeks under Napoleon Bonaparte as First Consul. This proved only his ability as administrator and as a statesman who had sensed the right time for his coup d'etat. It suggests also that if the time was truly ripe for an authoritarian regime, it might have come about under lesser men, though perhaps not quite as fast and with more violence. After the revolutionary drive had lost its impetus, such achievemests were not specific enough to assume a genuine restorative process based either primarily or fully on law and order established by an authoritarian regime. Law and order represent but the premise of restoration, by no means restoration itself.

Of the great achievements of the Napoleonic domestic administration, the establishment of the prefectures and the new tax-collecting system preserved and strengthened the departmentalization of France already brought about during the first revolutionary period. The same held true for the improvement of the civil service system, for the codification of French substantive and procedural civil and criminal law between 1804 and 1810, and for the whole impressive structure of higher education, the body known as the National University of France with its affiliated academies. There is no doubt that every single one of these and other domestic achievements would have been shaped very differently if they had matured under the Convention. The fact remains that to a varying degree all these institutions owed their origin to the revolutionary regimes, the administrative organization in particular to the initial one until 1791, the judicial and educational, primarily to the Convention. Relatively few such changes were effected in the middle period of the legislative assembly of 1791/92, whose attention was focused chiefly on constitutional questions and the growing crisis in international relations.

There is only one truly major issue in the concordat of 1801, in which the Consulate resumed an older tradition of state and church relations, not those of the ancient regime, to be sure, but official, reciprocal relations nevertheless. The maintenance of the revolutionary confiscation and subsequent sales of Church property, the clerical submission to a secular nationwide system of education, and the divided authority concerning the nomination and confirmation of the clergy counted little compared with the restoration of full freedom of worship and the recognition of the Roman Catholic Church, at least indirectly, as the state religion of France. Here we find, indeed, a genuine issue, where a synthesis of the ancient regime, the revolution, and the new order did occur.

It was only one issue to be sure. Except in the very broadest terms used by Tocqueville, reforms in the judicial and educational sphere had little relation to the ancient regime. In the field of local administration there was admittedly a common feature in the ancient regime and the Consulate—the appointment of local officials by the chief executive. Yet this was merely a procedural factor and had nothing to do with the philosophy of government, which was very different in the two regimes.

Here it is essential to look at the constitutional issue, the significance of a legislative body under the Consulate and the Empire and above all the establishment of the empire itself. The constitution of the year VIII, 1799/1800, merely ratified but not, as alleged, actually voted upon by a tremendous popular majority, established a legislative branch of government, which comprised three chambers—four, if we include with some justification the Council of State. Any one of them, by intent of the First Consul, checked the legislative authority of the others to a degree that reduced the overall strength of representative government to a minimum, though not quite yet absurdity.

The *senatus consultum* of the year X (August, 1802), in its basic principles approved again by a doubtful plebiscite, did just that. The establishment of the lifetime consulate for the First Consul constituted monarchical government in all but name. Subject to the approval of the Senate, the First Consul was to name his successor. Equally important, elections were now reduced for all practical purposes to nominations made by a small body of the most prosperous citizens in the departments. The authority of the Tribunate and the *corps législatif* of 300 members were further reduced, while the more powerful Senate became at least indirectly an appointive body. Thus it is fair to say that the constitution of 1802 introduced a regime of near absolutism.[9] Not only was this absolutism more efficient, in a social sense more adapted to changed conditions, than the divine-right monarchy under the ancient regime; it was also far more stringent and its powers far more comprehensive than the governmental machinery under the old regime. Part of this, it is true, was due to the inadequacies of the royal administration. It could largely be deduced, however, from a century-old tradition of evolving local autonomies and assemblies of estates, territorial, judicial, and other corporate bodies. They represented interests unequally, but at least they represented varied interests.[10] The connection of this system with the Napoleonic order in the domestic sphere was tenuous indeed.

One may be inclined to emphasize even more strongly the discrepancy between ancient regime and Bonapartism in international relations. Here the argument rests frequently on a comparison of the cautious foreign policy of France from the death of Louis XIV to 1792 and the subsequent ideological warfare of the revolution and the imperialism of Napoleon. Actually the problem is rather complex. There is a question whether

[9] John H. Rose, *The Life of Napoleon* (New York, 1907), I, 279 ff.; August Fournier, *Napoleon* (Vienna, 1904), I, 294 ff.; Louis Madelin, *The Consulate and the Empire* (London, 1934), I, 160 ff.; Adolphe Thiers, *History of the Consulate and the Empire,* trans. Frederick Shoberl (Philadelphia, 1893), I, 305 ff.; Leo Gershoy, *The French Revolution and Napoleon* (New York, 1946), pp. 349 ff.

[10] Tocqueville, *L'Ancien Régime* (see n. 2 above), pp. 179 ff.

political initiative (as distinguished from ideological) in the war of the First Coalition lay with the French or with the anti-French coalition. In the wars of the Second and of the Third Coalition it was clearly on the side of the Allies, and in that of 1809, on the side of Austria. The issues of war guilt and the revolutionary upset of European stability were not focused primarily on the responsibility for the outbreak of these wars but rather, until the peace of Luneville of 1801, on the revolutionary conduct of warfare and peacemaking. In neither respect was there a decisive difference between the wars directed by the Convention and the Directory and those under Napoleon's military and political leadership.

Such difference has to be looked for in another context. With the peace of Tilsit in 1807 it had become clear that since the peace of Campo Formio in 1797 France had very gradually ceased to be the feared and hated revolutionary outlaw in the family of states. She had become again a respected Great Power, a status not entirely lost even in the dark days from 1812 to 1815. This was not merely a matter of fear of French military might; this had existed under the revolution as well. Essentially this was a question of confidence in the domestic stability of France. However outrageous her territorial demands might be, it was not considered likely that she would ever return to revolutionary egalitarianism at home or to its export to conquered territories abroad. In this sense the Napoleonic regime had indeed brought about a kind of French restoration in international relations.

The reason for this basic confidence still underlying the manifold divergences and conflicts in territorial and economic matters could be found largely in Napoleon's overall pursuit of a policy of law and order within France. Particularly important in this context was the establishment of the First Empire itself in 1804. Its proclamation occurred under inauspicious circumstances—it followed by only a few weeks the kidnapping and execution of the Duke of Enghien, which aroused the indignation of Europe to a greater degree than anything the First Consul had done before. The proclamation of imperial dignity was partly meant to deter royalist conspiracies against the new order and at the same time to divert attention from them in the future. More important, however, the imperial constitution of the year XII did away with almost the last shreds of constitutional government. The reformed *corps législatif* now represented even more than after 1802 the very travesty of parliamentary institutions.

Yet in a larger sense and viewed at longer range, the new monarchical system had a quite different effect on the stability of the regime in foreign and domestic affairs. This had something to do with the response of men and not of governments to the new emperor—at that time a very appropriate distinction. Beethoven spoke for many enlightened people in France as well as across the civilized world when he tore up the dedication of the *Eroica* destined for the hero who had saved the accomplishments of the revolution, but who appeared to him now just as a man on horseback and usurper of the throne.

There was also a reverse side of the medal, namely the reaction of established tradition, and its effect was certainly not negligible. The replacement of one dynasty by another through revolutionary action is, from the point of the theory of divine right, a more revolutionary act than the conversion from monarchy to republic. Revolutionary methods are in fact compounded if to one act of illegitimacy a second is added, and if after allegiance to a sovereign and his dynasty has been rendered for a long time, active support of a new one is demanded.[11]

After all, the comparatively slight deviation in the English royal succession brought about by the revolution of 1688 proved to be, for years to come, a major stumbling block for William III, Queen Anne, and even the first Hanoverian king. What then is the significance of so revolutionary an action as the replacement of the hallowed tradition of the Most Christian King by a new upstart emperor fabricated in a semi-mythical image of Charlemagne? The major importance of the imperial declaration was its meaning as testimony to the world that this new regime intended to remain, not as a one-man rule but as the beginning of a system of new legitimacy. One might argue that the reestablishment of a monarchy, to be distinguished from the restoration of another one, implied that the possibility of a statute of limitations for revolutionary illegitimacy in decades to come had been sighted for the first time since 1789.[12] The imperial dressing of the new court and the emperor's marriage to a daughter of an ancient dynasty may be taken as further confirmation of the intention to establish legitimacy. These moves were not liked but were respected by contemporary Europe prior to the debacle of 1814, which made a more genuine restoration inevitable.

We do not think that Napoleon had established such genuine restora-

---

[11] Rose, I, 429 ff.; Thiers, I, 586 ff.; Madelin, *Consulate and Empire*, I, 212 ff.; Fournier, II (1889), 32 ff.; Ferrero, *Principles of Power*, pp. 107 ff.; Eugene Tarlé, *Bonaparte* (New York, 1937), pp. 143 ff.

[12] See also Ferrero's discussion of prelegitimate government in *Principles of Power*, pp. 188 ff; and George F. Rudé *Revolutionary Europe, 1783–1815* (New York, 1964), pp. 28 ff. While Rudé's overall concept of the revolutionary era agrees in essence with the one expressed in this chapter, we see no reason to perceive the initiation of the revolutionary era as early as 1783, the conclusion of the Peace of Paris between Great Britain and the United States. Madelin, *La Contre Révolution*, pp. 182 ff., perceives here a new restoration process.

tion, even though weighty factors in foreign policy and at least the one pertaining to church and state relations in the domestic domain may support such a view. The bulk of the evidence in that latter field points the other way. We believe, furthermore, that in the establishment of the empire, motivations of domestic stabilization and imperialist designs in foreign relations, closely associated with the idea of empire, outweighed in importance for some time to come the desire for legitimacy. Most important perhaps, the absolutism of the new regime was stronger and more comprehensive in intent as well as in performance than that of the ancient regime during the last generations of its existence.

Yet even though the legitimacy of the Napoleonic regime never materialized, we should not minimize the desire for such legitimacy. To say that the reestablishment of the Bourbons came closer to true restoration than the Napoleonic era is not meant to be a search for and confirmation of the obvious. Napoleon's administration as consul and his reign as emperor, both of which we perceive as part of the period of revolutionary change—though not of the revolution itself—might be considered by others to be the beginning of genuine restoration. We have here a border case, and only a relatively slight preponderance of evidence leads to the evaluation of this era as one preceding, but, not in initiating, true restoration.

The question before us, then, is whether the returns of the Bourbons in 1814 and 1815 and the *chartre constitutionelle* of June 4, 1814, introduced reasonable expectations of genuine restoration, which the Napoleonic regime had failed to establish. Only if this question is answered in the affirmative can the further one be pursued, whether genuine restoration was actually effected in the course of the years.

When Talleyrand in the early spring days of 1814 resolved definitely, and that meant at that time publicly, to work for the return of Bourbon rule in France, he had, according to his memoirs, the following main considerations in mind. They are slightly colored by what is frequently understood as a spirit of French *panache*, but they are incisive just the same.

France, in the midst of the horror of an invasion, wished to be free and respected. This was equivalent to wishing for the return of the House of Bourbon in the order prescribed by legitimacy. Europe, still anxious in the midst of France, wished her to disarm, and to resume her former limits so that peace should no longer need to be constantly guarded. She required for that guarantees; this was also to wish for the return of the House of Bourbon. . . .

The House of Bourbon alone could veil, in the eyes of the French nation, so jealous of her military glory, the impression of the reverses which had just befallen her flag.

The House of Bourbon alone could nobly aid France to again take possession of the secure frontiers indicated by policy and by nature. With the House of Bourbon, France would cease to be gigantic, but would become great. . . . The House of Bourbon alone, . . . could avert that vengeance that twenty years of violence had heaped up against her.

Every road was open to the Bourbons to reach a throne founded on a free constitution. After having tried all manner of organizations, and submitted to the most arbitrary of them, France could find rest only in a constitutional monarchy. The monarchy with the Bourbons, offered complete legitimacy, for even the most innovating minds; for it combined family legitimacy to that given by institutions, and it was that that France desired. . . .

The first need of Europe, her greatest interest, was then to banish the doctrines of usurpation, and to revive the principle of legitimacy, the only remedy for all the evils which had overwhelmed her, and the only one, which could prevent a relapse into them.

This principle . . . is not . . . solely a means of preservation of the power of kings, and the safety of their persons; it is especially a necessary element of the tranquility and happiness of nations, the most solid, or rather, the only guarantee of their strength and duration. The legitimacy of kings, or to say better, of governments, is the safeguard of nations. That is the reason, why it is sacred.

I speak of the legitimacy of governments in general, whatsoever be their form and not only of those of kings, because it applies to all governments. A lawful government, be it monarchical or republican, herediary or elective, aristocratic or democratic, is always one whose existence, form, and modification have been consolidated and consecrated by a long succession of years. . . .[13]

There is plenty of reason to question the political morality of Talleyrand throughout all phases of his eventful career. A certain amount of sophistry in his dialectics may be admitted as well, such as in this case the argument that "the principle of legitimacy be not less violated by the overthrow of a republican government than by the usurpation of a crown" . . . but legitimacy "does not require that the former be restored, whereas it does require that the crown be returned to him, to whom it belongs." [14]

There is no reason to assume, however, that a personality, who as statesman showed not only conspicuous diplomatic skill but also wisdom and foresight to a high degree, would degrade himself before posterity

[13] *Memoirs of the Prince de Talleyrand,* Duc de Broglie ed., (London, 1891–1892), II, 117 ff.
[14] *Ibid.,* p. 120.

with a line of argument that conflicted with political common sense. The contrary is the case. Whether Talleyrand was right or wrong, his line of reasoning quoted here is of logical conciseness and lucidity.[15] This applies above all to principles. As for tactics, Talleyrand offered his Bourbon proposals to the hesitating czar, Alexander, as the only conceivable solution after eliminating alternatives, such as—horrible to consider—a republic or, only little better, a regency under the empress Marie Louise for Napoleon's infant son, or a monarchy under Napoleon's stepson, Eugène Beauharnais, or the former French marshall Bernadotte. As proof of acceptance by the French nation Talleyrand furnished the approval of that shadowy body of yes-men, the Napoleonic Senate. Thus the chasm between principles and expediency was opened and continuously widened. In vain did Armand de Caulaincourt, the former Napoleonic ambassador to Russia, try to convince the czar that the foundations of restoration in regard to rigid tradition and alleged consent of the governed were equally feeble.[16] Alexander disregarded Caulaincourt's counsel in spite of his sympathies for an upright man as noble in his loyalties as he was sincere in his beliefs. He sided with Talleyrand whom he—like Napoleon before and the two Bourbon kings afterward—thoroughly distrusted.

Eugene Tarlé is probably right when he assumes, contrary to Charles Dupuis, that Alexander was by no means motivated by a preference for a sham constitutionalism of some sort. He acted, rather, on the strength of the simple fact that the undiluted restoration of the ancient regime would lead to the almost immediate collapse of the newly established regime and hence to the necessity of Russian intervention.[17] Yet at this time the czar had every reason to keep his powder dry and at the same time to avoid

[15] See in the same sense Alfred Duff Cooper, *Talleyrand* (London, 1932), chaps. 9, 10; Ferrero, *Principles of Power,* pp. 232 ff., 275 ff.; G. Ferrero, *The Reconstruction of Europe* (New York, 1941), pp. 77 ff.; Crane Brinton, *The Lives of Talleyrand* (New York, 1936), pp. 183 ff.; and Eugene Tarlé, *Talleyrand* (Leipzig, 1950), pp. 120 ff., 140 ff. These authors question from different viewpoints, moderate conservative, liberal democratic, Marxian, the motivations of Talleyrand, but they do not question the logics and skill of his policy. For an almost fully negative view, see Louis Madelin, *Talleyrand* (New York, 1948), pp. 194 ff. See also Golo Mann, *Secretary of Europe: The Life of Friedrich Gentz* . . . (New Haven, 1946), pp. 202 ff., 223 ff. Very illuminating is the historiographical essay by Peter Geyl, "The French Historians and Talleyrand," in *Encounters with History* (New York, 1958), pp. 225–237.

[16] Armand A. L. de Caulaincourt, *Mémoires* (Paris, 1933–1934), III, 94 ff., 115 ff., 135 ff.

[17] Tarlé, *Talleyrand,* pp. 139 f. with reference to Charles Dupuis, *Le Ministère de Talleyrand en 1814* (Paris, 1920), II, 2 ff. See also Madelin, *La Contre Révolution,* pp. 360 ff.

being drawn into a conflict with jealous allies. Alexander, Talleyrand, Louis XVIII, and soon Castlereagh and even Metternich, although they might otherwise differ, realized that the possibilities for political maneuvers outside of the Bourbon Restoration were blocked. The position of the Bourbons may have been doubly weak because of their complete dependence on the victorious Allied armies. The lack of popular support was surely compounded by the narrow-mindedness of the symbol of the ultra conservatives, the Count of Artois, who wanted to erase not only the traces of Bonapartism, the deeds and misdeeds of the revolution, but even the halting reform attempts of Louis XVI. The weakness of the new regime in international relations might not have been fatal in view of the general desire of the French people for peace. In any case, it could not be helped. Yet something could be done about the second problem, the blindness of the Ultras, by recognition of certain imponderabilia of historic change. The minimum of this inevitable change, tolerated rather than approved by the conservative powers, might be summarized as the preservation of the basic social and economic legislation of the revolution as stabilized under the Napoleonic administration. Furthermore, it meant a return by and large to the principles of the constitutional monarchy of July, 1790, although by no means to the extent of the constitutional liberties secured then.[18] Based on these considerations and on the dubious endorsement of the Senate and various municipal councils, the Count of Provence, unlike his brother a genuine political realist, in May, 1814, en route to Paris from his English exile pledged in a proclamation at St. Quen a declaration of intention concerning the introduction of constitutional government. A committee, now a royal committee of former moderate Napoleonic officials, converted this proclamation within a few days to the famous *chartre constitutionelle*. It was issued formally on June 4, 1814, a month after the return of the new king, about nine months prior to his sad flight following the exiled Napoleon's landing at Frejus. More hastily though not less skillfully prepared than either Charles II's Declaration of Breda in April, 1660, or William III's Declaration of Rights in

---

[18] Paul Bastid, *Les Institutions politiques de la monarchie Française (1814–1848)*, (Paris, 1954), pp. 19 ff.; G. de Bertier de Sauvigny, *La Restauration* (Paris, 1955), pp. 27 ff.; Henry A. Kissinger, *A World Restored* (Boston, 1957), pp. 137 ff., 197 ff.; Frederick B. Artz, *France Under the Bourbon Restoration* (Cambridge, Mass., 1931), pp. 10 ff.; L. Madelin *Consulate and Empire,* II, 339 ff. See also the accounts by some of the outstanding contemporary historians: Alphonse de Lamartine, *The History of the Restoration of Monarchy in France* (New York, 1951), I, 146 ff.; and Louis Blanc, *Révélations historiques* (Brusseles, 1859), I, 146 ff., who condemns the proceedings of the Senate.

1689, the Charter rested on much feebler constitutional foundations. As for backing by popular support, the conditions of the Bourbon return could not be compared to the transformation of government under the Stuart and Orange kings at all, unless one confounds a strong emotional desire for peace with that for royalism. Yet what this new regime lacked in internal strength through popular endorsement was made up by the backing of external forces, largely lacking in the English Restoration. This, of course, was only a brief advantage. As seen from a long-range viewpoint, it represented a lingering, almost fatal weakness, made up only in part by the skill of the new ruler and his closest advisers and beyond this by the content of the Charter itself.

These are the factors which have to be weighed and balanced against each other. The preservation of the achievements of the revolutionary periods, the Consulate, and the First Empire could be seen in substance in the following. Recognition of the principle of equality before the law, equal recognition of the right to hold public office, and habeas corpus were guaranteed. Freedom of religion was assured, although a preference for a Roman Catholic state religion was recognized. Priests and ministers of other Christian denominations were to be paid from public funds, a provision extended to the Jews only after the July revolution of 1830.[19] Freedom of the press, though with important reservations, was promised. Inviolability of private property was recognized, and general conscription—for the time being a truly popular move—was abolished.

Legislative power was divided between king and two chambers, of deputies and of peers. Legislative initiative rested in principle with the king; the validity of legislative action was dependent on royal sanction. An unusual feature of the Charter was a most restrictive franchise legislation based on a stiff property census and indirectly on a screening of the political loyalty of eligible candidates, partly incorporated in the constitution itself. The usual guarantee of immunity for parliamentary deputies was pledged, however. As for the judicial branch, the irremovability of judges was guaranteed except for justices of the peace. The publicity of trials and the preservation of the jury system was promised. Military ranks, titles of nobility, and even the Legion of Honor, with all rights and privileges deriving from appointments and distinctions awarded by the previous regimes, were in principle preserved. Finally, according to

---

[19] Discriminatory legislation imposed by Napoleon against the majority of French Jews, namely those in the Alsace, in force until 1818, was not renewed, however, by Louis XVIII. See Simon Dubnow, *Die neueste Geschichte des jüdischen Volkes* (Berlin, 1929), II, 263 ff.

Article 11, 'All investigations concerning opinions and votes taken up to the reestablishment of the present government were forbidden; the same policy was prescribed for the courts as well as the individual citizens." There was much reason to question the full sincerity of this assurance; there was no reason to consider it completely worthless under Louis XVIII's reign.

Against these concessions, which stabilized revolutionary and evolutionary development for a quarter of a century, the following factors must be balanced. There was first the issue that the Charter was granted by the king by the Grace of God under the *fleur de lis,* rather than under the Tricolor as Talleyrand had wisely and strongly recommended. Furthermore, the Charter was officially dated in the nineteenth year of Louis XVIII's reign, which commenced thus fictitiously with the execution of his elder brother. All this was due to the influence of the Ultras under the leadership of the Count of Artois and against the wishes of the new king himself. The worst aspect of such measures was indeed the exposure of the weakness of the new administration. All the same, they must not be interpreted as a decisive step toward failure of the restoration. They might be taken either as symbols of continuity between ancient regime and restoration or as forebodings of outright reaction. Only time could tell what course the restoration would take. Other factors were of more immediate importance, such as the restriction of the franchise to less than 100,000 people at most, the denial of the principle of equality of citizens as seen in the establishment of a house of peers whose deliberations were to be secret. There were, furthermore, reservations concerning the publicity of trials. These measures could be abused for political reasons and the same applied to the twisted guarantee of the freedom of the press.[20]

To sum up, a clear distinction must be drawn between the provisions of the Charter and the conduct of government from 1814 to 1830 with true or alleged distortions and violations of its provisions. Yet judged plainly by the letter of the law, the following was obvious. France under the new Charter was to be a genuine, though severely restricted constitutional monarchy, in which the executive branch of government was far stronger, the legislative correspondingly weaker than in the constitution of July, 1790. Moreover, the drastically restricted franchise reduced the power of

[20] See Emile Bourgeois, *History of Modern France* (Cambridge, 1922), I, 2 ff., who perhaps overstresses the similarity between the institutions of the empire and the reestablished Bourbon monarchy. For the text of the Charter see Leon Duguit and Henri Monnier, *Les Constitutions et les principales lois politiques de la France depuis 1789* (Paris, 1920); concerning the franchise provisions in political practice see Artz, pp. 80 ff., Bastid, pp. 251 ff.

the legislature still further. Yet even during the worst reaction under the Polignac ministry in 1829/30 the chambers had more influence than Napoleon's acquiescent legislatures after 1804 at any time. The same could be said concerning the restrictions of the freedom of the press. Beyond this, equality before the law and recognition of the status of the Church in terms of the Concordat of 1801 and of the inviolability of former ecclesiastic landed property acquired legally by civilians during the revolutionary period were fully secured, at least until 1825. The Napoleonic Codes in regard to substantive laws as well as procedure, both with strong ties to the various phases of revolutionary legislation, were preserved. The centralized system of higher education as planned by the Convention and developed under Napoleon was, however, largely departmentalized. Much depended on compliance with the prohibition of proscription and harassment of citizens for their former political allegiance.

Extensive, though certainly not fully adequate, concessions to the institutions of the intermediate system from 1789 to 1814 were thus guaranteed by the Charter. If these guarantees had been kept by the government on the one hand and if the French people on the other had been fully satisfied with the terms of the Charter, the reestablishment of 1814 might indeed be perceived as a remarkably far-reaching synthesis of an original, an intermediate, and a restored system. If the crown in the course of fifteen years had not consistently felt that it had granted too much, and the French nation, as represented chiefly by the urban middle class, that it had obtained too little, then the reestablishment of 1814 might have become an example of restoration, no less successful than the English one in the seventeenth century.

It could never have been a perfect synthesis of three systems. The range of social differences between them was far greater and, except for the religious issue, far more complex than in the English Restoration. There was also a greatly aggravating factor of foreign policy in which desire for peace, for national honor, and for Great Power status, and charges of appeasement of former enemies tore public opinion apart. But after all, no absolute standard of a successful synthesis of different systems exists, except one—its duration in time. That restoration would not endure is easier to predict now, with the benefit of hindsight, than it was in the midst of events in 1814/15.

Admirers of the Napoleonic regime as well as historians of various opinions have frequently perceived the collapse of the so-called first restoration of 1814/15 upon Napoleon's return from Elba and the Hundred Days regime not only as the foreboding of ultimate failure but as outright irremediable calamity.[21] I believe such interpretation does not correspond entirely to facts. There is no doubt that the reactionary activities of the Ultras, their threat to undo the major concessions granted by the Charter in regard to the distribution of land, the harassment of the Napoleonic officers, and the attacks against the imperial system of administration helped to sway public opinion in favor of the Napoleonic comeback. Yet on the other hand, this very Hundred Days regime proved, more convincingly than anything else could have, that only the Bourbons could preserve the Great Power status for France so wisely upheld by the Allies in May, 1814, and so little appreciated by French public opinion. It is inconceivable that another regime would have received again such relatively lenient terms as France received in the second Peace of Paris in November, 1815. While no one saw any reason to hail this defensive accomplishment, the message of the intrinsic connection of the survival of France with the passiveness of the Bourbon regime in foreign relations should not have been entirely lost.

After all, the impact on the public of Napoleon's *Acte additionel,* with its promise of ministerial responsibility and a far less restricted charter of civil liberties, was insignificant. The Ultras knew what they were doing when they opposed the evacuation of France by foreign troops in 1818. The greatest asset of the reestablished regime could be voided in the eyes of the French people. Yet, in spite of the White Terror following Napoleon's defeat, particularly in the south of France, despite new, though not unprovoked, political persecutions and new muzzlings of the press, the government after some concessions to the spirit of the *Chambre introuvable* elected by political hysteria, could for a time follow a line of moderation. The direct consequence of Napoleon's return from Elba was the short-lived terror of the Ultras. The indirect but more significant consequence which appeared clearly between 1816 and 1820, was the rising recognition that France's welfare was tied to the unheroic regime of Louis XVIII and that she had nothing to hope and much to fear from the reawakening of imperial dreams on the one side and revolutionary dreams on the other.[22]

Far more detrimental to the stability of the regime was the pressure of

[21] See particularly Madelin, II, 375 ff.; de Sauvigny, pp. 131 ff.; E. Tarlé, *Bonaparte* (New York; 1937), pp. 373 ff.; A. Fournier, *Napoleon,* III, 221 ff. See further Daniel P. Resnick, *The White Terror and the Political Reaction after Waterloo* (Cambridge, Mass., 1966), 63 ff.

[22] See Artz, pp. 15 ff.; Sauvigny, pp. 156 ff.; Bastid, pp. 94 ff.; see also B. de Sauvigny, ed., *France and the European Alliance 1816–21: The Private Correspondence between Metternich and Richelieu* (Notre Dame, 1958), pp. 6 ff., 36 ff.

irreconcilable forces of the Left and Right, of which, however, only the latter exercised any direct influence on the course of the government. Until the death of Louis XVIII the following factors were of particular significance in the context of this problem. To begin with the relatively most favorable one: The ascendancy of the moderates between 1816 and 1820 in a newly elected chamber, the evacuation of French territories by Allied troops, and the readmission of France to the council of the Great Powers certainly helped the regime, though in a passive rather than in an active sense.

This means that the absence of a new severe crisis in international relations protected the government from new trouble in one sphere; it does not mean that French public opinion was in any way impressed favorably by a policy of accommodating the victors. This pertains in particular to the psychological effect of counterrevolutionary missions such as the French intervention in 1822/23 in Spain in the service of the Concert of Europe.[23]

The administration was not entirely unwilling to tackle the problems of the incipient industrial revolution. This applies, however, merely to the economic and not to the human side of the question, as shown by the deplorable state of the industrial labor force. Quite apart from this, the overall tendency of the regimes from 1789 to 1814 had been to further the welfare of the propertied urban middle and upper-middle classes, as far as they were engaged in trade, industry, and commerce. This policy was gradually reversed in favor of landed property, big landed property at that. A regime that counted heavily on the support of the provincial nobility could not easily act differently. Although no major social changes came about under the administration of Louis XVIII and even something positively good was done in the field of public finances, the specter of an indemnification of nobility and Church at the taxpayers' expense for losses during the revolution after the execution of the king became increasingly manifest. The resulting lack of confidence in continued economic stability could only weaken the position of the administration further.[24]

---

[23] Bourgeois, I, 50 ff.; Jean Lucas-Dubreton, *The Restoration and the July Monarchy* (New York, 1929), pp. 93 ff.; Sauvigny, pp. 250 ff. See also Karl Hammer, *Die französische Diplomatie der Restauration und Deutschland, 1814–1830* (Stuttgart, 1963), pp. 113 ff.

[24] See Artz, pp. 170 ff.; Sauvigny, pp. 269 ff. The thesis of Artz that "The French governments between 1789 and 1815 showed a strong bourgeois bias," though in a very general way perfectly reasonable, requires modifications as to various times and places during this whole period. See also John Clapham, *Economic Develop-*

These feelings, supported by evidence of a different kind, were not based primarily on economic grounds. The episcopacy of France, in a very literal sense more papal and less enlightened than the pope, fought in vain the continuation of the Concordat of 1801. Yet the higher clergy was successful at least in the creation of new dioceses and the strengthening of the bishops' authority over that of the lower clergy. The activities of the new missionary movement and of congregations which, far beyond the intentions avowed in the Charter, wanted to completely undo institutional changes since 1789, and the tacit readmission of the Jesuits were strong cases in point.[25]

The influence of the aristocracy of old concerning indemnification was less direct and certainly less effective than demands for the strengthening of the power of the Church, particularly that of orders and congregations. Demands of the nobles were originally taken as mere claims to satisfy personal interests; ecclesiastic claims, on the other hand, were widely interpreted as important means to the end of a new Catholic Reformation. After the assassination of the Duke de Berry in 1820, a renewed ascendancy of the Ultras as a strictly counterrevolutionary movement became evident. First and second estates of old coalesced under the leadership of the Count of Artois. Apart from the dilution of the statutes governing higher education these objectives became especially clear in the lamentable handling of the electoral laws and in the heightened interference with the freedom of the press, limited as it was under Article 8 of the Charter.

As for the press, the laws of 1819 and 1820 and the policies for their administration, particularly after 1821, had led to an increased constriction in the expression of public opinion. Concerning the electoral laws, a temporary liberalization in 1817 was superseded in and after 1820 by renewed legal restrictions. To this must be added governmental interference in the administration of elections. The introduction of the "double vote" and the gerrymandering of electoral districts favored the big landed property in the country and therefore the claims of the old aristocracy. On the other side of the political ledger the inconspicuous but steady propaganda of the urban liberal secret societies, largely organized on the Carbonari patterns, made its influence felt in favor of republicanism and Gallicanism. The underground opposition of the workers' organizations,

---

ment of France and Germany, 1815-1914 (Cambridge, 1961), pp. 53 ff.; John Plamenatz, *The Revolutionary Movement in France, 1815-71* (London, 1952), pp. 21 ff.

[25] Artz, pp. 99 ff.; Bastid, pp. 366 ff., 388 f.; Sauvigny, pp. 406 ff.

hit by a rise in prices and a relative decline in purchasing power, represented a groundswell that within a few years assumed formidable
proportions. Even now bourgeois and labor opposition together markedly
weakened the position of the administration. No appreciable opposition, it
is true, came from the political passiveness of the peasant class, but no
reliable support either. Here, too, the reintroduction of conscription in a
roundabout way in 1818 did not win favor for the administration. Its only
clear-cut success, the preservation of external peace, was consistently and
unfairly compared with the triumphs, not with the disasters, of the
Napoleonic age.

It is not unfair to state that the regime in most domains of governmental activities—state and church relations, freedom of the press, education, administration of justice, and above all, institutions of representative
government, had fallen considerably behind the promises of the Charter.
This was felt all the more distinctly since the educated minority, whose
position counted most in the evaluation of public opinion, advocated
changes that would have extended rather than restricted the Charter. The
main point in favor of the crown, perhaps, was that the voice of this
opposition, though muffled, could still be heard.[26]

Not even Charles X, of whom Louis XVIII had said justly, "that the
fate of the monarchy depended on whether he survived his brother." [27]
succeeded in quelling it completely. Soon and understandably, Charles X
had to face widening and stiffening resistance. It became even more clear
in new deeds than in previous words that he was actually not for restoration of the ancient regime in the terms of the hapless but well-intentioned
attempts at reform of Louis XVIII. Charles X stood obviously for the re-
pudiation not only of the revolution but of the Enlightenment as well.
The Law of Indemnity of 1825, which reimbursed the nobles for the
loss of land during the revolution, could only be considered a halfway
measure to that effect, since the land itself and—even more dear to
the Ultras—the feudal rights connected with it could not be restored.
The good sense of the chamber of peers frustrated the passage of a law of
feudal primogeniture. Yet the Law of Sacrilege, enacted through royal
pressure on a passionate parliamentary minority (but an actual popular
majority), and the concomitant administrative policies which to a large
extent handed education over to missions and congregations, went far beyond the state of affairs in existence during the prerevolutionary reigns of

[26] Artz, pp. 50 ff., 99 ff., 270 ff.; Bastid, pp. 211 ff., 343 ff.; Sauvigny, pp. 317 ff.,
361 ff., 406 ff.; Clapham, pp. 75 ff., 158 ff., 189 ff.
[27] Artz, p. 25. See also Bourgeois, I, 67 f.; Plamenatz, pp. 29 ff.

Louis XVI and even of Louis XV. This action as well as the dissolution
of the national guard, the very symbol of constitutional government, carried little practical significance, yet as a declaration of intention to undo
the past in an almost Orwellian sense, they heralded not merely the
failure but the reversal of true restoration. The liberal victory in the elections of 1827, impressive and notable under then existing conditions—not
so much for the obvious sentiments revealed but for those courageously
expressed—gave the regime a lease on life for another two years. Had it
not been for the slightly liberalizing effect of the policies of the Martignac
ministry in 1828/29, which cooperated with the majority of the chamber
to a point, the revolution might have come even sooner than it did.

The following Polignac ministry, for all practical purposes, though not
technically, a coup d'état cabinet, made such revolution a certainty. In the
vain and naïve hope that the successful colonial expedition in Algiers
would sway public opinion in favor of the regime, the government called
for new elections. As to be expected by any observer with a measure of
common sense, a majority in strong opposition to the crown was returned. Thereupon the notorious Five Ordinances were issued, according
to which the new chamber was dissolved, the still existing limited freedom of the press suspended, and the franchise restricted to some 25,000
people, roughly one in a thousand inhabitants. Regardless even of the
highly dubious interpretation of Article 14 of the Charter, according to
which legislation by decree in national emergencies was claimed for the
king, this whole governmental policy collided with the traditions of the
Enlightenment, revolution, Napoleonic centralism, and even the earlier
efforts toward restoration under Louis XVIII to such a degree that open
conflict had now become inevitable.[28]

All this pertains only to the timing of the outbreak of revolution; the
events themselves had become fully predictable some time before. It is
widely agreed that the three-day revolution of July, 1830, was intentionally
brought about by the king's appointment in August, 1829, of a ministry
that represented only a parliamentary minority and only a fraction of a
minority as far as popular support was concerned. The moderately liberal
majority, which in an address to the throne censured the appointment of
the Polignac ministry, desired revolution as little as did the king. The new
elections, in which the king identified himself completely with the Ultras,
and, after their failure, the issuance of the July ordinances, led from the
defeat of an extremist royalist minority to the fleeting victory of an

[28] Sauvigny, pp. 538 ff., 576 ff.; Artz, pp. 25 ff., 161 ff., 168 ff.; Lucas-Dubreton,
pp. 102 ff.; Plamenatz pp. 33 ff.

equally unrepresentative radical republican minority in Paris. Moderates like Lafayette quickly dissociated themselves from this group when the specter of leadership by the radical Left and perhaps also of foreign intervention appeared on the horizon.

It has been asserted with some justification that the process of transition from the Bourbon to the Orléans monarchy, though strongly influenced by public pressure in Paris, was to a degree legitimate from the dynastic viewpoint. "The king at the moment of abdication appointed the Duc d'Orléans the regent of his grandson. Henry V was one day to be the legitimate successor of Charles X, of Louis XVIII, of Louis XVI, and of Louis XV. . . ." [29] Even according to this line of thought, however, the subsequent proclamation of Louis Philippe as king was an act of usurpation. The old monarchy in France fell not during the July uprising but on August 6. There and then was a definite break with the principle of legitimacy, "an irrevocable revolutionary act: because an illegal assembly without mandate or power had pretended to create a king. Louis Philippe's monarchy is not a monarchy of the old regime but a usurpation." Since Louis Philippe belonged, however, to the ancient royal house, since he recognized the right of opposition to a point, and "did not possess himself of the power by means of a new 18 Brumaire," he is partly forgiven by Guglielmo Ferrero. The July monarchy is considered not as legitimate as that of Louis XVIII, but not quite as illegitimate as Bonapartism. Ferrero perceives the new regime as quasi-legitimate. This means in effect that government was only partly, not fully, based on acceptance by the representatives of the people and only in some measure brought about by unlawful means.[30]

This interpretation is based to a large extent on rather narrow dynastic grounds. Authors like Emile Bourgeois, Jean Lucas-Dubreton, Paul M. de la Gorce, and contemporaries, above all Talleyrand, emphasize far more the importance of the continuation of monarchic government itself than the question whether it was exercised by Louis Philippe in his own right or as regent for the ten-year old Count of Chambord (Henry V). Nevertheless, they and many other distinguished authors are agreed that the

---

[29] Ferrero, *Principles of Power*, pp. 215 f.; Bourgeois, I, 114 ff., 160 ff.; Lucas-Dubreton, pp. 160 ff; Sauvigny, pp. 604 ff.; Paul M. de la Gorce, *Louis Philippe* (Paris, 1931), pp. 6 ff. See also *Memoirs of the Prince de Talleyrand* III, 225 ff., who considered the acceptance of the crown by Louis Philippe rather than the mere position as lieutenant of the kingdom as necessary act of expediency. See further Brinton, pp. 194 ff.

[30] Ferrero, *Principles of Power*, pp. 216, 217; see also pp. 107 ff., 138 ff.; see further Ferrero, *Reconstruction of Europe*, pp. 47 ff., 58 ff.; Plamenatz, pp. 35 ff.

restoration period ended with the year 1830 in failure and that the Orléans "citizen king" initiated an entirely new phase in French history.
This view is based primarily on the political and social differences between two regimes separated by a revolution, however brief.[31]

This study dissents from this view. We believe that the brief interruption of legitimate government and the ensuing constitutional and social
changes that resulted were not sweeping enough to assume that the
endeavors toward restoration had definitely failed by July, 1830. If we
focus our attention less on the specific dynastic question of the Bourbon
monarchy than on the continuation of the monarchy in general, the success or failure of endeavors toward restoration can be tested only by reviewing the common foundations and the course of action of Bourbon
and Orléans monarchies. Here a transition very different from that of the
Napoleonic to the Bourbon regime took place. As in the English revolution of 1688-89, ties between the previous Bourbon and the coming Orléans
regime—established after a brief revolution—are obvious. Stuart and
Orange dynasties were closely related, and the same was true, though not
to the same extent, for the Orléans and Bourbon lines, which both de-
scended from Louis XIII. In both cases, however, the relationship between the pre-revolution and post-revolution dynasties was intentionally
used to give the new regime a measure of legitimacy.

Far more important is the second point, the relationship of the
philosophy and policies of the two regimes. The crown of England before
and after 1688 shared, of course, the whole constitutional tradition of
England, clarified by the Declaration of Rights and strengthened by a
new Triennial Act and the Act of Settlement of Protestant succession,
within little more than a decade. The Charter of August 7, 1830, passed by
a rump legislature and modified by the law about the peerage of 1832,
stands not only in principle for the common grounds of restoration, as
stated in the Charter of 1814. The new acts represent actually only a revised form of the document of 1814. This revised Charter, like the original one, was redrawn quite skillfully within a few days, and was
solemnly sworn to by Louis Philippe.

Neither of the two major changes in the revised Charter made much
difference in practice. The preamble was eliminated, according to which
the king of France ruled by the Grace of God and granted the Charter by

---

[31] Artz, pp. 173 f., deviates from this view in the sphere of economics. "The
Restoration in itself is not a self-contained period in the economic development of
France. It stands mid-way in a gradual transformation which took place roughly
between 1750 and 1850."

his own free will to his people. The new king, now a mere king of the French, ruled by implication on the basis of a contract with the people after the throne of France had been declared vacant. Restrictions of the royal power as compared with the Charter of 1814 were, however, by no means deduced from this change. On the other hand, the main principle of parliamentary monarchy, namely that the cabinet was dependent on the confidence of parliament (Art. 69/2), was actually a none to clear affirmation of an already established tradition in writing. Violation of that previously unwritten provision had cost Charles X his throne, and it was clearly understood that Louis Philippe had to respect it if he did not want to vacate royal power too. Otherwise, freedom of the press was to be affirmed, the rights of the Catholic religion as that of the majority of the French people, but not any more as the state religion, were to be respected. Article 14 was to be reformulated in a way that barred the possibility of using it as a handle for royal emergency legislation by decree, and legislative initiative was to be shared by king and chambers. Of these the chamber of hereditary peers was to be transformed into a kind of senate of distinguished lifetime members in various walks of civil service, industry, and agriculture, and foremost intellectuals in the academies.[32]

These were not the only changes, but they were the major ones, and like the Charter of 1814 they were on shaky constitutional grounds. The idea originally underlying both charters was that a genuine synthesis of ancient regime, the revolution, and Napoleonic regime must be found. The implied principle of Talleyrand still stood unimpaired in theory. "One of the gravest mistakes committed by human indolence is the belief that order is best preserved by keeping it as it stands. It can only be preserved by continually reconstructing it. The only real guardians are those who reconstruct it." [33]

How did these guardians perform their task? Certainly, it was difficult as far as pressure from the moderate and radical Left was concerned. The bourgeois liberals felt that the abortive revolution had betrayed their wishes. The increasing rate of industrialization linked to the propaganda of a no longer entirely utopian socialism led to unrest on the part of the workers. On the other hand the king and the successive ministries of Laffitte, Casimir-Périer, Soult, the Duke of Broglie, Thiers, Molé, again Soult and above all the Guizot cabinet under its erudite but shortsighted chief, never had to face on the Right as determined and powerful an

[32] Duguit and Monnier, pp. 194 ff., 199 ff.; Bourgeois, I, 119 ff.; P. de la Gorce, pp. 11 ff.; Lucas-Dubreton, pp. 202 f.
[33] Ferrero, *Reconstruction,* pp. 342 ff.

opposition as the late Louis XVIII faced in the Ultras. The charge that the king and the former liberals had sold out to conservatism and reaction was thus understandable, though not quite correct. The choice was no longer that between ultra conservatism and moderate liberalism under the Bourbons; it was between a somewhat more moderate conservatism and a republican radicalism ranging from Thiers to the memories of Robespierre to the Left of him and the even more radical future of Louis Blanc.

Certainly the performance of the regime did not rise to the challenge it had to face. It was as incongruous as it was disconcerting. The electoral law of 1831 enfranchised less than 200,000, a drop in the bucket if matched with the concept of general franchise, which liberal propaganda held increasingly before the eyes of the public. In the same sense and with the same effect, the right to hold elective office was reduced to some 20,000 of the highest tax payers. Reestablishment of the national guard on a broader basis than before was seen by the public to be little more than a nice gesture. It could certainly not offset the effect of the suppression of the workers' revolt by force of arms in Lyon in the same year 1831. The Primary Education Law of 1833, which assured free though not compulsory elementary education throughout the land, may have been considered a reasonable agreement of some merit between state and church. Yet it would have been received with better grace if it had not been promoted by a professed but not actually enlightened conservative like François Guizot, who compromised on the issue of separation of church and state in educational matters to nobody's satisfaction. New riots of workers in Paris and Lyon were suppressed by unduly harsh means. The subsequent September Laws of 1845, following an assassination attempt against the king led to muzzling of the press and to suspension of trials by jury. Special court proceedings put teeth into the enforcement of a previously passed law against associations of less than twenty persons. This surely was in the worst tradition of the Polignac ministry. There was one important difference, however. The majority of the chamber that passed this legislation could rely at least on the support of the limited electorate, which was scared by the workers' agitation. The main accomplishment of this governmental policy was to drive the radical opposition underground, a factor which facilitated rather than impeded the coming February revolution of 1848.

Positive factors in the policies of the July monarchy were the limited democratization of the departmental and municipal councils by 1833 and an almost lone effective economic measure, the Railway Act of 1842. It recognized to some extent the need for governmental support of new means of communication. French foreign policy during the whole period of the July monarchy was necessarily as unheroic as that of the Bourbon reestablishment, but considerably less successful. Louis XVIII had after all restored France to the Concert of the Great European Powers. Under Louis Philippe schemes to establish dynastic ties with Belgium and Spain aroused only distrust in Europe. The indecisive backing of the national liberal movements in Poland and Italy did not even help the king win the support of the Catholics at a time when a friend of Italian unification, Pius IX, was elected pope in 1846. France on the side of England was more successful in her Eastern policy and in particular in the support of Mehemet Ali, viceroy of Egypt. This policy helped indirectly to block Russia's drive toward the Mediterranean. Yet the broad masses in France considered the Eastern question hardly of primary French interest.

The failure of the July monarchy was not entirely due to an often charged inefficiency, corruption, and a failure to read the trend of public opinion properly, a failure which after a few years gave even the revival of Bonapartism a fighting chance. The endeavors to bring about a Bourbon restoration, in spite of ill success in the end, could at least count on the forces that had been the pillars of the old regime, the Church and the nobility. Louis Philippe, on the other hand, was looked at with suspicion and contempt by the supporters of the old regime, whom he supported just strongly enough to alienate the bourgeois Center without ever gaining their confidence. This Center and the moderate Left felt betrayed by the expectations of the "three glorious days" of July, 1830, and a new monarchy which had restored neither any achievements of the bygone revolutionary period nor any shred of the glory of Bonapartism. This monarchy, which ignored the need for remedies of the social ills of the Industrial Revolution, appeared to many to be only a more shabby and more dubious second edition of the restoration efforts from 1814 to 1830. The July monarchy was really less conservative and less reactionary than the regimes of Louis XVIII and certainly of Charles X. Yet it had also aroused greater expectations and the times had not stood still. The pressure of the republican Left and the needs of the industrial working class had risen far beyond anticipations, and if the restoration of 1814 was already out of step with them, the July monarchy had fallen much farther and much faster behind.[34]

[34] Bourgeois, I, 150 ff., 208 ff.; Lucas-Dubreton, pp. 174 ff., 222 ff.; La Gorce, pp. 103 ff., 159 ff. See also Louis Blanc, *Révélations historiques* (Brussels, 1859), I, 9 ff.; Clapham, pp. 140 ff.; Plamenatz, pp. 38 ff., 57 ff.

Conservative historians have made much of the fact that Charles X abandoned the throne with a dignity which was absent in the seemingly heedless and certainly unexpectedly sudden flight of Louis Philippe in February, 1848.[35] Nevertheless, the relative insignificance of the event leading to it—the vehement response to the government's cancellation of a banquet sponsored by the republican opposition—offers little evidence for the impact of chance on the course of history. On the contrary, the disproportion between the minor importance of the action which set the ball of the revolutionary powers rolling, and its sweeping effect confirm only the conclusion that the inability of the regime under radical pressure had reached a point where revolution might have commenced at any time or place in the centers of French government and industry. The far-reaching effect of this revolution in action and reaction, between February and December, 1848, and the subsequent entrenchment of new Bonapartist authoritarianism by December, 1851, made it clear that the attempt at restoration initiated in 1814 had now decisively failed. It had been destroyed by a genuine social revolution in 1848 and it could be restored neither by the republic under Louis Napoleon Bonaparte's presidency nor by his empire. Napoleon III could not possibly install a restoration of the regime of Napoleon I, which in itself still belonged to the revolutionary period and was not in power long enough to be considered as a true original system; and even if the premises had been different, Napoleon III was not long enough in power either to accomplish genuine restoration.

Far more important is another consideration. The early radical stage of the February Revolution, the relatively moderate bourgeois phase of revolutionary proceedings, roughly from April to June, 1848, the subsequent radical rightist authoritarian turn in June, the fairly liberal republic under Louis Napoleon from December, 1848 to 1851, his subsequent dictatorship, and finally his usurpation of the throne—all this changed the structure of France profoundly. Even the new monarchy, seemingly in some respects similar to the July monarchy, despite all its obvious shortcomings recognized the Industrial Revolution, the rise of the fourth estate and of liberal nationalism, factors which had been largely ignored by Louis Philippe's regime. Yet even if this view should be contested, it could surely be proved that the changes between 1848 and 1852 were too sweeping and too profound to tie the Second Empire to the monarchy of the

[35] Bourgeois, I, 365; Ferrero, *Principles of Power*, by implication, pp. 128 ff., 161 ff., 234 ff. See also William L. Langer, "The Pattern of Urban Revolution in 1848," in *French Society and Culture since the Old Regime*, ed. Evelyn A. Acomb and Marvin L. Brown (New York, 1966), pp. 96 ff.

"citizen king." In evaluating restoration we may pass over the three so-called "glorious days" in July, 1830, and link the Orléans to the Bourbon monarchy. The same attempt in regard to a connection between Second Empire and July monarchy would mean the arbitrary erasure of a chapter of history, the consequences of which extended far beyond France. One may argue whether the Restoration, or as it is held here, the endeavors toward restoration, had come to an end in 1830 or 1848. It would be absurd to go further and plead that they had continued until 1870.

One final significant factor in the history of the French restoration movement must not be overlooked. The English Restoration was perhaps the first in which political theorists and historians dealt consciously with the problems of transition and reestablishment of government. Reference to James Harrington, John Milton, Algernon Sidney, and, of course, the Earl of Clarendon (so much greater as historian than as statesman) must suffice here. Yet the thought of these men as it was stated in their writing merely accompanied and reviewed the course of history of the English Restoration. In France, where political and historical thinking was focused on the restoration problem to a degree unparalleled before and afterward in almost any place, political theorists and historians shaped the course of the movement to a considerable extent and in several ways. For one thing, outstanding political thinkers and writers like Bonald and Chateaubriand held high office under the Bourbon reestab-lishment.[36] They influenced to a marked degree the actual course of political action. It is more important, however, that they, with Guizot, who served in top echelons of government under both monarchies, and others, like Courier, Benjamin Constant, and above all Lamennais, par-ticipated in the great debate on the basic questions of French political philosophy under Louis XVIII and Charles X. The same is true for Saint-Simon, Lamartine and again Lamennais, Fourier, Proudhon, Michelet, and Montalembert under Louis Philippe.

There is one obvious difference between the great intellectuals of the Bourbon reestablishment and those of the July monarchy. Outstanding men with strong political interests, like Auguste Comte, Jules Michelet, Augustin Thierry, or Victor Hugo, were not vitally concerned with the political philosophy of the ruling regime. Adolphe Thiers and Louis Blanc are here almost the exception to the rule, and inasmuch as their

[36] Roland Mousnier and Ernest Labrousse, *Le XVIIIe siècle, Revolution in-tellectuelle, technique et politique (1715–1815)* (Paris, 1953), pp. 510 ff.; Jacob P. Mayer, *Political Thought in France from the Revolution to the Fifth Republic* (London, 1961 [1943]), pp. 21 ff., 25 ff.; Hammer, pp. 112 ff., 122 ff.

rank as historians is controversial, it is a doubtful exception. During the
Bourbon administration from 1814 to 1830 a much larger stratum of the
political intelligentsia of high caliber was concerned with the basic political questions of the regime. This, of course, was partly due to the reaction
which is inevitable when a regime and an ideology are imposed from
above. Yet the very fact that these voices were heard, that the defenders of
the administration were attacked by a liberal opposition and the voice of
the liberals was at least not permanently suppressed, was one of the positive aspects of the regime, whatever its grave shortcomings otherwise.

If there ever was an official state philosophy of the restoration in a
literally narrow sense, it would be that of Bonald and De Maistre. They
should be credited with a perfect inner consistency and a corresponding
absence of political opportunism, in an age and place that was alive with
converts of various grades and shades of persuasion. They shared a hatred
of the revolution, a denial of the persuasiveness of human reason, a belief
in the basic inequality of men, and a negative view of human character
which served a skeptic like Thomas Hobbes better than a doctrine of
professed Christian charity. This meant also that the social unit, a unit of
caste and class, is of greater significance than men as individuals. The
teachings of the administrator of royal censorship and champion of the
notorious Law of Sacrilege, Bonald, implied also papal supremacy over the
king. He rejected the ancient French theories of Gallicanism in various
forms. De Maistre, actually a subject and later dignitary in the government of the Piedmontese kingdom, went even farther and pleaded
for the subordination of the temporal monarchy under the spiritual
authority of the pope. This doctrine differed not so much in degree as in
the lack of popular appeal from the teachings of the great medieval popes
Boniface VIII and Innocent III. In this respect the impact of Chateaubriand's view, as expressed in his *Génie de Christianisme,* a book worth
a hundred thousand men to Louis XVIII, as he put it, was much greater.
Yet it is not the romantic synthesis of Christianity and the medieval spirit
which won him acclaim; it was between royalism and parliamentarism
which secured respectability for the former Bonapartist. The usefulness of
this versatile man as ambassador to Prussia and England, as French
delegate at the Congress of Verona in 1822, and as subsequent foreign
minister was obvious. The distinguished and enlightened writer, who had
even dared to take a stand against the Ultras, could not be simply dismissed as a literary turncoat.[37]

Even more important in fundamental matters of political philosophy

[37] Mousnier and Labrousse, pp. 510 ff., 525; Mayer, pp. 21 ff.

was the lifework of Lamennais, particularly in his influence on an intellectually alert youth of France caught in the maelstrom of political currents and countercurrents. He repudiated the existing state as a hodgepodge of rationalism, individualism, intellectual anarchy, and pseudotolerance in favor of a Church, not as she was but as he wished her to become. This meant the termination of the century-old alliance between episcopacy, congregations, and religious orders—above all the Jesuits—with the feudal or semifeudal monarchy. In its place Lamennais demanded the establishment of new ties with a democratic, truly universal Church, a theocracy not in terms of a two-swords theory but of ecumenical philosophy. It required genuine new conversion on the part of the faithful. Lamennais' theories in their extreme form were eventually repudiated by the Church, but by that time he was as little concerned with the concrete problems of governmental policies as the utopian socialists.[38] The immediate future of the July monarchy belonged to the scholarly politicians and political literary men of the brand of Guizot, Thiers, Lamartine, and seemingly of Benjamin Constant, whose parliamentary royalism would have served him well under Louis Philippe had he not died a few months after the establishment of the new regime.

Altogether intellectuals had an opportunity to make their voices heard in the religious, constitutional and, as the cases of Fourier and Courier show, even in the rural agricultural sphere of the Bourbon monarchy. The political intellectuals of the July regime could offer only minor adaptions to the failing compromise between bourgeois revolution and monarchy. The interests and demands of the social reformers and thinkers of that period were hardly in touch with the reality of a system for which nobody saw much of a future. This seems to be a more important difference between Bourbon and Orléans monarchy than the constitutional changes that were passed in July and August, 1830. Yet even these intellectual variations are not distinctive enough to comprehend the whole period from 1814 to 1848 in terms of our study as anything but an historical unit which comprises Bourbon and Orléans monarchy.[39]

[38] See also Michael P. Fogarty, *Christliche Demokratie in Westeuropa 1820–1953* (Freiburg, i.B., 1959), pp. 178 ff.; Mayer, pp. 22 ff.; Plamenatz, pp. 48 ff.

[39] See Artz, *France Under the Bourbon Restoration*, pp. 59 ff., 105 ff.; Sauvigny, pp. 420 ff., 444 ff., 459 ff.; La Gorce, pp. 207 ff.; Mayer, pp. 8–44 *passim*. Heinrich Heine (Frankreich I), *Französische Maler, Französische Zustände, Über die französische Bühne,* and (Frankreich II), *Lutezia* (various editions), offer an amazing insight into some of the intellectual problems referred to here. Focused on the July monarchy, Heine's reflections pertain in part to the Bourbon monarchy as well. See (Frankreich I) *Französische Zustände,* published 1832, particularly sections I–IV,

Jean Lucas-Dubreton, who makes a clear and justified distinction between the regimes of Louis XVIII and Charles X, has this to say about the restoration:

> The restoration was a period of originality and power; there was a clash of ideas and doctrines; the old world that was striving to return to life was opposed by a new world fighting for breathing-space—it was a time, when cause for conflict lay ever latent and sometimes became acute. Ardent spirits met in conflict and allowed themselves free play in a fresh atmosphere. [From here, however, one might say he moves from the sublime to the ridiculous.] This frankness of outlook, this confidence and youth, not to mention his ingenuousness of mind, were never to be seen again.
>
> From the political point of view the restoration was the golden age of parliamentarism; people believed in the virtue of systems, in the value of reason, in the power of order, and it was not regarded as duty to despise the enemy. . . . Never since the seventeenth century had the administration of France been better. . . . But it was above all in the domain of thought that the restoration gave evidence of greatness. . . .[40]

Except for the reference to the significance of the ideological struggle itself, every contention here could be easily refuted in regard to the reign of Louis XVIII and even more so for that of Charles X. This refutation is applicable to the July monarchy as well. Even the statement that enemies were not bound to despise each other, while correct to a point, is ambiguous. The fast transition from one regime to the other may lead to tolerance indeed, but a tolerance frequently diluted by skeptical laxity as to the seriousness of convictions. Steadfastness of purpose in political philosophy, on the other hand, is frequently intermingled with a holier-than-thou bigotry. France from 1789 to the advent of the Third Republic was exposed to all these effects. Nevertheless, one could well agree that the restoration in the wide sense perceived in this chapter, namely from 1814 to 1848, as well as in the narrower one of the Bourbon monarchy, and here particularly until 1824, was a fertile period of historical action and thought. It represented a singular attempt in history, not merely to reestablish an original system with some inevitable concessions to the intermediate one, but to create by intent a genuine synthesis of the two.

This attempt was bound to fail for two main reasons. First, the forces which promoted the restoration idea were not impartial arbiters between

VII, VIII, IX (Frankreich II), published 1854, section I, entries February–April, May 20–30, Nov. 6, 1840; April 29, May 19, 1841; Jan. 24, 1842; section II, Sept. 17, Dec. 4, Dec. 31, 1842; June 22, 1843.

[40] Lucas-Dubreton, pp. 171 f.

the systems but were heavily committed to the ancient regime. Yet even if they had been men more wise and just than ordinary mortals, they would have failed in all probability. Too much had happened—and too much of a politically disparate nature—between 1789 and 1814 to crowd a new synthesis into the old frame. The best proof of this is the fact that, in spite of the clearly conservative sympathies of the leaders of the restoration movement under the Bourbons (and only thinly camouflaged under the Orléans as well), the major legislation during those times reflected the ideas of the revolutionary period and the Consulate far more than those of the royal monarchy and of the empire. This pertains to relations of church and state, the land settlement, the judicial sphere, the technical aspects of the administrative order, and the basic principles of representative government. To proceed in this course fully within the tradition of the ancient regime would have taxed the ingenuity of wiser and more resolute men than Louis XVIII, Talleyrand, Richelieu, Thiers, or Guizot, and they were not to be despised on the grounds of their intelligence, foresight, or knowledge. It is quite conceivable that men with a wider vision would have given up this hopeless struggle long before 1848.

What then was the solution? Certainly not another restoration attempt like the Second Empire, which lacked a long established tradition. Was it then the Third Republic, which barely lasted for two generations, encumbered by political catastrophes, one from which it evolved and another in which it submerged? The final answer to this question cannot be given even today, after the Third Republic has been followed by a Fourth and a Fifth. Yet, at least in a negative sense, a solution appeared to be more clearly visible in 1848 than in 1830, in 1870 than in 1848, and in 1965 than in 1940. There seems to exist some kind of principle of saturation in history. According to it the success of restoration is dependent not only on the lapse of time. Restoration may also be impossible—and at that quite irrespective of the time factor—if the extent and intensity of historical action bursts any given historical frame and demands new forms "um alten Wein in neue Schläuche zu giessen." Ancient regime, constitutional monarchy, liberal republic, parliamentary dictatorship, authoritarian republic, and monarchic imperialism with all their designs, ideas, institutions—good, bad, efficient, and ineffective—could not possibly be subordinated to any of the established patterns in France. Suggestive as it certainly was to select the one with the strongest tradition in the sense of continuity behind it, the image of the ancient regime had become too brittle to be stretched by merger with more recent forces of various kind. For a long time these newer social and political factors have not succeeded either in creating a new structure capable of withstanding the pressures from extreme wings. In the light of all this the failure of a restoration as notable in intellectual history as it was socially sterile is understandable. The inscriptions on the main pillars in the interior of the Panthéon in Paris: "A la gloire des géneraux de la révolution Française," and on the other sides, "Aux orateurs et aux publicistes de la restauration," which puts the original and restored systems apparently on an equal footing, may not be deserved, but they do not strike us as absurd either. This in itself is no mean testimony to the French efforts to accomplish the impossible under existing conditions: genuine restoration.

CHAPTER XVII

Restoration That Came Too Late

From the Dissolution of the Holy Roman Empire in 1806 to the
Proclamation of the Second German Empire in 1871

Original system (A)	1648–1806, period of decline of Holy Roman Empire
Intermediate period, approximating system (B)	1806–1871
Approximated restored system (C)	since 1871, imperfect identification with original system (A)

At what point may we consider an intermediate revolutionary system to be stabilized for good? The answer was, as suggested in chapter 6 and substantiated there as far as possible, that this process of stabilization might take place within the course of a political generation, that is, about thirty to forty years. We have observed further that even within such time stabilization can take place only if the intermediate system is no longer dictatorial in nature, and if its efficacy to rule has not been seriously challenged by sizeable strata of the population.

The intermediate part of the three systems—not necessarily a system itself—which we intend to study in this chapter, appears to be quite disparate in character. In the east and west, south and north of the German orbit it operated under different conditions of time and place. Although it arose in a revolutionary stage of international relations and led to a major revolution in 1848, it was otherwise by no means revolutionary in nature.

On the other hand, the original system and the supposedly restored one can be clearly visualized in the German case. The same is true for the intermediate one but only as far as the time element is concerned. Otherwise its incongruous content did not lead merely to incomplete, questionable, or imperfect restoration: the result was failure of restoration, though a failure that came rather close to success. Moreover, this failure sheds so much light on our previous assumptions and findings that the subsequent analysis seems fully justified.

The Holy Roman Empire from the Westphalian peace treaty of 1648 to its dissolution in 1806 is the original system we have to deal with. It is hardly possible to determine the precise constitutional structure of this strange complex of feudal and federal elements, particularly in these last centuries of its existence when its political status went through a terminal phase of continued and accelerated decline. It is well known that Pufendorf in his brilliant studies of the nature of the empire referred to it as early as 1667 as *Irregulare aliquod corpus et monstro simile.* "The more the empire appeared incapable of adjusting its constitution to actual conditions, the less could political theory cope with it. . . . Bodin and, within the storms of the Thirty Years' War, Hippolithus da Lappide saw the sovereignty in the whole body of the estates and called it an aristocracy. Others . . . argued that the emperor was the sovereign of the empire as successor to the Roman emperor. Again . . . others looked for a compromise of both views in the theory of the mixed state." Subsequent political theory tried to disprove Pufendorf's contention concerning the uniqueness of the empire's constitutional structure. They asserted that "the empire had the character of a state to the very last. Undoubtedly this is correct, but the term state does not help much to understand the nature of the empire in the seventeenth and eighteenth centuries. The empire is not a structure that can be compared with other contemporary states, but a state ossified in the form of previous times." According to Fritz Hartung, only the concept of federative associations helps to further insight.[1] The federate element which represented an essential factor in the empire's formation and transformation after 1648 was at the same time a major force in its dissolution. In principle this was as true for the Confederation of the Rhine of 1658 and for the League of Princes of 1785, sponsored by Prussia, as for the Rheinbund of 1806, dominated by the French.

As Georg Dahm sees the problem,

> The feudal bonds to the empire did not preclude the concept of princely power in the eighteenth century as original state power not deduced from emperor and empire, which the prince could exercise in his own right and name. This corresponded to political reality. In the estates of the empire the allegiance to the empire (*Reichsgesinnung*) was as good as extinguished. . . . In the West and South of the empire, associations of imperial estates developed independent of the empire. In fact the estates coalesced [with foreign powers] against the empire. . . . Thus the empire did not represent a state and it was accordingly a mystery for the thinking of political theorists. . . . It was impossible to determine the question of sovereignty for the empire. In constitutional theory a distinction was made between imperial and princely trends (*kaiserliche*

[1] Severinus de Mozambano (Samuel von Pufendorf), *De statu imperii Germanici,* in Ellinor von Puttkamer, ed., *Föderative Elemente im deutschen Staatsrecht* (Göttingen, 1955), pp. 39–42; Fritz Hartung, *Deutsche Verfassungsgeschichte vom 15.Jahrhundert bis zur Gegenwart,* 6th ed. (Stuttgart, 1954), pp. 157 f.; J. Goodehard Ebers, *Die Lehre vom Staatenbunde* (Breslau, 1910), pp. 21 f.; Ernst R. Huber, *Deutsche Verfassungsgeschichte seit 1789* (Stuttgart, 1957); I, 7 f.; Ricarda Huch, *Untergang des römischen Reiches deutscher Nation* (Munich-Hamburg, 1964), pp. 30 ff., 81 ff.; Hajo Holborn, *A History of Modern Germany* (New York, 1964), Vol. II, 1648–1840, pp. 4 ff. If not stated otherwise, quotations in this chapter were translated by the author.

und landesherrliche Richtung). This composite of monarchical, feudal, and estates patterns could not be understood in conceptual terms,

a fact noted already by Pufendorf.[2]

There is general agreement that the importance of the Holy Roman Empire in European power politics declined after the Thirty Years' War, when princely sovereignty became further enhanced and foreign alliances of princes were officially recognized. Even as obvious a restriction as the prohibition of alliances directed against emperor and empire was conveniently ignored as early as 1658 by the Confederation of the Rhine between German princes and France. More important violations of that principle followed in the course of the next century and a half, and the one major attempt to enforce imperial authority against a princely aggressor, the empire's war against Frederick II of Prussia, ended in disaster at Rossbach in 1757. But although the position of the empire had surely diminished, it was not reduced to complete insignificance, as the bulk of evidence shows.

To be sure, the preservation of the principles of the Religious Peace of Augsburg of 1555, *cuius regio eius religio,* and after 1648 the rigid application of religious parity between Catholics and Protestants in the voting procedures of the Reichstag must be rated as divisive factors. In particular, the parity device after 1648 pertained even to matters unrelated to religious questions and thus limited the possibility of empire reform and imperial administration itself. A further issue usually adduced to show the impotence of the empire—the establishment of the Reichstag of 1663 in Regensburg as a body to sit in permanence as an ambassadorial conference of imperial estates—presents a more complex problem. By no means does it demonstrate clearly the weakness of the empire. This new kind of Reichstag was incapable of assisting in the government of the empire, and even if we make due allowance for the curia of cities, it was in no way a socially representative estates assembly either. Its own order of procedure enabled it, however, at least potentially to work for empire reform. Moreover, the imperial estates in permanent session conspicuously symbolized the idea of empire-wide comprehensiveness. The passing of an imperial defense constitution in 1681, brought about under the threat of the

---

[2] Pufendorf in Puttkamer, ed., pp. 27–42; Georg Dahm, *Deutsches Recht* (Hamburg, 1944), pp. 157 f.; Hartung, pp. 164 ff.; see also Friedrich Meinecke, *Weltbürgertum und Nationalstaat* (Munich, 1911), pp. 21 ff.; and Frederick Hertz, *The Development of the German Public Mind* (London, 1962), II, 33; see also 13–37 *passim.*

Turkish advance in the East and leaning heavily on princely support, went an important step beyond such symbolic significance.[3]

The same was true for the position of the emperor. True, his power was severely curtailed by the stringency of the imperial capitulations (*Wahlkapitulationen*), the pledges he had to give to the princes prior to the coronation. Yet after 1648 these commitments were, owing to the transformation of the empire, actually of far less importance than at the time of their initiation, the election of Charles V more than a century before. Furthermore—a point missed entirely by James Bryce—the capitulations weakened the position of the emperor, but they strengthened the idea of the empire as a federate body.[4] Perhaps the most conspicuous aspect of imperial power, the judicial one—the position of the emperor as the supreme judge of the empire and the existence of two imperial judicial high courts—remained substantially unchanged. In the smaller principalities, to the very end of the empire, this was not without practical significance.[5]

In the age of a balance-of-power conflict in Europe, beginning with the wars of Louis XIV, the empire had little significance in power politics. This is true specifically in the eighteenth century with the growing struggle between the Habsburg power and Prussia for supremacy in Germany. As Frederick Hertz sees it, a distinct opportunity to overcome empire-wide particularism and to cement unity by giving the Holy Roman Empire a more representative constitutional structure was foiled by this struggle. "A certain movement toward these aims might have been possible when Germany had recuperated from the ravages of the Thirty Years' War and the aggression of Louis XIV, and when the ideas of enlightenment began to gain in strength. But just at this point Frederick II began a policy rendering the two great German powers mortal enemies and thus barring any development of national unity and freedom."[6]

[3] See the documents cited in Puttkamer, ed. pp. 27–42 *passim,* 50 ff.; Hartung, pp. 156 ff., 162 f.; Heinrich Brunner and Ernst Heymann, *Grundzüge der deutschen Rechtsgeschichte,* 7th ed. (Munich, Leipzig, 1927), pp. 289 ff., 296; James Bryce, *The Holy Roman Empire* (New York, 1914), pp. 394 ff.; Dahm, 142 ff.; Holborn, II, 9 ff.

[4] Bryce, pp. 371 f., 398 ff.; see also Hugo Preuss, *Staat, Recht und Freiheit* (Hildesheim, 1964), pp. 273 ff.; Hellmuth Rössler, *Österreichs Kampf um Deutschlands Befreiung,* 2 vols. (Hamburg, 1940); see I, 177 ff.; Hartung, *Volk und Staat in der deutschen Geschichte* (Leipzig, 1940), pp. 77 ff., 84 ff., 89 ff.

[5] Hartung, *Deutsche Verfassungsgeschichte,* pp. 140 ff.; Hertz, II, 33 ff.; Brunner and Heymann, pp. 283 ff.

[6] Hertz, II, 354.

Substantial evidence, such as the eighteenth century writings of father and son (Johann Jakob and Karl Friedrich) Moser, Justus Möser, and others, confirms this view quite clearly. Yet the idea of German unity in the Holy Roman Empire was in its historical development not primarily literary, not even cultural in a broad humanitarian sense. Above all, it was of a spiritual and, in the widest ecumenical sense, of a political nature.

We owe a great deal to the lifework of Heinrich von Srbik in this respect, even though the romantic trend in his conclusions must be counterbalanced by other considerations. The Christian universalist tradition of the Ottonian emperors in the tenth and early eleventh centuries, the concept of the great national state, as it emerged in however imperfect form at the turn from the fifteenth to the sixteenth century under Maximilian I, and the supernational crusade of his grandson Charles V in the service of a worldwide and counterreformatory imperialism all form part of this tradition. According to Srbik, universalism in a supernational, national, and ecumenical Christian sense was even shared by Protestantism to a large extent and blocked only by the Austro-Prussian power struggle in the eighteenth century. Blocked but not destroyed! "In the last analysis it was not the imperial idea, but the empire in its containment from the point of power politics within the Central European German realm, which was defeated at Münster and Osnabrück." [7] In the writings of Srbik the distinction between ideologies as the driving forces in history and the mere rationalization of such ideologies as the releasing factor for historical action is unfortunately not sufficiently acknowledged. Too little attention is paid to strictly political motives behind the course of action and to the action itself. Despite this important reservation, Christian universalism, which even in the time of Herder exercised a mild control over the national sphere, may well be accepted as the dominant theme of the idea of empire.

It is necessary to reflect here briefly on the well-worn counterargument that this idea of a universal empire was paralyzed by the egotistic policy of the house of Austria, the Habsburgs, who allegedly for three and a half centuries had perceived the Holy Roman Empire only as an appendage of their own territorial power and had used it as a tool to further their own political aims. Obviously there was no dynasty nor for that matter any sovereign power in medieval and early modern history which did not endeavor to promote its political interest and which did not equate this interest with that of the body politic. The Habsburgs were no exception,

[7] Heinrich von Srbik, *Deutsche Einheit, Idee und Wirklichkeit vom heiligen Reich bis Königgrätz* (Munich, 1936), I, 55; see also 23–55 *passim*.

and unquestionably their status was considerably enhanced by the imperial crown, for which that of the Austrian empire of 1804 was a poor substitute. Yet the empire needed the Habsburgs even more than the Habsburgs the empire. Naturally, Austria as a Great Power, as it had emerged at the time of the War of the Spanish Succession, could well use imperial prestige. The whole history of the empire under such rulers as Lothair of Supplinburg in the twelfth century, Adolf of Nassau in the thirteenth, and Charles VII of Bavaria as late as the eighteenth century convincingly proved, however, that the reality of the imperial idea was meaningless without the support of ample hereditary domains or, even better, a Great Power position in terms of European politics. In this sense the position of the Habsburgs with their international affiliation represented the idea of imperial universalism somewhat more convincingly than any other princely dynasty in Germany.[8] A proponent of German national union like Karl Friedrich Moser knew precisely what he was saying when he held, as late as the sixth and seventh decades of the eighteenth century, that only an empire under the Habsburgs could secure a modicum of German unity in diversity.[9] That empire may have been far removed from the direct and powerful impact of the Roman Christian tradition in strictly medieval terms. Yet, as long as it lasted and well beyond its demise, throughout the history of the German Confederation the ideological reflection of that tradition can never be gainsaid.

Recognition of the weakness of the empire in itself has in general not led to its condemnation even under the most adverse conditions of the French advance into Germany from the peace of Lunéville in 1801 to the establishment of the new Confederation of the Rhine in 1806 and the dissolution of the empire itself. As skeptical a thinker as Hegel was seriously concerned with the potentialities of empire reform in 1801/02. So in a wider sense was a statesman like Wilhelm von Humboldt, let alone romantics such as Novalis and August Wilhelm von Schlegel.[10] The real

[8] See also Oswald Redlich, *Das Werden einer Grossmacht. Österreich, 1700–1740* (Brünn, 1942), pp. 333 ff.; Hermann I. Bidermann, *Geschichte der österreichischen Gesamtstaatsidee, 1526–1804*, Part II, 1705–1740 (Innsbruck, 1889), pp. 26 ff.

[9] Hertz, II, 369 f.; Srbik, I, 107, 130 f., 141 ff.; Walter H. Bruford, *Germany in the Eighteenth Century* (Cambridge, 1952), pp. 261 ff., 287 f.; Fritz Valjavec, *Die Entstehung der politischen Strömungen in Deutschland, 1770–1815* (Munich, 1951), pp. 84 ff.; R. Huch, *op. cit.* (see n. 1 above), pp. 160 f., 221 f.

[10] See Georg H. F. Hegel, *Die Verfassung des deutschen Reiches,* ed. Georg Mollatt (Stuttgart, 1935), particularly pp. 118 ff.; Wilhelm von Humboldt, *Druckschrift über die deutsche Verfassung, 1813,* in Puttkamer, ed., *op. cit.* (see n. 1 above), pp. 71–94; Meinecke, *op. cit.* (see n. 2 above), pp. 36 ff.; Valjavec, pp. 328 ff. See further the earlier writings of Friedrich von Gentz, Metternich's later

disparagement of the empire, well to be distinguished from justified criticism, began with the historiography of the Second Reich, which glorified Bismarck's achievement in establishing it under Prussian leadership. Yet this ideology outdistances Bismarck insofar as its proponents maintained claims that he had technically never made. The federation of 1871 was perceived by them to be the very fulfillment of a genuine German empire in lieu of the allegedly rotten structure dissolved in 1806 and unlamented by extreme Prussian historiography.

There were two forces, according to Heinrich von Treitschke, that had led to restoration—nay, more than that, to salvation—"the force of religious freedom," which means the ascendancy of Protestantism over the Catholic Church, and "the force of the Prussian state. It was impossible that the reconstruction of the German state should now be effected by the emperor and the empire. With the rise of Protestantism, the imperial constitution, which had for long been in an extremely fragile condition, became a hateful lie. . . . As soon as the majority of the nation had adhered to the Protestant doctrine, the theocratic office of the emperor became as untenable as was its principal prop, the support of the spiritual princes." Catholicism merges with the house of Austria in the service of the Counter Reformation to bring the empire down, and with its victory Austria parts from the community of German life.[11] French imperialism joined the unholy triad of intriguing and mystical Catholicism and Habsburg's greed for power, which had been so alien to Prussian policy. And while Treitschke quite justly condemns the bartering of the German princes at the *Reichsdeputationshauptschluss* of 1803 (the convention of the delegates of the empire) for additional strips of German ecclesiastic territories by the grace of France he welcomes this development at the same time. "And yet this overthrow was a great necessity. All that was buried was already dead; all that was disturbed was that upon which the history of three centuries had already passed judgment. . . . The ridiculous falsehood of theocracy was at length done away with. . . . The new temporal Germany was capable of movement, of development . . . there might

chief adviser, who deplores the dissolution of the empire on clearly national grounds, in *Briefe von und an Friedrich von Gentz,* Friedrich K. Wittichen, ed., 3 vols. in 4 (Munich, Berlin, 1909–1913), See particularly Vol. II, Gentz's letters to Karl S. Brinckmann of Aug. 9, 1806, pp. 278 ff., and of Nov. 12, 1807, pp. 292 ff., where he states: "A people like ours, united by a genuine German emperor and led in the defense of the fatherland . . . what could it have done?" See also Reinhold Aris, *History of Political Thought in Germany from 1789 to 1815* (London, 1965), pp. 266 ff.

[11] Heinrich v. Treitschke, *History of Germany in the nineteenth century,* trans. Eden and Cedar Paul (New York, 1915), I, 6, 8 f.; see also 3–28 *passim.*

result upon the soil of temporal territorialism, the uprising of a national unified state which would be less of a falsehood than had been the Holy Empire." As to the final act, the abdication of the last emperor, Francis I, in 1806, Treitschke observes: "The empire had traversed the whole circle of earthly destiny; after being an ornament of Germany it had become a detestable creature; and when it at length collapsed it seemed as if a ghost had been laid. The nation remained silent and cold." [12] This doctrine represents actually a nationalist catastrophic theory, not unlike the Marxian social one, with the difference, however, that the true Marxians feel they have not yet reached their goal, whereas Treitschke looked with smug and complete satisfaction at the achievement of 1871. Different only in regard to the less obvious anti-Catholic and anti-Austrian bias, but otherwise essentially similar was Heinrich von Sybel's interpretation. He too saw the dissolution of the empire only as a necessary preliminary step for the future rise of a Prussian imperial synthesis which added to the political philosophy of Frederick II the missing element of Protestant German nationalism.[13] And Erich Marcks, a generation after Treitschke and Sybel, still followed in somewhat modified form the same line of thought. At a time when the official historical interpretation of the Third Reich put Ribbentrop on a par with Bismarck, the latter's small-German solution under Prussian leadership was, naturally enough, seen as merely a preliminary step to the more comprehensive unification of the future. Accordingly, there was even more reason to state, in view of the dissolution of the empire in 1806, "After all, this too was liberation, that now the slowly dying was really dead and gone. New paths were opened up for the whole and its parts." [14] That this "liberation" "liberated" also the *Machtstaatsgedanken,* the Leviathan of Thomas Hobbes, first in the ideological sphere and then in the political one, has been brilliantly shown by Ricarda Huch.[15]

While the aforementioned historians and many of their lesser followers, unlike Mrs. Huch, disparaged the old empire, it is not the purpose of this discussion to depreciate their achievements. Psychological prisoners of a seemingly foreordained Prussian victory under Bismarck, they could not comprehend history as anything but an inevitable course of events, working up to the Prussian triumphs at the battlefields of Königgrätz

[12] Treitschke, I, 216 f., 273.

[13] Heinrich von Sybel, *Die Begründung des Deutschen Reiches durch Wilhelm I.,* 2d. ed. (Munich, 1908), Vol. I; see 12–19 *passim.*

[14] Erich Marcks, *Der Aufstieg des Reiches. Deutsche Geschichte von 1807–1871/78* (Stuttgart, 1936), I, 9; see also in the Preface xiii-xvii; and II, 567 ff.

[15] R. Huch, *op. cit.* (see n. 1 above), pp. 255 ff.

and Sedan and their political consequences. Yet German historians working, by intest, necessity, or both, in a political straitjacket are less to blame in view of the fact that historians of exemplary neutrality in the English-speaking world also failed to see the significance of the first empire, even in its decline. Bryce, to take an outstanding example, observed that "During the later part of the Austrian period from Ferdinand II to Francis II, the Holy Roman Empire was to Germany a mere clog and encumbrance, which the unhappy nation bore, because she knew not how to rid herself of." And Geoffrey Barraclough notes, "Politically [the empire] left no gap, for it had been a nullity since 1648; but with it went the last exiguous bond between the German peoples, the one remaining symbol of German unity." [16]

But how could a political entity which presented in however imperfect form a bond between the German peoples be considered a "nullity"? The very idea of such unity, still clearly visible, surely was a factor of outstanding importance in itself, surpassing in significance the sum of grave institutional shortcomings. How could a political body be written off by historians as inconsequential in view of the fact that it could be replaced only with difficulty? And this difficulty becomes apparent by the very fact that it has not been replaced to this day. The Prussian dominated Kleindeutsche Second Reich of 1871 lacked national comprehensiveness and Hitler's short-lived Grossdeutsche Leviathan of the Third Reich was, of course, the very antithesis of federal union by peaceful means, which the Holy Roman Empire represented to a large measure. Moreover, this empire was allied with a Great Power, that of the Habsburgs, but not penetrated and partly controlled by it as Germany was by Prussia between 1866 and 1918.[17]

It seems fair to conclude that the legend of the harmfulness and at the same time nothingness of the empire—contradictory reproaches—is based on two principal factors. There is first the Prussian interpretation of German history with some built-in specific nationalist and religious patterns of bias, referred to before. Yet as noted also, the interpretation concerning the insignificance of the empire in the late stage of its history transcends by far the ideology of the Prussian school. Here an obvious though not fully rational motivation derived obviously from the unheroic

[16] Bryce, pp. 434; Geoffrey Barraclough, *The Origins of Modern Germany* (New York, 1963), p. 405.

[17] Concerning the use of the terms grossdeutsch and kleindeutsch rather than the inadequate translation Greater German and Small German see Robert A. Kann, *The Multinational Empire* (New York, 1950 and 1964), I, 73 f., 366.

and shabby process of dissolution. While Treitschke rightly denounces the course of action itself, his conclusions are far too sweeping. In fact the interpretation of the dissolution of the empire is linked to a fallacious logical *post hoc, ergo propter hoc*. To assume that nobody will put up a fight for a political body already in a process of gradual disintegration may be correct. To conclude that the absence of a struggle for the preservation of the empire proves a lack of its *raison d'être* is to put the cart before the horse, and precisely this is widely done in the historiography of the dissolution.

Its particulars, the Congress of Rastatt from 1797 to 1799, which failed to achieve agreement on the compensation of the dispossessed princes on the left bank of the Rhine, was uninspiring, to say the least. The same was true for the so-called success of the *Reichsdeputationshauptschluss* in 1803 in eliminating most of the ecclesiastic principalities, a number of the smaller secular ones, and all but six of the free cities. The beneficiaries were, as planned by the French, Prussia and the middle-sized German states. Apart from the principalities and cities deprived of their sovereignty, Austria, then a chief continental opponent of Napoleon, was also indirectly the chief loser. The combined effect of the Treaty of Campo Formio of 1797, the agreement of 1803, and the outcome of the War of the Third Coalition had reduced the Habsburg power in the peace of Pressburg in 1805 to such a degree that it could contribute no longer to the strength of the empire. On the other hand, none of the German states was strong enough to fill the vacated power position of the Habsburgs. The outcome was so certain that Napoleon did not wait to establish the Confederation of the Rhine until accounts with Prussia were settled in October, 1806. The Confederation was proclaimed in July, 1806, less than three months prior to the battle of Jena, and on August 6 Emperor Francis abdicated, thus indicating that he neither hoped for nor expected Prussian support in the preservation of the empire.

All these proceedings were deplorable enough—the greed of the German princes, their kowtowing before the French power, and Prussia's peculiar synthesis of political timidity and territorial ambitions under the leadership of Haugwitz. Equally significant was the narrow-mindedness of the emperor Francis, who did not quite understand either the political or the far-reaching ideological consequence of his abdication. And it was an abdication, not a dissolution, in a legal sense, for neither law nor tradition supported the presumption that the existence of the empire was bound to that of a specific emperor. As Ernst Huber put it, "It was the extinction of the will to maintain the empire not only on the part of . . .

the imperial estates, but within the nation itself, which after the abdication of the emperor . . . brought about not only actually but also in constitutional law the destruction of the empire. Not the legally problematical state act by the emperor, not even the concurring approval of the imperial estates, but the extinction of the will of the nation concerning the empire brought about, constitutionally, the dissolution of the empire." [18] This legal argument is true enough, though the psychological one is not provable. The profound effect of the foregoing events, which amounted to a dismemberment of the empire prior to its actual demise, cannot be denied. This impact of the seizure and dissolution of so many German political entities of long standing, not by the illegitimate descendant of the French revolution but at the behest of the German princes of the old order, answers the argumentation of the Prussian school. The disappearance of the small German states may have served the interests of efficiency, power politics, and economic necessity. Yet in the furthering of German unity the reverse was true. This action dealt a blow to it as far as it was anchored in the tradition of the past, and did not serve its projection in the future either. We can see now that these events furthered the coming renewed struggle for supremacy in Germany and finally and chiefly the Prussianization of Germany.

The ancient empire, on the other hand, represented the contrary trend, that of universality of the German peoples, aligned with but not subordinated to one Great Power. This particular relationship and the particular character of that far-flung multinational power added to the universality. The difference transcends in importance the choice between a grossdeutsch concept of empire including German Austria and one without it, controlled by Prussia. The old empire, with its aligned fringe territories in the eastern Czech, western Flemish and French, and southern Italian associations, did not represent the idea either of a union of German-speaking peoples or even less of the expansion of German national affiliation. It stood for an association of historic units within the frame of medieval traditions. As such the empire idea was in later generations perverted to a pretext for national expansion and oppression; but those who justified their occupation of Czechoslovakia by reference to the residence in Prague of the German emperor Charles IV would not have been at a loss for other specious reasons to rationalize and justify conquest.

On the other hand, the notion cannot easily be dismissed that the his-

---

[18] Ernst R. Huber, *Verfassungsgeschichte*, I, 73; see also 40 ff., 71 ff.; Hartung, *Deutsche Verfassungsgeschichte*, pp. 167 ff., 176 ff.; Holborn, *History of Modern Germany*, II, 366 ff.; Huch, pp. 248 ff.

toric traditional character of the imperial idea might possibly have led to the gradual loosening of nationalist sentiments. It is a fact, however, that the trends of nationalism followed another direction of authoritarian relationship not only between government and people but between government and states or lands. On the other hand the Holy Roman Empire in its time and place represented to the very end the idea of coordinate union between political units. Moreover, this idea was embodied in historical reality, though in the most imperfect form. Therefore it had an important head start as compared with integral nationalism or the doctrine of supremacy in the dualistic struggle for the control of Germany in the following generations. This opportunity to broaden and strengthen the idea of coordinate union was missed, by error, misjudgment, and self-interest of Austria, no less than of Prussia. All the same, the empire, while it lasted, in its synthesis of idea and reality, in its obvious shortcomings and less obvious assets, represented a genuine original system. The argument that it could not be revived because it had no true reality after 1648 may be countered not with a thesis but with a question. Was it perhaps not the weakness but the strength of the empire idea that made it impossible to rebuild an ancient, complex, but precious structure in thought and deed?

The two generations between the dissolution of the old empire and the establishment of a new one in 1871 were not dominated by any even faintly homogeneous ideology. The era from 1789 to 1814 in France was characterized by the one patent factor of revolutionary changes, although these changes were of very different kind and could not be encompassed under the concept of the same revolution. Yet between 1806 and 1871 we pass in the German sphere through various phases tending toward restoration. They include conservative power politics and only one relatively brief phase of revolution, although this revolution of 1848/49 is a landmark of high significance within these two generations. Seen as a whole, the intermediate period—hardly a system—between 1806 and 1871 was characterized by two consistent main themes. Through most of its history it was dominated by the struggle for supremacy in Germany, and at its beginning stood the dissolution of one empire and at its end the establishment of a new one.

Inasmuch as the victory of the North over the South proved to be decisive, the question of restoration should not come into play here at all. It ought, however, to be an issue germane to the establishment of a new empire. In spite of the complexities of the time element of more than sixty years, there is a real restoration problem, if not real restoration, involved here. This negative factor of the non-existence of a German empire for over half a century had not the same significance for the maintenance of law and order in the empire as the interregnum after the death of Frederick II in 1252, Schiller's "die kaiserlose, die schreckliche Zeit." Yet in the realm of political ideas and political power in international relations the issue of empire-wide national union transcended in importance any previous empire crisis.

The idea of national unification during that long middle period from 1806 to 1871 has, of course, many facets, from the mere reestablishment of the old empire with emphasis on restoration of the ecclesiastic and mediatized secular princely houses, to a concept of the constitutional imperial monarchy or republic. The idea of unions includes the grossdeutsch solution with Austria and the kleindeutsch without it, the latter presented again in various forms of Prussian hegemony. All these various shades, aspects, and conflicting trends have, of course, a long history. The purely ideological ones go back to the beginnings of the High Middle Ages. Nevertheless, another observation by Treitschke, whose brilliance, fortunately, is never fully overshadowed by his bias, seems to me in this respect very much to the point. He observes, concerning the state of Prussia after the humiliating defeat of 1806/07,

> It was of great moment for our political life and continues to influence us at the present day, that in the case of Germany the idea of national unity was not as it had been in France, the outcome of the slow ripening of centuries, the natural fruit of a continuous monarchical policy, directed always towards the same goal, but that it reawakened suddenly after prolonged slumber, amid passionate tears, amid dreams of times that had passed away. Hence also its morbid bitterness, for even after the rude hatred of the French which was the issue of that tormented time had passed away, there still remained in the hearts of the spirited Teutons a profound rancour against the foreign world. It seemed impossible to dream of Germany's future greatness without railing at the foreign nations which had sinned so often and so grossly against Central Europe. Hence, also, the remarkably confused nature of the political aspirations of the Germans. . . . Very slowly did the dream of German unity pass from the cultured classes into the masses of the peoples. . . . The honorable love for a united Germany was often led astray into a narrow-minded grasping particularism.[19]

This is the spirit which came into being during the Stein-Hardenberg reform period in Prussia after the peace of Tilsit in 1807. Somewhat less

[19] Treitschke, *op. cit.* (see n. 11 above), I, 351. See also Meinecke, *op. cit.* (see n. 2 above), pp. 80 ff.; Franz Schnabel, *Deutsche Geschichte im neunzehnten Jahrhundert* (Freiburg im Breisgau, 1947), I, 283 ff.

clearly it can be traced in Southern Germany as well and even in Austria during the war of 1809. Despite differences in emphasis, speed of development, and political alignments in the North and the South, all these national trends can be comprehended within one multifaceted union movement. Hartung is correct when he observes that events changed their course entirely at the very moment of the abdication of Francis II as German emperor in 1806, "when the territories with the achievement of full political independence seemed to have reached their objective. This reverse movement led from the German confederation of 1815 and the incorporation of the individual states into the German empire of 1871 to the reduction of the states to the level of lands in the Weimar constitution." [20] Hartung, like Treitschke, believes that French nationalism of the great revolution had channeled its German counterpart from a humanitarian cosmopolitan movement into a political one, which "demanded the reestablishment of a comprehensive political association, as it had existed in the old empire. The struggle of the unitary movement in the nation with the separatist tendencies of the individual states represents one part of the German constitutional history after 1806.

"The second aspect of German constitutional history is the fact that the nation—in contrast to earlier times when only emperor and imperial estates were active agents—now strives for a codetermining influence on her destiny." This means the constitutional movement, which received a chief impetus from the West, in this case from England and France, although an independent German element is present in the estates idea.[21] This development reaches far beyond the settlement of the German question in 1815. Its basic ideas are ably summarized by Ernst Huber. "The spiritual foundations of the strivings for German unity and freedom that continued after 1815 were the philosophy of enlightenment and of idealism, the political theory of romanticism, of liberalism and of democracy. Only a small radical minority of representatives of the idea of the German national state, which operated and argued on this basis, approved *direct action,* that means the decision to create the German national state by violent means." [22]

Does this mean then that the conservative or conservative romantic theories of a Gentz, of Adam Müller, or somewhat later of Friedrich Julius Stahl from the Prussian side moved inevitably in the direction of

[20] Hartung, *Deutsche Verfassungsgeschichte,* p. 173.
[21] *Ibid.,* pp. 173 f. See also F. Valjavec, *op. cit.* (see n. 9 above), pp. 328 ff., 343 ff.; Schnabel, I, 316 ff.; II (1949), 90 ff.; Aris, pp. 21 ff.
[22] Huber, II, 313.

political liberalism? Does the Holy Alliance, the Carlsbad Decrees, the commission to investigate demagogic activities in Mayence, in short all that is usually but too indiscriminately perceived as the "Metternich system" in domestic affairs, stand for nothing but opposition to the idea of union? Did the forces which represent the time span from 1814 to 1848, commonly understood as the restoration, and the subsequent, likewise conservative Pre-March period, stand only for particularism? Did the liberals and, in national matters, pro-liberal romantics monopolize the claims for German unity? This seems to be again the view of Huber. For once he observes a western, that is, French and English oriented, constitutional parliamentary trend in the so-called restoration period. It is checked by a conservative Eastern police-state order under Austro-Russian sponsorship. Prussia was caught between these alternative ideologies in power politics.

> The experience of the twenty-five years between the Congress of Vienna and the change of government in 1840 in Prussia had proved that the German states—even if transformed into constitutional regimes—were individually not capable of developing into members of a European system like that in the West. . . . The political separation of the German states by means of the German confederative system, determined their constitutional dependency from Austria and prevented the effective evolution of a democratic-liberal constitutional state on Western European patterns. Only as a national state could Germany separate from the supremacy of the dynastic-autocratic constitutional concept of the two Eastern powers and align herself with the European idea of the West. *Only as a national state could Germany take the road toward the Western constitutional state. The effective democratization and liberalization of Germany was impossible as long as Germany formed a confederation, even if the individual states introduced technically the institution of the democratic-liberal system.*[23]

These well-reasoned deductions could be challenged on a number of counts such as the ambiguous democratic constitutional character of the Western systems, particularly the French one at that time, and the unambiguous, unequivocally conservative Prussian position. Whether a union of the southern and western German states could have strengthened and sustained the efforts toward genuine constitutional regimes in the face of the pressure of the two great German powers is doubtful. The governments of Bavaria, Württemberg, and Baden had deviated from the moderately liberal course initiated between 1815 and 1820 long before

[23] Huber, II, 315 f. See also Wilhelm Mommsen, *Grösse und Versagen des deutschen Bürgertums* . . . (Stuttgart, 1949), pp. 21 ff.; Schnabel, II, 364 ff.

the revolution of 1848. This fact is hardly surprising in the setting of the overall German political structure between 1815 and 1848. This means above all the German confederation in terms of political and ideological restoration.

In a formal sense the Confederation of 1815, including the final act in Vienna in 1820 qualified as a restoration project insofar as no political continuity existed between the Holy Roman Empire and the new association. The old empire—because of the common judicial institutions and the limited legislative functions of the estates under the presidency of an emperor—could still be considered a quasi-federal body *sui generis*. Legal theory does not question, however, the fully confederate character of the organization of German states of 1815. Here a treaty of international law between sovereign states was the foundation of the new association. The existence of certain common institutions, such as both wider and narrower confederate assemblies in Frankfurt, a confederate army consisting of state contingents, and the obligations of the member states to mutual assistance in a theoretically indissoluble union, could not impair the sovereign status of the member states. These legal transactions required the consent of the individual states, rather than that of joint agencies to which they were subordinated.[24]

The Confederation was carefully designed to give the German states, including Austria and Prussia, a new and on the whole firmer organization.[25] At the same time, according to the ideas of its chief architect, Metternich, the Confederation was to be a bulwark against Jacobinism and any kind of representative democratic institutions associated rightly or wrongly with the French Revolution. Inasmuch as German nationalism, in its mighty upsurge between 1807 and 1814, was to a measure linked to these ideas, the Confederation was also meant to be a first line of defense against the idea of a supposedly liberal national state. This is generally seen as a main reason Metternich opposed the reestablishment of the Holy Roman Empire, which in spite of Prussian objectives would have been

[24] There is virtual unanimous agreement of political theorists on this point. See, for instance instead of many, Josef L. Kunz, *Die Lehre von den Staatenverbindungen* (Stuttgart, 1929), p. 437, and Georg Jellinek, *Allgemeine Staatslehre*, 2d ed. (Berlin, 1905), pp. 745 f. The view of Heinrich von Srbik in *Deutsche Einheit* (see n. 7 above), I, 210 f., that the members of the Confederation were sovereign only in regard to their subjects but not to the Confederation as such can be explained only by Srbik's unfamiliarity with constitutional theory and judicial concepts.

[25] This means, of course, Austria as well as Prussia exclusive of the eastern parts of their territories—basically the Croatian, Hungarian, and Polish lands in the Austrian case and the Polish in the Prussian. These domains had not been part of the Holy Roman Empire either.

within his reach. A compromise might have been possible if the state chancellor and his Prussian counterparts had made concessions to Stein's plans of a far more centralized federal empire. Yet even if Austria could not have agreed to such a proposal, conciliation between confederate and federal plans, as submitted by such a distinguished Prussian statesman, as Wilhelm von Humboldt, and the Prussian chancellor, Prince Hardenberg himself, would have been quite feasible. A federal authority, to which the German states in a limited sphere would have been subordinated, might have come into existence.[26]

There existed, of course, a variety of reasons for this settlement, as it were, such as mutual distrust of Austria and Prussia, the expansionism of Prussia toward the German west and of Austria toward Central Italy. Concern of the smaller states for their sovereignty played an important part. There was also justified fear that the Habsburg emperor could no longer command the single-handed authority to intervene as imperial arbiter in German affairs. All this contributed to the compromise concerning leadership between the two German Great Powers and built-in confederal safeguards. There are ideological factors involved here also, which cannot be determined precisely. Anxiety in regard to the rise of German nationalism was no doubt instrumental in the establishment of the German Confederation. Yet the extent and the intensity of such fears can hardly be measured.[27]

This difficulty is particularly great because the political philosophy of Metternich and, even more, of his adviser Gentz was in itself not adverse to the idea of German union, including even the ideological concept of a common German "fatherland." Both men were greatly concerned, however, about the potential excesses of such movement, as they saw it, such as the Wartburg Festival of 1817, the assassination of Kotzebue in 1819, the republican tendencies of the Hambach Festival of 1832, and the Frankfurt riots of 1833. Here the architects of the Confederation did not distinguish at all between the very different political directions from which the disturbances of the reestablished order arose. All manifestations of public dissent appeared to them only as tentacles of the same revolutionary monster.[28]

[26] Huber, I, 483 ff., 510 ff., 538, 538 ff.; see also Enno E. Kraehe, *Metternich's German Policy* (Princeton, 1963), I, 187 ff.

[27] Henry C. Meyer, *Mitteleuropa in German Thought and Action, 1815–1945* (The Hague, 1955), pp. 10 f.; Hartung, *Deutsche Verfassungsgeschichte*, pp. 176 ff.; Huber, I, 477 ff.; Holborn, *History of Modern Germany*, II, 450 f., 466 f.; for a different interpretation see Kraehe, pp. 78 f., 278 ff.

[28] See in particular E. v. Puttkamer, ed., *op. cit.* (see n. 1 above), documents 74–101; Prince Richard Metternich-Winneburg, ed., *Aus Metternichs nachgelassenen*

On the other hand, whatever the major ideological and minor administrative shortcomings of the German Confederation were, in terms of an enlightened social philosophy, the verdict of history leaves little doubt that it represented an organization superior in efficiency to that of the old empire. Hartung rightly observes that it would be wrong to match the structure of the Confederation against the hopes and dreams of German nationalism after the 'wars of liberty'—conveniently renamed as 'wars of liberation' from a foreign enemy. "Compared with the constitution of the old empire the Act of Confederation represents decidedly a step toward improvement. Not only were the borders with the foreign countries clearly and distinctly drawn now, but the Confederation in its foreign relations acted more decisively than the empire. All the members of the Confederation were obliged to support each other against any aggression." [29]

Papieren, 8 vols. (Vienna, 1880–1883); see Vol. III, pp. 270 ff. Metternich's instructions of September 1, 1819, pp. 270 ff., in which he outlines his whole policy in regard to the Confederation; see *ibid.* also, Metternich's letter to the minister of the grand duchy of Baden in Vienna, 372 ff., which expresses a measure of ideological affirmation of the idea of German unity. See further Vol. V, Metternich's welcoming speech to the conference of German ministers of January, 1834, in Vienna and his address closing the conference in June of the same year, 600 ff., 606 ff. Here emphasis is put equally on the fight against political radicalism, the representative constitutional system beyond the estates institutions, and concern for the dangers threatening "our common fatherland" (p. 607). See finally Vol. VIII, Metternich's memorandum to the Reichsverweser archduke John in Frankfurt of August, 1848, 443 ff., which summarizes Metternich's views, why he had opposed the restoration of the empire in 1814/15. See *ibid.,* also, the clear and precise argumentation, why a German federation in lieu of the Confederation of 1815 would only serve the interests of Prussian hegemonical claims.

See further Heinrich von Srbik, *Metternich,* 3 vols. (Munich, 1925–1954), I, 193 ff., concerning the establishment of the Confederation, and II, 85 ff., on Metternich's German policy in the 1840's.

See also Prince Richard Metternich-Winneburg, ed., *Friedrich von Gentz, Österreichs Theilnahme an den Befreiungskriegen, . . . 1813–1815* (Vienna, 1887); see particularly Gentz's notes of September, 1814, pp. 403 f., and June, 26, 1815, pp. 552 ff., in which he not only opposes the reestablishment of the empire, but appears far more skeptical than Metternich concerning the potential consequences of the German Confederation. See further F. K. Wittichen, ed., *Briefe von und an Friedrich von Gentz,* Vol. III/1, letter of Nov. 15, 1813, to Metternich in which Gentz perceives an Austro-Prussian alliance in the frame of a German Confederation implicit as substitute for an imperial organization. See also Eugen Guglia, *Friedrich von Gentz* (Vienna, 1901), pp. 248 ff.; Golo Mann, *Secretary of Europe* (New Haven, 1946), 265 ff.; and Paul Sweet, *Friedrich von Gentz, Defender of the Old Order* (Madison, 1941), pp. 264 ff. Gentz died shortly after the Hambach Festival, prior to the Frankfurt riots against the confederate assembly.

For a contrary view denying completely the national element in the Austrian policy in 1814/1815 see H. Rössler, *op. cit.* (see n. 4 above), II, 125 ff., 197 ff., 251.

[29] Hartung, p. 181; Holborn, II, 447.

This opportunity for decisive action existed only for the period of the congress system, roughly until 1822, and even then it was based more on cooperation with the major European powers than between the members of the Confederation themselves. Nevertheless, potentially the Confederation remained in regional affairs a more effective organization than the empire had been after 1648, if not after 1555. Dahm goes even farther in this respect than Hartung. Recognizing the obvious, the inability of the Confederation to represent the main currents of German national life, he acknowledges, nevertheless, that "The German Confederation has preserved order and peace for the center of Europe throughout half a century." [30] And Huber perceives a specific merit of the Confederation in the fact that it maintained for a long time the equilibrium between the two leading powers. Neither of them exploited its position, according to Huber. "The federalism of the German Confederation served well in the side-by-side position of equality and hegemonical hierarchy." [31] This again is probably an overly optimistic evaluation, though one on the part of a genuine authority. Still more positive is the judgment of the head of the moderate Prussian school, Erich Marcks, who expressly affirms the ideological significance of the Confederation in terms of German union. "The Confederation was grossdeutsch; that was its virtue. For that reason alone it certainly had to be loose. It continued the old empire in a less presumptuous but more effective frame. It was infinitely better, than it [the empire] had become. It was more dreary but more clear-cut [in its structure]. Under Austria [meaning Austrian leadership] the central European direction of the [bygone] empire continued, its advantages and potentialities remained unblocked." [32]

This indeed is the salient point. The Confederation, as an association of sovereign states, represented a grossdeutsch order. In that sense it was a genuine successor of the empire, inferior in ideological appeal, superior in organization and efficiency. It did not fall short of the institutions of the Holy Roman Empire either in a constitutional, a military defensive, an administrative, or even an economic sense. The reactionary measures initiated by the Carlsbad Decrees of 1819 and the political police control established at Mayence and operative until 1848, were rightly condemned by a liberal democratic philosophy. At the same time these actions offered convincing proof for the administrative effectiveness of the Confederation. Obviously it was not designed to represent in any way the consensus

[30] Georg Dahm, *Deutsches Recht* (Hamburg, 1944), p. 177.
[31] Huber, I, 674.
[32] *Der Aufstieg des Reiches* (see n. 14 above), I, 99.

of the people, let alone a genuine spirit of national union. According to its founding fathers, the representatives of the princes, it should not represent but should rather direct, though not necessarily outright oppress, the national spirit as it had developed since the downfall of Prussia in 1807 and the attempted rise of Austria in 1809.[33]

Shortcomings and strong points of the Confederation are obvious. Those who stress exclusively the former and deny the latter frequently commit the double error of confounding their own system of values with that of an organization whose objectives were by full intent at variance with the programs of national and liberal union. This attitude is found almost equally on the Right and the Left. Franz Mehring, the orthodox Marxian, condemns "the miserable contraption" of the German Confederation as Lassalle had done before him, since it did not represent democratic progress; and in the same negative but reverse sense Treitschke on the far Right rejoices: "As we look back upon the life-history of the Germanic Federation we see that it is upon this that depends its historic renown: it did not possess power to prevent the increase in strength of the only living German state, of the state that was destined at a later date to destroy the Federation and to bestow upon our unhappy nation a new and worthy order." [34] We face here the strange spectacle of a theory on the Right which hails catastrophes for the sake of radical change.

And yet Treitschke has a point insofar as the Prussian government between 1815 and 1866 did everything by fair means or foul—or perhaps before 1848 by efficient and more often inefficient means—to wreck the grossdeutsch solution and to establish instead not only Prussian leadership but Prussian hegemonical power. Of the situation until 1848, when the prospects for revolutionary or restorative change suddenly widen in either direction, it seems fair to say that the whole policy initiated by the *Zollverein* (the customs union) of 1819 was aimed at the Prussian dominance in Germany and against the dualistic leadership of the Confederation. True enough, from Fichte to Paul Pfizer, Friedrich von Hagen, Friedrich Julius Stahl—none of them born as Prussians—and from many others the message of German unification under Prussia was voiced and

---

[33] See for instance F. Meinecke, *op. cit.* (see n. 2 above), pp. 89 ff.; F. Valjavec, *op. cit.* (see n. 9 above), pp. 361 ff.; Walter C. Langsam, *The Napoleonic Wars and German Nationalism in Austria* (New York, 1930), pp. 83 ff.; H. Rössler, *op. cit.* (see n. 4 above), I, 436 ff.

[34] Franz Mehring, *Zur preussischen Geschichte von Tilsit bis zur Reichsgründung* (Berlin, 1930), pp. 220 f.; Treitschke, *op. cit.* (see n. 11 above), II, 135 f. The translation "Germanic Federation" for Deutscher Bund by E. and C. Paul is incorrect. The correct term would be German or Germanic confederation.

promoted. True, also, to these men, with the qualified exception of Stahl, German union was a primary aim and Prussian leadership a mere means to such end. Certainly also a sincere feeling of German nationalism and a rejection of the multinational Habsburg empire in the leadership of Germany was involved here.[35] Yet, although the Habsburg Great Power could exist without dominating Germany, Prussia's Great Power status was irretrievably bound to her status in Germany. In practical politics the issue of Prussian predominance had to take precedence over that of a comprehensive German union.

In this sense the period from the dissolution of the empire in 1806 to the revolution of 1848 was characterized by three main trends. First there was the fight against the threatened revolution and for the European status quo outside the Confederation, in which Austria and Prussia concurred; second, the Austrian endeavor to maintain the Confederation for the sake of political equilibrium in Germany; and third, the Prussian policy of hegemony. It is not always possible to draw a clear line between an Austrian policy directed toward a modified grossdeutsch union and a Prussian kleindeutsch anti-union policy. As to the factor of emphasis, there can be little doubt. The Confederation as designed and willed by Austria was meant to be a successor of the old empire and therefore the mainstay of a restorative process. Prussia's claim to hegemony was and had to be directed against a grossdeutsch union. In the end it stood also against any genuine federative principle altogether, except on Prussia's own terms. In the relations to the member states of the Confederation the Prussian policy was as revolutionary in principle as the Austrian policy was restorative. In a sense the outcome of the revolution of 1848–1849 represented not only the conflict but also the synthesis of both philosophies.

The German revolution, and the Austrian revolution of 1848–1849 as far as it pertains to Germany, had obviously a threefold character, a national, a constitutional, and—regionally very important—a social one as well. The first two principal issues represented not only the struggle between grossdeutsch and kleindeutsch programs, not only conflicts between republicans and adherents of hereditary or elective monarchy under Habsburg or Hohenzollern. There were not only conflicts between the two German Great Powers, based on Prussian and, after the appointment of Prince Felix Schwarzenberg as prime minister in November,

[35] Meinecke, pp. 256 ff., 332 ff., 491 f.; F. Schnabel, *op. cit.* (see n. 19 above), II, 364 ff., Theodore Hamerow, *Restoration, Revolution, Reaction, Economics and Politics in Germany, 1815–1871* (Princeton, 1958), pp. 56 ff.

1848, strongly emphasized Austrian claims for domination of the German sphere. What happened in Germany and in particular what occurred at the seat of the National Assembly in Frankfurt represented also honest and not entirely unsuccessful endeavors to reconcile these issues.

We cannot analyze here the manifold crosscurrents between political Right and Left on national constitutional issues and in particular the almost complete reversal of both fronts in connection with the national problem. In this context only one problem, the restoration of the empire, can be discussed. As Mommsen sees it, "The thinking at St. Paul's church was in strict conflict with the concept of empire which was linked to 1648. The conditions created by the Westphalian peace treaty were perceived as a rock-bottom point in German history. The planned federation was consciously understood in contrast to the old empire. . . . True, the terms empire and imperial power (*Reich und Reichsgewalt*) were taken over, because the word Reich corresponded to the continuity of our history. . . . But one cannot speak of an 'empire mythology.' . . ."[36]

It is interesting to see how the idea of empire transgressed the political fronts in various directions.

> Particularist deputies thought an empire would be a unitary state. The Prussian government proposed to eliminate the words empire and imperial power. One deputy compared an empire in Berlin with the decadent empire in Istanbul. Others thought one could speak of empire only if Austria was included. Representatives of the "Left" asserted [and this is particularly notable] that the word empire was popular with the people; the people had used the term prior to the national assembly. . . . This too had nothing to do with imperial tradition and veneration for the Middle Ages. Just the proponents of a hereditary empire . . . were against the "antediluvian memories." In 1848 the old empire was consistently referred to as a setup that represented neither national state nor federation. The particularist forces were castigated and it was said that the elective monarchy had failed. During the constitutional deliberations historians from all sides . . . misinterpreted history . . . but nobody idealized the medieval empire. Only very few thought here of a great tradition to be resumed.

In particular the champions of the idea of a hereditary empire shared with the Left a good deal of anti-Habsburg sentiments and the Grossdeutschen on the whole did not subscribe to the romantic cult of glorification of the Middle Ages.[37] The rejection of the imperial crown by

[36] W. Mommsen, *op. cit.* (see n. 23 above), p. 184.

[37] Mommsen, p. 185; see also 73 ff. The standard work on the issue is Veit Valentin, *Geschichte der deutschen Revolution 1848-49,* 2 vols. (Berlin, 1930-31);

Frederick William IV, a king indoctrinated with a full measure of admiration for medieval imperial rites, confirmed this overall view. The royal rebuff administered to the delegation of the Frankfurt Assembly on April 3, 1849 meant neither primarily contempt for a crown by the grace of Parliament nor rejection of German unity altogether. Even a weak Prussian king's position implied rather a scale of priority, first the crown of Prussia, then German union on Prussian terms, and thirdly, only the preservation of the status quo, princely power. This view is borne out in Bismarck's memoirs, when he states that the Frankfurt Assembly "honestly or dishonestly deceived itself as to the fact that, in the case of a conflict between a resolution of the Frankfurt Diet and a Prussian royal decree, the former, so far as seven-eighths of the Prussian population was concerned, would be regarded as of little or no weight." And further, "My satisfaction in those days at the refusal of the imperial crown by the king was not due to the judgment I had formed of his personal qualities, but rather to an increased sensibility for the prestige of the Prussian crown and its wearer, and still more to my distinctive distrust in the development after the barricades of 1848 and their parliamentary consequences." [38] As Bismarck put it in a different context, "Never, not even in Frankfurt did I doubt, that the key to German politics was to be found in princes and dynasties and not in publicists, whether in parliament and the press or on the barricades." [39]

All this and far more could be adduced to prove that if there was general consensus in Frankfurt and throughout the Germanies it was against the reestablishment of a revised replica of the Holy Roman Empire. Such a proposition seemed to be absurd as early as 1813, after the defeat of Napoleon had become inevitable, and it was even more so in 1848. Yet this was not really the issue. Neither was it, of course, the restoration of the empire of Charlemagne, of the Ottonian empire, of that of the Golden Bull of 1356, or that of 1648 or of any other time. The problem was one not of the restoration of a specific empire by approximation but of the empire itself beyond and irrespective of any of its specific and imperfect materializations in history. It would be tempting to say that the constitution adopted in Frankfurt on March 28, 1849, exemplary in many ways,

see particularly I, 467 ff., II, 11 ff., 297 ff., 448 ff. For the grossdeutsch and kleindeutsch issue with particular regard to Austria see also Robert A. Kann, *The Multinational Empire*, 2 vols. (New York, 1950, 1964), I, 68–84.

[38] Otto von Bismarck, *Reflections and Reminiscences*, 2 vols, translated under the supervision of J. A. Butler (New York and London, 1899), I, 61, 63.

[39] *Ibid.*, I, 318.

represented simply the empire idea itself, irrespective of its realization in the past.[40] Yet this would not be correct either.

The Frankfurt constitution revived the idea not merely of an empire but of a far more definite political concept: the association of the German peoples in a federation of sovereign states based on consent of the governed, rather than a confederation of sovereign states sponsored by their princes. This meant a distinct restorative drive of a political body which throughout its thousand years of history had shown many diverse facets, but also some common executive, legislative, and judicial functions in a semi-federal order. In the relationship between the princely rights and the German peoples, between the Habsburg and the Prussian power, the constitution meant compromise, but above all it meant a distinct and, as it turned out, terminal landmark of the German restorative process by peaceful means. Had the specific, albeit feeble empire structure of 1806 been replaced in actuality and not merely on paper by the constitutional model of 1849, we could indeed comprehend this as a true and successful restoration, brought about at the very end of the life-span of the political generation that, in its young manhood, had lived under the Holy Roman Empire.

This rather positive evaluation of the achievements at Frankfurt from the point of German union, not merely as a utopian scheme but as a positive step forward, is shared by a large number of distinguished historians from Sybel to Marcks, Srbik, Valentin, Hartung, and Huber.[41] Older historians like Sybel and more recently Marcks and Srbik emphasize a lack of a sense of political reality, a too far-reaching ambition and poor political strategy on the part of the fathers of the constitution of 1849. This is considered to be one of the reasons for the failure of the efforts to obtain a moderately unitary empire structure. Nevertheless there is general consensus that the Assembly in St. Paul's represented an important ideological step in the direction of future unity. As Huber puts it, "The urge for union in a national state remained alive beyond the defeat of 1814/15 and the defeat of 1848/49. . . . It is rare in history that a

---

[40] The official version of the *Verfassung des Deutschen Reiches* is the one printed by C. Krebs-Schmitt (Frankfurt am Main, 1849). See also Johannes Hohlfeld, ed., *Deutsche Reichsgeschichte in Dokumenten 1849–1934*, 2d ed., 4 vols. (Berlin, 1939), I, 1–27.

[41] H. von Sybel, *op. cit.* (see n. 13 above), I, 235, 125 ff., 201 ff.; E. Marcks, *op. cit.* (see n. 14 above), I, 270 ff., 295 ff., 311 ff.; Srbik, *op. cit.* (see n. 7 above), I, 317 ff., 386 ff., 437; Valentin, II, 297 ff., 359 f., 375 ff.; Hartung, *op. cit.* (see n. 1 above), pp. 187 ff., E. R. Huber, *op. cit.* (see n. 1 above), II, 791 ff.

political movement after a double failure . . . remained unbroken." [42]
Wilhelm Mommsen went far beyond this opinion and that of his fellow
historians when he observed in 1949, "If today the German people, in spite
of zone boundaries, land particularism, and the deep rift between East
and West, have remained a political community concerned with the same
problems and worries, this may be perhaps the most important political
consequence of the year 1848. Only the revolution has formed the German
people into a political community in spite of its failure. . . ." [43] This view
may possibly carry the significance of the revolution as far in one direction as the more customary views of pre-National Socialist German national historiography carried it in another. There the significance of the
revolution and within it the works of the Assembly in St. Paul's church is
seen mainly as a prelude to the establishment of the empire of 1871. One
might well say, the revolution was to the pre-Hitlerian nationalists what
the empire of 1871 was to the National Socialists: a prelude, here to the
Second Empire, there to the Third. Neither of these views understands the
Assembly at St. Paul's in its own democratic terms.

The chief error of such interpretations lies not so much in the differest
evaluations of political realism and utopianism or Grossdeutsche and
Kleindeutsche historical trends as in the belief that the revolution represented an intermediate step in the German unification movement. It was
actually a final one, unless we consider occupation and annexation by
force of arms—the National Socialist conquest of Austria and of the
Sudeten territories in 1938—as part of the union movement. If we disregard these tragic and sinister episodes, then the facts are obvious.
Neither the revolution of 1848 nor specifically the Frankfurt constitution
of 1849 can be associated with the victory of the grossdeutsch idea in the
realm of practical politics. And yet, never again in the course of the following four generations has the grossdeutsch union movement on a
democratic basis come as relatively close to realization as during the
revolution. The constitution of 1849 represents thus a final effort to reestablish the empire short of large-scale violence. The years 1848 and 1849
terminate a restorative process, though not yet the end of an intermediate
order that culminates in the establishment of the kleindeutsch solution
under Prussian hegemony between 1866 and 1871. We turn now to this
last phase of the intermediate political conditions between 1806 and 1871.

After the failure of the revolution in 1849 the struggle for supremacy in
Germany intensified. In the North the union scheme of an inner German

[42] Huber, II, 314.
[43] W. Mommsen, p. 216; see also 221 ff.

confederation under Prussian leadership was pressed forward. The conditional three kings' alliance between Prussia, Hanover, and Saxony and above all the activities of the Erfurt Parliament in 1849/50, which adopted a constitution for Prussian German union, were important steps in this direction. On the other hand, it is true that Schwarzenberg's Middle European schemes, preceded by demands that the entire Habsburg empire with all its Germanic and non-Germanic peoples should become part of the Confederation, indicated a clear expansionist policy in the South. The Austrian presidency in the Confederation, previously more or less an honorary vestige of ancient imperial rights, was now actually used to exercise supremacy in Germany. The short-range Austrian victory over Prussia, symbolized rather than manifested by the Punctation of Olmütz (Olomouc) in November, 1850, gave the old Confederation a brief renewed life. As with most concessions forced at the point of a gun, the Prussian retreat to the status quo was of short duration. Schwarzenberg's death in 1852 terminated Austria's daring imperialist policy.

It may well be argued that even before that time German nationalism and European power politics moved clearly in the Prussian direction. The weakness of the king, Frederick William IV, and the indifferent Prussian political leadership in the 1850's made little difference in this respect. Austria—involved in national conflicts, threatened by a potential Russian advance in the Balkans and the Italian unification movement in the south—could hardly have become truly supreme in Germany even if Schwarzenberg had stayed at the helm. With his death political developments until 1866, including the Austrian plan of 1863 to modernize the Confederation with a sprinkling of truly representative institutions, were actually rearguard actions. They could at best delay the inevitable Prussian victory.[44]

Much ink has been spilled over the question whether Bismarck's policy, initiated almost immediately after his appointment as Prussian prime minister in 1862, meant nothing but a straight fight to assert and extend the Great Power position of Prussia. In this struggle, German union,

---

[44] Hartung, pp. 194 ff.; Srbik, *op. cit.* (see n. 7 above), II, 17 ff., 56 ff., 92 ff., IV, 1–67. H. C Meyer, *Mitteleuropa* (The Hague, 1955), pp. 18 ff.; Robert A. Kann, *Das Nationalitätenproblem der Habsburgermonarchie* (Graz, Cologne, 1964), II, 72 ff.; Huber, II, 885 ff., III, 199 ff.; Heinrich Friedjung, *Der Kampf um die Vorherrschaft in Deutschland,* 2 vols. (Stuttgart 1897–98), I, 3–63 *passim,* Otto Pflanze, *Bismarck and the Development of Germany: The Period of Unification, 1815–1871* (Princeton, 1963), pp. 126 ff., 156 ff., 182 ff., Walter Bussmann, *Das Zeitalter Bismarcks,* Vol. III, Part 3 of *Handbuch der deutschen Geschichte,* ed. Leo Just (Konstanz, 1956), pp. 24 ff., 38 ff., 73 ff.

according to some, was merely the means to the end of Prussian hegemony in Germany and continental Europe and—equally important —of the preservation of the old Prussian Junker state of Frederick William I and Frederick II.[45] There are others—of German national, particularly pan-German, leanings as distinguished from liberals of grossdeutsch preference—who, until 1933, saw Bismarck almost exclusively as the architect of German union. This kind of historiography was then forced, between 1933 and 1945, to reduce him to the mere precursor of an alleged terminal union under Hitler. At far as such historians (and their number is large) are concerned with genuine historical evidence at all, they depend heavily on the views of the old Bismarck between his dismissal in 1890 and his death in 1898. At the time he allowed himself to be used by pan-German radical propaganda it is fair to assume that not only old age but defiance of the Kaiser played a major part in the motivations of his utterances. One is well advised to pay greater attention to Bismarck's actions in office and—with discrimination—to his recollections of these actions.

In this sense the more moderate leaders of the Prussian and the grossdeutsche trends in German historiography, though neither was entirely free from the influence of the National Socialist era, strike a far more sensible middle ground. Erich Marcks shows convincingly how the younger Bismarck at the time of the Erfurt Parliament and the Olmütz (Olomouc) punctations wanted the German question to be used merely as a tool to save and strengthen the position of Prussia in preparation for her future part in German affairs. Only through the opportunities unfolding after Königgrätz in the period of the North German Confederation did the union come more clearly into focus, although the major decisions were not taken prior to the outbreak of the war of 1870.[46] Srbik, though from a somewhat different ideological basis, concurs in essence with Marcks: "The architect of the second empire never became a Gross-

[45] This is basically, though not exclusively, the view of the Marxian Left. See for instance F. Mehring, *op. cit.* (See n. 34 above), pp. 381 f. In regard to the national question as distinguished from the social one, the view of some outstanding liberal writers comes at points close to this viewpoint. See for instance Erich Eyck, *Bismarck,* 3 vols. (Erlenbach-Zürich, 1941–44). See II, 145 ff.; 41 f., concerning Bismarck's relationship to the federalist Konstantin Frantz.

[46] Erich Marcks, *Bismarck* (Stuttgart, 1951), pp. 569 f., in reference to Bismarck, *Reflections and Reminiscences,* I, 44 ff., 59 ff., on the revolutionary era; concerning the period after 1866 see E. Marcks, *Der Aufstieg des Reiches,* II, 276 ff., 349 ff., 382 ff., 514 ff.; Bismarck, *Reflections and Reminiscences,* II, 76 ff., 126 ff. See also Theodor Schieder, *Das Kaiserreich von 1871 als Nationalstaat* (Cologne 1961), pp. 10 ff.; and Bussmann, pp. 100 ff.

deutscher; yet even in the peace negotiations of 1866 he did not yet strive for the kleindeutsch solution." Königgrätz means to Srbik final termination of the idea of the old empire and not yet the beginning of the new one.[47] These judgments conform to reality and not only to *realpolitik*. The Bismarckian idea of German union was no mere rationalization of Prussian imperialism and was certainly not devoid of traces which affirmed national union in an ideological sense. Yet this national policy was furnished with a built-in system of priorities and within this system the Prussian position always came first and the imperial second. The old king and first emperor, William I, in his initial protests against the imperial dignity represented certainly not Bismarck's policy in 1870/71 but his innermost feelings perhaps better than the chancellor himself.

Much more controversial is the line of argument that Bismarck intended to fulfill not only the national claims of the German people but their constitutional democratic ones as well. According to this view Bismarck was the true heir of the revolution of 1848, a democratic one at that. According to Huber, the "posthumous victory of the bourgeois revolution was all the more complete since Bismarck's establishment of the empire fulfilled not only the national union demands (*nationalstaatlichen*) but in principle also the democratic and liberal claims of 1848. . . . Compared with the preconstitutional authoritarian state of late absolutism, the Bismarckian empire, with its protection of freedom, its parliamentary rights to participate in decisions, and its equal franchise, could hardly be distinguished from revolutionary constitutional ideals of 1848/49. . . . Not only the national, but also the *liberal and democratic program* of 1848/49 exerted itself in 1870/71." [48] And Veit Valentin, a historian of definite liberal persuasion, states, "But the truly creative of his [Bismarck's] achievements consists in the fact that for a certain time he merged revolution and counterrevolution. . . . Only knowledge of the true domestic history of 1848/49 makes it understandable" that the imperial constitution of 1871—according to Valentin, under existing conditions a masterpiece—became what it was.[49] Here the democratic merits and above all the motivations of Bismarck are not as clearly stated as with Huber but are just as clearly implied. Bismarck himself, with extraordinary frankness, gives short shrift to this interpretation. "The acceptance of universal franchise was a weapon in the war against Austria and other foreign countries, in the war for German Unity, as well as a threat to use

---

[47] Srbik, *op. cit.* (see n. 7 above), IV, 466, 467.
[48] Huber, II, 314 f.
[49] V. Valentin, *op. cit.* (see n. 37 above), II, 591.

the last weapons in a struggle against coalitions. In a war of this sort, when it becomes a matter of life and death one does not look at the weapons that one seizes, nor the value of what one destroys in using them: one is guided at the moment by no other thought than the issue of the war, and the preservation of one's external independence; the settling of affairs and reparation of the damage has to take place after the peace." And in an almost naïve way Bismarck adds that he favors equal franchise as long as the secret ballot, not germane to the German character, is not demanded.[50]

He did not say, and did not really have to say, why he sustained a very unequal three-class franchise in Prussia. Although this was an important point, the main issue was the relationship between empire and Prussia or, more correctly, the steering of imperial policies by Prussia. Neither the constitution of the so-called North German Confederation of 1867— actually a federation—nor its offspring, the new imperial constitution of 1871, contained the Bill of Rights so firmly placed in the constitution of Frankfurt. Civil rights in Prussia—and this meant three-fifths of the population and more than three-fifths of the territory of the empire as a whole—were in substance based on the state constitution of 1850. General equal franchise was guaranteed for the Reichstag elections but not for any of the twenty-six state legislatures. Yet the center of domestic administration lay decidedly in the state administrations. Too often the principles of the federal constitution applied only in a restricted and indirect way (article 3 of the constitution). In the federal sphere the executive and legislative branches were in practice by no means coordinated and the superior position of the former partly invalidated the liberal constitutional provisions for the latter. The direction of foreign affairs rested largely with the emperor, and the military agenda in a somewhat devious way with the emperor in his capacity as king of Prussia. Inasmuch as the ingeniously designed Federal Council stabilized this constitutional setup, it became the true bulwark and guarantee of Prussian supremacy in Germany and of Bismarck's order in Prussia and therewith indirectly in the empire as well. This appears to be equally true socially and politically.

In view of the restrictions of the federal sphere of action in the domain of representative government, parallels between the new federal franchise system of 1871 and that envisaged in 1849 are not really meaningful. The same applies to analogies between a federal civil rights legislation under the control of the representatives of the people as planned in 1848/49 and one still largely administered by the princes in the individual states of the

[50] Bismarck, II, 65.

Second Empire. Despite obvious similarities in individual institutions and constitutional provisions, the trends of the assembly at St. Paul's and of the Berlin constitution of April, 1871, move in opposite directions: a strengthening of the rights of the individual citizen versus the state by way of federal protection there, an enhancement of the rights of the state with little interference on the part of the federation in the domestic sphere here. Where neither states nor individuals outside of Prussia had much say, that is, in the foreign and military sphere, the emperor in his added capacity as king of Prussia could step in.[51]

There is another point to be considered. The defenders of Bismarckian "liberalism" emphasize the fact that his constitutions of 1867 and 1871 had approached the spirit of the work at St. Paul's church. Yet even if this heavily contested supposition were granted for argument's sake, it should be remembered that the Western world had not stood still during these twenty-two years between 1849 and 1871. Labor legislation and the extension of the franchise in England, modifications of Napoleon III's dictatorship in France, to be followed by the democratic reforms of the Third Republic, and liberal constitutional movements in Austria, Italy, Spain, and other countries had moved in several respects far beyond the social and political setting of 1848. It did not mean too much that Germany had now in a merely legal, formal sense reached the stage of 1848 in the constitutional sphere and had not gone much beyond it in the social one.

Had Germany really advanced toward Union? Here historiography and the philosophy of nationalism outside of the sphere dominated by Prussia have somewhat overstated the failure to arrive at the grossdeutsch solution, barred since the peace at Prague with Austria in 1866. Correspondingly the same doctrines minimized the kleindeutsch settlement as a mere substitute for a grander design. In terms of national values the solution of 1871 was a painful compromise with an ideal extolled by moderate national liberals and for a time by integral nationalists. Yet in retrospect it is difficult to see how Bismarck could have ever established a viable na-

---

[51] For a convenient edition of the constitution of 1871 see J. Hohlfeld, ed., *op. cit.* (see n. 40 above), I, 87 ff. See also Philipp K. Zorn, *Die deutsche Reichsverfassung,* 3d ed. (Leipzig, 1933), pp. 32 ff.; see further Hartung, pp. 273 ff.; Huber, III, 641 ff., 702 ff.; Dahm, *Deutsches Recht,* pp. 186 ff.; T. Schieder, pp. 78 ff. The fact that two of the chancellors, Prince Hohenlohe and Count Hertling, were actually Bavarians did not change this arrangement substantially, since they were at the same time Prussian prime ministers and had to uphold the Prussian position. Only the appointment of Prince Max of Baden just a month prior to the collapse of 1918 initiated a belated change of the system.

tional community on the terms of the grossdeutsch solution. Furthermore, the antiliberal and militaristic spirit of the Second Empire was by no
means irretrievably associated with the concept of a kleindeutsch establishment. When Bismarck in his famous speech of 1862 declared that the
great questions of the day—including the national ones—would be decided through "blood and iron," he did not mean to imply that they could
not be settled otherwise. He wanted to say, and from his point of view
quite correctly, that any other solution would mean the establishment not
of a Prusso-German empire based on the principles of the Hohenzollern
soldier-state but a constitutional liberal body, very likely a democratic
republic. After all, quite a few honest German liberals had fought for the
kleindeutsch settlement. As they saw it, the movement toward this limited
goal was, throughout its history between 1815 and 1871, associated by and
large with somewhat more liberal ideas than those which prevailed in the
multinational Habsburg empire.[52] Only after Austria was forced to
withdraw from the German Confederation in 1866 was the issue of
liberalism versus conservatism settled in the North in favor of the latter.
In this sense the decision of Königgrätz, irrespective of liberal or antiliberal political currents in Austria, was indeed fateful but not necessarily
irrevocable. A more liberal empire, less strictly centralized in the Prussian
spirit, might have left the way open for an association with German
Austria, if and when the Habsburg monarchy should dissolve. The provisions of the treaties of Versailles and St. Germain made such an affiliation
certainly far more difficult. Hitler's aggression wrecked its possibility altogether for the foreseeable future.

Indeed, not the kleindeutsch solution in itself but the Prussian version
of a kleindeutsch solution undermined the chances for German union
short of violence. In stating this, the shallow and fake allegation that the
German North is ethnically and psychologically less adaptable than the
South and West to democratic reform is emphatically denied. It is certainly not the issue here. This study takes no position on whether German
union in itself would have been good or bad. It does take one with respect
to how far any planned or actual political order represented the idea of
genuine national union of the German peoples. This has little to do with
the specific form of political organization in the frame of federation or
confederation. It has everything to do with the problem of coordination
of peoples or states or their subordination to another power. The constitutional order of the Holy Roman Empire, cumbrous and, even by the

---

[52] See also F. Meinecke, *op. cit.* (see n. 2 above), pp. 499 ff.; O. Pflanze, *op. cit.*
(see n. 44 above), pp. 354 ff.; R. A. Kann, *Multinational Empire,* I, 90; II, 115 ff.

standard of its times, unrepresentative though it was, stood after all for a kind of federal coordination of states. As noted before, the Habsburg power did not dominate this semifederal union—it was associated with it. Its interests lay in diverse directions, some of them not related to the empire at all. This factor did in some ways impede relations between emperor and empire organization but it prevented also the danger that the empire could become a mere appendix of the Habsburg power. In the balance the non-German interests of this Habsburg power did not hurt the preservation of the identity and the image of the empire concept.

The German Confederation until 1848/1849 did not change this relationship substantially, although the aura of Christian universalism had been dissipated in the course of modern times. Yet in a more practical sense the concept of German union was not weakened by the looseness of the Confederation. It represented actually a far better organized political structure than the old empire even in its heyday. The continued and heightened struggle for supremacy between Austria and Prussia and above all the failure of the Confederation to build up an adequate system of social and political representation are the chief factors that distinguished the era between 1815 and 1848 from that of the empire prior to its dissolution. To be sure, the old empire had not solved these problems either. Before 1789, however, this did not mean an intentionally reactionary state of affairs. After the experience from 1789 to 1815 the Confederation had fallen back farther—not so much behind the spirit of the restoration period, but certainly behind the needs of the time.

The revolutionary period of 1848 was the last great attempt to restore peacefully an order of coordinate German states, this time on a democratic basis. Although the Frankfurt constitution differed from that of the old empire, its enactment would have meant restoration of German union in a new frame. In that case we could speak of a genuine intermediate system irrespective of the ups and downs of the union movement between 1815 and 1848.

The Austrian confederate reform plans, until 1850 and then again in 1863, represented little more than political episodes in the era from 1849 to 1866. This period was actually dominated by the ascendancy of Prussia. By 1866 she had secured the uncontested leadership in Germany; by 1871 an empire had been built after the image of her social structure. The German citizens were now fully equal only in the limited federal sphere, the German states under indirect Prussian hegemony not even there. Not coordination but subordination was the guiding principle of the Prusso-kleindeutsch solution. It was antidemocratic not because it was related to

Prussia, but because Prussia had remained socially as conservative as Bismarck and the king wanted her to be. Institutions of different generations can be compared only to a point. More than two generations after the destruction of the Holy Roman Empire, after the Industrial Revolution and the rise of Western European liberalism, the political order in the new empire was in absolute terms naturally more representative than in the old one. In relative terms the contrary was true. Germany in the constitutional political sphere had now fallen farther behind the spirit of the times than the Holy Roman Empire even in its abject decay after the Silesian wars.

From the viewpoint of this study the term "Second Empire" in reference to the federation of 1871 is, of course, a misnomer. Whatever it represented—and its economic, administrative and in several ways also its cultural achievements were truly respectable—it meant and stood for something basically different from the old empire. In accordance with the spirit of the past there was no democracy there, and contrary to the spirit of the new era a very imperfect one here. The old empire represented a grossdeutsch organization and coordination of states affiliated with Austria, the new empire a kleindeutsch structure and implied subordination of states under Prussia. Restoration of the Holy Roman Empire had finally and indisputably failed.

Was this failure inevitable due to the time element? Was the fate of German union sealed because the last of those who had affirmed the old empire and could still hail the union idea during the revolution were not destined to work for the movement later? Such assumption would put undue emphasis on somewhat controversial national heroes like Ernst Moritz Arndt (1769-1860) or the "Turnvater" Friedrich Ludwig Jahn (1778-1852), whose political activities had become anachronistic in their old age. The revolution came so late that the cooperation of one or the other contemporary of the old empire period in the union work could make little difference. And yet, seen from another angle, the time factor was of great significance indeed. In regard to the failure of the French Restoration we have noted that no restored regime, however well directed, could possibly have absorbed all the social and political changes brought about between 1789 and 1814. The German intermediate period between the two empires was not loaded with revolutionary social and political change like the French one. Yet that intermediate period, though less dramatic in action, was much longer in being (1806-1871) than in France (1789-1814). Old traditions had weakened more clearly than in the French case. Not the conflicts so much as the structure of international relations had changed even more markedly. Not institutions so much as their economic premises had altered conspicuously. The contingency of a return to a past more distant in time and social setting than in the French case, appeared even more complex and remote.

This does not mean at all that a free association of the German peoples had become inconceivable. What it does mean is that they could not rally any longer under the banners of the withered tradition of the past. The ways and means of establishing a second empire had destroyed the possibility to restore, renew, and reform the first one.

CHAPTER XVIII

The Dynastic Movements

When Time Stands Still

The endeavors of dynasties, driven from power, to make a comeback is our concern here, rather than broad sociopolitical movements. An objection might be made that in the majority of the chapters pertaining to specific cases we have already dealt with the issue either of restoration of dynasties or the establishment of them as part of would-be restored systems. The Stuart and Bourbon returns would represent specific restoration issues of dethroned dynasties; the problems of the Byzantine Empire under Justinian, the actions of the Ottonian and Habsburg emperors in the Holy Roman Empire and of the Angevin kings in England would be part of restoration movements concerned with reestablishment of royal and imperial power per se rather than the power of any specific dynasty. Nevertheless, all these cases, no matter whether the question of a specific dynastic succession is pertinent, were broad enough to perceive restoration in the frame of movements primarily concerned with the establishment of a particular social order. All of them are only in a secondary way related to the claims and interests of particular ruling houses.

In this chapter we look at the problem of dynastic reestablishment, not from the standpoint of a wide conservative or liberal movement of one kind or another, but from that of the dynasties themselves. The efforts to reestablish a dynasty may continue within an inner group for an unpredictably long time after the political and social restoration movement in a wider meaning has clearly failed. This would be the case of the Stuarts in their French exile after 1688 and of the Bourbons and Orléans abroad after 1830 and 1848. We face here the shift of onetime highly significant restoration movements from the broad avenues of social development into dead alleys of history. Yet there are also restoration efforts which have never led to a significant political movement at all, but within narrow circles they may have existed for a long time. They may still exist and there is no reason to assume that they would not continue to exist within close confines for an indefinite future. The Russian Romanov, the German Hohenzollern, and the Italian Savoy dynasties would be cases in point here, whereas the Austrian Habsburgs and Spanish Bourbons present more specific problems not easily placed in any category.

All these movements and others of the long-ruling dynasties in history have this much in common: with the possible exception of the Spanish case, they now represent dynastic claims without broad popular support. The good faith of most of the proponents of dynastic movements in the avowed sacredness of their objective, the establishment of an imperial or royal pretender on a vacant throne, may be readily granted. The social and political significance of such truly private royal and imperial enterprises must be strongly contested, however. Here the question arises: Why should we focus attention on problems whose limited importance seems to be acknowledged at the outset?

The answer is simple. The purely dynastic movement concerned with the specific claims of a dynasty and its very close group of followers, who had once benefited from its power or would like to share in restored power, reveals a challenging aspect of the overall restoration question. It pertains more to the theory of the problem than to its political impact, which in contemporary restoration movements is, more often than not, negligible. Previously we have discussed at some length the time factor involved in the restoration issue. We have suggested that restoration has little chance to succeed if it does not come about at the latest within the life-span of the generation which in its early manhood had still lived under the original system. We have further held that the success of restoration can only be tested within the course of another generation, when tradition, not direct orders from above, manifests the solidity of restored institutions.[1]

Accordingly, the additional insight which we may gain from a study of the purely dynastic movements in this: They are largely isolated from the major social and political factors that generally sustain restoration en-

[1] See particularly chapter 6 of this study and Robert A. Kann, "Was heisst Restauration?" *Wort und Wahrheit,* 1961, pp. 345–360, and "Wandel und Dauer im Donauraum," *ibid.,* March, 1964, pp. 184–194. In this second essay the problem is discussed in its specific application to the Danube area.

deavors, while the strictly dynastic tradition alone offers very little help for restoration. If we deal with the dynastic movement centered tightly and almost exclusively around a princely family, we face, so to speak, Kant's "thing in itself." How does the inner core of a restoration movement, the dynastic movement, look if it is separated, or in all probability will be separated, from the time element of the generation problem?

The answer to this question is interesting. The conditions—the initiation of restoration in the course of one generation and its tests of success within the following one—do not seem to apply to the purely dynastic movement. The genuine restoration movement supported by at least fairly broad social forces must come to grips with the social institutions of the regime that once had replaced it. The purely dynastic movement devoid of any sizeable popular support, which would bring restoration within the range of the conceivable, does not even need it to remain alive within its narrow confines. Permanently separated from the expectations of restoration and all that it involves in concessions to and confrontation with the spirit of the new times, such dynastic movement can concentrate on and indulge in one single idea within a social vacuum: dynastic legitimacy. On this all claims are based, for legitimacy answers all social questions in the sense that none need to be answered.

This, to be sure, is not the general problem of monarchical restoration; it is the specific one of dynastic restoration movements without popular support. In this limited sense such operations may last not only well beyond one political generation but throughout the centuries. Because of continuous failure they may be reduced from onetime vigorous restoration trends supported by broad strata of the population through contraction to mere dynastic movements. They may, on the other hand—and this is more often the case in modern times—begin with and remain confined to a narrow core of followers. In either case time stands still.

A great Austrian playwright, Arthur Schnitzler, has taken up this issue in the beautiful drama *Der junge Medardus,* whose setting is the Vienna of the war of 1809 against Napoleon. Here an old duke of Valois, a pretender to the French throne, resides in exile. The situation is only seemingly historical; actually it is completely fictitious. No such duke has ever existed, and the apparent but not actual relationship to reality makes the schemings of the ducal family appear even more ghostlike. The paradox is not that they live in the past but rather that they live and dream about a future which is built after the pattern of the past. Inasmuch as neither this past nor this future has any reality there is no need to compromise with reality.

It would be easy to trace a number of dynastic movements throughout history, movements which have never come to fruition, such as the numerous abortive attempts to change the English succession, from the time of the doomed Jane Grey in the sixteenth century to Bonny Prince Charles Stuart in the eighteenth. Some of the claims to the Russian throne by false or possibly genuine pretenders in the seventeenth and eighteenth centuries belong here, as do other examples of movements limited to strictly dynastic struggles without broad historical repercussions, from medieval Norway to Renaissance Italy. Yet in following these historical trails we would not meet the issue squarely. Any dynastic movement whose claim to reinvestment with sovereign dignity is based on legitimacy by the theory of divine right is not entirely cut off from the broad stream of social and political thought as long as the society in which these claims to the throne are made still recognizes the feudal tradition of sovereignty. This is one factor that helps us to understand why, for instance, as late as the mid-nineteenth century the conflict about the Spanish royal succession gave the so-called Carlist movement the impetus to unloose a civil war of wide social implications between conservative and liberal forces. Royal succession in itself was still a core issue of political thought which could be linked to any controversy in the body politic.[2] But what was still true for mid-nineteenth century Spain was true also for most continental European countries prior to the French Revolution of 1789.

Thus, if we want to study the relative or absolute isolation of the dynastic movements, we must move forward into the history of our own times where metaphysical preconditions of sovereign rule are no longer widely acknowledged. There exists even now wide variety in the historical situations that have conditioned dynastic movements. Yet they all are based on the most restricted concept of the restoration idea, namely "the restoration of legitimate rule that was temporarily interrupted by domestic or external force (revolution or conquest). The classical cases of such a restoration are the Restoration of the Stuarts in England (1660) and that of the Bourbons in France (1814). According to the legitimist theory applied there, the sovereignty interrupted by violent actions had never ceased to exist."[3] To be sure, the Stuart as well as the Bourbon restoration endeavors represented far more than purely dynastic movements. Fur-

[2] See particularly Theo Aronson, *Royal Vendetta: The Crown of Spain, 1829–1965* (Indianapolis, 1966), pp. 15 ff.; see also Raymond S. Carr, *Spain, 1808–1939* (Oxford, 1966), pp. 148 ff.

[3] Ernst R. Huber, *Deutsche Verfassungsgeschichte seit 1789* (Stuttgart, 1957), I, 531 (author's translation).

thermore, the rule of these dynasties was indeed only temporarily interrupted, although as it turned out, even in the English case in a strictly
dynasty sense it was only temporarily restored.

The dynasties in the movements we intend to discuss here were not
even temporarily restored to the throne, but this has not changed their
position that revolutionary movements may never become legitimate and
that a new order must be tied to the conditions of the old one. The
alleged temporary interruption of their rule may in reality become
permanent or, in other words, indefinite. To them, however, the term
temporary does not convey so much the notion of limited or unlimited
time but of illegitimate sovereignty, whether it is a matter of years or
centuries. Legitimacy based on the theory of divine right does not recognize any historical statute of limitations.

Six cases of theoretically feasible possibilities of restoration have evolved
within the last century among major European countries: in alphabetical
order, Austria-Hungary, France, Germany, Italy, Russia, and Spain. The
last-mentioned country, a particularly interesting case, may be substituted
for the Ottoman empire, which, as a non-European country in most
respects, would not fit in the context of our discussion. In the other cases,
the phrase "possibilities of restoration" means merely that in the six
countries listed the monarchical system of government has been superseded by other regimes, be it democracy or dictatorship. In theory
governments like these could be replaced by the monarchical regimes of
old. Possibility is thus by no means necessarily to be understood as actual
potentiality, let alone probability, of dynastic reestablishment.

Only in Italy and Spain has the elimination of monarchy taken place
within the course of the last political generation. In Spain the last
monarch ceased to rule in 1931, and the last political generation of royal
Bourbon Spain has almost seen the end of its active life.[4] In Italy, where
the constitutional change took place as late as 1945, this generation is still
represented in public affairs. This should suggest that monarchic restoration stands a better chance in Italy than in Spain. The contrary is
true, and if our other premises still hold, this would strengthen the
contention that the time factor ceases to operate where purely dynastic
movements are involved.

Yet it is always dangerous to draw far-reaching conclusions on one

---

[4] Through legislation of 1946 and 1947 Spain has become technically a kingdom
without a king. This means that in any but a merely formal sense the monarchy
has not (yet) been reestablished. See also Aronson, pp. 213 ff.

isolated factor alone. In this respect, the case of France could be adduced, where, among the six cases, monarchical government has for the longest time been absent—since 1870. While a dynastic movement there may be considered insignificant today, it certainly has played a far greater role in the history of the French Third Republic than has been true so far in Italy.[5]

In two countries, Spain and the Soviet Union, reestablishment of the monarchy could mean the end of dictatorial or at least one-party government.[6] Concerning the strength of the restoration movement, the question of state structure seems to be inconclusive again. In the first place, the experience of czarist Russia with genuine democratic institutions above the local level was negligible, and in royal Spain deficient indeed. It would be difficult, therefore, to speak of the appropriateness of the term restoration in these cases. Secondly, in regard to dynastic restoration, the very fact of dictatorship and totalitarianism does not seem in itself to be a decisive factor. Evidently, if some kind of "restoration" stood a chance at all it would be much greater in fascist Spain than in either totalitarian Communist Russia or democratic Italy. This leaves the possibility open that not the technical structure of dictatorship and the totalitarian philosophy themselves but in a more general way the Right or Left political content of government determined the turn of events.

In all but one of the six cases the territorial integrity of a country does not seem to be closely related to the possibility of dynastic reestablishment. Even in Germany the idea has never been seriously entertained that the question of reunification would be associated with the reestablishment of the German dynasties. Despite sundry republican schemes of Danube confederations, the idea, illusion, or possibility of the reestablishment of Austria as a Great Power is, on the other hand, quite clearly associated with the restoration of the Habsburgs.

First, there are three cases of democratic countries where the possibility of monarchic restoration seems obviously remote: France, Germany, and Italy. The problem—*sui generis*—of the former Habsburg monarchy will follow. Finally, we may expect some further insight from a comparison of the totalitarian system of Soviet Russia, obviously farthest removed from restoration, and the dictatorship in Spain, probably closest to it, relatively speaking. In none of these six cases will we be concerned with how restora-

[5] See for instance Samuel M. Osgood, *French Royalism Under the Third and Fourth Republics* (The Hague, 1960), pp. 5 ff., 54 ff.

[6] East Germany, where the same may be true, is not considered here as separated from the discussion of the overall German case.

tion could conceivably be brought about. What concerns us is alone the problem of how a dynastic movement represents itself in relation to systems which have superseded monarchy and whose rule may become permanent.

The case of France is particularly illuminating. For several reasons the movement for monarchic restoration could benefit there from a combination of specific, weighty issues. In the first place, the French monarchy fell at a time when Europe was, and remained until 1918, predominantly monarchical in its constitutional structure. France was during all these times the only republic among the Great Powers, a factor which not only increased suspicion between her and her chief opponent, Germany, but also aggravated relations with her chief ally, Russia. Bismarck's well-known policy in the 1870's to fight a French restoration and therewith to isolate the republic was not as unsuccessful as it is often pictured. Neither he nor his successors prevented republican France from becoming an ally of Czarist Russia. Yet his policy of cold-shouldering the French royalist movement probably delayed the establishment of the Franco-Russian alliance beyond his tenure of office. One may also doubt whether the alliance with Austria in 1879 could have been concluded easily if a royal France had been represented again by the fleur-de-lis of the Count of Chambord as King Henry V. This is, of course, partly conjecture, but it is not conjecture that royalism for some years after 1870 carried considerable weight in France. The French people, far more wrongly than rightly, blamed the republican government as much as Napoleon III for the defeat and particularly the armistice of January 28, 1871. The French elections of February 8 returned a clear monarchical majority, in which the followers of the older branch of the Bourbon dynasty outnumbered by far the supporters of the Orléans monarchy, while the Bonapartists hardly counted at that time.

Yet within a very few months monarchism had wasted its basic assets. The Bonapartes were saddled with defeat no less than the republic; the Orléans represented the slim tradition of a "citizen king" who lacked legitimacy as much as the firm hand of Monsieur Thiers. Conservatism probably would not have felt safe under the guidance of an Orléans king who was very conscious of the fact that as a mere second choice he owed precedence to the grandson of Charles X. Yet this Bourbon heir, the Count of Chambord, sworn to the tradition of the fleur-de-lis and an avowed opponent of the tricolor and the revolutionary tradition it stood for, was at the very most ready to recognize the dusty Charter of 1814. Otherwise he was ready to discuss further concessions to the spirit of the time only on the basis of the theory of divine right—after his installation as king, not prior to it. Yet according to all available evidence he neither believed he could become king on his own terms nor wished for restoration on any other. It is frequently held that the monarchic solution was wrecked only when the Count of Chambord, after he had come to an agreement with the Orléans pretender concerning the succession in 1873, still insisted on the royal banner. Only the acceptance of the permanent republican constitution of 1875 removed the monarchic question at least as an issue of current politics. The reconciliation with the Holy See in 1890 put its seal on this settlement. Yet there can be little doubt that the election of July, 1871, had already proved that monarchism was on the decline, and some subsequent slight increase of Bonapartist tendencies could not change this fact.[7]

Seemingly this does not mean the end of a restoration movement at all. In every French domestic crisis from Boulanger to Dreyfus in the 1880's and 90's, during the reactionary period following the anticlerical policy of the Combes ministry in 1906, during the revolt against the Daladier cabinet in 1934, and again throughout the Vichy regime from 1940 to 1945, monarchist agitation played an important part on the extreme Right. Yet whether we deal with the peculiar untraditional monarchism of Charles Maurras, his student, the strongly antialien and anti-Semitic Léon Daudet, and the more sophisticated writer, Maurice Barrès, the circles around the *Action Française,* the *Camelots du Roi,* and their successors the *Croix de Feu* under Colonel de la Roque, restoration was no longer the real issue. It had become a mere tool for the reactionary authoritarian and even outright fascist movements which used royalism as a symbol but not as a true political force. Yet as symbol it had become so feeble that not even Pétain and Laval were ready to take the final step to proclaim the monarchy in 1940, at a time when the Third Republic appeared utterly discredited.[8]

The strictly dynastic movement—primarily the Bourbon pretenders in exile—was never on top of any of these movements, was never leading, and was hardly found important enough to be led. The Bourbon Restora-

---

[7] See Osgood, pp. 1–27 *passim,* 51 ff., 73 ff., 81 ff., 102 ff., 163 ff.; D. W. Brogan, *The French Nation from Napoleon to Pétain, 1814–1890* (New York, 1957), pp. 151 ff.; Robert F. Brynes, *Anti-Semitism in Modern France* (New Brunswick, 1950), pp. 25 f.; Werner Richter, *Frankreich, von Gambetta zu Clemenceau,* (Erlenbach-Zürich, 1946), pp. 90 ff.

[8] Brogan, pp. 215 ff., 282 ff.; Brynes, pp. 179 ff.; Frederick L. Schuman, *War and Diplomacy in the French Republic* (New York, 1931), pp. 130 ff. For a viewpoint sympathetic to the French rightist movements, see the work of the National Socialist Walter Frank, *Nationalismus und Demokratie im Frankreich der dritten Republik (1871–1918),* 2d ed. (Hamburg, 1939–41), pp. 32 ff., 139 ff., 311 ff.

tion could not represent either fascism or conservatism of any brand, though lip service might be paid to them by the incongruous forces of the Right. The dynasty in exile represented nothing but its unaltered limited interest in restoration for restoration's sake, and that was too late and too little to put its stamp on the movements on the French Right.[9]

The German dynastic restoration movement lacks the advantages which the French had for a time and failed to use. The republic was established in 1918, not as in France in 1870 by a movement unique in its time, but as a corollary to the revolution in four great empires. In France the monarchical system was linked to defeat in 1870/71 only indirectly through pseudodynastic Bonapartism. German monarchism, despite the stab-in-the-back legend and the agitation against the republic, was clearly discredited by the Kaiser's flight to Holland. Dynastic monarchism had to leave it to other forces to rally the Right in the fight to destroy the democratic republic on the domestic front and to undo the Treaty of Versailles in foreign relations. It could well be argued that morally the inability of the German dynasties in this respect compares favorably with the short-lived success of National Socialism with its atrocious consequences. Yet the issue is not whether the dynastic movement was good or bad but whether it was effective or ineffective.

On this score little doubt exists. The dynastic idea and its proponents played an insignificant role in the fight for and against Hitlerism in 1933; it had no part in its overthrow and none in the shaping of German history ever since. This fact is not contradicted by the heroic actions of individual aristocrats in the resistance movement. The basic idea of German history after World War II is not that of restoration but of reunification. The powerful idea of union was for many centuries associated with that of emperor and empire. After World War II not even the slightest attempt was made to give it an imperial setting. This alone should clearly indicate that the monarchy, irrespective of the personal merits of claimants to the German thrones, does not move in the direction of any significant historical trend.

The contrary is the case; the monarchical idea can only inpede the idea of reunification. In the East the Prussian monarchy is associated with the social class system of a military junker state of warlike antidemocratic tendencies. Whether this assumption is correct is, in our context, beside the point. Democracy, a force far more important than the other Western asset, prosperity, is what the Federal republic has to offer to the people in the East. A major restoration movement in the German West would dilute

[9] Osgood, pp. 182 ff.

that attraction through historical reminiscences and would blur the democratic image there. Neither union nor democracy is associated in the minds
of the people with dynastic restoration and whether this is right or, as in
the case of the Wittelsbachs in Bavaria, not wrong in every respect, is beside the point. A restoration movement in the Germany of today represents
neither an idea nor a social system that transgresses dynastic interests for
any other reason than legitimacy.

The dynastic movement in France after the 1870's had been used only
for the ulterior purposes of the Right; in Germany after 1918 it had not
even such limited significance, and whatever shreds of it may have existed
at the time of the Kapp putsch in 1920 do not exist today. To be sure, the
issue of compensation for the dispossessed dynasties played a significant
part in the history of the Weimar republic. Yet the victory of the Right
against the Left on this question in the 1920's derived primarily from the
postulate to maintain inherited property rights, partly, it is true, from
sentimental remembrances of the past. Efforts toward restoration as a
direct political objective were hardly important and their political impact
dwindled further in the National Socialist era.[10] For the majority of people today the image of restoration is asssociated with the principles—not
the reality—of the Weimar republic; for a still sizeable minority, with the
transitory success of the National Socialist era; for the royal entourages
alone, with the princely dynasties.

The dynastic movement hardly offers better chances in Italy than in
Germany, although preconditions are, of course, different. In one respect
they seem to be favorable. The house of Savoy was never associated with
more than a passive tolerance of Fascism, and the last king and present
royal pretender with even a modicum of opposition. In fact, the fall of the
monarchy in Italy is the most recent case of the abolition of a monarchical
regime in any major European country. Yet new impetus may thus have
been given to the accelerated process of abolishing monarchical government, which started in 1918. This consideration does not bode well for the
chances of restoration. While nominally in power until 1945, the Italian
monarchy had actually abdicated politically to Fascism as early as 1922,
and few of the small group of monarchists active in the fight against the
dictatorship could return to the political scene.

Even more important is another factor. The rule of the Bourbons in

[10] Erich Eyck, *Geschichte der Weimarer Republik* (Erlenbach-Zürich, 1956), II,
87 ff.; Arthur Rosenberg, *Entstehung und Geschichte der Weimarer Republik*
(Frankfurt a/M, 1956–57), pp. 453 f. It is notable that even Rosenberg's leftist
interpretation does not perceive any direct relationship between indemnity for the
princes and a restoration movement.

France and of an emperor in the Holy Roman Empire stood for many a century in the forefront of French and German history; that of the Hohenzollern in Prussia, in the most powerful German state, had a long and virile tradition behind it as well. The state of Piedmont and its dynasty, the house of Savoy, played only a tangential part in Italian history until the middle of the nineteenth century. Largely by default of the other more centrally situated main areas of Italian culture and by the skill of one man, Cavour, did unification come about from the Italian northwest.

Political union in Italy is not an issue today, as it is in Germany. Even if it were, it would hardly be linked to the house of Savoy. Neither this nor any other issue of comparable significance is associated by the democratic Center with the reestablishment of the monarchy. As to the Right, Neo-Fascism has repudiated it. The communal elections of November, 1964, show that Neo-Fascism represents 5 percent of the Italian popular vote as compared with nearly 6 percent in 1960. Monarchists have fallen back, during that period, from almost 3 percent to 0.9 percent. The monarchical movement in Italy, in the no-man's-land of political warfare between communism, socialism, the Christian Democratic Center, and the Fascist Right, represents nothing but the dead-alley concept of dynastic legitimacy.[11]

Of greater significance for this study is the second group of cases, but not necessarily because they come closer to the problem of actual restoration. The Soviet Union certainly does not. Yet the problems of a dynastic restoration of the Habsburgs, Romanovs, or Spanish Bourbons are more directly associated with the main issues of this study.

To begin with the case of the Habsburg monarchy—as in Germany, it fell at a time that was as unfavorable to the maintenance of monarchic governments in defeated countries as it was unpromising for eventual restoration. As in Germany, the monarchy was rightly or wrongly, and in the Austrian instance far more wrongly than rightly burdened with responsibility for defeat. What is more important and indeed unique here is the fact that the monarchy stood also for the union of the bulk of the Danube peoples, as opposed to the Wilsonian principle of self-determination and ensuing separation. The significance of this juxtaposition has been only heightened by the erection of the Iron Curtain at the end of World War II. This odious situation, for which the old monarchy cannot con-

---

[11] See Leo Valiani in *Dieci anni dopo, 1945–55,* Antonio Battaglia, Pierro Calamandrei eds. (Bari, 1955), pp. 26 ff., 67 f.; see also Dennis MacSmith, *Italy: A modern history* (Ann Arbor, 1959), pp. 437 f., 494 ff.

ceivably be blamed any more than Wilsonian democracy, shows to many the clear advantages of the former union.

To many others it undoubtedly does not. We cannot deal here with the constitutional, political, and social shortcomings in the structure of the old empire. Neither can we discuss here why the Succession States failed to solve their national minority problems. The issue is not how the faults of the old monarchy should be weighed against those of imperfect democracies and authoritarian or even totalitarian regimes after 1918. The simple fact is that national self-determination and independence, no matter how poorly established or distorted by totalitarian regimes of various persuasions, represents a political idea of broad and powerful impact. Yet the same is true to a point for the idea of the union of the Danube peoples in the frame of the old empire. Proof of this is that the scores of plans for Danube federations of one kind or another drawn in the period between the two World Wars have apparently failed. Any one of them can be easily superseded by another and most of them have been.[12] The only patterns in which this issue has ever approached conceivable reality are within the frame of a restored and reformed Habsburg empire. This does not assume that a majority of the Danube peoples at any time after 1918 would have endorsed such plans. It does mean that a union of the Danube peoples within the frame of a Habsburg empire represents a live political idea, the like of which we do not see in the contemporary history of French, Italian, or German dynastic movements.

What kind of union and what kind of idea must we deal with here? The adherents of a Habsburg restoration would put up with almost any kind of federation or confederation scheme that would restore the image of an empire. Yet the Habsburg empire to which I refer, rather than to the somewhat artificial dualistic structure after the Compromise of 1867, was not a hazy affiliation of ethnic groups to be arranged or rearranged at will. In its time-honored historic setting it did not represent the ethnic union of peoples, although in the last decades of its existence it made concessions of some merit to the ethnic principle. With all the powers of a respectable tradition behind it, the Habsburg monarchy represented a union of historic entities only loosely attached to the ethnic principle.

This is not an arbitrary issue. The tradition of the Habsburg monarchy

[12] See Joachim Kühl, *Föderationsplane im Donauraum und in Ostmitteleuropa* (Munich, 1958), pp. 31 ff.; Rudolf Wierer, *Der Föderalismus im Donauraum* (Graz-Cologne, 1960), pp. 157 ff.; Feliks Gross, *Crossroads of Two Continents* (New York, 1945), pp. 29 ff.; Rudolf Schlesinger, *Federalism in Central and Eastern Europe* (London, 1945), pp. 419 ff.; Robert A. Kann, "Looking Across the Iron Curtain," *Journal of International Affairs,* Vol. XVI/1 (1962), 67 ff.

is not affiliated with a comprehensive southern Slav, Rumanian, or Polish state. With few qualifications these states—taken as separate entities—have neither a historic nor an ideological affiliation with the ancient empire whose tradition is linked only to sizeable parts of these political structures. Different, though not less weighty, ethnic factors would prevent the solution of the problems of the Ruthenian branch of the Ukrainian peoples or of the former Austro-Italians within the bygone empire structure. It is difficult to see how peoples of such diverse ethnic and historical affiliations and loyalties inside and outside the former monarchy could be expected to unite in a front strong enough ever to overcome the social and political barrier between Eastern and Western Europe, which is still sizeable, although the term Iron Curtain may no longer be fully appropriate.

Yet we are not concerned here with the political feasibility of any union based on the remote expectation of Russia's withdrawal from her Eastern and Central European sphere of interests. We have not even settled the preliminary question whether any of the Danube peoples East and West of what has been called the Iron Curtain could agree on a sociopolitical structure in line with the traditions of the empire. Such a realignment was impossible even prior to the National Socialist and Soviet threat; it appears even more imaginary now. It may be hoped that these tremendous historical experiences have alerted the common interest of the peoples in the Danube basin to fight the philosophy of the police state as much as that of the racial state in a spirit of cooperation. Yet it must be realized also that these experiences have moved their social and cultural environment and heritage much farther from the setting of the Habsburg empire.

The idea that this Habsburg monarchy, roughly with its previous boundaries and a moderately revised social structure, could be restored, seems absurd today, even though such concept has tradition behind it. A republican Danube federation or confederation of Succession States, more in line with current ethnic and political boundaries and more ready to absorb social changes brought about since 1918, has not even tradition behind it.

There exists no practical possibility of realizing either idea—a paradoxical structure with tradition behind it, or a less paradoxical one without it. This impossibility should explain why the Habsburg dynastic movement is bound to operate in the unreal world of the conflicting claims and memories of the various Habsburg crowns. A move away from these traditions will not bring the restoration designs of this dynastic movement closer to reality, but it will destroy the only force it still controls—tradition itself.

The last two cases, the Soviet Union and Spain, share with the major Eastern part of the area of the Habsburg empire the experience of subordination under totalitarian regimes. The obvious manifold and tremendous differences in social outlook and organization deriving from the basic difference between the Communist Left and the Spanish rightist regime cannot and do not have to be discussed here. Even in regard to political structure, only one distinction is really pertinent in the context of our investigation. While the Communist one-party state is ruled by an oligarchy of the so-called postrevolutionary elite, the fascist Falange system has only a limited influence on the administration of Spain, which is in essence a one-man authoritarian police state. Such divergence greatly affects, of course, the operation of any regime. What chiefly counts for our purpose beyond this is the simple fact that Spain is possibly closer to actual restoration and the Soviet Union infinitely farther from it than any other case under discussion.

To begin with the Russian case, it is obvious that the ruthless liquidation of the former ruling classes in Russia and the tremendous power of the state, combined with a far-reaching economic autarchy, represent a barrier to a restoration movement which could hardly be overcome. Yet only a superficial interpretation of Russian history after 1917 would base the absurdity of the idea of a Czarist restoration exclusively or predominantly on these facts. Few subscribe to the thesis that the basic features of a revolution which in the course of half a century has changed the social structure entirely could be reversed. Yet while the possibility of a slow process toward evolutionary transition to a pluralistic society is well conceivable, the notion that it could take place within the framework of Czarism is utterly inconceivable.[13] A social and political reform of such system under the former imperial dynasty would have to make such sweeping concessions to the changes brought about since 1917 that compared to this the systems of the French Convention of 1793 and of the Bourbons of 1814 would look almost alike. In other words, the changes required in a Russian restoration would be so great that the possibility of identification of the old and new regimes would be completely voided. Yet the absence of such changes would wreck attempts at restoration from the start. It was not frivolity on the part of Russian grand dukes,

---

[13] See the interesting observations in Richard Charques, *The Twilight of Imperial Russia* (London-Oxford, 1965), pp. 140 ff., 211 f., and in Hugh Seton-Watson, *Decline of Imperial Russia, 1855-1914* (New York, 1952), pp. 376 ff.

princes, and guard officers in the Parisian exile between the two World Wars which gave their schemings for dynastic reestablishment such ghost-like character. It is rather the impossibility of bridging the social abyss in time and place between imperial Czarism and totalitarian Communism. The destruction not only of the social structure before 1917 but of its very roots as well, has led the restoration idea here to the point of no return. And this would hold true even if the political preconditions for restoration were to exist in international relations, preconditions which most assuredly have no basis in fact. Any dynastic Russian restoration movement inevitably becomes absurd.

As indicated before, the differences between the Russian and Spanish cases lie not only in their alignments on the opposite sides of the political and social spectrum and the possible potential closeness to restoration here and the practical impossibility there. Disregarding the tremendous difference in power potential in domestic as well as international relations which sustains the Soviet regime and threatens that of Franco, there exists also a notable *constellatio oppositorum* in another way. As noted above, a chief theoretical difficulty or a Russian restoration consists in the fact that the differences between an original and a restored system could not be bridged, and if they could be bridged, the systems would still have to be so different that one could hardly speak of restoration at all.

The reverse would in all probability be true in the Spanish case. If the Spanish royal pretender, prince Juan (III), the son of Alfonso XIII, or the prince's own oldest son, Juan Carlos, should succeed Franco, the association with the dismal past of the intermediate dictatorial regime would appear to most people very close. Accordingly, the chances that the reestablished monarchy could maintain itself would seem slim indeed. After all, the return to the throne would take place according to the order of succession decreed by Franco in 1947 and confirmed only by a dubious plebiscite whose intent was to give the Franco regime the semblance of approval through the consent of the governed. A further declaration by Franco, of July, 1957, that Spain should be governed by the "traditional, representative and Catholic monarchy" [14] did not change matters in any way. A Spanish restoration incapable of absorbing the social change in the world after the abdication of Alfonso XIII in 1931 would thus seem doomed to failure from the start.

There are other interpretations possible, but it is doubtful whether they make the chances for restoration appear in a better light. As discussed

[14] Theo Aronson, *Royal Vendetta*, p. 222; see also 213–226 *passim;* and Salvador de Madariaga, *Spain, a Modern History* (New York, 1960), pp. 598 ff.

previously, we perceive restoration not just as the accession of the king of a deposed dynasty to the throne, but as the ability of the new regime to absorb a measure of revolutionary social change and to maintain itself in power. That a regime installed by Franco could do so seems highly doubtful. If it repudiated the dictator after his death and if it then, but only then, promised democratic reforms, such pledges might be looked at with suspicion even by the political Center. Opposition of extreme Right and Left would probably be unalterable in any case. Yet if the royal pretender, whoever he may be, should break formally with the Franco regime prior to his accession, he might never get the chance to assume power at all. In that case the door would probably be opened to extremism right from the start.

This interpretation is based on the assumption that the events after 1931, the Spanish republic, the civil war, and the Franco regime, are all part of a revolutionary period which comprises revolutionary and counterrevolutionary moves, with a profuse use of violence on either side. It is possible, of course, to perceive the Franco regime as a kind of restoration which by the length of its tenure of office—nearly thirty years—has to a good part stood the test of time according to the terms elaborated previously. If we follow this interpretation, the intermediate system would be limited to the republican regime and the civil war between 1931 and 1939, when Franco emerged victorious. In line with this thought the rule of a descendant of Alfonso XIII would mean merely the continuation of the restoration process, and inasmuch as the rule of the last king, almost to the end of his reign, was associated with the dictatorship of Primo de Rivera, the expectations of revolutionary change toward truly representative government would not seem very bright. Yet the success of a restored regime may depend to a great extent on the nature of such expectations. Of the question of a new Bourbon king as the originator of a restored regime by the grace of Franco or as a mere successor to him, it could truly be said, *plus ça change, plus c'est la même chose.*

All this is, of course, speculation. A new king, if he should ever come to power, might surprise the Spanish people, and the Spanish people might surprise him. As of now the chances for mere accession are certainly far greater than for true restoration. The prospect that the present dynastic movement could expand into a truly restorative movement in a democratic sense seems now less likely than that it would be overthrown again by a revolutionary regime. On the basis of ample precedent, monarchic restoration in Spain is not associated in general with a genuine desire for democratic government. An attempt in this direction seems at least more

likely than its chances for success. Whether a not improbable revolutionary change after the end of the present regime could be directed into
democratic channels is as unpredictable as the change of the present dynastic movement into a genuine restoration movement and subsequent
true restoration.

In general we have perceived, in this study, a genuine restoration
movement only if the protagonists of the original system can still be
active in the reestablished system's struggle for true, that is permanent,
restoration. The ideas of the intermediate system have to blend in various
ways with the restored one. We have observed further that this process
does not hold true for the purely dynastic movements, which represent a
rigid and unalterable idea of dynastic legitimacy. No symbiosis between
the three systems takes place. The hard core of the followers of these
movements have not participated in the social life of the new system in
power, to them eternally an intermediate and temporary one.

Consequently, dynastic movement of this kind have been attacked,
sneered at, but most often ridiculed. This is not the position taken here.
Apart from a fringe of followers whose motivation derives from sheer
snobbism or a delight in childish conspiracies, there are elements of
loyalty, steadfastness, respect for tradition, and devotion in such groups
which command respect, even if their efforts could be put to socially more
constructive use. In a sense, and this is a weighty factor in their favor,
their path is preordained. If a dynastic movement wants to preserve its
old loyalties—surely not a contemptible act—it is faced with an inevitable
choice. Either it must make such sweeping concessions to the spirit of the
times that its identity will be destroyed, or the movement must steer so
narrow a course of traditional political thought that it will be swept out
of the mainstream of thinking in the body politic. To keep its identity the
dynastic movement must bypass the spirit of the time; yet if it does, the
times will bypass it.

CHAPTER XIX

A Final Reflection

This inquiry has taken us far afield in time and place from the sixth century B.C. to our own age, from the Mediterranean coast of Asia to Spain, from the British Isles to Greece. The cases we have analyzed were varied and they conformed in varying degrees to the guiding principles of the restoration process outlined in the first part of the study.

The first case, that of Jewish history from the destruction of the kingdom of Judah through the Babylonian exile to the return to a homeland, now a mere vassal state, showed restoration rather successful in the area of social institutions but far less fortunate in the political sphere. The almost contemporaneous case of Athenian development from the rule of Solon through the tyrannis of Peisistratus and his sons to Cleisthenes revealed a remarkable expansion of democratic institutions. As seen from the angle of our problem the impact of the middle period, the tyrannis, was here not as strong as that of the comparable one, the Babylonian exile of the Jews. The synthesis of the three systems lacks clear focus.

The case of the Roman republic, roughly from the end of the Punic wars, through the Gracchan revolt to the death of Marius, proved to be very complex. Here the question of stability of the restored republican institutions remains controversial. The next problem, the restoration of the Roman Empire of Theodosius the Great under Justinian, did not represent a clear-cut case either. The question of relative durability remains problematical. The same pertains to the question of contemporaneous consciousness of the fact that the Roman Empire in the West and the East had really ceased to be a historical entity. The Ottonian restoration of the empire of Charlemagne in the second half of the tenth century was a historical transaction of political and even greater ideological significance. Yet if we take a long view, then the impact of the Holy Roman Empire on Christian Europe, and even on Central Europe alone, was intermittent rather than stable. England in the transition from the Norman kings to the Angevin rulers in the twelfth century, on the other hand, revealed a clear reestablishment and improvement of orderly government. However, the middle period under Stephen contributed so little to further development that it is difficult to perceive here a synthesis of three systems. The reestablishment of imperial power in Germany under Rudolf of Habsburg after the fall of the Ghibellines (Hohenstaufens) and the Great Interregnum proved to be successful from the point of law and order, but imperial authority was now based, far more than before, on the hereditary territorial power of princely dynasties and was at the same time more restricted. The question is here whether the similarity of the great Ghibelline empire and the new one under the houses of Habsburg, Luxemburg, or Wittelsbach was obvious enough to speak of genuine restoration.

From here we have moved to a somewhat more thorough discussion of four rather complex case studies in the history of modern times. In essence the question of similarity of systems dominates the first of these, like the preceding chapter on the transition from the Ghibellines to the Habsburgs. It deals with the reestablishment of an undivided faith in the Erblande under the rule of the Habsburgs in the late sixteenth and early seventeenth centuries after the far-reaching success of the Protestant Reformation in the intermediate period. Here in a sample case, primarily ideological in nature but within clearly established political boundaries, the question raised is this: To what extent could a society which had restored Catholic faith under the influence of the Catholic Reformation and the pressure of the Counter Reformation ever again resemble one which did not have to endure such severe tests? The negative answer to this question may be simple but the consequences of this historical process appear complex.

Of the two following cases commonly associated with the restoration problem, that of the Stuarts in England and of the Bourbons in France, we have perceived only the English one after 1688 as a really fully successful restoration and that of the Bourbons in France as a failure, though a failure which in its synthesis of the original, intermediate, and restorative reestablishment carried with it also some elements of success. We were unable to comprehend the establishment of the German Second Empire of 1871 as restoration of the Holy Roman Empire, but we believe that the constitutional developments in the Frankfurt Assembly in St.

Paul's church in 1848 and 1849 moved for a time toward genuine restoration. In this case as in the preceding French one the intermediate system presented specific problems. In France the full impact of the revolutionary era could not possibly be absorbed by a restored regime; in Germany the length of time of the intermediate period and the political and social disparateness of its setting led to the same consequences. We consider the purely dynastic movements discussed in the last chapter of the case studies to be largely separated from the social development of their time and place. Here we saw only in the Spanish case a very limited chance for true restoration, to be distinguished from mere reestablishment of monarchic government for a time.

To sum up: We believe the hypothesis of the first part of this study, that reestablishment of a system must come about within the life-span of a political generation and that its endurance must be tested within another one—has in substance been sustained. Little credit is claimed for this fact. We do not deny at all that a broader sample of cases might conceivably have led to different results. It should be remembered also that the purpose of this study was not to establish an airtight case for a highly problematical pioneer investigation. We merely wish to probe possibilities according to what seem to us plausible constellations in the diversity of history. This very diversity of history is to us its chief attraction, and it is this attraction which has motivated this study. Consequently, the fact that individual cases do not conform to tentative principles or that other concepts may be used does not disturb us in the least.

A different approach might lead to an analysis of the problem of restoration in a much wider sense. It might include reestablishment after conquest from outside as well. This, as noted in the general part of this study, would in our opinion inject in part an arbitrary factor of military or diplomatic success. Yet to others the reestablishment of Poland in 1918 or in a way also the conversion of the lands of the Bohemian crown as they existed prior to the battle of the White Mountain to modern Czechoslovakia, may appear to be genuine cases of restoration. To be sure, this would imply the change of the time factor of two generations as applied in this study. If it were once disregarded, then there is no reason why a process of restoration could not be perceived as extended over many centuries, as in Eire or Finland—or even millennia, as in Greece. On the other hand, the time factor could be contracted with equal justification, and in that case the transition of France from the Third to the Fourth or Fifth republic or that of Germany from Weimar to Bonn would be within the scope of the restoration problem. It would be very different indeed from the one discussed in this study, which is based on the process of domestic change within a strictly defined frame of time.

This means that the most basic changes take place under a dynamic intermediate system between a more sedate original and a restored one. In the case of Poland, which to many may appear as one of the most suggestive examples of restoration, the fundamental reforms in the social and political order had already occurred during the last years of the old kingdom's precarious existence between 1791 and 1795. In fact, they were far more sweeping than any changes under the auspices of the three partitioning powers during the long wait and heroic struggle for eventual reestablishment in 1918. Thus it is not only the problem of the time element, the question of reinstatement after conquest from outside, but also the necessity to perceive the three systems in a distinct consecutive order. All these factors have to be carefully weighed in the recognition and understanding of the restoration process.

This study takes a clear stand on all three issues: the two-generation test concerning success or failure of restoration, the elimination of conquest from outside as a largely arbitrary factor, and the demand that the three systems must appear separable and not intertwined. The fascinating Polish case is highly problematical on all three counts. In the case of the transition from the German Weimar republic throughout the revolutionary National Socialist era to the Federal republic of today, the first two factors, the partially arbitrary elements in conquest from outside and the lack of sufficient time as yet—two generations—would come into play. Unlike the Polish issue, the three systems can be separated quite clearly. Here, however, a different problem arises. Poland stands for the state as a whole even though its boundaries, after 1918, differed and continue to differ substantially from those of the state just prior to the third partition. The German Federal republic, because of the unfortunate division, cannot represent Germany as a whole. For partly identical and partly different reasons Germany after the Second World War is as poor an example as Poland after the First. Yet this does not mean that other interpreters could not take a different view on this and similar cases. New insights would strengthen our convictions that alleged historical laws must be reduced to propositions and that propositions must conform to facts, and not the other way around.

For this reason we do not intend to pursue, elaborate, and qualify any further the search for tentative historical guidelines governing the restoration process. It seems to us more useful to turn to another question not yet discussed in its major ramifications. If this investigation has established one thing beyond reasonable doubt, it is recognition of the fact that every restoration, indeed, every restoration movement, differs widely from any other. This in itself is a trite statement, yet it has far-reaching and perhaps even startling implications. If restorations, restoration movements, and potential restorations differ from each other across the board, then restoration implies and means change of one kind or another. Such recognition is at variance with the well-worn supposition that restoration means reestablishment of the same. We hope we were able to show that almost the contrary is true. Restoration stands a chance to succeed only if it absorbs a substantial part of the institutions and ideas of an intermediate system. It is bound to fail, as will the purely dynastic movements, if the intent is only to rebuild a faithful duplicate of the past. On the other hand it is, of course, true that restoration also includes a predominant element of the heritage of the past. Were it otherwise, the image of restoration could not be maintained and the very concept would become patently absurd.

Does all this mean that within the synthesis of the three systems the element of change implies progress and that of preservation reaction? Does it mean that the fewer genuine restoration situations there are, the more clearly is progress marching on? The answer to this legitimate question is a clear No. Outstanding scholars, to mention only Ernst Cassirer, R. G. Collingwood, or Karl Mannheim, have shown clearly the elusive and controversial character of a concept of progress, in J. B. Bury's terms, measurable in patterns of social development.[1] We may, of course well recognize that the response to social or ideological movements of some kind will never carry history all the way back to the basis from which the original movement started.[2] Change of one kind or another in line with new social situations is inevitable, but this does not signify necessarily a definite trend pertaining to the content of such change. Restoration may be to a greater or lesser degree subject to it, but the very degree of change has no intrinsic relationship to the political spectrum from Right to Left. Restoration may move in either sphere, and if it is in our times more frequently associated with the former, this is due

[1] See John B. Bury, *The Idea of Progress,* ed. Charles A. Beard (New York, 1955 ed.), see pp. 2 ff. and Beard's introduction pp. xix ff.; see R. G. Collingwood, *The Idea of History* (New York, 1957), pp. 114 ff.; with particular regard to Hegel's philosophy of history, see Karl Mannheim, *Ideology and Utopia* (New York, 1936), pp. 231 ff., 240 ff., Ernst Cassirer, *The Philosophy of the Enlightenment* (Princeton, 1951), pp. 251 ff.
[2] Robert A. Kann, *A Study in Austrian Intellectual History* (New York, 1960), pp. 294 ff.

primarily to the historical association with the monarchical form of government. Yet prior to the nineteenth century, restoration with few exceptions meant reestablishment not of monarchical government, which was generally taken for granted, but of a specific dynasty of sovereign. The issue of a concrete political philosophy was not inherent in the nature of the restoration problem. With the decline of monarchical government, beginning with the American Revolution, this situation has changed, but perhaps in the long run not as much as it may seem at first glance.

A shortage of illustrative cases pertaining to republican restoration after the breakdown of the ancient world limited this study largely to problems of monarchical restoration. Yet as indicated in the last chapter, on dynastic movements, it is quite likely that this may not be an important issue in the future. It seems probable that the question of the restoration of representative republican government, threatened by revolutionary rightist or leftist movements, will become the chief restoration issue in times to come. Yet there, too, the concept of restoration itself will reveal nothing about the direction of any specific political philosophy which may threaten the established order.

This does not mean that we can learn nothing further about the nature of the restoration process. Much of what has been discussed here may be confirmed, elaborated, or challenged by future research. Apart from the probable time limit in which restoration will take place, we were able to suggest that a genuine restoration movement must be backed by sizeable and markedly representative social forces, buttressed by a strong tradition and a spiritual idea which transgresses the mere claim of dynastic legitimacy. If this should be so, then we still may not be able to predict the success of a restoration movement, but we may be able to foretell that it will make an impression on society. And this after all is the issue here—not restoration of a regime in a technical sense but preservation of some of its main values. In this sense restoration and genuine restoration movements may merge into one.

Regardless of the specific impact of such movements on a new system from the standpoint of political party affiliations and ideologies, we believe that such change brought about by preserving old values and merging with new ones is not without ethical significance. The almost infinite varieties in which such synthesis will take place point to a pluralistic societal order. And in more than one sense pluralism is the best, perhaps the only guarantor of individual liberties in the domestic sphere and of peaceful adjustment in international relations. So much for the element of change, modified by respect for the values of the past—it controls the restoration process in its ties to the outside world. Yet we believe further that the idea of restoration does not lack comfort for the inner life of man, a comfort which he needs even more desperately in an increasingly complex society. In this sense the message of restoration is that what has been with us in times past is not lost and what will come will likewise be with us in one form or another. I have always felt a wonderful assurance in Schopenhauer's thought that we cannot fall off this world. This is precisely what restoration could and perhaps should mean to us.

APPENDIX

Restoration–The Terms

The noun *restoration* and the verb *to restore,* as we know them in the modern Romance and Teutonic languages, derive from the Latin.[1] There the terms mean *renewal, repair, to stand up again,* and *rebuild.* In classical Latin, *restauratio* was primarily used in a very literal, easily demonstrable sense, that is, the rebuilding or repair of a destroyed or damaged building.[2] However, Latin classical literature, as the Hellenic before it, was fully aware that the word could signify also the repair of destruction resulting from a great variety of causes, such as war, pestilence, unjust laws, loss of status, and so forth. It is suggestive that the metaphorical meanings of the term are closely associated with this diversity. Since the need for repairs, recovery, or renewal could derive from a

[1] To go farther back, classical Greek includes not less than three words, namely ἀναγωγή, ἀνακαίνωσις, and ἀποκατάστασις which the one term *restoration* comprises in all modern Western languages of today. Taking these words—none of which is etymologically related to *restoration*—in their proper alphabetical order, ἀναγωγή and the verb ἀν‑άγω refer here to leading back and being led back, as well as to a law suit in which the recovery of property, usually slaves, is demanded. However, these are merely secondary connotations of words, the primary meanings of which —departure, leaving, leading up,—have little to do with the term *restoration* and *to restore,* as discussed in the text below. Ἀνακαίνωσις or ανακαίνισις with the verbs ἀνακαινίζω and ἀνακαινόω on the other hand, hit a main target, namely one of the chief meanings of the terms as developed later, *renewal, to renew,* as well as *bringing up again.* The noun ἀποκατάστασις refers also to a chief purport of the English word *restoration,* that is, complete establishment of a previous condition, re-establishment, regular return (as applying for instance to seasons), righting of a previous wrong, as, in a legal sense, in restitution. See for instance H. G. Liddell & R. Scott, Greek-English Lexicon (Oxford), 1883, 2 vols.

[2] See for instance Harper's *Latin Dictionary* (New York); J. E. Riddle, *Latin-English Dictionary* (London); and Stowassers *Lateinisch-Deutsches Schul- und Handwörterbuch* (Vienna, Leipzig), all various editions. Tacitus uses the word *restauratio* in referring to the rebuilding of a theater destroyed by fire.

number of causes, subsequent literary development would then attempt to encompass them all as far as possible in the one word *restoration*. In this process the more general facets of the term would have to be emphasized, while the specific, often mutually contradictory ones, would have to be devalued. In other words, we observe the transition from a primarily concrete concept to a largely abstract one.

Moving ahead quickly in time, it is interesting to observe how this transition is reflected in the standard dictionary of the English language, the great unabridged *Oxford Dictionary*. In declining order of importance, the chief meanings of the term *restoration* as a later form of the more direct Latin derivative *restauration,* illustrated and documented by a considerable number of literary quotations, are listed there, as follows:

1. The action of restoring to a former state or position; the fact of being restored or reinstated: (a) of persons (here follows the first reference to the Stuart Restoration in England under Charles II in 1660); (b) of territory, condition, and things; (c) In a broad, non-legal, theological sense, meaning restitution, with reference to the English reformers and philosophers, such as John Wyclif or James Harrington.

Main meaning 2 of the term according to the *Oxford Dictionary* is clearly a historical and political one. Under the heading *History* it refers (a) to the "reestablishment of monarchy in England with the return of Charles II in 1660"; also, to "the period marked by these events"; (b) to the "reinstatement of the Bourbons in the sovereignty of France in 1814." While these are surely not the only cases of political restoration in modern history, they are the only two case histories consistently referred to as *Restoration* or *period of Restoration*.[3]

Heading 3 pertains to the recovery of physical strength. Much broader is the listing in the dictionary under 4: "The action or process of restoring something to an unimpaired or perfect condition."

Main heading 5 returns to the principal meaning listed under 1, but specifies the conditions under which it applies: "the action of restoring something to one who has been personally deprived of it." In other words, this means not just restoration of something that may have been destroyed for any reason, such as age, death, surrender, war; it means reestablishment under only one, although a very broad, condition: the restoration of something that had been destroyed by intent.

[3] See at this point the analysis of the political meanings of the term in Ernst Rudolf Huber, *Deutsche Verfassungsgeschichte seit 1789* (Stuttgart, 1957), I, 531 ff. In this sense of reference to definite historical actions and movements, such as those of 1660 and 1814/1815, or in direct quotation, should *restoration* be capitalized.

If we shift now from the noun *restoration* to the verb *restore,* we find a much greater variety of meanings, and at the same time a much greater stress on the specific than on the general. The primary meanings given here are: **1.** to give back, to make return or restitution of (anything previously taken away or lost); **2.** to make amends for, to compensate, to make good (loss or damage). All these meanings by denotation, rather than strict definition, refer pretty clearly to very specific actions of repairing a previous deficiency or wrong. Obviously all of them are specific rather than general.

Those meanings listed as follows, under **3**, are not only specific but doubtless concrete rather than abstract: "to build up again, to re-erect or reconstruct. Now specifically to repair and alter (a building), so as to bring it as nearly as possible to its original form."

The meanings under **4** (a, b, c, d) in their religious, legal, and physical aspects, retain this concrete denotation only partly: (a) to replace (mankind) in a state of grace; to be free from the effect of sin; (b) to reinstate or replace (a person) in a former office, dignity, or estate; (c) to bring (a person or a party of the body) back to a healthy or vigorous state; (d) to bring back to mental calm. Obviously only the references to physical and mental readjustment are clearly concrete, yet all four are specific in their relationships to well-defined human interests.[4]

Only group **5** (a, b) is clearly general in meaning: (a) to renew; to set up or bring into existence again, to reestablish, bring back into use, etc.; (b) to return to the original position. Subdivision (c), "to replace or insert (words or letters which are missing or illegible in a text)" returns again to the specific and concrete.

Meanings **6** and **7** follow this line further by emphasizing the reinstitution of individual rights, **6** "to bring back (a person or thing) to a previous, original, or normal condition," with the subdivision (b) "to grant or obtain (for a person) reinstatement to former rank, office or possession," and with (c) "to take or put back into, to convey or hand back, to a place." And **7**, "to recompense or compensate (a person) . . . "[5]

---

[4] For the sake of clarification it should be emphasized that the complementary concepts of *general/specific* and *abstract/concrete* are, though related, by no means identical. The former refers to concepts pertaining to the whole genus of one kind or another, as opposed to the species or the individual of some kind. *Abstract,* on the other hand, means expressing a quality apart from any object as opposed to one or more objects recognized by immediate experience. See for instance, H. Schmidt, J. Streber, *Philosophisches Wörterbuch* (Stuttgart, 1961).

[5] *The Oxford English Dictionary* (Oxford: Clarendon Press, 1933), Vol. VIII.

Before we leave the verb *restore* the following semantic points of difference between verb and noun should be noted. The verb encompasses a
decidedly greater variety of meanings than the noun, and is therefore
more frequently used in the English language. Yet, more frequently does
not necessarily mean more widely, that is, in a wider sense. In regard to
the verb a greater number of meanings refer to the readjustment of a
specific person, or recovery and repair of a thing, than is the case with the
noun. There, as far as the main connotations are concerned, emphasis on
the general and abstract is stronger than with the verb. Particularly interesting, however, is a distinction referring to the concrete and the specific.
The application to a definite historic situation, and in particular to that
exemplified by the return of the Stuarts to England in 1660 and of the
Bourbons in France in 1814, has no counterpart in the meanings of the
verb *restore.* To be sure, it may well be used to express the process of reestablishment of the Stuart and Bourbon dynasties in England and
France, as well, perhaps, as that of other sovereign houses in other countries. Yet, the use of the verb *restore* in that connection is not specific, let
alone exclusive. Unlike the term *Restoration,* which has a very definite—
in two cases practically exclusive—connection with a specific historical
situation, it may be replaced by a good many other verbs.

This particular difference between *restoration* as pertaining expressly
though not exclusively to political history, and the verb *restore,* without
this specific meaning is one of the reasons for further concentration on
the concepts comprised in the noun. In doing so, the view stating this
difference is strongly supported by the second most authoritative dictionary in the field, *Webster's Unabridged,* where the general meanings of the
concepts of *restoration* in its predominant applicability to phenomena of
social history are even more strongly emphasized than in the *Oxford Dictionary.* The various meanings of the verb, refer, as in the other reference
work, primarily to applications pertaining to the personal status of an
individual and to the repair or improvement of an object.[6]

Thus, after a brief comparative analysis of the terminology in the other
major Western languages—German, French, Italian, and Spanish—we
may be justified in dropping further investigation of the verb *restore*
altogether, and in turning exclusively to the significance of the main subject of investigation.

The major German dictionaries, the classic work sponsored by the
brothers Jakob and Wilhelm Grimm; as well as the more recent great

[6] *Webster's Third New International Dictionary of the English Language Unabridged* (Springfield, 1961).

dictionary by Trübner, do not list the words *Restauration* and *restaurieren* at all. According to their editorial policy, which is strictly based on etymological principles, these words cannot be regarded as German. Unlike the principle of selection in English-language dictionaries, emphasis is put on linguistic purity and not on colloquial use.[7] The point is not without significance for our discussion. Had the word been as widely used in German as in English, it probably would have been germanized. This means in turn that while in German the concept refers exactly to the same meanings as in English, in the sense of reestablishment, repair, recovery, restitution, renovation, and so forth, it has not quite the same significance as in English.[8] An obvious partial explanation would be that the concept of political restoration is not as important in German as in English, and only second to it, in French. Of course the political idea of restoration is frequently applied also to Central European conditions throughout the period from the Congress of Vienna to the Revolution of 1848. Yet the political and social changes which took place there during this era do not compare in social magnitude and intellectual penetration with the transition from Cromwell's Commonwealth to the Stuart monarchy.[9]

In French the principal meanings of the terms *restauration* and *restaurer* do not differ greatly from those in German or English. As in English, there is, however, greater stress on the concept of political restoration as exemplified by that of the Bourbons in 1814, than there is in German. Obviously this corresponds to the fact that the Restoration in France represents a more marked change from the French Revolution and the following Napoleonic era than that from the social status of the German states during this period to the postwar world after 1814/15.

No particular new aspects of the terminology are to be found in Italian. It is worth mentioning though that the concept of restoration may be expressed by two closely related nouns, *ristoramento* and *ristorazione,* while the verb would be in both cases *ristorare*. Although there is no

[7] Insofar as *restoration* represents the Norman linguistic roots in the English language, the affiliation of the word with the English is, of course, on etymological grounds, closer than the association with the German.

[8] See for instance *Der Sprach-Brockhaus* (Wiesbaden, 1959), or Duden, *Rechtschreibung der deutschen Sprache und der Fremdwörter* (Wiesbaden, 1949). The fact that the social concept of *restoration* is expressed by exactly the same word used for a public eating place (Restauration) may be dismissed as of little significance in this context. Obviously the connection (place for recovery, restrengthening of the body) is the same as with the French word *restaurant* (also used in English) and the Italian *ristorante*.

[9] See Huber, *op. cit.* (see n. 3 above), I, 531 ff.

clearly marked semantic distinction between these terms, *ristorazione,* which is by sound and grammar closer to the Latin origin, as well as to the terms in the other Romance languages, is usually referred to in the social and historical context of the term *restoration.*

Finally, a word about the concept in the Spanish language. There is again a not very noteworthy difference between *restauración* and *restaurar* in Spanish and the corresponding terms in other languages. However, one exception to be found in a Spanish-English dictionary of very recent vintage strikes a new and very notable chord. Two meanings of *restauración* are given here, as follows: (1) restoration, reintegration, restoring, (2) restoration, liberty recovered by an oppressed or subjugated people.[10] Something has been added here. The concept of *restoration* has been given a political connotation of a strongly affirmative nature. Considering the obvious fact that hardly any words in any language are subject to so much misinterpretation and misunderstanding as *freedom* and *liberty,* this peculiar remark of a decidedly subjective nature has, for the first time, injected the main issue—whether restoration in a social and political sense means merely return to a previous state of affairs, or to a state of affairs of a particular kind.

Discussion from here on will deal exclusively with the paraphrases of the noun. We will match it with the following principal terms, which are all frequently used to define *restoration:* recovery, reform or reformation, renewal, renovation, repair, reestablishment, restitution, and revival.[11]

All these concepts have as common denominator the prefix *re,* with its different meanings, indicating, in general, notions of *back, backward, anew, again,* and so forth. Somewhat more specifically they pertain also, with reference to the words discussed here, to the concept of "back with return to previous state, after lapse or cessation of occurrence of opposite state or action."[12] It is of great importance to keep this common denominator in mind, namely, the change from an original status by way of an intermediate one to a new one.

All nine nouns repeated in alphabetical order—*recovery, reestablishment, reform, reformation, renewal, renovation, repair, restitution,* and *re-*

[10] Velasquez, *Spanish and English Dictionaary* (Chicago, New York, 1960).

[11] Terms like *preservation, reconstruction, resurrection,* and several others might be surveyed as well, but it is deemed sufficient here to confine the survey to some of the words most frequently used in the standard dictionaries, such as partial synonyms of *restoration.*

[12] *The Concise Oxford Dictionary of Current English* (Oxford, 1938).

vival—have meanings partly overlapping that of *restoration,* though to very different extents.

Three of them, *recovery, repair,* and *restitution,* refer primarily to concrete specific changes in the physical world. The chief meaning of *recovery* pertains to the restoration of physical health, getting well again. However, the word is used also in a far more general sense, namely, the regaining of balance, the restrengthening of the administration, economy, and so forth. In this latter context there is a strong relationship to the social aspects of the term *restoration,* with one important difference: *recovery* implies that a previous deficiency has been righted; *restoration,* merely that a previous status has been reestablished. In that sense, *recovery* is more specific, and deviates from the general meaning of *restoration.*

Repair also refers primarily to the process of putting something back into good condition, of correcting some shortcomings, of restoring to a sound state after an injury. In this latter sense, *repair* may be, but does not necessarily have to be, related to *restitution. Repair* differs from *recovery* primarily insofar as it refers above all to the refitting of an object, for instance in architecture. Also *repair,* unlike *recovery* and *restoration,* pertains mostly to a partial and not a general overhauling of a deficiency.

Restitution, the third and last term in this group, refers predominantly to the redressing of individual claims and rights, frequently in a legal sense, as making good for loss or damage, reimbursement, return to a former specific condition. This undoubtedly pertains also to one of the meanings of *restoration,* though not to the general social one we are primarily interested in. *Restitution* may well, if not predominantly, refer to the reestablishment of the claims and/or rights of the whole social body, and in that sense it shares one connotation of meaning with *restoration.*

The six other concepts are of a more general, though not necessarily of an abstract nature. *Renewal* means to give new lease on life to an obligation or agreement that is expected to lapse. Whereas in *restoration* a situation is restored that has lapsed for some time, the overall connotation of *renewal*—and for that matter of the verb *renew*—links a previous state of affairs to a new one. Therewith the meaning of giving a new lease on life to a certain state of affairs that had existed for some time, as in *restoration,* is preserved. On the other hand, *renewal* means far more often than not continuation or extension in time of a prior state of affairs rather than the return to it after interruption, as it is in *restoration.* The middle phase of the restoration concept is not emphasized in *renewal* and *renew,* if it is not altogether lacking.

More concrete than *renewal* is the term *reestablishment*. It means primarily to have established something anew. This may be a household, a kind of business, or—more important and more usual—an organized body of men maintained for a purpose, which by the process of *reestablishment* is returned to its previous state. In addition to this the word conveys also a very specific meaning in religious terms, namely the setting up anew of a religious body, in particular the Church of England, and the "Kirk," the Presbyterian Church of Scotland, both to be considered as state churches.[13] The relationship of *reestablishment* to *restoration* is thus manifestly quite strong, and in its religious aspects tied to the political concept of the Stuart Restoration. However, *reestablishment* emphasizes the organizational aspects in general and the religious in particular more strongly than *restoration*, and is thus, broadly speaking, a narrower concept with somewhat different overtones than *restoration*.

Obviously of great importance is the unequal pair of the words *reform* and *reformation* in regard to our subject. *Reform* has a general meaning, referring primarily, though not exclusively, to social factors. It implies in a broad way and not merely in isolated cases, improvement of a previous state of affairs by removing faults and defects and setting up a better standard of character, conduct, and above all the many different functions of the body politic. *Reform,* in a sense, is also reestablishment of a previous condition, but definitely of a very much changed condition, righted possibly by general measures.

Reform, in this context, thus refers to a kind of change that clearly goes beyond the meaning implied in the formal change from one system to a previous one, entailed in the word *restoration*. Yet there exists a fairly strong relationship to it insofar as both terms refer to a reorganization of the social body, though *reform* is more precise in the extent and kind of change implied.

Probably most specific among the terms investigated here is the concept of *reformation*. It may be used not seldom in the sense of *reform* in its predominantly general aspects, though with a definite underlining of the spiritual aspects involved in such *reform* or *reformation*.[14] There is the very specific meaning of *Reformation*—hence its capitalization—as the broad religious movement in the first half of the sixteenth century re-

[13] See in particular *Webster's Third New International Dictionary Unabridged* under "renewal," and *The Concise Oxford English Dictionary,* and *Webster's New World Dictionary,* also under *establishment*.

[14] See at this point also, Gerhard B. Ladner, *The Idea of Reform: Its Impact on Christian Thought and Action in the Age of the Fathers* (Cambridge, Mass., 1959), particularly pp. 39–48.

ferred to as either "the Reformation" or the "Protestant Reformation." It is frequently put into juxtaposition with the "Catholic Reformation," more often, and many times incorrectly, also referred to as the "Counter Reformation." The distinction is of considerable interest. The term *Counter Reformation,* the more widely used of the two, is employed primarily but not exclusively by non-Catholic historians, who perceive the Counter Reformation as a movement, the primary aim of which was to undo the changes brought about by the Protestant Reformation, to them *the* Reformation, and to restore the status quo. To most Catholic historians, but not to Catholic historians alone, the term "Catholic Reformation seems to be far more appropriate than "Counter Reformation." According to these historians the Catholic Reformation was a spiritual reform movement in its own right, within the Church. It partly responded to the Protestant Reformation by original reform ideas of its own. Some of them antedated the reforms of the Protestant Reformation by many a century.

There is a third possible way of delineating the distinction between the concepts of Counter Reformation and Catholic Reformation. It may be tenable to apply the former term to politically motivated actions of Catholic powers, such as those of the Spanish Habsburg power under Charles V and Philip II, and later, particularly in the Thirty Years' War, of the German-Austrian Habsburgs as well, when religious issues played a limited part only. The concept of the Catholic Reformation would then be reserved for the primarily religious Catholic movement, above all in the second half of the sixteenth century, which centered largely around the Council of Trent.

The discourse on the relationship between *Reformation, Counter Reformation,* and *Catholic Reformation* has carried us only seemingly far afield. In fact, we have touched here upon one of the major aspects of the problem. The term *reformation,* whether pertaining specifically to the Protestant Reformation or not, is generally understood as a primarily spiritual movement, far more so than *reform* or *restoration.* It may be opposed by two concepts of different kind, that of a *counter reformation* of some sort, which merely wants to nullify the preceding *reformation,* or it may be answered by a reformation of a very different nature. This means that the new *reformation* intends to undo the previous reformation, not simply by restoring the conditions prior to it but by developing them by way of the injection and evolution of new ideas, albeit without denial of the values of the old spiritual heritage.

The momentous implications in terms of an analogy to *restoration* are obvious. Is *restoration* a mere counter movement or counter stage of some sort, which only wants to restore the status quo? Or does the term imply the further development of the status quo, differing from that of the re-form period, but differing also from the original state of affairs? Yet if differing at all, to what extent? If the difference is considerable, funda-mental as to principles and broad in application, can we then still speak of a *restoration,* or is something entirely new the issue now? On the other hand, if there is no change at all, does the term *restoration* imply simply the precise reconstruction of past social conditions by way of a counter movement? Would or could such movement be of a counterrevolutionary character, including the use of violence? Would the revolutionary or counterrevolutionary means not destroy the purpose of *restoration,* which may be the reestablishment of a previous legal order, that is, of legal con-tinuity? Quite clearly, the semantic questions raised here are closely re-lated to the content matter discussed in the general part of this study.

The next concept in this group is *renovation. Renovation* is in a sense the counterpart of reformation in the physical world, though a counter-part of a rather general nature. If we think of making something new or like new, of restoring it to full vigor of life, we speak of renovation. The term does not have the specific spiritual meaning of *reformation,* though it definitely does not rule out a spiritual meaning. It certainly pertains less exclusively to mundane affairs than *renewal.* It does not clearly refer pre-dominantly to a specific concrete act of restoring something physical, as does, for instance the word *reconstruction.* The latter may be used, like *renovation* and *restoration,* in a metaphorical sense as well, but primarily it would be understood as a physical aspect of restoration, as a compre-hensive large-scale application of repairs, as for instance during the Re-construction period after the Civil War. Thus *renovation* holds a kind of middle ground between spiritual *reformation* and physical *reconstruction,* and is in both cases related to *restoration.* The most distinctive feature of the term *renovation* is its comprehensive character.

This factor is lacking in our final concept, *revival.* Far more than the verb *revive,* it emphasizes the spiritual sphere in the sense of religious awakening, reanimation, a restoration to the consciousness of life.[15] The organizational and even political side aspects of *reformation* do not come into play. *Revival* is synonymous with restoration primarily in the reli-

[15] *Webster's Third New International Dictionary Unabridged; Oxford English Dictionary,* Vol. VII, ed. I933.

gious area, but without any strictly ecclesiastic connotation. Still it adds another facet to our concept while it maintains the basic feature of revitalizing something that had been lost.

At this point a brief summary is in order. After the comparative semantic review of the noun *restoration* and the verb *restore* in the principal Western languages and primarily in English, we have concluded that the verb, with its great variety of meanings with regard to the correction of flaws in individual subjects and objects of the physical world, yields relatively little specific insight into the general social and political meanings of the concepts of restoration. The general aspects expressed in the noun, insofar as they pertain to the reestablishment and preservation of a state of social and political affairs after a protracted intermediate period, are, on the other hand, of major importance for our purpose.

In Lieu of a Bibliography

Neither the scores of works cited in the notes to the general part of this study nor the hundreds of references in the case studies will be repeated or even abstracted here. The reason is simple. With regard to the specific cases of restoration, the best works on the political history of the periods and areas we have dealt with are also the best on our problem. A small selection of these works will be found in the notes to the individual chapters. To single out the few works which emphasize only the restoration aspects would convey the misleading impression that other sources are less important. Moreover, if we were to focus our attention mainly on works of political history which are concerned with the restoration problem per se, we would also imply that restoration is only a specific problem of certain times and places. Contrary to this assumption, we believe that it is a pervasive one.

A much better case could be made for a summarization of the works referred to in the general part of the study. The relationship of several of them to the restoration problem is far more direct than that of most references in the second part of the book. Such works as John B. Bury, *The Idea of Progress;* Crane Brinton, *The Anatomy of Revolution;* Hannah Arendt, *On Revolution;* Karl Griewank, *Der neuzeitliche Revolutionsbegriff,* and *Der Wiener Kongress und die europäische Restauration;* Guglielmo Ferrero, *Principles of Power,* and *Reconstruction of Europe;* the studies by Jacques Godechot, *Les Révolutions, 1770–99,* and *La Contre Révolution, doctrine et action, 1789–1804;* Robert Palmer, *The Age of the Democratic Revolution,* have indeed a very specific bearing on the problems discussed. I am greatly indebted to these authors and to many others referred to in the general part of the study. Yet their comprehensive or selective listing could not offer a bibliography of the theory of the restoration concept since none of them deals exclusively with the restoration problem. There are, to my knowledge, no books in existence which discuss the problem in any sense other than with regard to specific situations or more often as an aspect of other topics. A bibliography of the theory of our subject would thus be somewhat artificial and certainly tangential to the main issue.

I would rather refer here to some eminent intellectual ancestors of the history of the restoration problem. While I subscribe fully to none of their philosophies, they have undoubtedly greatly influenced my thinking, as they influenced to some extent that of many authorities referred to in this study. In the first place I would have to mention the cyclic philosophies of history and some of the methods used by their creators. The dialectical method of Hegel in its original sense, prior to the adaptation by Marxian materialistic interpretation of history, should be mentioned here before and above the others. Secondly, the philosophy of law of Hans Kelsen helped me greatly to focus problems of the kind discussed in this study. As to matters of content, the political sociology of Max Weber balances in a most fortunate manner the logocratic approach of Hegel and Kelsen. Acknowledgment of the inspiration received from these great minds is appropriate and it should also give more than bibliographical insight into what this study is built on and where it is heading.

INDEX

Index

Basic concepts discussed in this volume, such as change, cycle, revolution, system, time element, tradition, and so on, and above all restoration are listed in the index only where they are discussed and not merely referred to. An *n* after a page number refers to discussion of a specific entry in a note. Subdivisions of historical subjects are in general listed in chronological order, others in alphabetical order.

Date Due
